Leasehold enfranchisement explained

Authors
Ellodie Gibbons and James Wilson

Consulting editor
Professor James Driscoll

Acknowledgements

Crown copyright material is reproduced with the permission of the Controller of HMSO and the Queen's Printer for Scotland.

Please note: References to the masculine include, where appropriate, the feminine.

Published by the Royal Institution of Chartered Surveyors (RICS)

Surveyor Court

Westwood Business Park

Coventry CV4 8JE

UK

www.ricsbooks.com

No responsibility for loss or damage caused to any person acting or refraining from action as a result of the material included in this publication can be accepted by the authors or RICS.

ISBN 978 1 84219 584 0

© Royal Institution of Chartered Surveyors (RICS) May 2010. Copyright in all or part of this publication rests with RICS, and save by prior consent of RICS, no part or parts shall be reproduced by any means electronic, mechanical, photocopying or otherwise, now known or to be devised.

Typeset in Great Britain by Columns Design Ltd, Reading, Berks

Printed by Page Bros, Norwich

Contents

Foreword	ix
Lists of Acts, Statutory Instruments and abbreviations	xi
Table of cases	xiii
Enfranchisement explained	**1**
Introduction	1
House leases	3
How the *Leasehold Reform Act* 1967 has been amended	4
Amendments to the *Leasehold Reform Act* 1967	4
Summary of these amendments	7
Procedures and valuation	7
Valuation	8
Flat leases: enfranchisement and new lease claims	9
Claiming the grant of a new lease	11
Flat new lease claims: procedures, valuation and costs	11
Valuation: hope value and marriage value in all leasehold claims	12
Investment value	12
Marriage value	12
Hope value: is this a relevant factor in valuing house and flat new lease claims?	12
Hope value	13
Proceedings in the tribunal	13
Hope value and *Sportelli* in the Court of Appeal	14
Deferment rates and *Sportelli* in the Court of Appeal	14
Hope value and *Sportelli* in the House of Lords	15
Summary of the *Sportelli* decisions	16
Recent decisions on hope value and the generic deferment rate	16
Intermediate leases	20
Other recent decisions in enfranchisement and new lease claims	21
Redevelopment as a ground for resisting a claim	25
Can an intermediate lease qualify for a new lease?	26
Adjudication	27
What this book does not cover	28
Writing this book	29

Contents

1 Flats: the individual right of a tenant to a acquire a new lease — 30
   Introduction — 30
   Who qualifies? — 31
      The qualifying tenant — 31
      The qualifying flat — 32
      The qualifying lease — 32
      Checklist for tenants — 35
   Who is the landlord? — 36
      Special categories of landlord — 38
      Missing landlords — 38
   Starting the claim — 40
      Restrictions on serving an effective tenant's notice — 40
      Contents of a tenant's notice — 41
      Who to serve with the tenant's notice — 46
      How to serve the tenant's notice — 47
      Registering the tenant's notice — 48
      Effect of the tenant's notice — 48
      Assigning the tenant's notice — 49
      Suspension of the tenant's notice — 50
      Withdrawing the tenant's notice — 50
   Receipt of a tenant's notice — 50
      Other landlords — 51
      The competent landlord — 51
      Landlord's counter-notice — 55
      Checklist for landlords — 57
      Conduct of proceedings by competent landlord — 57
      Other landlords acting independently — 58
   Preparing and executing the new lease — 59
   Applications to the court or LVT — 60
      Landlord fails to serve a counter-notice — 61
      Landlord serves a non-admitting counter-notice — 64
      Landlord intends to redevelop — 66
      Application where terms are in dispute or there has been failure to enter into a new lease — 69

2 Flats: new lease claims: valuation issues — 74
   Introduction — 74
   Starting the claim — 75
   The tenant's enquiry — 75
   Schedule 13 — 76
      Timing of the notice of claim — 81
      The diminution in value of the landlord's interest — 82
      The statutory provisions — 82
      The term — 83
      The capitalisation rate — 84

The reversion	85
The share of freehold/999 years' lease vacant possession value	86
Apply an appropriate deferment rate to reflect the postponement to the end of the term	86
What is the deferment rate?	87
Why does a lower deferment rate result in a higher premium?	87
The deferment rate and where we are now	88
A synopsis of the decisions of *Sportelli*	89
Specific factors	90
A chronological analysis of *Pockney, Arbib* and *Sportelli*	92
Settlement evidence	94
Outside the PCL	102
Leases below 20 years	103
Long terms unexpired:	103
What is PCL?	104
Section 9(1) v section 9(1A)	107
Further examples	109
Marriage value	111
Landlord's share of marriage value	111
Relativity	121
What is relativity?	121
Benefit of the Act or Act rights	122
Onerous ground rents	125
Checklist for the tenant's valuer	133
The landlord's view	133
Checklist for the landlord's valuer	135
Intermediate landlords – intermediate leasehold interests (ILIs)	135
Schedule 13, Part III	135
The interest to be valued	139
The total profit rent and capitalisation approaches	142
The single rate approach	143
Checklist	144
Intermediate lease reversion	164
Further valuation examples	170
A flat occupied by a statutory tenant (*Rent Act* 1977)	176
A flat occupied by an assured tenant (*Housing Act* 1988)	181
Compensation	182
Summary	195

Contents

3 Flats: collective enfranchisement — 196
- Introduction — 196
- What can be acquired? — 198
  - Freehold interests — 198
  - Leasehold interests — 199
  - Other interests — 200
  - Leasebacks — 201
- Qualifying criteria — 202
  - Qualifying premises — 202
  - Qualifying tenants — 206
  - Qualifying leases — 207
  - Tenants unable to participate — 207
- Who is the landlord? — 208
  - Finding the landlords — 210
  - Missing landlords — 212
- Starting the claim — 213
  - Restrictions on serving an effective initial notice — 214
  - Requirements of an initial notice — 214
  - How to serve the initial notice — 218
  - Giving copies of the initial notice — 219
  - Registering the initial notice — 220
  - Effect of the initial notice — 220
  - The nominee purchaser — 221
  - The participating tenants — 223
  - Withdrawing the initial notice — 224
- Receipt of an initial notice — 225
  - Relevant landlords — 225
  - The reversioner — 226
  - Reversioner's counter-notice — 227
  - Checklist for landlords — 231
  - Conduct of proceedings by the reversioner — 232
  - Relevant landlords acting independently — 232
- Preparing the conveyance — 233
- Applications to the court or LVT — 233
  - The reversioner fails to serve a counter-notice — 234
  - The reversioner serves a non-admitting counter-notice — 237
  - Landlord intends to redevelop — 240
  - Application where terms are in dispute or there has been a failure to enter into a binding contract — 243

4 Flats: collective enfranchisement valuation issues — 248
- Introduction — 248
  - The valuation principles — 249
  - The tenants' enquiry — 250

Schedule 6	250
The capitalisation rate	255
The deferment rate	256
Marriage value	257
Value of the participating tenants' existing interests	260
Participators and non-participators	262
Hope value	263
What is hope value?	263
How is hope value to be calculated?	264
Hope value in relation to a section 42 notice	269
Tenant's hope value	271
Further valuation issues	272
Checklist for the tenants' valuer	274
Further points on hope value	280
Checklist for the freeholder's valuer	291
Compensation	293
Development value	295
Summary	303

5 Houses: the right of a tenant to acquire the freehold — 305

Introduction	305
What is a house?	305
Designed or adapted for living in	305
Reasonably called a house	306
Divided buildings	308
Non-detached buildings	309
The extent of the freehold to be acquired	309
Qualification criteria	312
Exceptions	313
What is a long tenancy?	316
Basis of valuation	320
Checklist	321
Basis of qualification	322
Low rent	323
Starting the claim	328
Serving the notice of tenant's claim	335
Registering the notice of tenant's claim	338
Effect of serving the notice of tenant's claim	338
Assigning the notice of tenant's claim	340
Missing landlords	340
Receipt of a notice of tenant's claim	343
Landlord's notice in reply	346
The landlord intends to apply for possession	349

Contents

Terms of acquisition	350
The purchase price	351
Costs	352
Withdrawal	352
Applications to the court or LVT	353

6 Houses: the right of a tenant to acquire an extended lease   355

Introduction	355
Meaning of terms used	355
Qualification criteria	356
Starting the claim	357
Receipt of notice of tenant's claim	359
Redevelopment rights	359
Terms of acquisition	359
Costs	361
Execution of the new lease	362
Terms of the new lease	362
Rent	363
Rights under the new lease	364
Applications to the court or LVT	364

7 Houses: extended leases and enfranchisement valuation issues   366

Introduction	366
An extended lease	368
Section 1, 'tenants entitled to enfranchisement or extension'	369
Section 4, 'meaning of low rent'	369
Letting value	369
Rateable value	371
The section 15 rent	379
Decapitalise the site value	383
The 'adverse differential'	384
Freehold – purchase price	386
Valuations under section 9(1)	386
Further considerations	394
Section 9(1A)	397
Section 9(1B)	407
Section 9(1C)	407
Section 9A – compensation	409
Summary	416

Glossary	**418**
Index	**426**

Foreword

Leasehold enfranchisement can be a challenge both for those who are experienced in the field and for those who are new to the subject. For lawyers, this is a niche area of the law. It requires precision and efficiency. The valuation aspects of lease extension and enfranchisement require an expertise that valuers may not have encountered in their day to day practice. This book is therefore very welcome. It is the result of the collaboration between a lawyer, Ellodie Gibbons and a valuer, James Wilson under the consulting editorship of Professor James Driscoll.

There are several striking aspects of the text. The first is the order in which the authors have tackled the four main areas of acquisition. Instead of taking matters chronologically, they start with the individual right of a tenant to acquire a new lease under the *Leasehold Reform, Housing and Urban Development Act* 1993. This is probably the area most commonly encountered in practice and therefore it is logical that the book should start in this way. This reflects a desire to ensure that the book is, above all, intended to be a practical guide. It is therefore not surprising that the next section deals with the collective enfranchisement of flats before moving on to deal with houses and the acquisition of the freehold under the *Leasehold Reform Act* 1967 and finally the right to acquire an extended lease of a house.

The law is explained in clear and straightforward language and is written with refreshing confidence. Valuation is tackled by an expert in the field who does not shy away from an explanation of difficult concepts. What becomes clear to the reader is that the authors have approached the issues in the order and in the manner that they would be tackled by a practitioner. The statutory requirements and case law are put together like building blocks and the whole is pulled together with lists, timetables and flowcharts. Where illustration is required, examples are given and where possible these are drawn from case law. In the valuation sections, worked examples are provided and explained.

Foreword

'Enfranchisement explained' is an ambitious title for a book concerning law where, in 2008 alone, four cases were considered by the (then) House of Lords and this book does not hold itself out to be the definitive guide on all matters of acquisition. However, what it does do is provide a timely guide and a clear explanation, which I am happy to recommend.

Siobhan McGrath

Senior President of the Residential Property Tribunal Service

List of Acts, Statutory Instruments and abbreviations

The following Acts and Statutory Instruments are referred to in this publication. Where an Act or Statutory Instrument is mentioned frequently, it is referred to by the abbreviation in brackets that follows.

Agricultural Holdings Act 1986
Agricultural Tenancies Act 1995
Commonhold and Leasehold Reform Act 2002 (**CLRA 2002**)
Companies Act 1985
Companies Act 2006
Finance Act 2003
Finance Act 2009
Housing Act 1969
Housing Act 1974
Housing Act 1980
Housing Act 1985
Housing Act 1988
Housing Act 1996
Housing and Planning Act 1986
Housing and Regeneration Act 2008
Inheritance Tax Act 1984
Interpretation Act 1978
Landlord and Tenant Act 1927
Landlord and Tenant Act 1954
Landlord and Tenant Act 1985
Landlord and Tenant Act 1987
Land Charges Act 1972
Land Registration Act 2002
Law of Property Act 1925
Leasehold Reform Act 1967 (**LRA 1967**)
Leasehold Reform Act 1979
Leasehold Reform, Housing and Urban Development Act 1993 (**LRHUDA 1993**)
Limitation Act 1980
Local Government and Housing Act 1988
Local Government and Housing Act 1989 (**LGHA 1989**)
Recorded Delivery Service Act 1962
Rent Act 1977

Rent (Agriculture) Act 1976
Leasehold Reform (Collective Enfranchisement and Lease Renewal) Regulations 1993 (SI 1993/2407)
Leasehold Reform (Collective Enfranchisement) (Counter-notices) (England) Regulations 2002 (SI 2002/3208)
Leasehold Reform (Collective Enfranchisement) (Counter-notices) (Wales) Regulations 2003
Leasehold Reform (Enfranchisement and Extension) Regulations 1967 (SI 1967/1879)
Leasehold Reform (Enfranchisement and Extension) (Amendment) (England) Regulations 2003 (SI 2003/1989)
Leasehold Reform (Enfranchisement and Extension) (Amendment) (Wales) Regulations 2004 (SI 2004/699)
Leasehold Reform (Notices) Regulations 1997 (SI 1997/640)
Leasehold Reform (Notices) (Amendment) (England) Regulations 2002 (SI 2002/1715)
Leasehold Reform (Notices) (Amendment) (Wales) Regulations 2002 (SI 2002/3187)
Leasehold Reform (Notices) (Amendment) (No.2) (England) Regulations 2002 (SI 2002/3209)
Leasehold Reform (Notices) (Amendment) (Wales) Regulations 2003 (SI 2003/991)
Rating (Housing) Regulations 1990
The Service Charges (Consultation Requirements) (England) Regulations 2003
Civil Procedure Rules 1998
Unfair Terms in Consumer Contracts Regulations 1999

For the full statutory extracts, please visit:
www.isurv.com/leaseholdfranchisement

Table of cases

9 Cornwall Crescent London Ltd v Royal Borough of Kensington and Chelsea	[2005] EWCA Civ 324
10 Cheniston Gardens Ltd v Catherine Fiona Atkins	Unreported 2008, LVT
Arbib v Earl Cadogan	[2005] 3 EGLR 139
Arrowdell Ltd v Coniston Court (North) Hove Ltd	[2007] RVR 39
Blendcrown Limited v The Church Commissioners for England	[2004] 1 EGLR 143
Boss Holdings Limited v Grosvenor West End Properties	[2008] UKHL 5
Buckley House (Freehold) Limited v Copper Smith Corporation	Unreported 2004, LVT
Byrnlea Property Investments Ltd v Ramsay	[1969] 2 QB 252
Cadogan Holdings Limited v Charles Carey-Morgan and Jonathan Money	Unreported 2009, LVT
Cadogan Holdings Limited v Pockney	[2005] RVR 197
Cadogan v 26 Cadogan Square Limited	Unreported, 2009, LVT
Cadogan Estates Limited v Hows	[1989] 2 EGLR 216
Cadogan v McGirk	[1996] 4 All ER 643
Carl v Grosvenor Estate Belgravia	[2000] 38 EG 195, Lands Tr
Cascades and Quayside Ltd v Cascades Freehold Ltd	[2008] L&TR 23
Chelsea Properties Limited v Earl Cadogan	Unreported 2007, Lands Tr
Cik v Chavda	Unreported 2008, Lands Tr
City of Westminister v CH2006 Ltd	[2009] UKUT 174 (CC)
Clinker & Ash Limited v Southern Gas Board	(1967) 203 EG 735
Collins v Howard de Walden Estates Ltd	[2003] HLR 70
Cresswell v Duke of Westminster	[1985] 2 EGLR 151
Culley v Daejan Properties Limited	[2009] UKUT 168 (LC)
Daejan Investments Ltd v The Holt (Freehold) Ltd	Unreported 2008, Lands Tr

xiii

Table of cases

Delaforce v Evans and Evans	(1970) 215 EG 315
Dependable Homes Limited v Mann & Mann	[2009] UKUT 171 (LC)
Dickins v Howard De Walden Estates Ltd	Unreported 2008, LVT
Dugan-Chapman v Grosvenor Estates	[1997] 1 EGLR 96
Earl Cadogan v 2 Herbert Crescent Freehold limited	Unreported 2009, Lands Tr
Earl Cadogan v Sportelli	[2007] 1 EGLR 153
Farr v Millerson's Investments Ltd	(1971) 22 P&CR 1055
Fitzgerald v Safflane Ltd	[2010] UKUT 37 (LC)
Forty-Five Holdings Limited v Grosvenor (Mayfair) Estate	(2010) PLSCS 2
Free Grammar School of John Lyon v Secchi	[1999] 3 EGLR 49
Freehold Properties Ltd	[2009] UKUT 172 (LC)
Gaidowski v Gonville & Caius College, Cambridge	[1975] 1 WLR 1066
Gajewski v Anderton and Kershaw	(1971) 217 EG 885
Gallagher Estates Limited v Walker	(1973) 28 P&CR 113
Gidlow-Jackson v Middlegate Properties Limited	[1974] QB 361
Grosvenor Estates Limited v Prospect Estates Limited	[2008] EWCA Civ 1281
Hall v Davies and Davies	(1971) 22 P & CR 780
Hareford Ltd v Barnet London Borough Council	[2005] 2 EGLR 72
Haresign v St John the Baptist's College, Oxford	(1980) 225 EG 711, Lands Tr
Hildron Finance Ltd v Greenhill Hampstead Ltd	[2008] 1 EGLR 179
HILMI & Associates Ltd v 20 Pembridge Villas Freehold Ltd	[2010] EWCA Civ 314
Hosebay Limited v Day (and another)	(2009) PLSCS 318, CC
Howard de Walden Estates Ltd v Aggio	[2009] 1 AC 39
James v United Kingdom	(1986) 8 EHRR 123
John Lyon's Charity v Red Earl Ltd	Unreported 2008, LVT
Johnston v Duke of Westminster	[1986] AC 839

Table of cases

Jones v Wrotham Park Settled Estates	[1980] AC 74
Lake v Bennett	[1970] QB 663
Lewis v James	(1981) 258 EG 651, Lands Tr
Lloyd-Jones v Church Commissioners for England	(1981) 261 EG 471
Majorstake Ltd v Curtis	[2008] 1 AC 787
Malekshad v Howard de Walden Estates Ltd	[2003] 1 AC 1013
Mannai Investment Co Ltd v Eagle Star Assurance Co. Ltd	[1997] AC 749
Mansal Securities & other appeals	[2009] 10 EG 110
Maurice v Hollow-Ware Productions	[2005] EWHC 815 (Ch)
McHale v Earl Cadogan	[2008] PLSCS 298 LU/UT
Methuen-Campbell v Walters	[1979] 1 QB 525
Millard Investments Limited v The Earl Cadogan	Unreported 2004, LVT
Mosley v Hickman	[1986] 1 EGLR 161
Ms Betul Erkman v Earl Cadogan	Unreported 2007, LVT
Nailrile Limited v Earl Cadogan	[2009] RVR 95
Nell Gwynne House Freehold Ltd v various	Unreported 2009, LVT
Nicholson v Goff	[2007] 1 EGLR 83
Norfolk v Trinity College, Cambridge	(1976) 32 P&CR 147
Official Custodian for Charities v Goldridge	(1973) 26 P&CR 191
Peck v Anicar Properties Ltd	[1971] 1 All ER 517
Pitts v Cadogan and others	[2007] 42 EG 296
Pitt & Wang v Earl of Cadogan	
Roberts v Church Commissioners for England	[1972] 1 QB 278
Sarum Properties Limited v Webb, Webb & Webb	[2009] UKUT 188 (LC)
Sherwood Hall (East End Road) v Magnolia Tree Limited	[2009] UKUT 158 (LC)
Shortdean Place (Eastbourne) Resident's Association Limited v Lynari Properties Ltd	[2003] 3 EGLR 147, Lands Tr

xv

Table of cases

Sinclair Gardens Investments (Kensington) Ltd v Poets Chase Freehold Co Ltd	[2008] 1 WLR 768
St Ermins Property Co v Tingay	[2002] 2 EGLR 53
Stylo Shoes Ltd v Prices Tailors Ltd	[1960] Ch. 396
Tandon v Trustees of Spurgeon Homes	[1982] AC 755
Tsiapkinis v Cadogan (2008)	[2008] L&TR 21, Lands Tr
Ulterra Ltd v Glenbarr (RTE) Co Ltd	[2008] 1 EGLR 103
Visible Information Packaged Systems Ltd v Squarepoint (London) Ltd	[2002] 2 EGLR 93, Lands Tr
Watton v The Trustees of the Ilchester Estates	Unreported 2002, Lands Tr
Waitt v Morris	[1994] 2 EGLR 224
Willingdale v Globalrange Ltd	[2000] 2 EGLR 55
Wolf v Crutchley	[1971] 1 WLR 99
Zuckerman (and others) v Trustees of the Calthorpe Estate	[2009] UKUT 235

Enfranchisement explained

Introduction

Surveyors, lawyers and others involved in residential property are often instructed to advise on a wide range of matters affecting long leases of residential property. According to official statistics, there are nearly one million houses that are owned leasehold (rather than freehold). These are to be found predominantly in the Midlands and north-west of England but there are also significant concentrations of leasehold houses in Wales (from where the pressure for the original legislation sprang) and in London. Official statistics also suggest that there are nearly two million flats which are owned leasehold. As the building of blocks of flats has become an important feature of housing development in this country, the numbers of leasehold flats will continue to increase.

So far as we know, this is the first book on leasehold enfranchisement to be written by a team of two lawyers and a valuer. We start with an account of a claim by a flat owner for a new lease. The legal analysis of the principles and the procedures is followed by a detailed examination of how valuation of the price payable is determined. This approach has been adopted as these are the most common types of claim made by flat leaseholders. With these issues in mind, we then turn to collective enfranchisement and consider the law and the procedures, followed again by a detailed examination of valuation. Finally, we turn to house lease claims, where again, the legal issues are first examined followed by an account of the valuation of the premium. The law and valuation of house lease extensions is also undertaken (though there are few house leases which qualify for an extended lease).

Residential leasehold law is a notoriously complex subject. One has to consult the *Leasehold Reform Act* 1967 for house leases; Part I of the *Leasehold Reform, Housing and Urban Development Act* 1993 for flat leases; the *Landlord and Tenant Acts* 1985 and 1987 for other features of leasehold management, and the *Local Government and Housing Act* 1989 for occupation rights at the end of a long lease. An additional source of complications lies in the numerous statutory amendments made to all of this legislation.

Decades after the legislation was enacted, the courts and the tribunals are still frequently asked to adjudicate disputes often involving very complex valuation and legal issues. In 2008, for example, there were no fewer than four cases that went to the House of Lords (now called the Supreme Court) and they are summarised later in this chapter. Other leasehold issues are often adjudicated on by the Court of Appeal and the High Court. Leasehold matters are also a common type of litigation in the County Court, the Lands Tribunal (the Upper Tribunal (Lands Chamber) as it is now known) and the Leasehold Valuation Tribunal.

At the time of writing this book, there is an outstanding decision on valuing intermediate leases awaited from the Upper Tribunal, some statutory amendments to the house enfranchisement legislation came into force a few months before publication and the results of a departmental consultation on flat enfranchisement are awaited.

There is a large demand for advice on valuation and on how to make claims or how to resist them, where one is instructed by a landlord. The purpose of this new work is to provide an explanation of the principles and procedures that apply to residential long leases, looking respectively at the legal and the valuation issues. It is written for busy surveyors, solicitors and others who advise on leasehold matters, or who are considering specialising in this field.

In this introductory chapter, I summarise the basic principles; how they have evolved, and I also elaborate on the scope and ambit of this new work.

However well-drafted leases may be (and sadly, evidence and experience suggest that many leases are very poorly drafted), many leaseholders would prefer to have a greater degree of control over their homes, either through acquiring the freehold or, as the lease gets shorter, the ability to extend that lease.

Landlords faced with a claim by a leaseholder to acquire the freehold, or a new lease, also need expert advice on questions such as whether the leaseholder is following the correct procedures and whether the leaseholder's proposals on price and costs are fair and reasonable.

In the most general of terms, the current position so far as residential leases of houses and flats are concerned is simple to state: the holder of a qualifying lease has a right to enfranchise and in many cases the right to a new lease. With limited exceptions, there is no residence test and a lease usually qualifies if it was originally granted for a term longer than 21 years.

House leases

Now just over 40 years old, the *Leasehold Reform Act* 1967 is the landmark legislation in enfranchisement claims. For the first time in English law, a qualifying leaseholder of a house was given the right to purchase the freehold (through a process that is now commonly known as 'enfranchisement') and also the right to an extended lease 50 years longer than the current term. Unlike the later leasehold legislation, this original measure was quite controversial, both during its parliamentary passage and later. In a famous challenge to the validity of the legislation, one landlord took proceedings in the European Court of Justice (see *James v United Kingdom* (1986) 8 EHRR123), arguing that there had been a breach of Article 6 of the European Convention on Human Rights by allowing a leaseholder to compulsorily acquire the freehold whether the landlord was willing to sell or not. The challenge was unsuccessful, the court holding that signatory state legislatures must be accorded a wide margin of discretion in framing legislation that has a defined social need. In this case, the social need was to give rights to residential leaseholders of houses, whose leases are coming to an end, and who have no rights at the end of the lease, unless the landlord is willing to grant them a new lease. As it was originally enacted, the legislation applied only to qualifying leases of houses of lower value (formerly known as rateable values). Higher value dwellings were, therefore, excluded. A brief history of the amendments since 1967 may assist in understanding the current statutory framework.

How the Leasehold Reform Act 1967 has been amended

Part I of the *Leasehold Reform Act* 1967 (most of which came into force on 1 January 1968), gives the right to compulsorily acquire the freehold, or to obtain an extension for a further 50 years term. As originally enacted, a lessee qualified if he had a long lease (broadly speaking, a lease which was originally granted for a term longer than 21 years), at a low rent, having occupied the house as his only or main residence for the past five years, or for periods totalling five years during the past ten years. Enfranchisement was limited to houses with lower rateable values: higher value houses were originally excluded from the right to enfranchise.

Amendments to the Leasehold Reform Act 1967

The original legislation has been amended on several occasions. Some amendments are of a technical nature; others (such as extending the numbers of houses that qualify), are more substantial.

In 1969, technical changes were made to valuation (s.82 of the *Housing Act* 1969). More substantial amendments followed with the passage of the *Housing Act* 1974, which extended the number of eligible houses by increasing the rateable value limits for enfranchisement (but allowing a more generous basis for valuation for such houses). These amendments also made provision for landlords to apply for an estate management scheme (EMS) to be approved. This allowed landlords with a portfolio of leasehold houses to apply for such a scheme to be registered. Under an EMS, a landlord can retain rights over properties even though some of the leaseholders have acquired the freehold.

Amendments were also made to valuation to take account of any increase in value caused by improvements carried out by the lessee or any previous lessee. Any increase in value is to be discounted in assessing the price payable for the freehold.

The *Leasehold Reform Act* 1979 was introduced to prevent landlords from artificially increasing the price payable on enfranchisement by a device which had been upheld in litigation by the House of Lords in a case called *Jones v Wrotham Park Settled Estates [1979] 38 P&CR 77*.

The next set of amendments were contained in the *Housing Act* 1980 (legislation which is best known for the introduction of the right to buy, security of tenure and other new statutory rights, for tenants of local authorities and other public sector landlords). It amended the *Leasehold Reform Act* 1967 by reducing the five-year qualification period to three years. Certain types of shared ownership leases (under which tenants purchase part of an interest in the house, paying a rent and having the right to purchase further interests in the property), became excluded from enfranchisement.

Leasehold Valuation Tribunals (LVTs) were created to deal with disputes over valuation in place of the Lands Tribunal, whilst allowing an appeal to the Lands Tribunal against their decisions. Other minor amendments were also made, including a change to the definition of a long lease (to combat an avoidance device), and a change to the way in which intermediate leases were valued on enfranchisement.

Further changes (of a technical character) were made by the *Housing and Planning Act* 1986 to prevent lessees from taking advantage of a quirk in the 1967 Act which allowed them (in effect), to purchase more cheaply by combining an application to extend the lease with a claim to acquire the freehold. Also, the statutory basis on which some shared ownership leases are excluded from enfranchisement was reformulated.

Substantial amendments were made to the *Leasehold Reform Act* 1967 by the *Leasehold Reform, Housing and Urban Development Act 1993*. Perhaps the most important change was the removal of the higher rateable value limits thus bringing all otherwise eligible leasehold houses within enfranchisement under the 1967 Act. The major leasehold changes made by the 1993 Act also introduced the collective right to enfranchise for flat leaseholders and an individual right to a new lease, which are examined further later in this chapter.

As might be expected, a different valuation basis was introduced for house leases, which now qualified (including the landlord's right to receive additional compensation for any additional losses, such as a loss of development value following enfranchisement).

The numbers of qualifying leases were extended by changes to the low rent test condition and changes made to the definition of long leases so as to include certain leases which terminate after death or marriage. But house leases granted by charitable housing trusts, and houses transferred for the public benefit, became excluded from enfranchisement. Landlords were given new rights to apply for an EMS in relation to houses which became eligible for enfranchisement under these amendments, and the procedures for the approval of such schemes were greatly simplified.

Further amendments were made to the 1967 Act by the *Housing Act* 1996. The most substantial change was the reform to the low rent test by rendering leases which failed the test, qualifying leases, provided they were originally granted for a period of more than 35 years. Reforms were also made to cases where a dwelling failed the low rent test because it did not have a rateable value at the date on which the test is applied. Once again, the landlord's right to apply for an EMS to be approved was extended to cases where house leases became enfranchiseable following these amendments; however, the low rent test was not abolished for shared ownership leases granted by registered social landlords. [The position was simplified by amendments under the *Housing and Regeneration Act*, Part 3, which came into force on 9 September 2009.]

Landlords were also given a new right to compensation where an ineffective enfranchisement claim was made at the end of the term of the lease. The lessee becomes a statutory tenant or an assured tenant and the landlord loses the increased rent whilst the enfranchisement claim is pending. LVTs were also given jurisdiction to determine the costs payable by the enfranchising lessee when the parties fail to agree them.

A substantial number of changes were made to the 1967 Act by Part 2 of the *Commonhold and Leasehold Reform Act* 2002 (plus major changes for flat lease enfranchisement rights, and radical new leasehold management provisions, such as new service charge consultation procedures). These changes included the virtual repeal of the residence qualifying condition and this has paved the way for investors to exercise rights. Another change was to allow leaseholders who have the right to an extended lease, the right to enfranchise and the right to an assured tenancy at the end of that extended lease. Before these amendments, a leaseholder with an extended lease had no right to enfranchise or to stay in the house under a statutory tenancy once the extended period had started. This may make the right to an extended lease more attractive than was previously the case. Another change is procedural; applications in relation to missing landlords can now be made to the County Court (and not the High Court as was previously the case).

Additional amendments were recently made by Part 3 of the *Housing and Regeneration Act* 2008. These changes repeal the remaining vestiges of the low rent test, except that it remains a qualifying condition for extended lease claims. Schedule 4A to the 1967 Act has been amended to allow all landlords (not just social landlords), to grant shared ownership leases, which will not qualify for enfranchisement unless the leaseholder has first acquired 100 per cent of the equity. Also, under regulations, shared ownership leases in prescribed protected areas will remain social housing. A shared ownership leaseholder of a house in such a protected area will either not have the right to acquire the whole of the equity, or will be required to offer the house to the landlord before selling it. These amendments came into force on 9 September 2009 and apply only to leases granted on or after this date.

Summary of these amendments

The effects of these reforms have (a) removed the higher value exclusions for house leases, with the result that all houses held on qualifying leases can enfranchise, and (b) have simplified the qualifying rules by such matters as abolishing the low rent tests and the residence test for qualification. However, it is very important to note that as more and more house leases became enfranchiseable so the valuation bases changed in a way that favoured landlords. This accounts for the section 9(1) valuation based on 'site value' for leases which originally qualified in 1967, and sections 9(1A) and 9(1C) which require payment of 'marriage value'. The 2002 Act also simplified marriage value by amendments to the 1967 Act: in all cases any marriage value is shared 50:50 except where the term of the current lease exceeds 80 years, in which case the marriage value is treated as nil. It should also be noted that the right to an extended lease only applies if the original qualifying conditions (e.g. rateable value, low rent test and so on), apply. In other words, the reforms that have allowed more houses to qualify for enfranchisement have not included the right to an extended lease.

Procedures and valuation

The 1967 Act sets out the procedures. The forms used have been prescribed by regulations made under the Act. In summary, the leaseholder initiates the claim by giving notice in the prescribed form to the landlord who must reply with a notice stating, amongst other things, whether or not the claim is admitted. The Act prescribes time limits for the exchange of notices but these limits are not as strict as they are in flat lease claims.

Additional commentary on valuation, marriage value and hope value, and how this affects house and flat lease claims appears later in this chapter.

Valuation

One of the criticisms of the 1967 Act, when it was first enacted, was the policy on which valuation was based. It was based on the principle that, in equity, the leaseholder owns the house whilst the landlord owns the land on which it is built. This led to the enactment of a principle that, in enfranchising, the leaseholder had to pay, in effect, the site value. The landlord was not entitled to any 'marriage value', that is to say the additional value that is generated where the leaseholder of the house acquires both the leasehold and the freehold. Another way of describing marriage value is that it is the additional price a leaseholder, as a special purchaser will pay, compared with a third party investor, to acquire the freehold.

As the later amendments to the higher value limits unfolded, on each occasion the right to acquire the freehold was extended, a different valuation basis was introduced, namely those in sections 9(1A) and 9(1C) of the 1967 Act. An important characteristic of this is that the landlord is entitled to a share of marriage value. Since another of the amendments made by Part 2 of the 2002 Act, this share is fixed at 50:50 between the landlord and leaseholder in all cases other than where the unexpired length of the lease exceeds 80 years; however, as Parliament amended the legislation by extending the enfranchisement rights to higher value houses, the right to a lease extension was not accorded. This remains, therefore, confined to leases that qualify under the original rules.

As will be seen, a qualifying holder of a lease has the right to an extended lease 50 years longer than the current term. No premium is payable but a higher rent is payable from the term date of the expired lease. The computation of the higher rent is also provided for in the legislation by reference to the site value of the property and other factors

Under the House of Lords ruling in *Sportelli v Cadogan Estate and others* [2008] UKHL 71, 'hope value' cannot in law be claimed in a house lease enfranchisement claim. There was no appeal against the decision of the Court of Appeal which upheld the Lands Tribunal's promulgation of a generic deferment rate of 4.75 per cent for house lease claims.

Leaseholders also have to pay the landlord's reasonable professional costs and where these are not agreed, application can be made to the LVT for a determination.

Flat leases: enfranchisement and new lease claims

Part I of the 1993 Act introduced a collective right to buy the freehold and an individual right to the grant of a new lease. Some amendments were made to valuation and related matters by the *Housing Act* 1996. Far more substantial changes were made under Part 2 of the 2002 Act; the residence test was repealed in its entirety, the numbers of leaseholders who have to participate was reduced from two-thirds to one-half, and buildings with up to 25 per cent non-residential floor use became eligible (previously up to ten per cent). So, as things currently stand, a block of flats qualifies in principle for enfranchisement rights provided any non-residential parts do not exceed 25 per cent; provided that there are at least two flats in the building, and provided that not less than one half of the leaseholders in the building support the application. Taken together, these amendments have extended flat leaseholder rights to a larger group of blocks of flats, and have relaxed the qualifying conditions.

A procedural change made by the 2002 Act was a requirement that leaseholders of flats who want to acquire the freehold to their block, must set up a right to enfranchise (RTE) company to act as their nominee purchaser. Under that reform, the company would serve the enfranchisement notice under section 13 of the *Leasehold Reform, Housing and Urban Development Act* 1993, act as the nominee purchaser under the claim and, on acquiring the freehold, become the landlord under the leases. All qualifying leaseholders would have a statutory right to become a member of the company and so join in the claim. Since the enfranchisement notice would be given by the RTE company, the participating leaseholders would not have to sign the notice, thereby avoiding the practical problems (for larger blocks) caused by the requirement that participants must all personally sign: see *Cascades & Quayside Ltd v Cascades Freehold Ltd* [2007] EWCA Civ 1555; [2008] L&TR 23, where the block contained 174 flats.

A year after the 2002 Act was enacted, a Stamp Duty land tax (SDLT) concession was made whereby the duty payable would be divided between the participants should an RTE company acquire the freehold (see section 74 of the *Finance Act* 2003). Since RTE has not commenced, this concession could not come into force. It has been replaced with a different SDLT concession for enfranchisement in the *Finance Act* 2009.

At present, participating leaseholders usually form a company to act as the nominee purchaser. They are best advised also to enter into a participation agreement in respect of their contributions to the costs of the acquisition, the appointment of professional advisers and other matters.

Turning these steps into a statutory requirement would not, in practical terms, represent a significant change. RTE would also have the advantage of using a company whose constitution is specially designed to enable it to act as a landlord of residential premises. Moreover, every leaseholder in the block would have the right to join in the purchase, which has added importance since the 2002 Act reduced the required minimum proportion of participating leaseholders from not less than two-thirds, to not less than one-half. As previously noted, it also offers SDLT advantages.

Seven years after the statutory changes received royal assent, RTE has not yet been brought into effect. Doubts have emerged as to whether, as drafted, it can work and this has delayed its commencement. The Department of Communities and Local Government has recently published a consultation paper: The right to enfranchise (RTE) provisions: Consultation, seeking comments on the proposal that RTE, far from being introduced, should be repealed.

It now appears, therefore, that these procedural changes will not be brought into force and will be repealed in due course.

On valuation, the 2002 Act amended marriage value with the result that it is shared 50:50 between the landlord and the leaseholders except in relation to any participating lease which has more than 80 years unexpired. In the *Sportelli* decision, the House of Lords decided (by a majority), that 'hope value' may be claimed in a collective enfranchisement claim where there are leaseholders in the block who have not participated. Such hope value can be claimed for the prospect that a non-participant might in future negotiate a new lease/share of freehold and this would release marriage value.

Claiming the grant of a new lease

Turning to the right to acquire a new lease; this is an important right for an owner of a flat as they have the right to seek the grant of a new lease. The new lease is for a term 90 years longer than the current term; it is at a peppercorn rent, but otherwise usually on the same terms as the current lease. A premium must be paid representing the deferment of the landlord's reversion in the flat and also for the loss of the ground rent. Marriage value is also payable where the current lease does not exceed 80 years. However, the House of Lords decided in *Sportelli*, that hope value cannot be claimed, though it can in a collective enfranchisement claim where there are non-participating leaseholders. There was no appeal against the Court of Appeal's decision which upheld the Lands Tribunal's promulgation of a generic deferment rate of five per cent for flat lease claims.

(The law governing leasehold enfranchisement and new leases for leaseholders of flats is not affected by the amendments in Part 3 of the *Housing and Regeneration Act* 2008.)

Flat lease claims: procedures, valuation and costs

Unlike house claims, there are no prescribed forms for flat lease enfranchisement and new lease claims. The 1993 Act sets out a timetable for the exchange of notices and the time periods for applications to the court or the tribunal. In contrast to the 1967 Act, these time limits are strict and failure to comply can result in the leaseholder being treated as having withdrawn the claim, or in the landlord's case, being unable to question the leaseholder's premium proposals.

In addition to paying a premium, leaseholders have to pay the landlord's reasonable professional costs and where these are not agreed, application can be made to the LVT for a determination.

Valuation is examined further later in this chapter.

Leasehold enfranchisement explained

Valuation: hope value and marriage value in all leasehold claims

Many of the issues that divide leaseholders and landlords have been determined by recent Court of Appeal and House of Lords (now the 'Supreme Court') decisions, known popularly as the *Sportelli* litigation. These decisions concerned appeals against various LVT decisions in both house and flat lease claims.

Investment value

Leaseholders have to pay the landlord its freehold investment value, which has two elements – the capitalised loss of ground rent income before the term date of the lease (or leases) **and** the present vacant possession value of the freehold discounted to term by applying, on an annual basis, an appropriate deferment rate. So clearly, the deferment rate is important particularly in claims involving the more expensive leasehold houses or flat claims. (Though the point may seem counter-intuitive to a non-valuer, the higher the deferment rate, the lower the premium payable.)

Marriage value

The leaseholder (or leaseholders) must pay 50 per cent of any marriage value, which may be described as the additional value generated when an enfranchising leaseholder owns both the lease and freehold estates. The value of the freehold and leasehold estates in separate ownership is less than in common ownership, as the leaseholder is a special purchaser who will pay more than an investor for the freehold. As previously noted, as a result of statutory amendments in 2002, marriage value has to be split 50:50 between the landlord and the leaseholder(s) except where the unexpired term of the lease exceeds 80 years, in which case the marriage value is treated as nil.

Hope value: is this a relevant factor in valuing house and flat lease claims?

The House of Lords decision in the appeals, commonly known as the *Sportelli* case, is the final episode (for now) in a long-running litigation over the correct approach to be taken in valuing lease enfranchisement and new lease claims.

In summary, the Lords decided unanimously that a landlord is not in law entitled to claim 'hope value' in either a house lease enfranchisement claim, or a flat new lease claim. But the House was divided on the issue in flat lease collective enfranchisement claims. The majority of the Lords (Lord Hoffman dissenting) held (overruling the Court of Appeal), that here the landlord is entitled to claim hope value if there are leaseholders who are not participating in the claim. Such 'hope value' may be claimed in relation to the expectation that a non-participant leaseholder may in future seek to negotiate a new lease or share of freehold.

There was no appeal against the Court of Appeal's decision that a generic deferment rate is to be applied in valuing the investment value of the freehold. So the Court of Appeal's decision on deferment rates is undisturbed. In that decision, the Court of Appeal confirmed the approach of the Lands Tribunal that a generic deferment rate of five per cent should be applied in flat lease enfranchisement or new lease claims.

Hope value

Hope value is a concept known to valuers, but not one that is defined, let alone referred to, in the enfranchisement legislation. Broadly speaking, hope value may be described as the additional value of the freehold that accrues where an investor is buying subject to a leasehold property and the leaseholder is not in the market. It resides, so it is argued, in the expectation that the investor will pay the landlord more for the freehold in the anticipation that the leaseholder will, in time, seek to purchase it, thereby releasing the marriage value which is split between the parties.

Disputes over these two elements of valuation – the deferment rate and hope value - underlay the *Sportelli* litigation.

Proceedings in the tribunal

On the first element, should financial market evidence be used instead of 'market' evidence in arriving at the appropriate deferment rate? If so, should this generic deferment rate be applied in all claims?

On the second issue, as a matter of statutory construction, is a landlord entitled in law to hope value?

These issues were tested in many house enfranchisement claims under the *Leasehold Reform Act* 1967, and new lease and collective enfranchisement claims under Part I of the *Leasehold*

Reform, Housing and Urban Development Act 1993. In order to clarify the position, the Lands Tribunal heard together, various conjoined appeals from the decisions of the LVTs. All of the claims concerned high value properties in what was described as the 'Prime Central London' (PCL) location.

In September 2006, the Lands Tribunal decided that in valuing the vacant possession of the dwelling, general deferment rates should be used: 4.75 per cent for house claims and five per cent for flat new lease or enfranchisement claims. More controversially, the tribunal ruled that such rates should be applied instead of market evidence as that is tainted by the very existence of leaseholder's statutory rights and, in consequence, is unreliable. In arriving at these conclusions, the tribunal heard expert evidence from four financial experts and four valuers. These generic rates were deduced by applying a formula derived from financial evidence adduced at the hearing, based on a 'risk-free rate' of 2.25 per cent, less real growth rate of two per cent, plus a risk premium of 4.5 per cent for houses and 4.75 per cent for flats, producing deferment rates of 4.75 per cent for houses and five per cent for flats.

Originally, the tribunal also decided that except for certain house lease claims (under s.9(1A) of the 1967 Act), a landlord is not entitled to hope value in either enfranchisement or new lease claims. But in a later decision (*Pitts v Cadogan and others* [2007] 42 EG 296), the Tribunal decided that hope value cannot in law be included as an element of a valuation under section 9(1A).

Hope value and Sportelli in the Court of Appeal

The Court of Appeal upheld the tribunal's decisions, including that on hope value. (In a later decision the court dismissed a separate appeal against the *Pitts* decision.) A landlord is not entitled in law to claim hope value, ruled the court, in any claim under the 1967 or 1993 Acts. The landlords obtained permission to appeal the hope value issue to the House of Lords.

Deferment rates and Sportelli in the Court of Appeal

The court also upheld the tribunal's decision on the use of deferment rates based on financial evidence and by rejecting market evidence. But in an important qualification to this it was said:

'The judgement that the same deferment rate should apply outside the PCL area was made, and only could be made, on the evidence then available'. This leaves open the possibility of further evidence being called in areas outside the PCL. The deferment rate adopted by the tribunal will no doubt be the starting point; and their conclusions on the methodology of including the limitations on market evidence, are likely to remain valid'.

As an example, evidence was given on issues relevant to the risk premium for residential property in different areas. There was no appeal against the deferment rate issues to the House of Lords.

Hope value and Sportelli in the House of Lords

The sole issue for the Lords, therefore, was hope value. Dismissing the appeals in the house lease claims and new lease flat claims, the Lords held unanimously that hope value is not in law a valid issue with such claims. To allow it, along with the 50 per cent share of marriage value, would amount to double counting. Further, there is no hope value where the remaining term of the lease is such that no marriage value is payable. (Any element of a leaseholder's hope value should also be left out of account.)

But the Lords held by a majority that in collective enfranchisement claims, if there are any leaseholders in the block of flats who are not participating in the claim, in law hope value can be claimed arising from the possibility that, in future, they may seek, on a voluntary basis, a new lease/share of freehold. This can be taken into account in valuing the investment value of the freehold. The fact that all leaseholders are deemed not to be in the market (under Schedule 6 to the 1993 Act) does not prevent hope value in relation to non-participating leaseholders. The participants are acquiring an investment in relation to those flats and it is only fair that they should pay the market price.

The majority of the Lords emphasised that these conclusions are based on a construction of the legislation; whether or not there is, in any individual case, additional hope value will be a matter for expert valuation evidence. (The Lands Tribunal had heard evidence that there are two approaches: one based on a different deferment rate; the other based on an addition of a proportion of marriage value and it preferred the second approach. Lord Neuberger indicated that he agreed with the tribunal's conclusion on that point).

Leasehold enfranchisement explained

Summary of the *Sportelli* decisions

On the deferment rate two uncertainties remain; what is the extent of the PCL and when can evidence justify a departure from the generic rates?

Hope value has been to a large extent settled. A landlord cannot claim it in house lease claims or flat new lease claims. This applies also to these cases even though there is no marriage value payable. (Lord Neuberger added that any leaseholder 'hope value' should also be excluded from consideration).

But hope value can be claimed in collective claims in relation to the possibility that non-participating leaseholders may seek new leases, etc. at some point in the future by negotiation (not under the Act).

Recent decisions on hope value and the generic deferment rate

Two recent decisions of the Upper Tribunal (Lands Chamber) are of the first importance to enfranchisement claims. They affect valuation issues in flat lease claims. These are the decisions in *Culley v Daejan Properties Limited* [2009] UKHT 168 and *Zuckerman (and others) v the Calthorpe Estate* [2009] UKUT 235. *Culley* is the first Lands Tribunal decision on the assessment of hope value post *Sportelli;* it also deals with the deferment rate. *Zuckerman* is the first decision where the UT has sanctioned a higher deferment rate than the generic rate decisions in *Sportelli*.

Hope value

In *Sportelli,* the Lands Tribunal decided that hope value cannot be claimed in any enfranchisement or new lease claim. (That aspect of their decision was upheld by the Court of Appeal). They did, however, consider how hope value could be assessed: should it be assessed as a proportion of marriage value or by an adjustment to the deferment rate? They preferred the former approach.

Culley v Daejan Properties Limited [2009] UKHT 168 concerned an appeal against a decision of the LVT in a collective enfranchisement claim of a block of four flats in Eastcote, Hillingdon in Greater London. The LVT determined the price

Enfranchisement explained

payable, applying a deferment rate of five per cent. That tribunal also followed the Lands Tribunal *Sportelli* decision and made no allowance for hope value.

One of the issues on appeal was what is the appropriate allowance for hope value in this case, where only two of the four leaseholders were participating? The two non-participating leaseholders had unexpired terms of just over 65 years at the valuation date. If they had participated, the price would have reflected marriage value in relation to their leases (payable for a lease with 80 years or less). As a result of this non-participation, the landlord would only share the marriage value in relation to the two participating leaseholders.

On appeal, the claimant leaseholders argued for an allowance based on five per cent of marriage value (with a deferment rate of eight per cent, on which see below), whilst the respondent landlords claimed an allowance based on 20 per cent of this value. Each party relied on past Lands Tribunal decisions on the application of hope value (that is prior to *Sportelli*), where hope value has been taken, as the Upper Tribunal (UT) concluded that hope value should be expressed as ten per cent of marriage value (in relation to the non-participating leaseholders). In reaching this conclusion, the UT stated that 'considerable care' should be taken before giving weight to specific percentages adopted in other cases. It added:

> 'Hope value is not a matter to be taken into account in the deferment rate, and the deferment rate has no influence on what the appropriate allowance for hope value should be' (para. 62).

The Lands Tribunal made two other points: first, the hope value allowance is likely to be greater if the proportion of non-participating leaseholders is relatively large, and second, that it will be lower if the unexpired terms are particularly long. In this case, where 50 per cent of the leaseholders were participating and the unexpired terms were just over 65 years (and 'bearing in mind the essentially speculative nature of hope value') hope value was expressed as ten per cent of marriage value.

It will be interesting to see how valuers will argue cases following this decision. This appeal concerned a claim where the non-participation could not be any lower (as not less than 50 per cent of leaseholders must support an enfranchisement claim). Presumably, if three of the four leaseholders had participated, the hope value allowance would have been lower? And, if the unexpired leases had longer terms than they did in this case, the allowance might have been lower? Or, if just 50 per cent of the leaseholders participated and they had longer leases, presumably a lower allowance would be appropriate? It is possible that applying hope value as ten per cent of marriage value may prove to be the maximum allowable in these claims.

The deferment rate

In *Sportelli,* the Court of Appeal upheld the Lands Tribunal on both hope value and on the decision on the general application of a deferment rate of five per cent for flat claims (4.75 per cent for houses). In *Sportelli,* the UT decided the five per cent generic deferment rate as the 'risk-free rate' of 2.25 per cent, minus the 'real growth rate' of two per cent, plus a 'risk premium' of 4.5 per cent, plus an increased figure for the management risks of 0.25 per cent. The Court of Appeal left open the issue of whether a higher rate could be justified in claims outside the PCL.

So far, valuers acting for leaseholders have been unsuccessful in the UT, in contending for a higher deferment rate to take account of matters such as poor location. The UT has been steadfast in ruling that such factors are already taken into account in valuing the freehold reversion and do not of themselves justify a higher deferment rate.

In the *Culley* appeal, the claimant's valuer contended for an eight per cent deferment rate on account of the current condition of the property (built in the 1930s); its likely deterioration and its obsolescence, which justified departure from the generic five per cent rate. Other factors included the risk of different property growth rates in different areas. These submissions were firmly rejected, as was the valuer's challenge to UT's general approach to the deferment rate (hardly surprising as this approach has been upheld by the Court of Appeal).

It is noteworthy that both valuers would have supported higher deferment rates (as would the LVT), in this case, were it not for the *Sportelli* edicts on the use of generic rates.

Such challenges were also firmly rejected in another recent decision of the UT in *Sherwood Hall (East End Road) v Magnolia Tree Limited* [2009] UKUT 158. Here, the valuer's evidence that a higher deferment rate is justified for leases with unexpired terms in excess of 80 years was also firmly rejected.

Enfranchisement explained

This brings us to the *Zuckerman* decision where 11 leaseholders were claiming new leases under the 1993 Act. They appealed against decisions of the LVT, which decided in favour of the estate, that the standard five per cent rate should be applied. (The appeal properties are located on the Calthorpe estate in the Midlands, which comprises six three-storey blocks of flats built in the 1970s.) Their appeal succeeded on three grounds; 'deterioration and obsolescence', 'prospects of future growth' and the appropriate 'allowance for flats'.

On the first ground, the Lands Tribunal accepted the leaseholder's expert evidence that there is a greater risk of deterioration in the properties than is the case for properties in the PCL. This was not reflected in vacant possession values so that a potential purchaser would, concluded the tribunal, require an increase in the risk premium of 0.25 per cent (to 4.75 per cent).

On future growth, the Lands Tribunal also accepted the expert evidence that 'despite its undoubted limitations' the available statistical evidence demonstrated a 'significantly slower long-term growth rate' in the West Midlands than in PCL. An investor would therefore be less confident of achieving a two per cent growth, and to compensate for this, a further increase of 0.5 per cent in the risk premium to 5.25 per cent should be made.

On the third ground, the tribunal accepted the evidence and expert opinion that the greater risks suffered by landlords since the introduction of the new regulations on service charges has affected the attitude of the market (these requirements came into force on 31 October 2003).

> 'I am satisfied that by September 2007, the first date with which I am concerned, the market was more aware of the dangers posed by the regulations than was the case in *Sportelli*, where the properties fell to be valued between two and a quarter and three and three quarter years earlier'.

This led the tribunal to decide that in the 11 properties concerned, an addition of 0.5 per cent was justified.

In summary, on the basis of the expert evidence, the case for a departure from the *Sportelli* starting point of five per cent was allowed by increasing the risk premium from 4.5 per cent to 5.25 per cent, and the allowance for flats was increased from 0.25 per cent to 0.5 per cent. This resulted in a deferment rate of six per cent. This is the first decision that has introduced a different rate to the generic rate and it comes just after the *Culley* decision. The difference in the results appears to be that, in the *Zuckerman* case, there was convincing evidence to justify a different deferment rate.

It would be surprising if valuers instructed by leaseholders do not in future press the case for a higher rate where such evidence can be produced. The point on the increased rate for allowances for flats is particularly interesting, as presumably there will be evidence in most parts of the country that the impact of the service charge consultation regulations is something that the local market is aware of. (The same might apply to properties in prime central London?). There may also be evidence that the market is aware of other risks as well, such as the prospect of a landlord losing control of the management of a block of flats where the leaseholders exercise the no-fault right to manage (under Part 2 of the *Commonhold and Leasehold Reform Act 2002*, which also came into force in October 2003).

Intermediate leases

It is sometimes the case that there is a lease (or leases) superior to the house lease held by a qualifying leaseholder. The 1967 Act takes account of this in its procedures and in the valuation of the claim. So too, with flat lease claims for the grant of a new lease where the claim has to be made of the competent landlord; that is the freeholder, or the holder of a superior lease where that leaseholder has a sufficient interest as to be able to grant a new lease 90 years longer than the current lease. In collective claims, there may be intermediate leases. In all such cases, holders of such leases are entitled to payments for either the loss of the superior lease, or its diminution in value, along with an appropriate share of any marriage value. These issues are all considered in the legal and the valuation chapters that follow.

A number of issues were considered by the Lands Tribunal in several conjoined appeals in what has become known as the 'Nailrile' litigation. Certain preliminary decisions were announced by the tribunal in December 2008 (*Nailrile v Cadogan Estate and others* [2009] RVR 95). A final decision is expected in 2010.

Enfranchisement explained

Other recent decisions in enfranchisement and new lease claims

As previously noted, in 2008 there were four House of Lords decisions and a major Court of Appeal decision. One of these cases – the *Sportelli* litigation has just been considered. In addition, this chapter summarises decisions on the meaning of a 'house', a decision on when a landlord can use redevelopment to oppose claims, and whether a head lease of a block of flats is a qualifying lease.

Is the building a 'house'?

For someone unfamiliar with leasehold house enfranchisement, the breadth of the definition of which buildings can be treated as houses may come as a surprise. Section 2(1) of the *Leasehold Reform Act* 1967 (LRA 1967) defines the word 'house' as follows:

> '(1) For purposes of this Part of this Act, "house" includes any building designed or adapted for living in and reasonably so called, notwithstanding that the building is not structurally detached, or was or is not solely designed or adapted for living in, or is divided horizontally into flats or maisonettes: and (a) where a building is divided horizontally, the flats or other units into which it is so divided are not separate "houses", though the building as a whole may be; and (b) where a building is divided vertically, the building as a whole is not a "house", though any of the units into which it is divided may be.'

The application of this definition to individual cases has been the subject of no fewer than four appeals to the House of Lords, and there are also several Court of Appeal decisions as well.

In considering whether a particular building is a house or not, one question is whether it was 'designed or adapted for living in', a question that was easier to answer when there was a residence test. Another issue (assuming the building was designed or adapted for living in), is whether it is a house 'reasonably so called'. The first of these two related issues was considered by the House of Lords in *Boss Holdings Limited v Grosvenor West End Properties* [2008] UKHL 5, [2008] 2 All ER 759; the second issue was considered by the Court of Appeal in *Grosvenor Estates Limited v Prospect Estates Limited* [2008] EWCA Civ 1281, [2008] All ER (D) 202 (Nov).

Was the building designed or adapted for living in?

This was the issue for the Lords (now the Supreme Court), in the *Boss* case, which concerned a building built in the mid-18th century as a large single dwelling in central London consisting of a basement, ground, and four upper floors. From 1946, the building was held on a lease under which the lower three floors were used for a dressmaking business, the second and third floors as a self-contained flat, while the upper floor was used by employees. With the passing of time this changed: the commercial use finished in 1990 since when those floors became vacant, and the residential use finished later whereupon those floors also became vacant. The upper three floors were completely dilapidated and the whole of the building became unoccupied.

In October 2003, the then leaseholder (a company) served a notice seeking to enfranchise under LRA 1967 and shortly afterwards assigned the lease with the benefit of the notice to Boss Holdings. The Grosvenor Estate gave a counter-notice denying that the building was a house at the date the enfranchisement notice was given. In the ensuing County Court proceedings, the court upheld the landlord's contention and the Court of Appeal dismissed the leaseholder's appeal. In essence, the courts held that at the date of the notice, the building was not physically fit for immediate residential occupation.

Allowing the leaseholder's appeal, the Lords unanimously held that at the date of the enfranchisement notice the building was a 'house'. The Lords concluded that as at the date the enfranchisement notice was given, the fact that the building had become internally dilapidated and incapable of occupation did not detract from the fact that the building was originally designed for living in; that nothing that has happened since it was built changed this conclusion. The key question is first for what purpose was the building originally designed and whether any works since carried out have adapted the building for a different use – the key question being, was the building designed or adapted for living in? Applied to this case, the Lords concluded the building was designed for living in and that, despite what may have happened in recent years, most of the interior of the building remained designed to be lived in.

The question whether a building that was originally designed for living in might through later adaptation cease to be a 'house' was left open, though it was hinted that it is the original design that is the key issue and that the approach adopted by the

Court of Appeal of examining whether the building is capable of immediate residential use is an uncertain one. The Lords' decision has the merit of a degree of certainty. A building is a house if it was originally designed as such and, if it was, this will usually determine the issue of whether the building is a house when an enfranchisement notice is given.

Is a building a 'house' reasonably so called?

The Lords' decision in *Boss* was published early in 2008. Some ten months later came the Court of Appeal decision in the *Prospect Estates* case, where the building appears from the reports to be very similar to the one in *Boss*. It was built in the mid-19th century as a house for living in and later two floors were added. As the court put it: 'It still looks like a house' (para. 4) and 'To a passer-by, the building still looks like a house' (para. 7). A difference between this and the *Boss* building is that 88.5 per cent of the floor space is in commercial use, the remainder is residential for occupation by employees of the leaseholder.

The issue in this appeal was whether it was reasonable to call the building a house. The leaseholder of the building gave notice to enfranchise and the landlord served a counter-notice denying the claim, contending that it was not reasonable to call the building a house. The landlord accepted that, at the date of the notice, it was correct to say that the building had not ceased to be designed as a house. But the landlord contended that as the only living accommodation was on the fourth floor and this was linked to occupation of the remainder of the building, which could only be used for offices, this meant that it was not reasonable to call the building a house.

Both parties relied on an earlier House of Lords decision in *Tandon v Trustees of Spurgeon Homes* [1982] AC 755, [1982] 1 All ER 1086, the leading case on this issue. Applying the reasoning in that decision, the Court of Appeal concluded that the words: 'a house reasonably so-called' is a limitation or qualification. It serves to exclude certain buildings which might be 'houses' under other legislation (such as the Rent Acts) from being houses within LRA 1967. Thus purpose-built hotels, for example, cannot be a house under LRA 1967, while a building designed for living in does not cease to be a house simply because part of it is no longer used for living in. The court went on to say:

'In between these kinds of building, there is a grey area of varying degrees of mixed use. Depending on the particular circumstances of the case, such a building may, or may not, as a matter of law be a house reasonably so called' (para. 14).

In this case, the Court of Appeal concluded that the County Court paid insufficient attention to the 'peculiar, even exceptional' circumstances of this case where under the lease of the building there is a prescribed and a predominant office use. Giving sufficient attention to the commercial use required by the lease, the actual uses of the building and the relative proportions of mixed-use, the judge should have concluded that it was no longer reasonable to call the building a house (although the building had been designed as a house).

In the *Boss* case, the County Court concluded that, had it decided that the building had been designed or adapted for living in, it would have concluded that it was reasonable to call it a house. The Lords stated that this conclusion was 'plainly correct' (para. 15). Of course, this particular issue did not have to be considered in any detail by the Lords who had to concentrate on the primary issue of whether the building was designed or adapted for living in. In *Prospect Estates*, in contrast, it was accepted that the building was still correctly described as having being designed for living in, but the extent of commercial use meant that it was no longer reasonable to call it a house. This was so even though, from an external view, one would call the building a house and even though the internal design had not been materially altered since it was built as a house. (It is understood that Prospect Estates are not pursuing an application for permission to appeal.)

Where does this leave the position? Well, it seems clear that a building which was originally designed for living in is, and remains, a house even though it is no longer occupied, or in part is incapable of occupation. It also seems likely that a later adaption of the building will not necessarily point to the conclusion that it is no longer a house. Where, however, a building can only be used exclusively or predominantly for commercial use, it may not be reasonable to call it a house.

If a house is subject to a business lease, this is one of the two residual cases where there is still a residence test (and the lease must have been granted for a term longer than 35 years (see: s.1(1)(1ZC) and s.1(1)(9IA) of LRA 1967). In this case, the commercial units were underlettings so the leaseholder was not occupying under a business lease (as defined in Part II of the *Landlord and Tenant Act* 1985). The leaseholder did not, therefore, have to satisfy the residence test (which as a company it could not, of course, by itself or through occupation by its employees (s.37(5)).

One wonders if Parliament anticipated the full implications of repealing the residence test. Did it really intend that commercial interests or investors should be able to take advantage of enfranchisement rights, which until 2002, were justified as protecting home owners? Why should a tenant with a business lease have enfranchisement rights? *Prospect Holdings* allows the courts to take a more flexible approach to whether it is reasonable to call a building a house or not. Many will see this approach as a fairer policy to this, at times, complex issue.

This same issue was recently considered by the County Court in *Hosebay Limited v Day (and another)* [November, 2009] where it was held that it was reasonable to call buildings which were constructed as houses, but used for the letting of rooms, a 'house'. Permission to appeal this decision to the Court of Appeal has been given and the appeal is likely to be heard in 2010.

Redevelopment as a ground for resisting a claim

During the last five years of the lease, the landlord may oppose a new lease claim by application to the court where the landlord needs possession to redevelop and must demolish, reconstruct or carry out substantial construction works to the whole or a substantial part of the premises in which the flat is contained. The House of Lords examined this issue in *Majorstake Limited v Curtis* [2008] UKHL 10. In a unanimous decision, the House of Lords has allowed a leaseholder's appeal from a decision from the Court of Appeal ([2006] EWCA Civ 1171). The Court of Appeal, by a majority, held that the landlord was entitled to oppose the leaseholder's claim for a new lease under the provisions in Part I of the *Leasehold Reform, Housing and Development Act* 1993 as the landlord intended to recover possession of the flat in order to carry out redevelopment works to premises in which the flat formed part. In that decision the Court of Appeal overruled a decision of the County Court. By allowing the leaseholder's appeal, the House of Lords has now reinstated that decision.

The House of Lords held unanimously that the expression 'any premises in which the flat is contained' could not be the combination of the two flats.

The House of Lords concluded that the problem with the Court of Appeal's construction is that it could lead to the conclusion that the landlord would succeed under section 47, by establishing an intention to redevelop the tenant's flat, together with a wholly insignificant area such as a box room or a broom cupboard.

This issue can also arise with a claim for a new lease of a flat under the 1993 Act as the landlord has a right to seek possession in the last year of the current lease or during the last five years of the new lease (s. 61 of the1993 Act). Similarly, a landlord can seek possession where not less than two-thirds of the leases have less than five years unexpired and the landlord intends to redevelop.

Can an intermediate lease qualify for a new lease?

Where the lease is an intermediate lease, can that leaseholder exercise the right to a new lease in relation to any of the flats which are held under that intermediate lease? This was the issue for the Court of Appeal in the following case: *Howard de Walden Estate v Aggio (and others)* [2007] L&TR 129. This case involved two appeals on the same issue. In the first, the *de Walden Estate* case, there was a single building with five flats of which three were held on long leases. There was also a head lease which included internal common parts and external parking areas. The head leaseholder sought to extend the head lease in relation to two of the flats and the landlord served a counter-notice denying that a head leaseholder can be a qualifying tenant for a new lease claim.

In the second case, the *Cadogan* claim, there is a five storey building and a head lease to the building except for the basement and part of the ground floor. The head lease includes common parts and parking areas and the flat is three stories. The head leaseholder sought to extend the lease of the flat and the landlord served a counter-notice denying the claim, arguing that the head lease is not a qualifying lease for new lease purposes.

In both cases, the Court of Appeal, noting that Part I of the Act makes no specific provision for such cases, held that such intermediate and head leases are not qualifying leases under the Act. The court overruled *Maurice v Hollow-Ware Productions*

[2005] 26 EG 132, a case involving a head lessee of a block of 28 flats who was clearly not entitled to enfranchise under the 1993 Act (owns more than three flats), but the court decided that the leaseholder was entitled to new leases for each. This was overruled by the Court of Appeal by the *de Walden v Aggio* [2007] decision: a head lessee has no right to seek lease extensions.

The decision was overruled by the House of Lords ([2008] UKHL 44) where the court held that such leaseholders have qualifying leases for the purposes of claiming a new lease. The fact that the lease contained property other than a flat is irrelevant. The House confirmed that the *Maurice* decision was correctly decided. In summary, the Lords decided that a lessee who has a lease of property which includes a flat can be a 'qualifying tenant' of that flat for the purpose of Chapter II of Part I of the *Leasehold Reform, Housing and Urban Development Act* 1993 irrespective of the nature or extent of the other property included in the demise and therefore does have the right to a new lease in respect of that flat under the 1993 Act.

Adjudication

Both the 1967 and the 1993 Acts make provision for the settlement of disputes. In the most general of terms, any dispute over entitlement must be referred to the County Court. For example, if the landlord argues that the building is not in law a 'house' this is a matter that must be referred to the County Court for a decision. Another example is where a landlord claims the right to oppose a grant of a new flat lease because the landlord intends to redevelop the premises containing the flat, and another is whether the holder of a head lease of a block of flats has a qualifying lease for new lease purposes. These are all matters that can only be resolved where there is a dispute by reference to the County Court. Of course, in the usual way, appeals lie from the County Court decision to the Court of Appeal and, in some cases, beyond that to the Supreme Court.

Issues relating to valuation (which it is thought are far more common in practice than issues over entitlement), and related issues over the terms of a transfer or grant of a new lease, belonged to the Leasehold Valuation Tribunal (part of the Residential Property Tribunal service). Appeals proceed from that Tribunal to the Lands Tribunal which is now known as the Upper Tribunal (Lands Chamber) and from there to the Court of Appeal (on legal issues only), with a further appeal possible to the House of Lords. It was appeals on these valuation decisions that were the subject of the fourth House of Lords case in 2008 that is the *Sportelli* litigation, which was considered earlier in this chapter. (For ease of reference, the UT will be described in this work as the Lands Tribunal (or the tribunal)).

What this book does not cover

Qualifying leaseholders of flats have two other ways in which they may be able to acquire the freehold. (This does not apply to qualifying leases of houses.)

First, the landlord that wishes to dispose of an interest in a qualifying block of flats, that is to say a block where the non-residential use does not exceed 50 per cent and there are two or more leases, which are qualifying leases (which rather anomalously can include protected tenancies). The landlord must first offer the interest to the qualifying leaseholders. The principles and statutory procedures (which can be complicated), are provided for in Part I of the *Landlord and Tenant Act* 1987. Failure by a landlord to dispose in breach of these obligations is an offence and the leaseholders have rights to acquire the interest which has been transferred from the new landlords.

Under Part III of the 1987 Act, qualifying leaseholders may, in certain circumstances, apply to the County Court to acquire the freehold, broadly speaking, in cases where the current landlord cannot be found or is in default of his obligations. The costs to the acquiring leaseholders may be considerably less than the cost in exercising enfranchisement rights under the 1993 Act. This is because no marriage value is payable regardless of the length of the leases, and where the court makes an order, costs will usually follow the event.

All leaseholders have other rights and landlords have obligations under other legislation, which applies to leasehold management. These include matters that are far more relevant to blocks of flats than they are to houses. They include regulation of service charges and related matters under the *Landlord & Tenant Act* 1985; the right for a manager to be appointed under Part II of the 1987 Act, and the no fault based right to manage under Part 2 of the 2002 Act. The changes made by Part 2 of the 2002 Act have made massive changes to leasehold management.

Finally, leaseholders may have the right to stay on the property when the long lease expires. For leases which expire on or after 15 January 1999, the leaseholder has the right to an assured tenancy under the provisions in section 186 and Schedule 10 to the *Local Government and Housing Act* 1989. Assured tenancies are provided for in Part I of the *Housing Act* 1988. The leaseholder must live in the property as their only or principal home and the rent must not exceed £25,000 per annum. Clearly, this excludes a company leaseholder from the right to an assured tenancy and higher value properties may command a rent above the current £25,000 limit. It appears that the 1988 Act may be amended in 2010 to increase the maximum rent to £100,000 per annum, which will bring even higher value properties within the scope of the assured tenancy regime.

Writing this book

This introductory chapter was written by James Driscoll who is the consulting editor to the work. Chapters 1, 3, 5 and 6 were written by Ellodie Gibbons. James Wilson wrote chapters 2, 4 and 7.

We hope that readers will find this work useful and we will be pleased to receive comments on it.

1

Flats: the individual right of a tenant to acquire a new lease

Introduction

Whilst it is common to talk about tenants having a right to extend their leases, it is important to be clear at the outset as to what, in fact, a tenant has a right to acquire under Chapter II of Part 1 of the *Leasehold Reform, Housing and Urban Development Act 1993*. A tenant does not have a right to acquire an extension to their existing lease, but rather a new lease in substitution for the existing lease, which is:

- at a peppercorn (i.e. a nominal) rent; and
- for a term expiring 90 years after the term date of the existing lease (s.56(1)).

In order to obtain a new lease the tenant must pay:

- a premium determined in accordance with Schedule 13;
- such amounts, determined in accordance with Schedule 13, as are payable to the owners of any intermediate leasehold interests;
- any outstanding rent;
- the landlord's professional costs in connection with the new lease; and
- any other sums due and payable by the tenant to any other party to the tenant's lease.

If the amount of any of the above sums cannot be fully ascertained, then the tenant must offer reasonable security in respect of the payment of them (s.56(3)).

Who qualifies?

The following persons have the right to acquire a new lease:

- a tenant who has for the last two years been a qualifying tenant of the flat (s.39(1));
- the personal representatives of a tenant who has for the two years prior to his death been a qualifying tenant of the flat (s.39(3A)), if they make claim within two years of the grant of probate or letters of administration (s.42(4A)); and
- the assignee of a tenant's notice served by a tenant who has for the previous two years been a qualifying tenant of the flat.

It is only upon registration at HM Land Registry that a tenant becomes the legal owner of the lease. Consequently, the tenant must have been the registered proprietor of the lease for at least two years in order to have the right to acquire a new lease. However, as the definition of a 'lease' includes an agreement for a lease (s.101(2)), a tenant could include a period prior to the grant of the lease or a period between the grant and registration within the two years, although it is probably safest to wait for two years post-registration.

The qualifying tenant

Pursuant to section 5(1), a tenant is a qualifying tenant of a flat if he is the tenant of the flat under a long lease. Where there are joint tenants, they are regarded as jointly constituting the qualifying tenant of the flat (s.5(4)(b)). Further, a tenant can be the qualifying tenant of two or more flats in the building at the same time (s.39(4)) and a head lessee can be a qualifying tenant: *Howard de Walden Estates Ltd v Aggio* [2009] 1 AC. 39.

> *Example*
>
> A head lessee was a long lessee of a five-storey building containing residential flats, none of which were sub-let on long leases. The building contained internal common parts and external areas for parking, all of which were included in the head lease. The head lessee was, in relation to each of the flats, a tenant of a flat for the purposes of section 39(1): *Aggio*.

However, in relation to claims under Chapter II, there are two situations where tenants who would otherwise be qualifying tenants for the purposes of subsection 1, do not in fact qualify.

These are where:

- the tenant's lease falls within one of the exceptions contained in section 5(2), as to which see below; or
- there is also a qualifying tenant of an inferior lease (s.5(4)(a)).

> *Example*
>
> A grants B a lease of a flat for a term of 99 years. B grants C a sub-lease of the flat for a term of 90 years. C is a qualifying tenant and therefore B cannot also be a qualifying tenant by virtue of section 5(3) and 5(4)(a).

The qualifying flat

The tenant must be a tenant of a flat. 'Flat' is defined in section 101(1) as being a separate set of premises (whether or not on the same floor):

- which forms part of a building; and
- which is constructed or adapted for use for the purposes of a dwelling, and
- either the whole or a material part of which lies above or below some other part of the building.

By virtue of section 62(2) a flat includes any garage, outhouse, garden, yard and appurtenances belonging to, or usually enjoyed with, the flat and let to the tenant with the flat. This definition is almost identical to the meaning given to 'premises' in section 2(3) of the *Leasehold Reform Act* 1967 and regard should be had to chapter 5 where that meaning is discussed.

> *Example*
>
> A storeroom on the sixth floor of a block of flats, which was not included in the lease of a flat to the tenant, but let to the tenant separately for the same term as the lease was not an 'outhouse' as it was not outside the main building. However, it was an 'appurtenance' as it was within the curtilage of the block: *Cadogan v McGirk* [1996] 4 All ER. 643.

The qualifying lease

A qualifying lease is a 'long lease'. Most commonly, this is a lease for a fixed term of more than 21 years (s.7(1)(a)). However, other leases can be long leases, for example, right to buy leases and shared ownership leases where the tenant's total share is 100 per cent. Consequently, when considering whether a lease is a long lease, the starting point ought to be to look to see whether or not it has been granted for a fixed term of more than 21 years and if it has not, refer to section 7(1) to ascertain whether it may fall within any of the other categories.

In order to establish whether a lease has been granted for a fixed term of more than 21 years, it is necessary to ascertain:

- What is the length of the term specified in the lease?
- When did the term commence? This will be the later of the date of the lease and the date specified in the lease as being the commencement of the term: see *Roberts v Church Commissioners for England* [1972] 1 QB 278.

Example

(1) A lease is dated 6 September 1990 and stated to be for a term of 22 years, commencing on 29 September 1990.

The term commences on 29 September 1990 and expires on 28 September 2012 and is therefore more than 21 years. Consequently, the lease is a 'long lease' within the meaning of the Act.

(2) A lease is dated 30 September 1991 and stated to be for a term of 22 years, commencing on 29 September 1990.

The term commences on 30 September 1991 and expires on 28 September 2012 and is therefore less than 21 years. Consequently, the lease is not a 'long lease' within the meaning of the Act.

A second consideration, if the lease is not, on its face, for a fixed term of more than 21 years, is whether the lease is in some way a continuation of a previous lease. For example, where the tenant was a tenant of any property under a long lease and on the coming to an end of that lease became the tenant of the property, or any part of it, under a subsequent tenancy (whether by express grant or implication of law), then by virtue of section 7(3), that tenancy is deemed to be a long lease irrespective of its terms.

Alternatively, a lease may not have been granted for a fixed term of more than 21 years, but may contain a covenant or obligation for renewal without payment of a premium. If the lease is, or has been renewed, so as to bring to more than 21 years the total of the terms granted, then the lease will be treated, by virtue of section 7(4), as having been granted originally for a fixed term of more than 21 years. A lease may also have continued or be continuing under statute, for example, under Part I of the *Landlord and Tenant Act* 1954 or Schedule 10 to the *Local Government and Housing Act* 1989. Where this is the case, any period during which the lease is so continuing is included within the meaning of a long lease by virtue of section 7(5).

Certain leases are excluded from the definition of a long lease and these are leases which are terminable by notice after death, marriage or the formation of a civil partnership. Such leases are not to be treated as long leases by virtue of section 7(2) if:

- the notice is capable of being given at any time after the death or marriage of, or the formation of a civil partnership by, the tenant;
- the length of the notice is not more than three months; and
- the terms of the lease preclude both –
    (i) its assignment otherwise than by virtue of section 92 of the *Housing Act* 1985 (assignments by way of exchange); and
    (ii) the sub-letting of the whole of the premises comprised in it.

A common example of this type of lease is one which has been granted in pursuance of an equity release scheme. A company buys a property from its owners and then leases the property back to the former owners to allow them to continue to reside in the property for the remainder of their lives. In order to protect the company's interest, the lease is likely to contain, among other clauses, an absolute prohibition against assignment or sub-letting of the whole of the property and will be terminable on the death of the previous owners.

Some leases are long leases within the meaning of section 7, but, as stated above, are such that any tenant under them is not to be regarded as a qualifying tenant. These leases are listed in section 5(2) and are:

- business leases;
- leases under which the immediate landlord is a charitable housing trust and the flat forms part of the housing accommodation provided by it in the pursuit of its charitable purposes; and
- leases granted by a sub-demise out of a superior lease, which is not a long lease, where the grant was made in breach of the terms of the superior lease and there has been no waiver of the breach by the superior landlord.

> *Example*
>
> A grants B a lease of residential premises for a fixed term of 90 years from 1 January 2001. The lease is terminable on the death of B upon one month's notice being given any time after B's death. The lease contains an absolute prohibition against assignment and sub-letting the whole of the premises. Unbeknown to A, B grants C a lease of the premises for a fixed term of 83 years from 1 January 2008, which is not terminable on death. By 1 February 2010, C, knowing that he has a lease for a fixed term of more than 21 years and has been the registered proprietor of the premises for at least two years, wants to acquire a new lease under the Act. Is he a qualifying tenant?
>
> Answer: The lease of the premises from A to B is not a long lease by virtue of section 7(2). The grant of a lease by B is a breach of covenant. As A does not know about the breach, he cannot have waived it. Consequently, the lease of the premises from B to C falls within section 5(2)(c); section 5(1) does not apply and C is not a qualifying tenant.

Checklist for tenants

The first step is to identify the person seeking to acquire a new lease and the lease pursuant to which they own the flat. If the person seeking to acquire a new lease is a personal representative or an assignee of a notice of claim, then it is necessary to identify who it is said was the qualifying tenant and the lease pursuant to which they owned the flat. Once the purported qualifying tenant and lease have been identified, it is then necessary to check the following.

- Has that tenant been (or had that tenant been), the registered proprietor of the lease for at least two years?
- Is there an inferior lease? If so, is there a qualifying tenant under that lease?
- Does the flat fall within the definition contained in section 101(1)?
- Has the lease been granted for a term of more than 21 years?
- If not, does the lease fall within subsections (b) to (e) of section 7(1) or sections 7(3) or (4)?
- If the lease is for a fixed term of more than 21 years, is it terminable upon death or marriage?
- If it is, does it fulfil the criteria in section 7(2)?
- Does the lease fall within section 5(2)?

Who is the landlord?

Before making a claim it is important to identify who the landlord is for the purposes of Chapter II. This landlord is known as the 'competent landlord'. The competent landlord will be the landlord with either a freehold or a leasehold interest whose duration is such as to enable him to grant a new lease in accordance with Chapter II, and who is not the superior landlord to a landlord who also fulfils these criteria (s.40(1)). Any landlord intermediate between the competent landlord and the tenant is an 'other landlord'.

> *Examples*
>
> (1) The tenant's lease is for a term expiring on 24 December 2059. The tenant's immediate landlord holds under a lease from the freehold owner expiring on 31 December 2059. The freehold owner is the competent landlord as the immediate landlord's interest is of insufficient duration to enable him to grant a new lease of 90 years from the expiry of the existing lease on 24 December 2059. The immediate landlord is an other landlord.
>
> (2) The tenant's lease is for a term expiring on 24 December 2059. The tenant's immediate landlord holds under a lease from another leasehold owner expiring on 31 December 2149. The superior landlord holds under a lease from the freeholder expiring on 1 January 2150. Both the immediate landlord and the superior landlord have an interest of sufficient duration to enable them to grant a new lease of 90 years from the expiry of the existing lease on 24 December 2059. However, in such circumstances, the immediate landlord is the competent landlord and there are no other landlords.

It ought to be obvious from the above that it is necessary to ascertain not only the identities of all those with interests superior to the tenant, but also the duration of those interests. In order to do this, the first step will be to look at the Land Register. This may not provide all the information required and if so, it will be necessary to serve a notice under section 41. There are three notices which may be served under this section, which can be summarised as follows:

- a notice to the immediate landlord or any person receiving rent on behalf of the immediate landlord (s.41(1) and (2));
- a notice to the freeholder requiring him to give details of the intermediate leaseholders (s.41(3)(a)); and
- a notice to the intermediate leaseholders requiring them to give particulars of their leases (s.41(3)(b)).

Flats: the individual right of a tenant to acquire a new lease

A notice under section 41(1) may be served requiring the recipient to state whether the immediate landlord is the owner of the freehold interest in the flat and, if not, to give the tenant as much of the following information as is known to the recipient:

- the name and address of the person who owns the freehold interest in the flat;
- the duration of the leasehold interest in the flat of the tenant's immediate landlord and the extent of the premises in which it subsists; and
- the name and address of the person who has a leasehold interest in the flat, which is superior to that of the tenant's immediate landlord, the duration of any such interest and the extent of the premises in which it subsists.

There is no prescribed form of notice. However, any notice given under section 41 shall also require the recipient to state whether there is a current claim for collective enfranchisement in respect of the premises containing the flat and to give certain information regarding any such claim (s.41(4)). Further, any information sought by virtue of a notice served under section 41 must be given to the tenant within 28 days of the giving of the notice.

Example

**Leasehold Reform, Housing and Urban Development Act 1993
Section 41(1),(2)**

Notice

Re: [*Address of the flat*]

To: [*Name of recipient*]

TAKE notice that I/we [*Name of the tenant(s)*] are the qualifying tenants of the above flat within the meaning of the above Act.

You are required under section 41 of the above Act to state whether [*Name of recipient*] is the owner of the freehold interest in the above flat and, if not, to give me/us (so far as you know) the following information:

(1) the name and address of the person who owns the freehold interest in the flat;
(2) the duration of the leasehold interest in the flat of my immediate landlord and the extent of the premises in which it subsists;
(3) the name and address of every person who has a leasehold interest in the above flat which is superior to that of my immediate landlord, the duration of that interest, and the extent of the premises in which it subsists.

37

> If you have received a notice under section 13, you are required to state the date on which that notice was given, and the name and address of the nominee purchaser for the time being appointed for the purposes of section 15 of the above Act in relation to that claim.
>
> You must give me all the information required by this notice within 28 days of receiving it.
>
> Dated, etc.

If the recipient of a notice served under section 41 fails to provide the information sought, then it will be necessary to serve a default notice under section 92 and seek an order from the court requiring him to make good the default, if he has not done so within 14 days of the giving of the notice. An example of a default notice follows.

Special categories of landlords

Schedule 2 contains provisions relating to special categories of landlords, those categories being as follows:

- mortgagees in possession of the landlord's interest;
- custodian trustees in whom the landlord's interest is vested;
- landlords under a disability;
- landlords whose interest is held in trust;
- landlords whose interest is subject to a settlement;
- university and college landlords; and
- ecclesiastical landlords.

If the landlord falls into one of the above categories, then regard ought to be had to Schedule 2.

Missing landlords

It may be that the competent landlord cannot be found or that his identity cannot be ascertained. In such circumstances the court may, on the application of the tenant, make a vesting order under section 50(1). The court must be satisfied that:

- on the date of the making of the application, the tenant had the right to acquire a new lease of his flat; and
- on that date he would not have been precluded by any provision of Chapter II from giving a valid notice under section 42 with respect to his flat (s.50(3)).

As to the tenant having the right to acquire a new lease of his flat, see the 'Checklist for tenants'. As to being precluded from giving a valid notice, see 'Restrictions on serving an effective tenant's notice' to follow.

It will also be necessary to prove on an application under section 50(1), not only that the tenant has right to acquire a new lease and to serve a notice under section 42, but that the competent landlord cannot be found or that his identity cannot be ascertained. This will be done by showing that all reasonable enquiries have been made of him and have proved fruitless. Depending upon the circumstances, it is suggested that the following steps could be taken:

- check the Land Register;
- serve all relevant section 41 notices;
- check when ground rent and service charges were last demanded/collected and whether there is an address on any such demands;
- check the occupation and ownership of any address given for the competent landlord on the Land Register, in any response to a section 41 notice or on any demand for ground rent and service charges;
- make enquiries with previous leasehold owners as to any contact they may have had with any landlord;
- check the National Deaths Register;
- place an advertisement in the national and/or local press; and/or
- employ a firm of enquiry agents to trace the competent landlord.

If there are reasonable steps which could have been taken and have not, then the court may require the tenant to take such steps before making an order under section 50(1) (s.50(4)). As to the position if the landlord is subsequently traced, or the tenant wishes to withdraw the application for a vesting order, see sections 50(4) and (5).

A vesting order under section 50(1) is an order providing for the surrender of the tenant's existing lease and the grant of a new lease on terms determined by a leasehold valuation tribunal (LVT) (s.51(1)). Consequently, once the court has made a vesting order, the LVT must determine those terms and approve a form of lease. In doing so, the LVT will determine the appropriate amount, which is the aggregate of:

- the premium payable under Schedule 13;
- any other amounts payable under Schedule 13; and
- any amounts or estimated amounts, at the time of execution of the new lease, due to the landlord from the tenant.

It may be that the landlord has been missing for some time, in which case no rent will have been paid for a number of years. Given that section 19 of the *Limitation Act* 1980 provides that no action to recover rent shall be brought after six years, no more than six years' worth of rent will be due to the landlord at the time of execution of the new lease.

On the tenant paying the appropriate sum into court, a person designated by the court will execute the lease, the form of which having been approved by the LVT. The tenant is likely to incur significant costs in relation to the proceedings, both before the court and the LVT, through no fault of anyone other than the landlord who has neglected his property interests; whilst the appropriate sum will languish in the court's funds and can be claimed by the landlord at any time. It seems only fair, therefore, that the tenant should be able to recover his costs from the money in court. It is not possible to deduct the costs from the appropriate sum and pay the difference into court as the Act requires 'the appropriate sum' and not some lesser amount to be paid into court as a condition of the lease being executed. However, it is possible to obtain an order from the court, which provides that having paid the appropriate sum into court, the tenant is then entitled to have paid out to him his costs as assessed by the court.

Starting the claim

A claim to acquire a new lease starts with the service of a tenant's notice pursuant to section 42. The date the notice is given is known as the 'relevant date' and the tenant must be a qualifying tenant and have been so for the last two years on that date (s.39(8)). Unless the notice is delivered by hand, the date of the notice is unlikely to be the date the notice is 'given', as to which see the following.

Restrictions on serving an effective tenant's notice

A tenant's ability to serve an effective tenant's notice is restricted in the following circumstances.

- Where a valid notice has previously been given under section 42, no further notice may be given in respect of the flat, whilst the first notice continues in force (s.42(6)).

- If a prior notice is withdrawn, deemed to have been withdrawn, or the landlord has successfully defeated the tenant's claim to a new lease on the ground that he intends to redevelop (i.e. he has obtained an order under section 47(1)), then no further notice can be given in respect of the flat within the period of 12 months beginning with the date of withdrawal, deemed withdrawal or the order under section 47(1) becoming final (s.42(7)).
- Where the notice is being served by personal representatives and more than two years have elapsed since the grant of probate or letters of administration (s.42(4A)).
- There has been a prior notice by the tenant or the landlord terminating the lease (Sch. 12, paras. 1 and 2).
- An order for possession has been made or there are pending forfeiture proceedings (Sch. 12, para. 3).

Contents of a tenant's notice

Unlike the position under the *Leasehold Reform Act* 1967, there are no prescribed forms. However, the tenant's notice must:

- state the full name of the tenant and the address of the flat (s.42(3)(a));
- contain sufficient particulars of that flat to identify the property to which the claim extends (s.42(3)(b)(i));
- contain particulars of the tenant's lease including the date it was entered into, the term for which it was granted and the date of the commencement of the term (s.42(3)(b)(ii));
- specify the premium which the tenant proposes to pay (s.42(3)(c));
- where any other amount will be payable by the tenant in accordance with any provision of Schedule 13, i.e. to any other landlord, the amount which he proposes to pay in accordance with that provision (s.42(3)(c));
- specify the terms which the tenant proposes should be contained in the new lease (s.42(3)(d));
- state the name of the person (if any) appointed by the tenant to act for him in connection with his claim, and an address in England and Wales at which notices may be given to such a person (s.42(3)(e));
- specify the date by which the landlord must respond to the notice (s.42(3)(f)) (the date must be not less than two months after the date the notice is given (s.42(5)));
- where an order has been made under section 50(2) dispensing with the need to give a copy of the notice to a person who

cannot be found, or whose identity cannot be ascertained, and in reliance on that order a copy of the notice is not to be given to that person, state this (s.50(6)); and
- be signed personally by the tenant, or each joint tenant (s.99(5)(a)).

In addition, the tenant's notice shall state whether copies are being given in accordance with paragraph 2 of Schedule 11 to anyone other than the recipient and, if so, to whom (Sch. 11, para. 2(3)).

One of the most common reasons why a notice is invalid is because it has not been signed personally by the tenant. It is not sufficient for an agent or the holder of the tenant's power of attorney to sign the notice: *St Ermins Property Co v Tingay* [2002] 2 EGLR 53.

In *HILMI & Associates Ltd v 20 Pembridge Villas Freehold Ltd* [2010] EWCA Civ 314 it was held that where the tenant is a company, the requirements of section 36A of the *Companies Act* 1985 must be met in order for a notice to have been signed by the company itself. That section has now been replaced by section 44 of the *Companies Act* 2006. This section provides that a document is executed by a company by affixing the company's common seal to it or by being signed by the company's director and secretary, by two directors, or one director in the presence of a witness who attests the signature and expressing it to be executed by the company.

The tenant's notice will not be invalid because of any inaccuracy in any of the 'particulars' required, i.e. those required under sections 42(3)(b)(i) and (ii). Neither will it be invalid because of any misdescription of any of the property to which the claim extends. Where the tenant's notice specifies any property which the tenant is not entitled to have demised to him under the new lease, or fails to specify any property which the tenant is entitled to have so demised to him, the notice may be amended with the leave of the court (Sch. 12, para. 9).

Any other mistakes in the tenant's notice will not invalidate it if a reasonable recipient would nevertheless understand the notice (*Mannai Investment Co Ltd v Eagle Star Assurance Co. Ltd* [1997] AC 749). For example, an obvious typographical error would not cause a problem. As to the consequences of serving an invalid notice, see the section on 'Receipt of a tenant's notice'.

Proposed terms

Whilst the landlord and tenant are free to agree the terms of the new lease (s.57(6)), in default of agreement, the freedom of the parties to dictate such terms is severely limited. Section 57 provides that the new lease is to be on the same terms as the existing lease. There are exceptions to this and the circumstances in which departure from the terms of the existing lease may be permissible (or is obligatory), can be summarised as follows:

- where the existing lease includes property, which is not to be included in the new lease (s.57(1)(a));
- where alterations have been made to the property demised since the grant of the existing lease (s.57(1)(b));
- where the existing lease derives from one or more separate leases (s.57(1)(c));
- where the service charge provisions in the existing lease are such that the landlord is unable to recover the cost of complying with any obligation for the provision of services, or for repairs, maintenance or insurance (s.57(2));
- where there are any agreements collateral to the existing lease (s.57(3));
- where in the existing lease there is a term which:
  - provides for or relates to the renewal of the lease;
  - confers any option to purchase or right of pre-emption in relation to the flat demised by the existing lease; or
  - provides for the termination of the existing lease before its term date otherwise than in the event of a breach of its terms (s.57(4));
- where the new lease is granted after the term date of the existing lease (s.57(5));
- where there is a defect in the existing lease, which requires remedying (s.57(6)(a); and
- where changes occurring since the date of commencement of the existing lease affect the suitability of the provisions of that lease (s.57(6)(b)).

If any of these exceptions apply, then reference should be had to the particular subsection of section 57.

In addition, unless the parties agree otherwise, the new lease must contain the following provisions:

- a statement that the lease is granted under section 56 (s.57(11));

- a provision that any sub-lease is not to confer, as against the tenant's landlord, any right under the Act to acquire a new lease (ss.57(7)(a) and 59(3)); and
- a reservation, to the tenant's immediate landlord, of the right to obtain possession of the flat in accordance with section 61 (s.57(7)(b)).

Section 61 provides that a lease granted under the Act may be terminated on the grounds of redevelopment. In order to successfully rely on this ground, the landlord must show that he intends to demolish or reconstruct, or to carry out substantial works of construction on the whole or a substantial part of any premises in which the flat is contained, and that he could not reasonably do so without obtaining possession of the flat. Any application under section 61 can only be made during the last 12 months of the existing lease or the last five years of the new lease (s.61(2)). The wording of section 61 is identical to that contained in section 47, which provides that a landlord is able to defeat a tenant's claim where he intends to redevelop, and reference should be made to the discussion of section 47 which follows.

Landlords often see the grant of a new lease as an opportunity to modernise the terms of the existing lease (as may tenants) and section 57(6) is often relied upon for this purpose. There are two limbs to section 57(6), however, it is clear that neither limb allows for the addition of a wholly new term: *Gordon v Church Commissioners for England* (unreported, 25 May 2007, Lands Tribunal).

Under subsection 57(6)(a) any term of the existing lease shall be excluded or modified in so far as it is necessary to do so in order to remedy a defect in the existing lease. Simply because a term is 'convenient', does not mean that it is 'necessary': *Waitt v Morris* [1994] 2 EGLR 224 at 226C. Further, a 'defect' is a shortcoming, fault, flaw or imperfection and a lease can only properly be described as containing a defect when viewed objectively from the standpoint of both a reasonable landlord and a reasonable tenant: *Gordon*.

Under subsection 57(6)(b) any term of the existing lease shall be excluded or modified in so far as it would be unreasonable in the circumstances to include, or include without modification, the term in question in view of changes occurring since the date of commencement of the existing lease which affect the suitability on the relevant date of the provisions of that lease. 'Changes' is

Flats: the individual right of a tenant to acquire a new lease

not defined and there is little guidance as to what changes may fall within section 57(6)(b). However, it is suggested that changes in acceptable conveyancing practice, the law and the property market could be relied upon. For example, in 1999 the Unfair Terms in Consumer Contracts Regulations were introduced, paragraph 7 of which provides that a seller or supplier shall ensure that any written term of a contract is expressed in plain, intelligible language.

It is a good idea, particularly if it is sought to modify the existing lease in any material way, to attach a draft lease to the tenant's notice. That way, disputes as to what terms were or were not proposed in the notice can be avoided further down the line.

Proposed premium

The proposal figure must be made in good faith. It can be an opening shot in negotiations and does not have to be justified by valuation evidence: *9 Cornwall Crescent London Ltd v Royal Borough of Kensington and Chelsea* [2005] EWCA Civ 324.

Example

**Leasehold Reform, Housing and Urban Development Act 1993
Section 42**

Notice of Claim

Re: [*address of the flat*]

To: [*The competent landlord*]

1. We/I, [*name of the tenant(s)*], claim a new lease of [*address of the flat*] being the flat contained in title number [*title number*], numbered [*flat number*] and being on the [*floor*] floor of the building situate and known as [*address of the building containing the flat*].
2. The lease under which I hold the flat was entered into on [*date of the lease*] and granted for a term from [*commencement of lease term*] to [*expiry of lease term*].
3. I propose to pay a premium of £[*proposed premium*] in respect of the grant of the new lease, and £[*amount*] by way of other amounts under Schedule 13.
4. I propose that the terms of the new lease should be the same as those contained in the lease identified at paragraph 2 above.
5. The name of the person appointed to act for me in connection with the claim is [*name*], and his address for service is [*address in England and Wales at which notices may be given to such a person*].
6. The landlord must respond to this notice by giving a counter-notice by [*date*].

> 7. A copy of this notice is being given to [*name of anyone other than the recipient to whom copies are being given*] in accordance with Schedule 11, paragraph 2.
>
> Date:
> Signed: [*the tenant's personal signature*]
> Name: [*name of the tenant(s)*]

Who to serve with the tenant's notice

The notice must be given to:

- the competent landlord (s.42(2)(a)); and
- any third party to the lease – this is any person who is a party to the lease apart from the tenant and his immediate landlord (s.42(2)(b) and s.62(1)), e.g. a management company or surety.

However, the notice is to be regarded as given to the competent landlord if it is given to any of the other landlords (Sch. 11, para. 1).

The notice is not 'given' until it is given to both the competent (or other) landlord and any third party (*Free Grammar School of John Lyon v Secchi* [1999] 3 EGLR 49). Consequently, as the date specified in the notice by which the landlord must respond to the notice, must be not less than two months after the date the notice is given, sufficient time needs to be allowed to ensure that both the competent landlord and any third party can be served at least two months before the specified date.

Copies of the tenant's notice must be given to everyone the tenant knows or believes to be the competent landlord or one of the other landlords (Sch.11, paras. 2(1) and (2)). However, each recipient of a tenant's notice, or a copy of a tenant's notice, must give a copy to anyone they know or believe to be the competent landlord or one of the other landlords, who is not stated in the notice or known by the recipient to have received a copy (Sch. 11, para. 3). The consequences of failing to comply with paragraphs 2 or 3 are set out in paragraph 4 of the Schedule.

Where the identity of the competent landlord is known and he can be found, but it is not possible to give a copy of the notice to an other landlord in accordance with Part I of Schedule 11 because that person cannot be found, or his identity cannot be ascertained, then the court may make an order dispensing with the need to give a copy of the notice to that person (s.50(2)).

How to serve the tenant's notice

The notice may be given to a landlord at an address provided pursuant to sections 47 or 48 of the *Landlord and Tenant* Act 1987 (s.99(3)), i.e. an address in England and Wales at which notices (including notices in proceedings) may be served on him by the tenant. Further, the notice is regarded as given to the competent landlord if it is given to any of the other landlords instead (Sch. 11, para. 1).

'Given' is not defined in the Act and therefore bears its ordinary and natural meaning. Further, unlike, for example, in the Civil Procedure Rules, which do not apply to a notice served under the Act, there is no deeming provision in the Act. In other words, the Act does not provide that if a notice is posted on a particular day it is deemed to have been given two days later, for example. However, by virtue of section 99(1)(b), the notice may be sent by post and pursuant to section 7 of the *Interpretation Act* 1978, service is deemed to be effected by properly addressing, pre-paying and posting a letter containing the notice, and unless the contrary is proved, to have been effected at the time at which the letter would be delivered in the ordinary course of post. Consequently, if the notice is posted and the recipient does not subsequently prove that he did not receive it, then the notice is 'given' when it would be delivered in the ordinary course of post. Otherwise, when the notice is given will be a question of fact.

The lack of more detailed provisions as to service in the Act can cause significant problems. If a landlord does not in fact receive a notice, then proceedings may have reached an advanced stage before it is realised that the notice has not been validly served and the proceedings have to be abandoned (with the associated waste of costs). Consequently, and where possible, it is advisable to make contact with the landlord, his legal advisors or managing agents prior to serving the notice and to ascertain from them, preferably in writing, where and how they will accept service of the notice.

Registering the tenant's notice

The tenant's notice ought to be registered at the Land Registry once served. Otherwise, it will be void against a purchaser of the freehold if the current landlord sells. For guidance as to how to register the notice, see paragraph 6.4.1 of the Land Registry Practice Guide 27 available at www.landregistry.gov.uk

Effect of the tenant's notice

By virtue of section 43(1), a tenant's notice has 'contractual' effect. In other words, the rights and obligations which arise from the notice, arise as if they were rights and obligations arising under a contract. Among other things, this means that the tenant's notice can be assigned. There are, however, other effects of a tenant's notice:

- once a valid tenant's notice is given, no further notice may be given in respect of the flat, whilst the first notice continues in force (s.42(6));
- service of a tenant's notice restricts the landlord's ability to terminate the tenant's lease (see Sch. 12);
- the tenant serving the notice becomes liable for the landlord's costs (s.60(1)). This is likely to be so whether or not the notice is valid; and
- the landlord may, by notice, require the tenant to pay a deposit on account of the premium payable for the lease: Schedule 2, paragraph 2 of the Leasehold Reform (Collective Enfranchisement and Lease Renewal) Regulations 1993 ('the Regulations').

The costs in respect of which the tenant is liable are the reasonable costs that are incurred by the competent landlord, an other landlord or a third party to the lease in pursuance of the tenant's notice, and are of, and incidental to:

- any investigation reasonably undertaken of the tenant's right to a new lease;
- any valuation of the tenant's flat obtained for the purpose of fixing the premium or any other amount payable by virtue of Schedule 13 in connection with the grant of the new lease (as to what is a reasonable amount in this regard see *Fitzgerald v Safflane Ltd* [2010] UKUT 37 (LC)); and

- the grant of the new lease (ss.60(1) and (6)), i.e. 'the costs of and incidental to the drafting and execution of the new lease': *Huff v Trustees of the Sloane Stanley Estate* Unreported 1997, LVT.

A tenant is not liable under section 60 for any costs which a party to any proceedings under the Act before a leasehold valuation tribunal incurs in connection with those proceedings (s.60(5)). However, if a party behaves frivolously, vexatiously, abusively, disruptively or otherwise unreasonably in connection with the proceedings, then that party can be ordered to pay up to £500 in respect of the other side's costs (Sch.12, para.10(2) of the *Commonhold and Leasehold Reform Act* 2002).

'Reasonable' costs are such costs which a landlord would incur if he were paying the costs himself, i.e. if a landlord increases the costs he incurs because the tenant is paying, such increase is not recoverable (s.60(2)).

Assigning the tenant's notice

As stated, the tenant's notice can be assigned and the assignee of a tenant's notice can thereby acquire a new lease. This is particularly useful for the purchaser of a short lease. The purchaser of a lease must wait until he has been the registered proprietor of that lease for two years before he can serve a tenant's notice. Where the unexpired term of the lease is short, the premium payable on the grant of the new lease could increase significantly in two years. Similarly, if the unexpired term of the lease were to fall below 80 years during those two years, such that marriage value became payable, this would also cause a significant increase in the premium. By requiring the vendor of the lease, who has been the registered proprietor for at least two years, to serve a tenant's notice and to assign the benefit of that notice, the purchaser avoids the two year wait and the potential increase in premium.

Section 43(3) provides that the rights (and obligations) of the tenant arising from the notice are not capable of subsisting apart from the lease of the entire flat. This means that (1) the notice can only be assigned upon the assignment of the lease; and (2) completion of the assignment of the notice must take place upon completion of the assignment of the lease. If the lease is assigned without the benefit of the notice, then the notice is deemed to have been withdrawn as at the date of assignment.

Suspension of the tenant's notice

A claim to collectively enfranchise any premises containing the tenant's flat has the effect of suspending the operation of the tenant's notice during the currency of that claim. No further notice can be given and no application can be made in respect of the notice (s.54(1) and (2)).

Withdrawing the tenant's notice

At any time before a new lease is entered into in pursuance of the tenant's notice, the tenant may withdraw the notice, by giving a 'notice of withdrawal' under section 52(1). A notice of withdrawal must be given to:

- the competent landlord;
- every other landlord; and
- any third party to the tenant's lease (s.52(2)).

If a tenant's notice is withdrawn, no further notice can be given in respect of the flat within the period of 12 months beginning with the date of withdrawal (s.42(7)). Further, if the notice is withdrawn, then the tenant's liability for costs is a liability for costs incurred by each of the persons down to the time when the notice of withdrawal is given to that person (s.52(3)). This is also the case if the tenant's notice ceases to have effect or is deemed withdrawn (s.60(3)).

Following the withdrawal of the tenant's notice, the tenant may give the landlord notice requiring the return of any deposit paid. The landlord must comply with such a request within 14 days, but is entitled to deduct from the deposit any amount due to him from the tenant under section 60, i.e. his costs (Sch. 2, para. 3 to the Regulations). Once again, these provisions also apply if the tenant's notice ceases to have effect or is deemed withdrawn.

Receipt of a tenant's notice

Anyone receiving a tenant's notice will want, in the first instance, to ascertain in what capacity they have received it, i.e. are they a competent landlord, an other landlord or a third party? If they are a competent or other landlord, then they must:

- give a copy to anyone they know or believe to be the competent landlord or one of the other landlords if that person is not stated in the notice or known by the recipient to have received a copy (Sch. 11, para. 3(1)(a));
- if they do so, add to the notice the names of anyone they are giving copies of the notice to or who are known to them to have received a copy and notify the tenant of the names they have added (Sch. 11, para. 3(2)); and
- if they know, or they believe themselves to be, the competent landlord, they must give a notice to the tenant stating who is thought by them to be the competent landlord (Sch. 11, para. 3(1)(b)).

Other landlords

By virtue of section 40(2), the competent landlord conducts all proceedings arising out of a tenant's notice on behalf of all the other landlords. Consequently, other than distributing copies of the notice as set out previously, an other landlord cannot take any independent steps in those proceedings prior to a counter-notice being served. An other landlord, however, will be required to contribute to the competent landlord's costs so far as they are not recoverable or recovered from the tenant (Sch. 11, para. 8(2)). Further, it is the duty of an other landlord to give the competent landlord all such information and assistance as he may reasonably require. If the other landlord fails to provide such information and assistance, he will be liable to indemnify the competent landlord in respect of any loss so caused (Sch. 11, para. 8(1)).

There follows a discussion of the conduct of proceedings by the competent landlord and the circumstances in which an other landlord may act independently following service of a counter-notice. Of course, an other landlord may, in any event, want to investigate for himself whether the tenant is entitled to acquire a new lease and/or obtain a valuation of his interest and, therefore, regard should be had to the following.

The competent landlord

Before he takes any steps and thereby incurs any costs, the landlord may want to require the tenant to pay a deposit. Pursuant to Schedule 2, paragraph 2 of the Regulations, as soon as the tenant's notice has been served and at any time whilst it continues in force, the landlord can serve on the tenant a notice requiring him to pay whichever is the greater of £250 and ten per cent of the total amount proposed in the tenant's notice as being payable on the grant of the lease. If the tenant's notice is withdrawn, deemed withdrawn or ceases to have effect, the landlord can, by notice, be required to return the deposit. However, he is entitled to deduct from the deposit any amount due to him from the tenant under section 60, i.e. his costs (Sch. 2, para. 3 of the Regulations).

In the first instance the landlord will want to ascertain whether the notice is valid. In this regard, reference should be made to the paragraph above dealing with the contents of a tenant's notice. If any of the mandatory requirements are not met, then the notice will be invalid and of no effect. One of the simplest and most common errors in tenants' notices is the failure of the tenant to sign the notice personally. Many tenants' representatives will look in detail at the provisions of section 42, but will overlook section 99 and assume that they are able to sign the notice on their client's behalf.

Even if the tenant's notice is believed to be invalid, it is often advisable to serve a counter-notice, but to serve such a notice without prejudice to the contention that the tenant's notice is invalid. This avoids a situation in which the tenant's notice is in fact found to be valid, and the premium and terms of the new lease are then those stated in the tenant's notice, by virtue of the landlord having failed to serve a counter-notice, as to which, see the discussion of section 49(1).

The Act is silent as to the procedure to be followed where a tenant serves an invalid notice. However, by virtue of section 90(2) the County Court has jurisdiction to determine the validity of a notice. Consequently, if the tenant refuses to accept the invalidity of his notice, an application ought to be made to the County Court for a declaration that the notice is invalid.

> *Example*
> (To be inserted into a CPR Part 8 Claim Form, N208)
> Details of Claim
> Part 8 of the Civil Procedure Rules 1998 applies to this claim.
>
> The Claimant, [*landlord's name*], applies to the Court
> (1) For a Declaration that a purported notice under section 42 of the Leasehold Reform, Housing and Urban Development Act 1993 given on [*date*] was not a valid notice; and
> (2) for an order that the Defendant does pay the costs of this application.
>
> The grounds upon which the Claimant claims to be entitled to the Order are:
>
> 1. The Claimant is the freehold owner of the [*address of the flat*] ('the Premises').
> 2. The Defendant is the leasehold owner of the Premises by virtue of a lease dated [*date*] and made between [*original landlord*] of the one part and [*original tenant(s)*] of the other part.
> 3. By a purported notice given on [*date*], the Defendant claimed to be entitled to a new lease of the Premises under the provisions of the above-mentioned Act. A copy of the said purported notice and accompanying letter is annexed hereto.
> 4. The said purported notice is invalid and of no effect because it was not signed in accordance with section 99(5)(a) of the above-mentioned Act in that it was signed by the tenant's solicitor and not by the tenant personally.
> 5. As permitted by Practice Direction 8, paragraphs 5.1 and 5.2, the Claimant relies on this Claim Form as its evidence.

Where a tenant has served an invalid notice, he is not precluded from serving a further notice immediately (see *Sinclair Gardens Investments (Kensington) Ltd v Poets Chase Freehold Co Ltd* [2008] 1 WLR 768 in relation to section 13 notices). Consequently, the landlord may see little point in incurring the costs of a County Court application and may prefer to proceed as if the notice were valid. However, where the tenant has assigned the invalid notice, the assignee will need to wait two years before being able to serve a fresh notice. In such circumstances, the landlord may wish to seek a declaration that the notice is invalid and thereby prevent the tenant from acquiring a new lease for two years, particularly if the market is rising or the unexpired term of the lease will drop below 80 years (so that marriage value will become payable) within those two years.

If the notice is, on its face, valid, the next step is to check whether there is anything which would preclude service of an effective tenant's notice. In this regard, reference should be had to the 'Restrictions on serving an effective tenant's notice' covered previously.

Having ascertained that the notice is, on its face, valid and that the tenant (or personal representative of the tenant) is not precluded from serving it, it is necessary to check whether the tenant does in fact have the right to acquire a new lease. At this stage, reference should be had to the checklist for tenants. In considering the checklist, and, in particular, whether the tenant has been the owner of the lease for at least two years, it may be necessary to require the tenant to deduce title to the lease. Schedule 2, paragraph 4 to the Regulations provides that, within 21 days of service of the tenant's notice, the landlord may serve a notice on the tenant requiring him to deduce title to his lease within 21 days. The landlord's reasonable costs of, and incidental to any investigation reasonably undertaken of the tenant's right to a new lease, are recoverable from the tenant pursuant to section 60(1)(a).

If a tenant fails to comply with a request either to pay a deposit or to deduce his title, then it will be necessary to serve a default notice under section 92 and then seek an order from the court requiring him to make good the default, if he has not done so, within 14 days of the giving of the notice.

Example

Leasehold Reform, Housing and Urban Development Act 1993 Section 92(2)

Landlord to tenant, notice

Re: [*address of the flat*]

To: [*name of the tenant*]

And its Solicitors, [*name and address of the tenant's solicitors*]

TAKE NOTICE that you have failed to;

1. deduce title to your tenancy pursuant to a notice dated [*date*] served on behalf of your landlord, [*landlord's name*], under Schedule 2, paragraph 4 to the Leasehold Reform (Collective Enfranchisement and Lease Renewal) Regulations 1993; and
2. pay a deposit of £[*amount*] on account of the total amount payable on the grant of a new lease pursuant to a notice dated [*date*] served on behalf of your landlord, [*landlord's name*], under Schedule 2, paragraph 2 to the Leasehold Reform (Collective Enfranchisement and Lease Renewal) Regulations 1993.

We hereby require you under section 92 of the above Act to make good the default. If you fail to comply with this notice within 14 days we will apply to the court for an order requiring you to make good such default.

Date:

Signed:

[*The name and address of the landlord's solicitors*] Solicitors for [*landlord's name*]

Having concluded that the tenant is entitled to acquire a new lease, the landlord will be keen to ascertain what premium he is entitled to upon the grant of a new lease. To enable him to do this, whether he is the competent landlord or an other landlord, he, and any person authorised to act on his behalf, has a right of access to the flat pursuant to section 41. The right is exercisable at any reasonable time and on giving not less than three days' notice to the tenant. Further, the landlord's reasonable costs of, and incidental to, any valuation of the tenant's flat obtaining for the purpose of fixing the premium or any other amount payable by virtue of Schedule 13, are recoverable from the tenant by virtue of section 60(1)(b).

Landlord's counter-notice

Any counter-notice is given under section 45 and must be given by the date specified in the tenant's notice. The counter-notice must:

- be given by the competent landlord;
- specify the other landlords on whose behalf the competent landlord is acting (Sch. 11, para. 5);
- comply with one of the three following requirements (s.42(2));
  - state that the landlord admits that the tenant had the right to a new lease on the date of service of the notice of claim;
  - state that for such reasons as are specified in the counter-notice, the landlord does not admit that the tenant had such a right; or
  - comply with either of the above two requirements but state that the landlord intends to apply for an order under s.47(1) on the grounds that he intends to redevelop the premises containing the flat. For these purposes, the landlord wishing to make the application can be the competent landlord, any other landlord, or any combination of landlords acting together (Sch. 11, para 9(2));
- if the counter-notice admits the claim, state which (if any) of the proposals contained in the tenant's notice are accepted and which (if any) are not and in relation to each proposal, which is not accepted, specify the landlord's counter-proposal (s.42(3)); and
- specify an address in England and Wales at which notices may be given to the landlord.

As to any counter-proposals by the landlord as to the terms of the new lease, regard ought to be had to the paragraph above dealing with proposed terms.

Leasehold enfranchisement explained

It is a good idea, particularly if it is sought to modify the existing lease in any material way, to attach a draft lease to the notice. That way, disputes as to what terms were or were not counter-proposed in the counter-notice can be avoided further down the line.

Example

**Leasehold Reform, Housing and Urban Development Act 1993
Section 45(2)(b)**

Counter-notice not admitting claim

Re: [*The address of the flat*]

To: [*the name of the tenant*]
And its Solicitors, [*the name of the tenant's solicitors*]

[*Landlord's name*] does not admit that you had on the relevant date the right to acquire a new lease of your flat.

The reason for not admitting the claim is that on the relevant date you had not been the registered proprietor of the lease [*particulars of the lease*] for two years.

The following is the address at which notices may be given to [*landlord's name*]:
[*Solicitor's name and address*]

Date:

Signed:
[*Solicitor's name and address*]
Solicitors for [*landlord's name*]

Example

**Leasehold Reform, Housing and Urban Development Act 1993
Section 45(2)(a)**

Counter-notice admitting claim

Re: [*the address of the flat*]

To: [*the name of the tenant*]
And its solicitors, [*the name of the tenant's solicitors*]

[*Landlord*] admits that you had on the relevant date the right to acquire a new lease of your flat.

[*Landlord*] accepts the following proposal contained in the tenant's notice:
1) That the ground rent under the new lease is to be a peppercorn; and
2) That the new lease will be for a term expiring 90 years after the term date of the existing lease.

> [*Landlord*] does not accept the following proposals contained in the tenant's notice:
> 1) That the premium payable for the grant of a new lease is £41,000;
> 2) That the amount payable under Schedule 13 to the intermediate landlord is £500; and
> 3) That the terms of the new lease are to be the same as the existing lease.
>
> In respect of each proposal which the [*landlord*] does not accept, it is proposed that:
> 1) The premium payable for the grant of a new lease is £128,393; and
> 2) The amount payable to the intermediate landlord pursuant to Schedule 13 is £1,182; and
> 3) The terms to be contained in the new lease should be those set out in the draft lease annexed hereto.
>
> The following is the address at which notices may be given to [*landlord*]: [*Solicitor's name and address*]
>
> This counter-notice is given on behalf of [*names of any other landlords on whose behalf the competent landlord is acting*]
>
> Date:
>
> Signed:
> [*Solicitor's name and address*] Solicitors for [*landlord*]

Checklist for landlords

In summary, upon receipt of a tenant's notice, a landlord ought to check.

- Is there anyone he knows or believes to be the competent landlord or one of the other landlords and who is not stated in the notice or known by him to have received a copy?
- Is the notice, on its face, a valid notice? See the Requirements of a tenant's notice above.
- Are there any restrictions on serving a tenant's notice? See 'Restrictions on serving an effective tenant's notice'.
- Does the tenant have the right to acquire a new lease? See the 'Checklist for tenants'.

Conduct of proceedings by competent landlord

Save for any application under section 47(1), the competent landlord conducts all proceedings arising out of a tenant's notice on behalf of all the other landlords. In particular:

- any notice given under Chapter II by the competent landlord to the tenant;
- any agreement for the purposes of Chapter II between the competent landlord and the tenant; and
- any determination of the court or LVT under Chapter II in proceedings between the competent landlord and the tenant,

is binding on the other landlords (Sch. 11, para. 6(1)).

However, in the event of a dispute, the competent landlord may apply to the court for directions as to the manner in which the competent landlord should act in the dispute (Sch. 11, para. 6(1)). Further, the competent landlord may receive on behalf of any other landlord any amount payable to that person on the grant of the new lease (Sch. 11, para. 6(2)). For the circumstances in which that amount is not to be received by the competent landlord, see paragraph 7 of Schedule 11.

If any of the other landlords cannot be found, or their identity cannot be ascertained, the competent landlord must apply to the court for directions as to how to proceed (Sch. 11, para. 6(3)). If the competent landlord acts in good faith and with reasonable care and diligence, then he shall not be liable to any of the other landlords for any loss and damage caused by any act or omission of his (Sch. 11, para. 6(4)).

Other landlords acting independently

Following service of the counter-notice and by giving notice to both the competent landlord and the tenant, any other landlord may:

- be separately represented in any legal proceedings in which his title to his property comes into question (Sch. 11, para. 7(1)(a));
- be separately represented in any legal proceedings relating to the determination of any amount payable to him by virtue of Schedule 13 (Sch. 11, para. 7(1)(b)); and
- require that any such amount shall be paid by the tenant to him or to a person authorised by him to receive it, instead of the competent landlord (Sch. 11, para. 7(2)).

In any event, an other landlord may make an application under section 47(1) on the grounds that he intends to redevelop any premises in which the flat is contained (Sch. 11, para. 9(1)).

Preparing and executing the new lease

Once the counter-notice is served, there is usually a period of negotiation between the landlord and the tenant as to the terms of the new lease and the premium to be paid. Once these terms of acquisition have been agreed, or if it has not been possible to agree them, an LVT has determined them the lease can then be prepared and executed. The timetable for preparing and executing the lease is set out in Schedule 2, paragraph 7 of the Leasehold Reform Regulations 1993 ('the Regulations') and is as follows:

- the landlord must prepare a draft lease and give it to the tenant within the period of 14 days of the terms of acquisition being agreed or determined by an LVT;
- the tenant must give to the landlord a statement of any proposals for amending the draft lease within 14 days of being given the draft lease, and if no statement is given within those 14 days, the tenant is deemed to have approved the draft lease;
- the landlord must give the tenant an answer giving any objections to or comments on the tenant's proposals within 14 days of being given them and if no answer is given within those 14 days, the landlord is deemed to have approved the tenant's amendments to the draft lease;
- the landlord must prepare the lease and as many counterparts as he may reasonably require and must give the counterparts to the tenant a reasonable time before completion; and
- the tenant must give the counterparts, duly executed, to the landlord and the landlord must give the lease, duly executed, to the tenant on the completion date or as soon as possible thereafter.

The completion date will be:

- such date as the landlord and tenant agree;
- the first working day 21 days after a completion notice is given by either the landlord or the tenant under paragraph 8 of the Regulations; or

- such date as the court orders under section 48(3) or 49(4). (These are orders made where there has been a failure to enter into a new lease.)

Applications to the court or LVT

The procedures to be followed where the landlord is missing or the tenant serves an invalid notice have been set out previously. What this section aims to deal with is the applications which follow from service of a valid notice.

It is unlikely that not only will the tenant's right to acquire a new lease be admitted, but that all the tenant's proposals contained in the tenant's notice will be accepted. It may be that the parties can come to a negotiated agreement. However, it is often the case that one or more applications will need to be made to the court or the LVT before the tenant's claim is finally determined. Most commonly, the parties will not be able to agree as to the premium payable for the new lease and/or its terms.

Whilst the cost of proceedings before the court may be recoverable if an application succeeds, costs incurred in relation to any proceedings before the LVT are not recoverable unless a party behaves frivolously, vexatiously, abusively, disruptively or otherwise unreasonably in connection with the proceedings, in which case costs are limited to £500 (Sch. 12, para. 10(2) of the *Commonhold and Leasehold Reform Act* 2002). Costs incurred in relation to proceedings before the LVT are not recoverable from a tenant under section 60 (s.60(5)).

There are numerous applications which can be made and careful attention must be paid to the deadlines for making each application. In most cases, the Act provides that if the deadline is missed, the tenant's notice is deemed withdrawn. As stated, if the tenant's notice is deemed to have been withdrawn, then no further notice can be given in respect of the flat within the period of 12 months beginning with the date of the deemed withdrawal (s.42(7)). As the lease is a diminishing asset, the need to wait a further 12 months before serving a further tenant's notice can have a significant impact on the cost of acquiring a new lease, particularly in a rising market or if the unexpired term drops below 80 years and marriage value becomes payable.

It is also important to remember that if a claim collectively to enfranchise any premises containing the tenant's flat is made, then the tenant's notice is suspended during the currency of that claim and no applications can be made (s.54(1) and (2)). As to the operation of the various time limits, once a tenant's notice ceases to be suspended, regard must be had to section 54.

Landlord fails to serve a counter-notice

Reference has already been made to applications under section 50 where the competent landlord or one of the other landlord's cannot be found. Where the competent landlord's identity is known and he has been properly served, but he fails to serve a counter-notice, then an application can be made to the court under section 49(1) for an order determining the terms on which the tenant is to acquire a new lease. Whilst section 49(1) states that:

> 'the court <u>may</u>, on the application of the tenant, make an order <u>determining</u>, in accordance with the proposals contained in the tenant's notice, the terms of acquisition' (emphasis added),

the court has no discretion and must make an order on the terms proposed in the tenant's notice: see *Willingdale v Globalrange Ltd* [2000] 2 EGLR 55.

The requirements to be satisfied prior to an order being made are as follows:

- on the relevant date the tenant had the right to acquire a new lease of his flat (s.49(a));
- if applicable, the requirements of Part I of Schedule 11 have been complied with as respects the giving of copies of the tenant's notice (s.49(b)); and
- the application must be made not later than the end of the period of six months beginning with the date by which the counter-notice was required to be given (s.49(3)).

If no application is made within six months, then the tenant's notice will be deemed to have been withdrawn at the end of those six months (s.53(2)).

> *Example*
> (To be inserted into a CPR Part 8 Claim Form, N208)
> Details of Claim
>
> I, [*tenant's name*], claim a new lease of [*address of the flat*] ('the Flat') on the terms set out in the notice dated [*date*] which I served upon the Defendant under Section 42 of the Leasehold Reform and Urban Development Act 1993.
>
> The grounds upon which I claim to be entitled to the Order are the following:
>
> 1. I am the tenant of the Flat by virtue of a lease, which was entered into on [*date*] and granted for a term of [*term*] years from [*commencement of term*] at an initial rent of [*rent*] per annum. A copy of the said lease and up to date office copy entries in respect of the leasehold and freehold interests are annexed hereto at Schedule 1. On the date of the notice referred to in paragraph 3 below, I had for the last two years been a qualifying tenant of the Flat.
> 2. Under the provisions of the above-mentioned Act I am entitled to a new lease of the Flat.
> 3. By notice dated [*date*] and served upon [*landlord's name*], my landlord and the freeholder of the premises which contain the Flat, I claimed to be entitled to a new lease of the Flat and set out particulars of the terms which I proposed should be contained in the new lease and the premium which I proposed to pay in respect of the grant of such a new lease. A copy of the said notice and statement of service is annexed hereto at Schedule 2.
> 4. The Defendant failed by the date specified in my notice or at all to serve a counter-notice as required by Section 45 of the above-mentioned Act.
> 5. Under Section 49 of the above-mentioned Act, I request the court to determine the terms on which I may acquire a new lease of the Flat in accordance with the terms set out in my notice referred to in paragraph 3 above.
> 6. As permitted by CPR 8.5(7), I rely on the matters set out in this Claim Form and the schedules hereto as my evidence.
>
> Part 8 of the Civil Procedure Rules 1998 applies to this claim.

Once an order has been obtained under section 49(1) and if a new lease has not been entered into within two months of the order becoming final or within such other period as may have been fixed by the court when making the order ('the appropriate period'), a further application can be made to the court under section 49(4). Upon such an application, the court can make such order as it thinks fit with respect to the performance or discharge of any obligations arising out of the tenant's notice. For example, if it is the landlord making the application, he may ask the court to make an order providing that the tenant's notice is deemed to have been withdrawn at the end of the appropriate period (s.49(5)). However, the tenant is likely to want to require the landlord to enter into a new lease. An order of the court becomes final if not appealed against on the expiry of the time for bringing an appeal (s.101(9)(a)). Pursuant to rule 52.4 of the Civil Procedure Rules, unless the lower court directs otherwise, an appellant must file an appellant's notice at the appeal court within 21 days after the date of the decision of the lower court.

Any application under section 49(4) must be made not later than two months from the end of the appropriate period (s.49(6)). If no application is made within two months, then the tenant's notice will be deemed to have been withdrawn at the end of those two months (s.53(2)).

Timetable of required steps

In order to illustrate what steps are required to be taken when in circumstances where the landlord fails to serve a counter-notice, the following assumes that the tenant's notice has been given on 1 January 2010.

Date	Time allowed	Steps, significant dates and deadlines
1 January 2010		**1.** Service of the tenant's notice under section 42.
15 March 2010	At least two months after step 1.	**2.** Date specified in the tenant's notice by which the landlord must respond to the notice by giving a counter-notice under section 45.
14 September 2010	Six months after date 2.	Deadline for an application under section 49(1) for an order determining the terms of acquisition.
9 November 2010		**3.** Decision of court.
Midnight 30 November– 1 December 2010	21 days after date 3.	**4.** Order under section 49(1) becomes final.
31 January 2011	Two months after date 4.	**5.** Appropriate period under section 49(7) ends. If a new lease has not been entered into, an application can be made under section 49(4).
31 March 2011	Two months after date 5.	Deadline for an application under section 49(4).

Landlord serves a non-admitting counter-notice

Where the landlord serves a counter-notice, but does not admit that, on the relevant date, the tenant had a right to acquire a new lease, an application can be made to the court by the landlord under section 46(1) for a declaration that the tenant had no such right. Any application under section 46(1) must be made within two months of the giving of the counter-notice to the tenant (s.46(2)). Pursuant to section 46, there are therefore, three possible outcomes following the service of a non-admitting counter-notice.

No application is made

If no application under section 46(1) is made within the two months or an application is made but withdrawn, then section 49 applies as if the landlord had not given the counter-notice (s.46(2)).

A declaration is made under section 46(1)

If the court makes a declaration that, on the relevant date, the tenant had no right to acquire a new lease, then the tenant's notice shall cease to have effect on the order becoming final (s.46(3)).

An application under section 46(1) is dismissed

If the court dismisses the landlord's application under section 46(1), then it must make an order:

- declaring that the landlord's counter-notice shall be of no effect; and
- requiring the landlord to give a further counter-notice to the tenant by such date as is specified in the order. This notice must admit the tenant's right to acquire a new lease.

However, the above does not apply if the landlord has stated in the counter-notice that he intends to make an application under section 47(1) on the grounds that he intends to redevelop premises in which the flat is contained and an application for such an order has not been made or the period for doing so has not expired (s.46(5)).

If the landlord is required to give a further counter-notice and does not do so by the date specified in the order, then section 49 applies (s.49(1)(b)).

Flats: the individual right of a tenant to acquire a new lease

> *Example*
> (To be inserted into a CPR Part 8 Claim Form, N208)
>
> Details of Claim
> Part 8 of the Civil Procedure Rules 1998 applies to this claim.
>
> The Claimant, [*landlord's name*], applies to the court
> (1) For an order under section 46 of the *Leasehold Reform, Housing and Urban Development Act* 1993 that the Defendants had no right on [*the relevant date*] to acquire a new lease of [*the address of the flat*] ('the Premises') under the provisions of the above-mentioned Act; and
> (2) for an order that the Defendants do pay the costs of this application.
>
> The grounds upon which the Claimant claims to be entitled to the order are:
> 1. The Claimant is the freehold owner of the premises.
> 2. The First Defendant held the premises by virtue of a lease dated [*date*] and made between [*original landlord*] of the one part and [*original tenant(s)*] of the other part.
> 3. On or around [*date of transfer*] the First Defendant transferred his leasehold interest in the Premises to the Second and Third Defendants. A copy of the notice of transfer and an up to date office copy entry are annexed hereto at Schedule 1.
> 4. By a deed dated [*date of deed of assignment*] the First Defendant purported to assign to the Second and Third Defendants the benefit of a tenant's notice. A copy of the said deed is annexed hereto at Schedule 2.
> 5. By a purported notice given on [*date*], the First Defendant claimed to be entitled to a new lease of the premises under the provisions of the above-mentioned Act. A copy of the said purported notice and accompanying letter is annexed hereto at Schedule 3.
> 6. By a counter-notice dated [*date*], a copy of which appears at Schedule 4, the Claimant informed the Defendants that it did not admit any of their right to a new lease and specified its reasons, which are set out in paragraph 7 below.
> 7. At the date the said purported notice was given, which is the 'relevant date' for the purposes of the above-mentioned Act, the First Defendant was not the tenant of the Premises and had no right to a new lease. The purported assignment referred to in paragraph 4 above was ineffective and invalid as it pre-dated the giving of the said purported notice.
> 8. As permitted by Practice Direction 8, paragraphs 5.1 and 5.2, the Claimant relies on this Claim Form as its evidence.

Timetable of required steps

In order to illustrate what steps are required to be taken when in circumstances where the landlord serves a counter-notice, which does not admit that the tenant had a right to acquire a new lease, the following assumes that the tenant's notice has been given on 1 January 2010.

Date	Time allowed	Steps, significant dates and deadlines
1 January 2010		Service of the tenant's notice under section 42.
1 March 2010		1. Landlord serves a counter-notice under section 45.
30 April 2010	Two months after step 1.	Deadline for an application under section 46(1) for a declaration that the tenant had no right to acquire a new lease.

Landlord intends to redevelop

A landlord may apply to the court for an order pursuant to section 47(1) declaring that the right to acquire a new lease shall not be exercisable by the tenant by reason of the landlord's intention to redevelop any premises in which the flat is contained. For these purposes 'flat' does not include any garage, outhouse, garden, yard or appurtenance (s.62(3)) and 'premises' must be an objectively recognisable physical space, something which the landlord, the tenant, the visitor, and the prospective purchaser would recognise as 'premises': *Majorstake Ltd v Curtis* [2008] 1 AC 787.

> **Example**
>
> The tenant's flat was on the seventh floor of a block containing 50 flats on nine floors. The upper floors of the block each contained six flats and the common parts. The tenant gave notice to his landlord claiming to exercise his right to acquire a new lease. The landlord responded by serving a counter-notice stating its intention to apply to the court for an order under section 47(1) that the tenant's right to acquire a new lease should not be exercisable on the ground that the landlord intended to redevelop 'the whole or a substantial part of the premises in which the tenant's flat [was] contained'. The landlord proposed to combine the tenant's flat with the one on the floor below, so as to form a larger 'duplex' apartment.
>
> The two flats taken together were not 'premises' within the meaning of section 47. If a visitor was asked: what were the premises in which the tenant's flat was contained? the visitor would say the block and would not further sub-divide the space: *Majorstake*

The prerequisites for an order under section 47(1) are as follows:

- the landlord has given the tenant a counter-notice stating that he intends to make an application for an order under section 47(1);
- the tenant's lease is due to terminate within five years of the relevant date, i.e. the service of the tenant's notice (s.47(2)(a)); and
- for the purposes of redevelopment the landlord intends, once the lease has terminated, to:
  - demolish or reconstruct; or
  - carry out substantial works of construction on,
  - the whole or a substantial part of any premises in which the flat is contained (s.47(2)(b)). (It was taken for granted in *Majorstake* that two flats out of 50 did not constitute 'a substantial part of' the premises);
- the landlord cannot reasonably carry out the proposed works without obtaining possession of the flat (s.47(2)(c)); and
- the application must be made within two months of giving the counter-notice (s.47(3)).

Whilst the application under section 47(1) must be made within two months of giving the counter-notice, where the landlord has served a counter-notice which does not admit the tenant's right to acquire a new lease, the application cannot be proceeded with until any application under section 46 has been dismissed (s.47(3)). Obviously, if the application under section 46 is not dismissed, i.e. it is declared that the tenant does not have the right to acquire a new lease; there will be no need to proceed with the application under section 47(1).

Pursuant to section 47, there are various possible outcomes following the service of a counter-notice which states the landlord intends to redevelop.

No application is made

Where the landlord gives a counter-notice stating that he intends to make an application under section 47(1), but he fails to make that application within two months of giving the counter-notice, then the landlord can give a further counter-notice (s.47(5)). Any further counter-notice must be given within two months of the expiry of the deadline for making the application under section 47(1) (s.47(5) and (6)). The above does not apply where an application has been made under section 46, i.e. for an order declaring that the tenant does not have the right to acquire a new lease, so that the question of the tenant's right to acquire a new lease can be determined in the first instance.

If the landlord fails to give a further counter-notice within the time specified, then section 49 applies (s.49(1)(b)).

An application is made, but subsequently withdrawn

Where an application under section 47(1) is made, but subsequently withdrawn, the landlord can give a further counter-notice. Such further counter-notice must be given within two months of the withdrawal of the application. This does not apply, however, where an application has been made under section 46, i.e. for an order declaring that the tenant does not have the right to acquire a new lease. If the landlord fails to give a further counter-notice within the time specified, then section 49 applies (s.49(1)(b)).

An application succeeds

Where the application succeeds and the court makes the order sought, then the tenant's notice will cease to have effect upon that order becoming final. In such circumstances, the tenant is not liable for any of the landlord's costs under section 60 (s.60(4)).

An application is dismissed

Where an application under section 47(1) is dismissed, the court must make an order:

- declaring that the landlord's counter-notice shall be of no effect; and
- requiring the landlord to give a further counter-notice to the tenant by such date as is specified in the order (s.47(4)).

If the landlord fails to give a further counter-notice within the time specified, then section 49 applies.

Timetable of required steps

In order to illustrate what steps are required to be taken when in circumstances where the landlord gives a counter-notice stating that he intends to make an application under section 47(1), the following assumes that the tenant's notice has been given on 1 January 2010.

Date	Time allowed	Steps, significant dates and deadlines
1 January 2010		Service of the tenant's notice under section 42.
1 March 2010		1. Landlord serves a counter-notice under section 45.
30 April 2010	Two months after step 1.	2. Deadline for application under section 47(1) for an order declaring that the right to acquire a new lease shall not be exercisable by the tenant by reason of the landlord's intention to redevelop.
15 May 2010		3. An application made under section 47(1) is withdrawn.
30 June 2010	Two months after date 2.	Date by which landlord must serve a further counter-notice, where he has stated that he intends to make an application under section 47(1), but has failed to do so.
14 July 2010	Two months after date 3.	Date by which landlord must serve a further counter-notice, where he has made an application under section 47(1), which he has subsequently withdrawn.

Application where terms are in dispute or there has been a failure to enter into a new lease

Where the landlord has given the tenant a counter-notice (or a further counter-notice pursuant to sections 46 or 47), admitting the tenant's right to acquire a new lease, but any of the terms of acquisition remain in dispute two months after that notice was given, either the tenant or the landlord may apply to the LVT under section 48(1) for a determination of the matters in dispute. Any such application must be made within six months of the counter-notice (or further counter-notice) being given (s.48(2)). If no application is made within six months, then the tenant's notice will be deemed to have been withdrawn at the end of those six months (s.53(1)). Consequently, the landlord may prefer not to make an application under section 48(1), but to wait to see if the tenant fails to do so.

'The terms of acquisition', by virtue of section 48(7), mean the terms on which the tenant is to acquire a new lease of his flat, whether they relate to the terms to be contained in the lease or to the premium or any other amount payable by virtue of Schedule 13 in connection with the grant of the lease, or otherwise.

Example
Residential Property Tribunal Service
10 Alfred Place
London WC1E 7LR

[Date]

Dear Sirs,

In the matter of [address of the flat]
And in the matter of section 48 of the Leasehold Reform Housing and Urban Development Act 1993

We hereby apply on behalf of our client [*the tenant*] of [*address of the flat*] ('the Premises') for a determination pursuant to section 48 of the Leasehold Reform Housing and Urban Development Act 1993 ('the Act') of the terms of acquisition of a new lease of the Premises in accordance with section 56 of the Act.

[*The tenant*] has been the registered proprietor of the leasehold interest in the premises since [*date*] pursuant to a lease dated [*date*] and made between [*original landlord*] of the one part and [*original tenant*] of the other part ('the lease'). The lease was for a term of [*term*] years from [*date*]. [*Landlord's name*] is the landlord of the premises for the purposes of Chapter II of the Act. Up to date office copy entries in respect of both the freehold and leasehold interests in the premises are enclosed together with a copy of the lease.

[*The tenant*] served a notice pursuant to section 42 of the Act dated [*date*] and a copy of that notice is attached. [*The landlord*] served a counter-notice pursuant to section 45 of the Act dated [*date*] and admitting [*the tenant*] had a right to acquire a new lease of the premises. A copy of that notice is also enclosed.

Since service of the said counter-notice, none of the terms of acquisition have been agreed.

[*The tenant*] proposed that she acquire a lease on the terms of her existing lease. [*The landlord*] has counter-proposed a lease on the terms it currently uses and has provided a draft lease, a copy of which is enclosed.

[*The tenant*] proposed that she acquire a lease upon payment of a premium of £1,750. [*The landlord*]'s counter proposal as to price is £16,500.

We trust that the above information is sufficient for you to process [*the tenant*]'s application. However, if you require any further information or documentation from us, we would be grateful if you would let us know.

We confirm that we have sent a copy of this letter to the [*the landlord*], its address for service being [*landlord's address for service*] and we look forward to receiving directions from you in due course.

Yours faithfully,
[*Tenant's representative*]

Where all the terms of acquisition have been agreed or determined by the LVT, but a new lease has not been entered into within two months of the agreement or determination, or within a period fixed by the LVT, known as 'the appropriate period', either the landlord or the tenant may make an application to the court pursuant to section 48(3). Pursuant to s.101(9), a decision of the LVT is to be treated as becoming final if it is not appealed against on the expiry of the time for bringing an appeal. Pursuant to Regulation 20 of the Leasehold Valuation Tribunals (Procedure) (England) Regulations 2003, the expiry of the time for bringing an appeal is the end of the period of 21 days starting with the date the decision is sent to the parties.

The court has a discretion as to what order to make on an application under section 48(3). If it is the landlord making the application, he may ask the court to make order providing that the tenant's notice is deemed to have been withdrawn at the end of the appropriate period (s.48(4)). However, the tenant is likely to want to require the landlord to enter into a new lease. Any application under section 48(3) must be made not later than two months after the end of the appropriate period (s.48(5)). If no application is made within two months, then the tenant's notice will be deemed to have been withdrawn at the end of those two months (s.53(1)).

Timetable of required steps

In order to illustrate what steps are required to be taken when in circumstances where the landlord has given the tenant a counter-notice admitting the tenants right to acquire a new lease, but any of the terms of acquisition remain in dispute, the following assumes that the tenant's notice has been given on 1 January 2010.

Date	Time allowed	Steps, significant dates and deadlines
1 January 2010		Service of the tenant's notice under section 42.
1 March 2010		1. Landlord serves a counter-notice under section 45.
30 April 2010	Two months after step 1.	Date after which an application can be made to the LVT under section 48(1) for a determination of the matters in dispute.
30 September 2010	Six months after date 1.	Deadline for an application under section 48(1).

71

5 April 2011		**2.** Date LVT decision determining the terms of acquisition under section 48(1) is sent to the parties.
Midnight 25/26 April 2011	21 days after date 2.	**3.** LVT decision has not been appealed against and therefore becomes final.
25 June 2011	Two months after date 3.	**4.** The appropriate period under section 48(6) ends. If a new lease has not been entered into, an application can be made under section 48(3).
25 August 2011	Two months after date 4.	Deadline for an application under section 48(3).

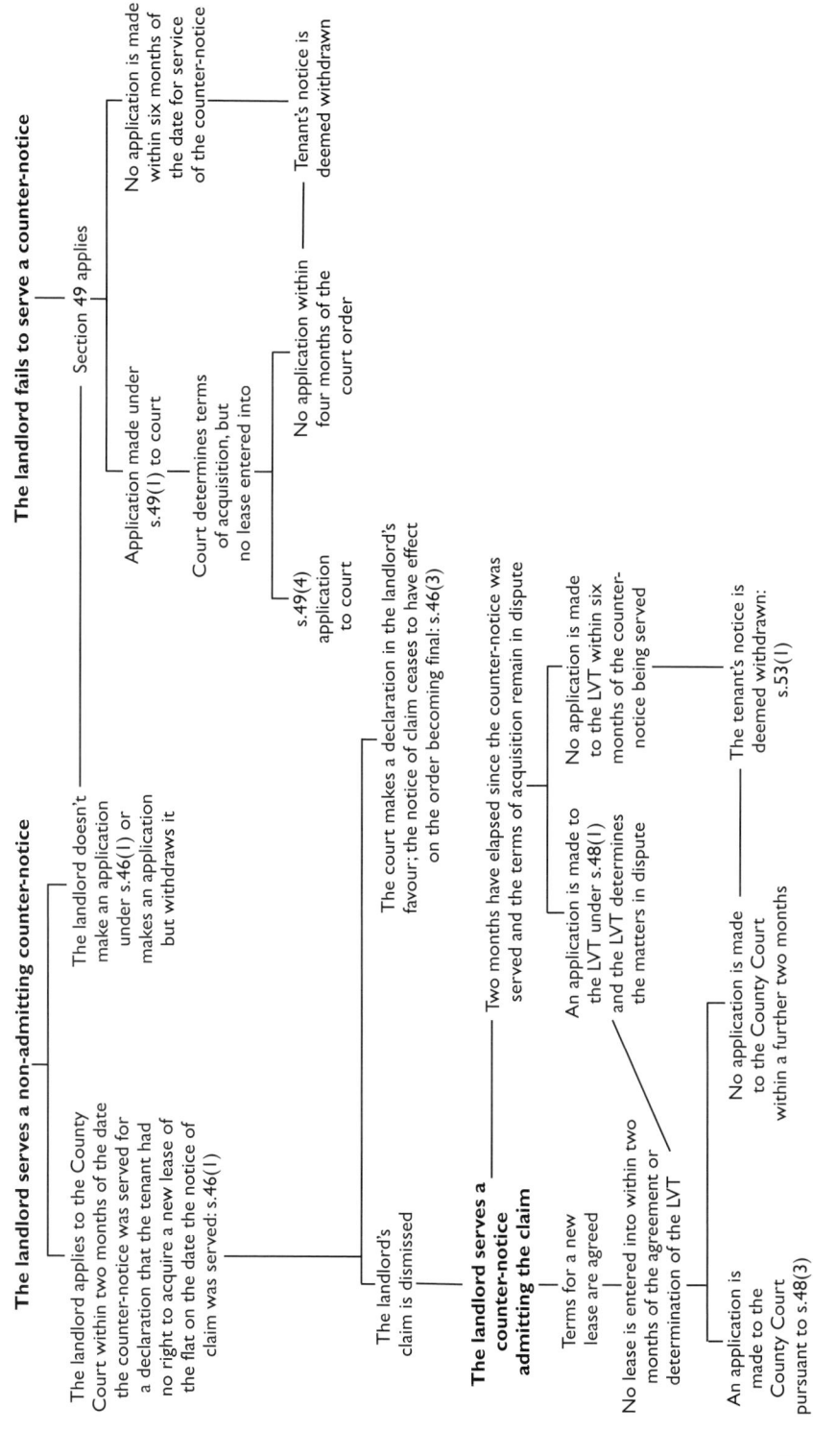

Flats: the individual right of a tenant to acquire a new lease

The landlord serves a non-admitting counter-notice

The landlord applies to the County Court within two months of the date the counter-notice was served for a declaration that the tenant had no right to acquire a new lease of the flat on the date the notice of claim was served: s.46(1)

— The landlord doesn't make an application under s.46(1) or makes an application but withdraws it

The landlord's claim is dismissed

— The court makes a declaration in the landlord's favour; the notice of claim ceases to have effect on the order becoming final: s.46(3)

The landlord serves a counter-notice admitting the claim

Terms for a new lease are agreed

No lease is entered into within two months of the agreement or determination of the LVT

An application is made to the County Court pursuant to s.48(3)

— Two months have elapsed since the counter-notice was served and the terms of acquisition remain in dispute

An application is made to the LVT under s.48(1) and the LVT determines the matters in dispute

— No application is made to the County Court within a further two months

— No application is made to the LVT within six months of the counter-notice being served

The tenant's notice is deemed withdrawn: s.53(1)

The landlord fails to serve a counter-notice

— Section 49 applies

Application made under s.49(1) to court

Court determines terms of acquisition, but no lease entered into

s.49(4) application to court

— No application within four months of the court order

— No application is made within six months of the date for service of the counter-notice

Tenant's notice is deemed withdrawn

73

2

Flats: new lease claims: valuation issues

Introduction

The valuation issues in leasehold reform are covered starting with new leases; thereafter collective enfranchisement is considered in chapter 4. We have taken this approach as not only do many of the principles apply equally to enfranchisement claims, but also since the 1993 Act came into being, most claims for flats in leasehold reform have been for new leases. This is due, in the main, to the somewhat cumbersome nature of collective enfranchisement, coupled with the practicalities of tenants grouping together to submit a notice, and the doggedness required to negotiate their way through to completion.

Whereas in an enfranchisement claim for house leases under the *Leasehold Reform Act* 1967, and a collective enfranchisement claim under the 1993 Act, the purchaser acquires the freehold interest outright and all interests in between, new leases, in effect, perpetuate the landlord and tenant relationship. The difference is that the tenant has a new lease for a term 90 years longer than the existing lease. There are additional complications where there are superior leases.

The valuer has to bear in mind that the only interest that is extinguished is the existing lease – it is replaced by the new lease. Accordingly, the valuer is required to consider all of those interests that are affected by the new lease claim.

Sportelli, Arbib, Pockney, Arrowdell, Nailrile et al

It is anticipated that the reader will have a broad understanding and knowledge of the statutory provisions, and similarly, how to carry out the various valuations. Having said that, there is no escaping the fact that leasehold reform legislation and its accompanying valuations is complicated. In addition to which, over the last few years there have been a number of high profile Lands Tribunal hearings cases referred to the Court of Appeal and the House of Lords. The decisions of these are of paramount importance and need to be understood; we shall both summarise and analyse each of them.

Starting the claim

The process is instigated by a tenant serving a notice for a new lease. The valuation issues from the tenant's perspective are covered initially; thereafter the practical and valuation issues from the landlord's view, upon receipt of a notice, are examined. The tenant needs advice on what he is likely to pay, and the landlord needs independent advice on what he may be entitled to.

The tenant's enquiry

The initial enquiry could come from a telephone call, an email or a letter, and if your offices are on the High Street, you may meet your potential client straight off the pavement.

The first question you ask any tenant considering making a claim is: 'what is the unexpired term of your lease?' With marriage value taken as 'nil' for any notice where the unexpired term exceeds 80 years (Sch. 13, para. 4, s.2A), and the date of valuation being the date the landlord receives the notice of claim; if a tenant is to realise this potential benefit, time is of the essence. It is not that the original term exceeds 80 years, but that which remains unexpired on the date of receipt of notice.

From that initial enquiry, the valuer needs to establish various basic facts, gain access to inspect, and be provided with the relevant lease documentation to carry out the valuations.

It is the author's experience, with an Agency background, that tenants make their initial enquiries to the local estate agent – as a valuer you can expect to be asked a number of legal questions in addition to those on the valuation issues.

The basic facts that the valuer needs to establish include the following (see chapter 1, 'Who qualifies?'):

- does the tenant satisfy the two year ownership rule; or
- is an assignment of the benefit of a notice being taken and/or contemplated; and
- is the tenant considering a sale – to which an assignment of the benefit of the notice is considered?

On the assumption that the unexpired term exceeds 80 years and that there is sufficient leeway before the cut off point is reached, an inspection should be arranged and duly carried out. At the inspection, a copy lease should be provided, and if applicable, any licence to alter and/or deed of variation.

The next step is for the valuer to provide his report and valuations, and assuming a valid claim can be submitted, the tenant needs to be advised as to:

- the premium he might reasonably expect to pay for the new lease plus costs; and
- the sum(s) to be included in the notice (s.42(3)(c)).

The valuer has to bear in mind that a valid claim is one that includes a sum(s) which meets the statutory requirement; the proposed figure(s) must be made in good faith. All of which, in addition, will give the tenant an idea of the market value of his existing lease.

The premium and other amounts payable by the tenant on grant of a new lease are set out in Schedule 13.

In short, the premium payable by the tenant is made up of three parts (Sch. 13, para. 2), as follows:

- the diminution in value of the landlord's interest;
- the landlord's share of the marriage value; and
- any compensation payable.

We now look at Schedule 13 in broad terms to assist the valuer in navigating his way through the various provisions.

Schedule 13

In outline, Schedule 13 is made up of three Parts and ten paragraphs as follows:

Part I: General (paragraph 1)

Paragraph 1: Definition of an 'intermediate leasehold interest'.

Part II: Premium payable in respect of grant of new lease (paragraphs 2, 3, 4 and 5)

Paragraph 2: Premium payable by tenant.

2. The premium payable by the tenant in respect of the grant of the new lease shall be the aggregate of–

- the diminution in value of the landlord's interest in the tenant's flat as determined in accordance with paragraph 3;
- the landlord's share of the marriage value as determined in accordance with paragraph 4; and
- any amount of compensation payable to the landlord under paragraph 5.

Thereafter, paragraphs 3, 4 and 5 are as follows:

Paragraph 3: Diminution in value of landlord's interest.

Paragraph 4: Landlord's share of marriage value.

Paragraph 5: Compensation for loss arising out of grant of new lease.

Part III: Amounts payable to owners of intermediate leasehold interests (paragraphs 6, 7, 8, 9 and 10)

Paragraph 6: Amount payable to owner of intermediate interest.

Paragraph 7: Diminution in value of intermediate interest.

Paragraph 8: Value of intermediate interests.

Paragraph 9: Compensation for loss arising out of grant of new lease.

Paragraph 10: Owners of intermediate interests entitled to part of marriage value.

Each element under paragraphs 3 to 10 inclusive will be examined by way of examples, starting with a new lease claim where the unexpired term exceeds 80 years at the date of valuation, and the premium payable by the tenant is under paragraph 3 only.

Diminution in value of landlord's interest

Paragraph 3

3(1) The diminution in value of the landlord's interest is the difference between:
  (a) the value of the landlord's interest in the tenant's flat prior to the grant of the new lease; and
  (b) the value of his interest in the flat once the new lease is granted.

(2) Subject to the provisions of this paragraph, the value of any such interest of the landlord as is mentioned in sub-paragraph (1)(a) or (b) is the amount which at the relevant date that interest might be expected to realise if sold on the open market by a willing seller (with neither the tenant nor any owner of an intermediate leasehold interest buying or seeking to buy) on the following assumptions–
  (a) on the assumption that the vendor is selling for an estate in fee simple or (as the case may be) such other interest as is held by the landlord, subject to the relevant lease and any intermediate leasehold interests;
  (b) on the assumption that Chapter I and this Chapter confer no right to acquire any interest in any premises containing the tenant's flat or to acquire any new lease;
  (c) on the assumption that any increase in the value of the flat which is attributable to an improvement carried out at his own expense by the tenant or by any predecessor in title is to be disregarded; and
  (d) on the assumption that (subject to paragraph (b)) the vendor is selling with and subject to the rights and burdens with and subject to which the relevant lease has effect or (as the case may be) is to be granted.

(3) In sub-paragraph (2) 'the relevant lease' means either the tenant's existing lease or the new lease, depending on whether the valuation is for the purposes of paragraph (a) or paragraph (b) of sub-paragraph (1).

(4) It is hereby declared that the fact that sub-paragraph (2) requires assumptions to be made as to the matters specified in paragraphs (a) to (d) of that sub-paragraph does not preclude the making of assumptions as to other matters where those assumptions are appropriate for determining the amount which at the relevant date any such interest

Flats: new lease claims: valuation issues

of the landlord as is mentioned in sub-paragraph (1)(a) or (b) might be expected to realise if sold as mentioned in sub-paragraph (2).

(5) In determining any such amount there shall be made such deduction (if any) in respect of any defect in title as on a sale of that interest on the open market might be expected to be allowed between a willing seller and a willing buyer.

(6) The value of any such interest of the landlord as is mentioned in sub-paragraph (1)(a) or (b) shall not be increased by reason of–
    (a) any transaction which–
        (i) is entered into on or after the date of the passing of this Act (otherwise than in pursuance of a contract entered into before that date), and
        (ii) involves the creation or transfer of an interest superior to (whether or not preceding) any interest held by the tenant; or
    (b) any alteration on or after that date of the terms on which any such superior interest is held.

From 3 (1)(a) and (b) above, the valuer has to have it in mind that as the premium payable is based on a 'diminution' in value, it is a 'before and after' exercise.

The new lease is at a peppercorn (i.e. nominal) rent (s.56 (1)), and the landlord's reversionary interest is effectively postponed for 90 years. So to calculate the diminution in value of the landlord's interest adopting the 'term and reversion' method of valuation, the computation is the difference between:

    (a) the aggregate of the value of the rent lost under the existing lease calculated by capitalisation; and the value of the reversionary interest calculated by applying an appropriate deferment rate to the share of freehold/999 years lease value over the existing lease term;

less

    (b) the value of the reversionary interest calculated by applying an appropriate deferment rate to the share of freehold/999 years lease value over the new lease term.

In the following Examples 1 to 8, we examine in detail paragraphs 3 and 4 of Schedule 13.

Leasehold enfranchisement explained

Example 1

Calculation of the new lease premium for a flat within a prime south west London residential location (PCL), unexpired term of 81 years, at a fixed ground rent of £50 per annum, with a new lease (171 years) value of £500,000; and advice for the sum to be proposed in the notice of claim.

Take the computation as read and to reflect established principles in leasehold reform valuations; further explanation and clarification on the constituent parts is detailed later.

New lease – premium computation

In accordance with Schedule 13, paragraph 3 incorporating the various assumptions.

Date of valuation: 25 March 2010

Lease expiry date: 25 March 2091

<u>Diminution in value of landlord's interest</u>

Difference between the value before grant of the new lease

<u>Term</u>

Rent	£50 p.a.		
YP 81 years @ 8%	12.4755	£624	

<u>Reversion</u>

To 'share of freehold' with vacant possession value	£505,050		
(new lease value – 99% FHVP)			
Deferred 81 years @ 5%	0.0192	£9,697	£10,321

minus

and the value after the new lease is granted

<u>Term</u>

New lease at a peppercorn rent	£0	£0	

<u>Reversion</u>

To share of freehold with vacant possession value – as above	£505,050		
Deferred 171 years @ 5%	0.0002	£101	£101

Diminution in value of landlord's interest	£10,220

> plus
>
> | Marriage value – as 81 years unexpired, if any, taken as 'nil' | | £0 |
> |---|---|---|
> | New lease premium (excluding costs) | | £10,220 |
> | | Say | £10,200 |
>
> For the purposes of the sum to be included in the notice, there is little margin in these circumstances – the valuer may feel a new lease value of £450,000 should be applied. Two valuations are reported: (1) the anticipated premium to pay and (2) the premium to be proposed in the notice.

Timing of the notice of claim

As the date the competent landlord receives the claim is the date of valuation, whether market values are rising or falling will have an effect on the premium to be paid. It is beneficial to the tenant to submit the notice when values are depressed. Conversely, if the notice has been served with the benefit of hindsight, at a peak or near thereto in the market, it may be beneficial to the tenant to withdraw the claim, incur the costs, wait the appropriate time (which will be a minimum of one year, and up to two years if an assignment of the existing lease has been taken and the ownership period has to be satisfied), and then serve a further notice.

Typically, from the period summer/autumn 2007 to March 2009, capital values fell from their peak, according to Savills PCL Indices. The downturn in the market was mirrored in the reduction in the number of tenants who submitted claims. Similarly, during that period, there were an increased number of withdrawals where claims had been made towards and at the peak of the market.

A downturn in the market will lead to pent up demand amongst claimants, who will seek advice on the legal and valuation issues for new leases, and an assessment of the anticipated premium. Having said that, potential claimants may continue to wait and see if further benefit can be gained if capital values continue to fall.

From March 2009 to December 2009 (at the time of writing this chapter) there has been a recovery in capital values generally, which in turn has seen an increase in the number of new lease claims.

The exception to the 'wait and see' option is the short unexpired existing lease term, where any potential gain through a fall in capital value is offset by the decrease in the term of the lease, and thus an increase in the landlord's reversionary interest. The valuer should also be ever aware of the 80 years plus cut off point for marriage value.

We now look at the premium payable under paragraph 3 in detail.

The diminution in value of the landlord's interest

In Example 1, the diminution in value of the landlord's interest is calculated adopting the 'term and reversion' method of valuation. Pursuant to the House of Lords' decisions in *Sportelli*, whereas it is accepted that hope value forms part of the landlord's interest in the open market, where there is marriage value in the computation, there is no separate sum for hope value. Hope value is discussed further in chapter 4.

The statutory provisions

The statutory provisions to assess the landlord's interest as part of the premium payable for a new lease are essentially similar to those for the freeholder's interest of high value houses under the 1967 Act, and for collective enfranchisement under Schedule 6 of the 1993 Act.

The valuer is required to determine the amount at the date of valuation that the interest (para. 3 (2)) 'might be expected to realise if sold on the open market by a willing seller (with neither the tenant nor any owner of an intermediate leasehold interest buying or seeking to buy) on the following assumptions'.

The basic assumption is that of an open market sale and a willing seller.

The four further assumptions, in outline, are:

- …the vendor is selling for an estate in fee simple…;
- …Chapter I and this Chapter confer no right to acquire any interest…or to acquire any new lease;

- ...that any increase in the value of the flat which is attributable to an improvement carried out at his own expense by the tenant or any predecessor in title is to be disregarded; and
- ...the vendor is selling with and subject to the rights and burdens with and subject to which the relevant lease has effect or...is to be granted.

Accordingly, it is to be assumed, amongst other things, that neither the tenant nor other parties with special interests are buying or seeking to buy. This is generally known as the 'exclusion of the tenant's bid assumption'.

In short, the interest to be valued is one that is on the open market for sale by a willing seller of an estate in fee simple, where the right to acquire a new lease is ignored, with any value attributable to improvements disregarded and on the terms of the relevant lease.

The assumption that the Act does not confer the right to any new lease is known as the 'no Act world'. However, it is important to understand that this doesn't mean the Act has not been passed, but that the rights the Act provides haven't been granted to the tenant, to whom the rights have in fact been granted.

To recap, the value of the landlord's interest is the aggregate of two elements: (1) the right to receive the rent under the existing lease for the remainder of the term; and (2) the right to vacant possession at the end of the term (subject to the tenant's right to remain in occupation, of which more later).

The two elements are known as the 'term'; and the 'reversion'; which we will now consider in depth in relation to Example 1.

It is fundamental to understand that under Schedule 13, two hypothetical sales are assumed to take place (i.e. two valuations are required), whereas under sections 9(1), 9(1A), 9(1C) and Schedule 6, there is only one.

The term

The value equivalent in lieu of the right to receive the ground rent income per annum (or at the appropriate intervals as the case may be). Calculated by applying a capitalisation rate (Years' Purchase), over the term to the rental stream.

The ground rent (£50 per annum) is a nominal sum fixed for the duration of the term of the existing lease. In valuing the diminution of the landlord's interest, the ground rent is capitalised applying single rate tables, with an eight per cent rate of return. Ultimately, the capitalisation rate will depend on market evidence and the valuer's opinion. The diminution in value of the landlord's interest must include a sum for the loss of ground rent income, as following the grant of the new lease, the new lease is at a peppercorn ground rent.

In many cases, a change of one or two percentage points to the capitalisation rate has a relatively small effect on the premium, accordingly the question of appropriate capitalisation rate is not generally contentious. In the balance of cases, the costs of testing the argument at the tribunal far outweigh any potential increase or decrease in premium.

The capitalisation rate

There is much debate amongst valuers as to the appropriate capitalisation rate to be applied to the rent passing in the term calculation. Ultimately, it is market evidence that guides the valuer to the rate of return to be adopted. Whereas there are sales of ground rent investments in the auction rooms and at private treaty, analysis of these to establish the capitalisation rate is often difficult, and any two valuers may analyse the sale price differently based on the information and facts of the case available to them. The valuer may have to rely solely on his experience and opinion.

There are nevertheless a number of general valuation points to consider:

- Where the ground rent is a nominal sum (say £50 per annum), with nominal reviews (say doubling every 25 years), the investment might be regarded as undynamic and unattractive and a capitalisation rate in the region of seven per cent to ten per cent might be appropriate.
- If, on the other hand, the current ground rent is nominal, but there is an early review (say within five years) to a substantially higher sum, the investment might be described as 'dynamic' and a lower capitalisation rate (say five per cent to seven per cent) might be appropriate. Having said that, one also has to consider the security of the investment, which might lead to an increase from the five per cent to seven per cent suggested.
- Some leases have ground rent reviews to a percentage of either notional capital or market value. Typically, those

to say, 0.2 per cent of corresponding freehold with vacant possession value, or ten per cent of market rental value can result in substantial uplifts.

Example 1 – a current ground rent of £50 per annum with review in 18 months time to 0.2 per cent of freehold with vacant possession value (assessed at £500,000), rent on review equals £1,000 per annum.

Example 2 – a current ground rent of £50 per annum with review in 18 months time to ten per cent of market rental value (assessed at £25,000 per annum), rent on review equals £2,500 per annum.

Factors relevant to the choice of capitalisation rate are listed in *Nicholson v Goff* [2007] 1 EGLR 83 as follows:

- the length of the lease term;
- the security of recovery;
- the size of the ground rent (a larger ground rent being more attractive);
- whether there is provision for review of the ground rent; and
- if there is provision for review, the nature of it.

The factors relevant to the choice of capitalisation rate differ from those for deferment rate, so there is no valuation rationale to adopt a capitalisation rate in line with the deferment rate – having said that, there may be circumstances where the two are the same.

Single rate tables are applied, by convention, to the rental stream for a number of years to a reversion to freehold possession. Dual rate tables, which may include provision for tax, are applied where the income is for a limited number of years, and the reversion is to a nominal term (of which more later).

The reversion

The value equivalent in lieu of the right to vacant possession of the flat (or house, as the case may be), at some future date. Calculated by applying a deferment rate (Present Value) over the term to the share of freehold/999 years' lease vacant possession value.

At the expiration of the lease, the property (save where the tenant has a statutory right to occupation), reverts to the landlord. Accordingly, the landlord's reversion is to a 'share of freehold/999 years' interest. In the example, the proposed new lease value represents 99 per cent of corresponding share of freehold/999 years' lease value. The subject of relativity (which is the relationship between an existing lease value and corresponding share of freehold value) is discussed later.

By valuation convention the value of the reversionary interest is calculated as follows:

- by establishing the share of freehold/999 years' lease vacant possession value; and thereafter
- applying an appropriate deferment rate to reflect the postponement of vacant possession to the end of the term.

The share of freehold/999 years' lease vacant possession value

To calculate the share of freehold/999 years' lease vacant possession value, a relativity of 99 per cent has been applied to the new lease value; which in turn is valued by reference to comparable sales where the evidence is available.

In an ideal world, there would be comparable sales of share of freehold and new lease interests to refer to. Notwithstanding the passage of time since the flat legislation took effect, there remain cases where comparable sales evidence of new leases is unavailable. In those cases, the valuer might apply an appropriate 'market value' relativity schedule; be obliged to widen the net for comparable sales evidence; have regard to any further new lease claims if available; and consider any existing lease sales coupled with new lease premiums and/or sums proposed in new lease claims.

Apply an appropriate deferment rate to reflect the postponement to the end of the term

Following the Lands Tribunal decisions (upheld by the Court of Appeal) in *Sportelli*, the generic deferment rate of five per cent must be applied to this property in a prime central London (PCL) location.

The deferment rate is applied to the share of freehold/999 years' vacant possession value to compensate the landlord for his loss. In the case of a new lease, the flat will not revert to the landlord for a further 90 years; nevertheless the price computation has to reflect the fact that the property will revert to the landlord, albeit at a distant future date.

What is the deferment rate?

There are various definitions of deferment rate, which include the following:

- 'the present value of £1';
- 'the rate of compound interest that would be needed to be earned on an investment made at the valuation date, in order to produce at the end of the term, the capital value which has been determined as being the value as at the valuation date of the interest, which value will however accrue only at the end of the term'. *Arbib v Earl Cadogan* [2005] 3 EGLR 139, para. 87;
- an All Risks Yield (ARY), which can be defined as 'a yield figure which reflects within it the future benefits and risks to which the investment is subject' (Paper 8991V7-0 Glossary of Terms, College of Estate Management, Reading, 2007); and
- 'the deferment rate is an annual discount of a future receipt, the vacant possession value of the house or flat at term'. *Earl Cadogan v Sportelli* [2007] 1 EGLR 153, para. 51.

Why does a lower deferment rate result in a higher premium?

Following on from the second bullet point above, the deferment rate is the rate of compound interest that would be needed to be earned on an investment, in order to produce the capital value at the end of the term. The right is to receive the property with vacant possession at the end of the term.

In Example 1, the 'capital value' is £505,050.

The amount to which £1 invested now will accumulate at compound interest is calculated by the formula: $(1 + i)^n$;

where 'i' is the rate of interest; and

'n' is the number of years.

For a fixed number of years (n), the lower the compound interest rate (i) applied, the greater the initial investment required to apply thereto to produce the capital value. Hence, the lower the deferment rate, the higher the diminution in landlord's interest, and thus increase in premium.

Example 1

$i = 5\%$

$n = 81$.

$(1 + 0.05)^{81} = 52.0395$

× £9,705 equals £505,050.

The initial investment is £9,705.

If the deferment rate (i) is, say, six per cent, the investment required is less, as follows:

$i = 6\%$

$n = 81$.

$(1 + 0.06)^{81} = 112.14375$

× £4,504 equals £505,050.

The initial investment is £4,504.

Fundamentally, the lower the deferment rate, the higher the premium for the new lease.

It was the belief amongst a number of valuers in central London, experienced in leasehold reform, that the 'established' six per cent deferment rate applied in valuations was too high that led to the three hearings of the Lands Tribunal (known as *Pockney*, *Arbib* and *Sportelli*), and ultimately to the generic five per cent deferment rate with associated specific factors.

The deferment rate and where we are now

We now examine and consider *Pockney*, *Arbib* and *Sportelli* to understand how and why the generic deferment rate evolved. As the decisions of the tribunals are fundamental, and their effects wide ranging, the analyses are lengthy.

The approach adopted is as follows:

- a synopsis of the decisions in *Sportelli*;
- a chronological analysis of *Pockney*, *Arbib* and *Sportelli*; and
- a review of the various tribunal cases that have been heard subsequently where variations from *Sportelli* have been sought.

A synopsis of the decisions of Sportelli

Further to their decision in *Arbib*, the evidence before them in *Sportelli*, including the agreed definitions and the component parts that go to make up the risk-free rate and the risk premium of the financial experts, the Lands Tribunal state how the deferment rate can be calculated being 'the addition of an appropriate risk-free rate and an appropriate risk-free premium, with a deduction for capital growth'. (*Sportelli*, paras. 15 and 16).

Which in turn is represented as follows:

$$DR = RFR - RGR + RP$$

Where, DR is the deferment rate;

RFR is the risk-free rate;

RGR is the real growth rate; and

RP is the risk premium.

The risk-free rate is 2.25 per cent (para. 70).

The risk-free rate is defined as 'the return demanded by investors for holding an asset with no risk, often proxied by the return on a government security held to redemption' (para. 16).

(2.25 per cent is also the annual sinking fund rate in the total profit rent approach to valuing an intermediate leasehold interest (ILI) where dual rate tables apply);

the real growth rate is 2.0 per cent (para. 73); and

the risk premium is 4.5 per cent (para. 79).

The risk premium is 'the additional return required by investors to compensate for the risk of not receiving a guaranteed return' (para. 16 also).

Which results in the 'generic' deferment rate for houses of 4.75 per cent, as follows:

$$DR = RFR - RGR + RP$$

$$DR = 2.25\% - 2\% + 4.5\%$$

$$\underline{DR = 4.75\%}$$

The generic deferment rate being 'one that is applicable to long-term residential property reversions in general' (para. 80).

Specific factors

Thereafter, the tribunal considers as to whether the generic rate needs to be adjusted in any particular case for 'specific factors'.

All the subject properties in *Sportelli*, and thus those to which all the valuers evidence was directed, were in the PCL area. However, both the valuers and the financial experts were asked more general questions during the hearing on the following topics, from which the tribunal concluded as follows.

Length of term (para. 85):

- the deferment rate is constant beyond 20 years;
- below 20 years, the rate would need to have regard to the property cycle at the date of valuation; and
- beyond 75 years, on the evidence before them, there was no reason to conclude the rate would be either higher or lower.

Location (para. 88):

- the tribunal accepted the view of the valuers that the deferment rate could require adjustment for location, but saw no justification for making any adjustment to reflect regional or local considerations either generally or in relation to the subject cases; and
- the tribunal went on to say that on the evidence of the financial experts, no adjustment to the real growth rate is appropriate given the long-term basis of the deferment rate, and locational differences of a local nature are, in the absence of clear evidence suggesting otherwise, to be assumed to be properly reflected in the freehold vacant possession value.

Obsolescence and condition (para. 91):

Flats: new lease claims: valuation issues

- as with location, the tribunal concluded that whilst they did not rule out the possible need to adjust the deferment rate to take account of such matters as obsolescence and condition, they thought it would only exceptionally be the case that such factors were not fully reflected in the vacant possession value and the risk premium.

Flats v houses (paras. 92, 95 & 96):

- In *Arbib*, the tribunal concluded that there should be a 0.25 per cent differential between houses and flats (increasing the deferment rate for the latter), having regard to the lesser management problems of a single house and the possibility that there might be a better prospect of growth in the house as opposed to the flat market. Also, it was determined that it was not necessary to assume a different risk factor for the reversion upon a single flat compared to a block of flats.
- In *Sportelli*, the tribunal concluded that any disparity between growth rates for flats and houses would likely even out over time, so no adjustment was required. However, there should be an adjustment to reflect the management problems, although there is no differentiation between flats subject to head leases, and those that are not. Nor did they believe that management concerns were any different between a single flat and a block, to warrant further adjustment. Such is the nature of the management of flats, problems inevitably occur over the term of the lease. An adjustment of an additional 0.25 per cent for flats was concluded.
- The tribunal went on to say that they did not rule out the possibility that there could be a case for an additional allowance where exceptional difficulties are in prospect, but this would need to be the subject of compelling evidence.

Special factors – transaction costs:

- there is to be neither adjustment to the deferment rate nor the vacant possession value for transaction costs.

All the above result in a generic deferment rate as follows:

- houses – DR = 2.25% – 2% + 4.5% = 4.75%;

to which an adjustment of an additional 0.25 per cent is made for flats;

- flats – DR = 2.25% – 2% + 4.75% = 5.00%.

A chronological analysis of Pockney, Arbib and Sportelli

Cadogan Holdings Limited v Pockney [2005] RVR 197.

The first case where the established six per cent deferment rate was appealed to the Lands Tribunal is known as *Pockney*.

For these purposes, it is helpful to know that the appeal was further to the LVT's determination of the price payable for the freehold interest under section 9(1C) at 57 Shawfield Street, London SW3.

The house is described as a modern end of terrace built in about 1970, which at the time was in good repair and decorative condition throughout. The date of valuation is 11 June 2002, and the tenant's lease had an unexpired term of 32.54 years.

There were two 'issues' to be determined:

- the leasehold value (which is irrelevant here); and
- the deferment rate.

Mr K D Gibbs FRICS of Messrs Gerald Eve gave evidence that the value the freehold vacant possession should be deferred at is 5.25 per cent.

Mr Justin Shingles, practising as Justin Shingles Ltd, gave evidence that the deferment rate should be no lower than six per cent.

The Tribunal Member, Mr N J Rose FRICS, stated that the previously established deferment rate of six per cent was too high in June 2002 and found that the 'rate of 5.25 per cent suggested by Mr Gibbs is not too low' (para 76).

The reasons stated at paragraph 76 of the decision for the departure from the established six per cent are as follows:

- the yields obtained from central London residential investments let on assured shorthold tenancies had declined from 6.8 per cent in 1993 to approximately three per cent in 2002; and
- in 1995, investors in the Freehold Income Trust, secured on residential ground rents throughout the country, could obtain a yield of 11.5 per cent and this had fallen to 5.6 per cent by 2002.

The reasons for the departure above are, as is evident later, not the source of what is to become the generic deferment rate.

What is important in this decision is what the member (Mr N J Rose FRICS) said at paragraphs 74 and 75:

Paragraph 74:

> 'It is clear that, since the mid 1990s, yields in the central London residential market have fallen very considerably. During that period, however, the rate at which freehold reversions are deferred for leasehold enfranchisement purposes has remained virtually unchanged at or about six per cent. In the course of cross-examination, Mr Shingles [who gave evidence in the case on behalf of the tenant] suggested that this could be explained by the fact that the hypothetical purchaser of the appeal property will not secure his reversion until the termination of the lease in 32.5 years time. In fact, however, he will be free to dispose of his investment – with the possibility of securing a capital profit – at any time. The rate at which he chooses to discount the freehold vacant possession value will reflect, among other matters, the rate at which he can borrow; the returns available from alternative investments, and his perception of likely future changes in vacant possession values. Inevitably, all these factors will change over time. It is in my view inconceivable that they could result in an identical discount rate being applied consistently for ten years or more. In particular, I can discern no reason in economic theory to explain why the bids of investors for the type of freehold reversion with which this appeal is concerned should have remained completely unaffected by changes in yields obtainable from alternative residential property investments.'

Paragraph 75:

> 'In my judgment, the deferment rate has remained at six per cent for so long because of the lack of reliable evidence of yields in the no-Act world, not because such yields have not changed over time.'

We now look at the second case to be heard.

Arbib v Earl Cadogan [2005] 3 EGLR 139

The second case concerned five conjoined appeals from decisions of the LVT.

Again it may be helpful to know that the appeal properties were located in London SW1, SW3 and SW7 postcodes (all PCL); and the valuations fell under section 9(1C) to the 1967 Act, and Schedules 6 and 13 to the 1993 Act, respectively.

For these purposes, we shall consider the issues on deferment rate only; at Part 3 of the decision from paragraph 78 onwards.

Paragraph 119: Mr Walker in his submissions pointed out that the 'all risks yield' (ARY) which is the deferment rate, is the resultant of adding to the risk-free rate of return (RFR), a risk premium (RP), and subtracting an allowance for the prospect of growth (g), i.e. as follows:

DR = RFR + RP – g.

Paragraph 126, in reference to *Gallagher Estates Limited v Walker* (1973) 28 P&CR 113:

> '...it is only in the absence of dependable open market transactions concerning the subject matter to be valued that resort should be made for guidance to other markets, including non-property markets; also highlighting that where the subject market differs from that which it is being compared with, it is an essential part of the valuer's task to identify the differences between the two markets and to make appropriate adjustments'.

Settlement evidence

Three main criticisms are listed with respect to settlement evidence (para.127):

- they are usually evidence only of the price agreed and not of the component parts of that price;
- they may be affected by the '*Delaforce*' effect, that is to say the anxiety on the part of the tenant or landlord to reach agreement, even at a figure above or below the proper price, without the stress and expense of tribunal proceedings; and
- they tend to become self-perpetuating and a substitute for proper consideration and valuation in the particular case.

At paragraph 139, the tribunal said:

> 'It is in these circumstances that we have concluded that resort must be made to the financial markets in order to assess the range of deferment rates to be used in these cases, subject to appropriate adjustment for each property.'

At paragraph 143:

> 'If material from financial markets is to be used, there is common agreement that it is necessary to select a suitable risk-free investment and to apply an appropriate risk premium net of growth, as was postulated by Mr Walker [Counsel for 55/57 Cadogan Square Freehold Limited and Dorrit Moussaieff] in his submissions'.

Thus the formula for the generic deferment rate evolved from *Arbib*, where the tribunal concluded that resort had to be had to the financial markets, though there was not a financial expert giving evidence.

The paragraph continues

> '…a deferment rate is the yield obtained from a long-term investment providing no income until maturity, but providing for capital growth and the possibility of early profit if, for example, the tenant wishes in the "no-Act" world to negotiate the purchase of the freehold or an extension of his lease. In these respects it corresponds to a nominal zero coupon gilt…'

The tribunal determined the risk-free rate to be two per cent (paras. 145 and 147), and included commentary on the availability since 1985 of index-linked gilts, which without the benefit of careful financial analysis (unavailable to them) are taken as the most comparable financial risk-free investment market product to the deferment rate.

To this risk-free yield, an adjustment is required for 'risk net of growth measured in real terms'. And from that resultant figure it will be further necessary to make adjustments for any particular advantage or disadvantage of the particular case, which justifies a departure from such rate.

After further discussion on volatility, and what are called 'general risks', including:

- the market fearing a failure of values to keep pace with inflation;
- risks inherent in an investment in a freehold reversion are only marginally offset by the prospect of growth as compared with index-linked gilts;
- comparative illiquidity; and
- adverse legislation;

the tribunal concluded that the deferment rate of 4.5 per cent makes a sufficient differential for a reversion in a high value house on the Cadogan Estate as compared with index-linked gilts.

Thereafter the following 'specific factors' in relation to differences between types of property were discussed.

Statutory assumptions:

- under section 9(1A) *Leasehold Reform Act* 1967, there is no liability to repair, whereas under Schedules 6 and 13, there is no such assumption;
- risk factor with respect to condition, house v flats;
- no differential in risk factor between a single flat and a block of flats.

On the basis of the above, the tribunal concluded in the circumstances of these cases there is no statutory assumption requiring a differential deferment rate as between one exercise of rights or another.

Physical differences:

- in which case any differential between flats and houses on the Cadogan Estate is limited to such judgment as is appropriate, having regard to the lesser management problems of a single house, and a possible better prospect of growth in the house market as opposed to the flat market. An adjustment of 0.25 per cent is concluded.

Length of unexpired term:

- no change in these circumstances.

Size:

- an adjustment of 0.25 per cent is made for an unusually large investment in a single house.

Flats: new lease claims: valuation issues

Valuation date:

- the valuation dates for the cases range from 1 April 2003 to 23 June 2004 and the tribunal concluded that there is no adjustment for the following principal reason:

    '…it is not until a change in the trend in risk-free yields has been established over a period of years, so that it is recognisable in the market for long term investments, … that there will be changes that can properly be reflected by step gradations in deferment rates…' (para. 179).

Finally, turning to the Summary at page 42 of the decision, the following conclusions highlight the main points to carry forward (using the sub paragraph numbers of the decision):

(2)   Although market evidence is usually the best evidence of value, the extent of the right to enfranchise or to a lease extension is now so wide that there is unlikely to be dependable market evidence in any particular case. There is none in these appeals (paras. 99 and 109).

(3)   There is not, and has never been, a binding 'convention' that a fixed and constant deferment rate of six per cent should be universally used. The deferment rate in each case must be individually determined on the evidence (para. 112).

(4)   Decisions of LVTs and this tribunal on questions of fact and opinion should not be treated as evidence of value in later cases. Such decisions do not establish any conventions or precedents (paras. 112–116). A decision of this tribunal setting out general guidance on valuation or procedure, however, may be applied or referred to in subsequent cases (para. 116).

(5)   It is unlikely that there could be a constant deferment rate over a period of several years despite changes in the investment market and financial indicators (paras. 118–120).

(6)   In the absence of dependable market transactions to provide evidence of value, it is permissible to consider the money market and this was decided by the decision in *Gallagher Estates Limited v Walker* (paras. 124–126).

(7) Settlements relating to comparable properties are admissible as evidence of value but are subject to criticism, and will usually be given weight only where a detailed analysis of the price or value has been agreed and the agreement has not been influenced by the *Delaforce* effect (paras. 127 and 129). No settlements are helpful in the *Cadogan* appeals (para. 129).

(9) In the absence of reliable land market evidence in these appeals, resort must be had to the financial or money market in order to assess deferment rates (para. 139).

(10) The starting point is a risk-free investment and this, on the evidence available to us, appears to be best represented by index-linked gilts (para. 145).

(11) For the Cadogan Estate a deferment yield of 4.5 per cent compared to index-linked gilts at two per cent makes sufficient allowance for the general risks perceived by the market to attach to these properties compared to index-linked gilts. That is the norm to be applied to houses by reference to the specific qualities and circumstances of each property (para. 152).

(12) The assumption under section 9(1A) of the 1967 Act that the tenant has no liability for repairs is agreed to have no application to the houses in these appeals on the Cadogan Estate (para. 157).

(13) The assumption under Schedule 13, paragraph 3(2) to the 1993 Act, that the vendor is selling for an estate in fee simple subject to the lease, does preserve the assumption of a sale of the freehold reversion to the flat as if sold with the rest of the block (para. 161).

(14) Having regard to the preceding two paragraphs, it is not necessary to assume a different risk factor for the reversion upon a single flat compared to a block of flats (para. 163).

(15) Lesser management problems for houses compared to flats, and the possibility of greater growth in the house market, indicate a 0.25 per cent differential, increasing the general deferment rate for Cadogan flats to 4.75 per cent (para. 163).

(19) Changes in deferment rates will not occur until a change in the trend in risk-free yields has become established or the continuation of a trend establishes a new level of yields. In the circumstances, in these appeals, no adjustments are to be made for the different dates of valuation (para. 179).

Fundamentally, the approach to determining the deferment rate has been established without the assistance of financial expertise, and for Cadogan Estate properties the rates are, in effect, 4.5 per cent for houses and 4.75 per cent for flats.

Earl Cadogan v Sportelli [2007] 1 EGLR 153

The third case concerned five further conjoined appeals from decisions of the LVT.

The tribunal had the benefit of both valuation and financial evidence in this case and it is again helpful to know that the appeal properties were all located in London SW1, SW3, SW7 and W1 postcodes (all PCL). The valuations fell under section 9(1C) to the 1967 Act, and Schedules 6 and 13 to the 1993 Act, respectively.

The Lands Tribunal decision in *Sportelli* saw the process of calculating a deferment rate based on market evidence evolve slightly further, resulting in the equation:

$$DR = RFR - RGR + RP$$

At paragraph 52 of the decision, the tribunal enunciates the 'nature of the investment' to which the deferment is to be applied:

> 'The nature of the investment being assumed may be analysed thus: the value of the asset consists of its prospect of appreciation; it will appreciate through the lapse of time as the term date gets nearer (inherent growth); if, however, the vacant possession value of the property increases in real terms, the reversion will appreciate through real growth in the same way as the property in possession. On the other hand, set against the relatively secure long-term nature of the investment that the asset represents, are the risks and disadvantages that are associated with it. There is volatility in the market in residential property, and there are prolonged periods of downturn. The property is illiquid in the sense that any sale will take time to achieve. While it is a tradeable asset,

therefore, the reversion is subject to the risk that a sale may only be achievable after a delay and at a time when the market is low. It is also an asset that may become obsolescent and deteriorate physically.'

The methodology for determining deferment rate is that adopted in *Arbib*, and is briefly as follows:

A form of financial valuation known as CAPM (Capital Asset Pricing Model), which expresses deferment by the formula DR = RFR – RGR + RP; with RP being reached by independent assessment.

Risk-free rate: 'the return demanded by investors for holding an asset with no risk, often proxied by the return on a government security held to redemption', with government bonds being agreed to be the usual source of information.

The risk-free rate is taken as 2.25 per cent, rather than the 2.0 per cent assumed in *Arbib*.

The rate of 2.25 per cent was taken because

'...the average index-linked yields on a five year rolling basis over the last decade suggested that a more stable market based risk-free rate would be in the range 2.0 per cent – 2.5 per cent'.

The tribunal chose the midrange figure. The apparent decline in yields on long-term gilts should be compared with the more consistent rates for ten-year gilts, before drawing conclusions as to the risk-free rate.

'The choice of period for assessing the risk-free rate should be as long as is necessary for identifying from self-consistent information a steady long-run rate'.

Real growth rate: two features are highlighted for particular consideration:

- the very substantial difference over a long period that can arise from different rates; and
- the fact that real house prices fluctuate significantly, so that at any one time they may be substantially above or substantially below the level that would have resulted from a projection of past average growth rates.

Flats: new lease claims: valuation issues

Two per cent is adopted as the assumed growth rate.

Risk premium: 'the additional return required by investors to compensate for the risk of not receiving a guaranteed return'.

Having rejected the use of CAPM, risk premium is to be assessed by considering the individual components of the risks of investment in long reversions, namely:

- volatility;
- illiquidity;
- deterioration; and
- obsolescence.

Physical deterioration and obsolescence are factors that need to be reflected in the generic deferment rate insofar as the risk related to them is common to all residential property considered in the long term. To the extent that they are property specific, volatility and illiquidity have the most impact on the risk premium.

Since real house prices fluctuate, are prone to shocks and are strongly cyclical, an investor in a long-term reversion would be conscious of the risk that the market could be depressed at the time he wishes to dispose of his interest, even though the residential property market is less volatile than the equities market. The illiquidity resulting from high transaction costs, and the time taken for it to complete a transaction when compared with equities, adds to the risk associated with volatility.

The tribunal decided that after offsetting the extra volatility of equities against the relative illiquidity of property, plus additional allowance for the possibility of physical and functional depreciation, 4.5 per cent was appropriate.

Therefore:

Deferment Rate = RFR − RGR + RP
= 2.25% − 2% + 4.5%
= 4.75%

In *Arbib*, the 0.25 per cent upwards adjustment for flats was intended to reflect both the greater management problems and the possibility that there might be a greater prospect of growth in the house as opposed to the flat market (para. 95). The tribunal confirmed the *Arbib* adjustment upwards of 0.25 per cent for

101

flats due to the greater management problems, regardless of whether the flat or block of flats is subject to a head lease or not. There could be a case for an additional allowance where there are exceptional difficulties, but there must be compelling evidence to support this.

As to the prospect of better growth in the house as opposed to flat market, the tribunal concluded that any disparity is likely to even out over the longer term.

Departure from the rates (para. 123)

> 'The application of the deferment rate of five per cent for flats and 4.75 per cent for houses that we have found to be generally applicable will need to be considered in relation to the facts of each individual case. Before applying a rate that is different from this, however, a valuer or an LVT should be satisfied that there are particular features that fall outside the matters that are reflected in the vacant possession value of the house or flat or in the deferment rate itself and can be shown to make a departure from the rate appropriate.'

In other words, *Sportelli* did not purport to be 'the last word'. The guidance was to stand 'in the absence of compelling evidence to the contrary'.

The Lands Tribunal decisions in *Sportelli* were upheld in the Court of Appeal (paras. 98 & 99). The court confirming that the tribunal:

> '...could hardly have done more to ensure that the issues were fully ventilated and exhaustively examined...it is difficult to envisage a better qualified panel of experts for the purpose than those called in this case, or of specialist counsel on both sides of the argument'.

Outside the PCL

The court concluded that whereas the tribunal in its guidance did not distinguish in terms between the PCL area and other parts of London or the country, there must be an implicit distinction. The evidence before the tribunal wholly related to PCL, and notwithstanding the fact that those giving evidence were asked whether the deferment rate would vary with location, the court makes it clear that the possibility remains for further evidence to be called by other parties in other cases directly concerned with different areas.

The generic rate will be the starting point, including methodology to reach the same, but the opportunity remains to present further evidence, typically with respect to the risk premium. Each case to be handled on its merits.

We now review various tribunal cases that have been heard subsequently, where variations from the generic rates of *Sportelli* have been sought.

Leases below 20 years

In *Sportelli,* the tribunal concluded that for a lease with less than 20 years unexpired, the deferment rate would need to have regard to the property cycle at the time of valuation (para. 85).

In *John Lyon's Charity v Red Earl Ltd* (LVT 13 October 2008 unreported) a house in St John's Wood, London NW8, where the term was only 3.38 years, the tribunal concluded that market perception at the date of valuation of anticipated real growth over the remainder of the term was less than the long term trend and assumed a real growth rate of only one per cent (as opposed to two per cent), therefore adding one per cent to the deferment rate in *Sportelli*.

In *Dickins v Howard De Walden Estates Ltd* (LVT 19 September 2008 unreported) two flats in Marylebone, London W1, where the terms were only 5.12 years, the tribunal similarly concluded that departure from the five per cent rate was justified and applied six per cent, having regard to the position within the property cycle at the date of valuation and where short term considerations were more likely to apply.

Long terms unexpired:

In *Sherwood Hall (East End Road) Management Company Ltd v Magnolia Tree Ltd* [2009] UKUT 158 (LC), the five per cent deferment rate in *Sportelli* was upheld by the Lands Tribunal in a collective enfranchisement claim where the unexpired terms were approximately 88 years. The property is also outside the PCL area, but the deferment was not challenged on that basis.

The tribunal confirmed that it was satisfied it is open to a party to call evidence seeking to demonstrate that a different deferment rate is appropriate in the case of longer dated reversions (para. 16); this following the comments of Carnwath LJ at paragraph 102 of the Court of Appeal's decision.

The tribunal go on to say at paragraph 18 that there are a number of components to the deferment rate – the risk-free rate, real growth and the risk premium. An assessment of the latter involves a consideration of the risks of investment in long reversions, namely volatility, illiquidity, deterioration and obsolescence. Whether one or more of these risks increase over a period of time is a matter for evidence.

Whereas the tribunal acknowledged the principle that a departure from the *Sportelli* rate may be justified for 88 year reversions as opposed to shorter terms, on the basis of the evidence before it, five per cent was determined.

The LVT came to the same conclusion on the basis of the evidence before it in their decision pursuant to the collective enfranchisement in *10 Cheniston Gardens Ltd v Catherine Fiona Atkins* (5 January 2008 unreported), a mid-terrace building converted into flats close to Kensington High Street, London W8, where the unexpired terms ranged from 106 years to 152 years. Accordingly, the five per cent deferment rate in *Sportelli* was not departed from.

Conversely, in the collective enfranchisement claim of *Nell Gwynn House Freehold Ltd v various* (LVT 21 April 2009, unreported), a substantial 1930s block of flats on Sloane Avenue, London SW3, the tribunal concluded that the deferment rate for flats with leases of 91.68 years unexpired was 6.5 per cent and those with 119.68 years unexpired had no reversionary value.

What is PCL?

The earliest reference to Prime Central London (PCL) of which the author of this chapter is aware, is the Hampton & Sons (now known as Hamptons), Prime Residential Property Index which dates from January 1974. The index charts the movement of prices of prime properties in Mayfair, Belgravia, Knightsbridge, Kensington, Chelsea, Regent's Park and St John's Wood.

Flats: new lease claims: valuation issues

The Savills PCL indices cover all property in Mayfair, Belgravia, Knightsbridge, Chelsea, Kensington, Holland Park, Notting Hill, St John's Wood, Regent's Park and Hampstead. This index dates from June 1979.

In *Sportelli,* whilst the Lands Tribunal accepts that the deferment rate could require adjustment for location, on the evidence before it, no adjustment is justified to reflect regional or local considerations, either generally or in relation to the particular cases (all within PCL) para. 88. They go on to say at paragraph 121 that the prospect of varying conclusions on the deferment rate in different cases can be avoided by LVTs adopting the guidance of this decision, unless there is compelling evidence to the contrary.

What the tribunal was in effect saying is that the *Sportelli* rates were to apply countrywide, unless there was compelling evidence to depart from them.

However, the Lands Tribunal's decision in *Sherwood Hall* shows that the tribunal is now of the view, pursuant to the Court of Appeal's observations at para. 102, that the threshold to apply outside PCL is to be less than compelling. The court confirms the methodology in *Sportelli* to reach the deferment rate; accordingly evidence is required to show long-term regional variations in volatility, illiquidity, deterioration and obsolescence to justify departure.

Various challenges to the generic rate in *Sportelli* outside PCL have hitherto been made at the Lands Tribunal. In chronological order, these are as follows:

Nicholson v Goff [2007] 1 EGLR 83

The tribunal applied a deferment rate of five per cent for a flat in Birmingham as there were no special factors that would have made it appropriate to move away from the Sportelli rate for this 25 year lease. It is noted that the appeal was unopposed.

Hildron Finance Ltd v Greenhill Hampstead Ltd [2008] 1 EGLR 197

The tribunal concluded that the property in Hampstead is to be taken as falling outside the PCL, but said that none of the evidence in this appeal had persuaded them that the deferment rate should be different from five per cent in *Sportelli* (para. 38).

Daejan Investments Ltd v The Holt (Freehold) Ltd (LT 2 May 2008, unreported)

There was no evidence before the tribunal to show that Morden (The Holt) was subject to lower real growth than PCL; accordingly two per cent was adopted as the real rate of growth (para. 82).

In addition, the tribunal was not persuaded that the age, physical condition, design and construction of The Holt are such as to constitute an exception that these are factors that will be fully reflected in the vacant possession value and the (generic) risk premium. The Holt is not a building that is especially prone to the risk of deterioration and obsolescence (para. 85).

Cik v Chavda (LT 7 August 2008 unreported)

The LVT had determined a deferment rate of 6.5 per cent to be applicable for a number of new lease claims for flats in Hounslow; however the Lands Tribunal overturned this due to the fact that the adverse factors which the LVT had relied upon in order to depart from *Sportelli* were all ones that would be taken into account when reaching the vacant possession value.

The adverse factors identified by the LVT were:

- the continuing history of litigation between landlord and tenants about services and charges;
- the 'very poor tenants' that made up half the occupancy of the flats;
- the poor external condition of the premises;
- noise from the A3006 Bath Road and the overhead flight path; and
- the flanking road to the industrial estate to the rear (para. 32).

The tribunal found there was no justification to depart from a deferment rate of five per cent.

Mansal Securities & other appeals [2009] 10 EG 110 [2009] EG 104 LT 24 February 2009, (the 'Midlands 22')

The LVT had determined a deferment rate of 5.5 per cent for these various cases under section 9(1); the houses being located in the West Midlands area, thus outside PCL.

At the Lands Tribunal, two issues were highlighted to be decided to determine whether a departure from the 4.75 per cent generic rate in *Sportelli* is justified:

- are the factors that led to 4.75 per cent in *Sportelli* under section 9(1A) sufficiently different to those under section 9(1); and
- is there any evidence to justify a deferment rate for houses in the West Midlands which is different from that applying to houses in the PCL area?

Section 9(1) v section 9(1A)

The tribunal concluded that a 0.25 per cent increase in the risk premium is appropriate to compensate for the increased volatility and illiquidity for a reversion to a ground rent only (section 9(1)) as opposed to a house standing on the site (section 9(1A)), para. 27.

As to the second point, the tribunal concluded that the evidence before it was insufficient to displace the *Sportelli* rate of 4.75 per cent. Having said that, further explanation is required here, which, in turn, is referred to later.

The evidence before the LVT was that from limited Nationwide statistics it could be shown that real growth rate was lower in the West Midlands than PCL. The tribunal concluded that this evidence was insufficient to justify a departure from *Sportelli*, but the Member's comments at paragraph 34 are important.

The leaseholders were not represented; and the information on the Nationwide statistics was inadequate.

> 'Valuers who give evidence in similar cases in future are to bear in mind their professional duty to investigate as fully as possible the matters before this tribunal, in particular the Nationwide statistics.'

The implication being that the Member had it in mind that with further in depth analysis and supporting material to the Nationwide statistics before him, he may have concluded that there is sufficient evidence to show that real growth in the West Midlands is less than PCL, and thus an adjustment to the *Sportelli* rate is justified.

The tribunal determined a deferment rate of five per cent, an increase of 0.25 per cent, to reflect the increased risk premium an investor would seek for a section 9(1) case as opposed to section 9(1A).

Culley v Daejan Properties [2009] UKUT 168 (LC)

In this case the tribunal confirmed the LVT's determination of a five per cent deferment rate applicable for a collective enfranchisement of a 1930s block of flats in Middlesex. Two issues in relation to deferment rate were challenged: (a) location, hence real growth rate; and (b) obsolescence.

On both points, the tribunal determined on the evidence before it, that there was no justification to depart from the five per cent rate in *Sportelli*. There is, however, a discussion on 'obsolescence', and what it means in relation to deferment rate.

> 'Obsolescence is concerned with the risk that a building will decline, not that the value for another purpose will increase' (para 41).

Redevelopment of city centres is founded on the latter, and would suggest a lowering of deferment rate, rather than an increase.

In *Freehold Properties Ltd* [2009] UKUT 172 (LC), the tribunal upheld the decisions of the LVT for various houses in the West Midlands where the deferment rate was determined at 5.5 per cent under section 9(1). The increase of 0.75 per cent from the *Sportelli* rate of 4.75 per cent to reflect the lower growth rate in the West Midlands as opposed to PCL, and the differences between section 9(1) and section 9(1A).

The Member draws attention to the fact that he is not persuaded that the independent analysis required of the Nationwide statistics presented in *Mansal* had been carried out sufficient to show that the appropriate deferment rate in this case should not depart from the *Sportelli* 4.75 per cent rate (paras. 17 & 18).

Zuckerman v Trustees of the Calthorpe Estates [2009] UKUT 235 (LC)

This appeal to LT/UT was pursuant to the LVT's determination of a five per cent deferment rate for 11 new lease claims in Dudley, West Midlands. The flats are of 1970s construction and were held on existing leases for terms of 64 years.

Flats: new lease claims: valuation issues

The appeal succeeded on three grounds as follows:

- greater risk of deterioration in Kelton Court than PCL (not reflected in vacant possession values), increase in risk premium of 0.25 per cent;
- significantly slower long-term growth rate in West Midlands than in PCL, increase in risk premium of 0.5 per cent; and
- greater risks associated with flats pursuant to the introduction of The Service Charges (Consultation Requirements) (England) Regulations 2003, increase in the addition for flats to reflect greater management problems from 0.25 per cent to 0.5 per cent. It is noted that the Member comments that he would not have made this adjustment if the head lease had still been in existence.

In summary the six per cent deferment rate is reached as follows:

Risk-free rate: no change from 2.25 per cent; minus

Real growth rate; no change from two per cent, but see below; plus

Risk premium: increase from 4.5 per cent to 5.25 per cent (see above); and plus

Increase in adjustment for flats (management) from 0.25 per cent to 0.5 per cent equals six per cent.

Further examples

We now consider the effect on premium of the five per cent deferment rate, where hitherto a higher rate might have been adopted.

Prior to *Sportelli*, the deferment rate established for flats and houses in PCL was six per cent, with corresponding deferment rates in the suburbs and provinces typically in the region of seven per cent to ten per cent.

Five per cent is now applicable to flats in PCL unless there is compelling evidence to the contrary; and similarly five per cent countrywide, save where there is evidence to the contrary (note the difference in threshold required pursuant to the Court of Appeal's decision in *Sportelli*).

Example 2

As per Example 1, save that a deferment rate of seven per cent is applied.

New lease – premium computation

Date of valuation: 25 March 2010

Lease expiry date: 25 March 2091

Diminution in value of landlord's interest

Difference between the value before grant of the new lease

Term

Rent	£50 p.a.			
YP 81 years @ 8%		12.4755	£624	

Reversion

To 'share of freehold' with vacant possession value (new lease value – 99% FHVP)		£505,050		
Deferred 81 years @ 7%		0.0042	£2,121	£2,745

minus

and the value after the new lease is granted

Term

New lease at a peppercorn rent		£0	£0	

Reversion

To share of freehold with vacant possession value – as above		£505,050		
Deferred 171 years @ 7%		0.00001	£5	£5

Diminution in value of landlord's interest	£2,740

plus

Marriage value – as 81 years unexpired, if any, taken as 'nil'	£0

New lease premium (excluding costs)		£2,740
	Say	£2,750

The new lease premium is approximately one quarter that of Example 1; whereas the generic deferment rates affect enfranchisement prices within PCL, the greater impact is on premiums in the suburbs and provinces.

Marriage value

Marriage value is that released by the coalescence of the interests – in its simplest form – the landlord's and tenant's interests. It is calculated by aggregating the values of the interests after the new lease has been granted, and deducting the corresponding values prior.

Landlord's share of marriage value

Schedule 13, paragraph 4

4(1) The marriage value is the amount referred to in sub-paragraph (2), and the landlord's share of the marriage value is 50 per cent of that amount.

(2) Subject to sub-paragraph (2A), the marriage value is the difference between the following amounts, namely–
 (a) the aggregate of –
  (i) the value of the interest of the tenant under his existing lease,
  (ii) the value of the landlord's interest in the tenant's flat prior to the grant of the new lease, and
  (iii) the values prior to the grant of that lease of all intermediate leasehold interests (if any);
and
 (b) the aggregate of –
  (i) the value of the interest to be held by the tenant under the new lease,
  (ii) the value of the landlord's interest in the tenant's flat once the new lease is granted, and
  (iii) the values of all intermediate leasehold interests (if any) once that new lease is granted.

(2A) Where at the relevant date the unexpired term of the tenant's existing lease exceeds eighty years, the marriage value shall be taken to be nil.

(3) For the purposes of sub-paragraph (2)–
 (a) the value of the interest of the tenant under his existing lease shall be determined in accordance with paragraph 4A;
 (aa) the value of the interest to be held by the tenant under the new lease shall be determined in accordance with paragraph 4B;

(b) the value of any such interest of the landlord as is mentioned in paragraph (a) or paragraph (b) of sub-paragraph (2) is the amount determined for the purposes of paragraph 3(1)(a) or paragraph 3(1)(b) (as the case may be); and

(c) the value of any intermediate leasehold interest shall be determined in accordance with paragraph 8, and shall be so determined as at the relevant date.

Paragraphs 4A and 4B are not detailed here, but were introduced under s.110 of *The Housing Act* 1996. When Schedule 13 was originally drafted, it was unclear as to whether the same assumptions to value the landlord's interests in the marriage value computation were to apply in valuing the tenant's interests. Section 110 introduces a similar set of assumptions to apply in valuing the tenant's existing and new leases in the marriage value computation.

We now look at examples which include the marriage value computation.

Example 3

Following on from Example 1, we look at a 79 years' unexpired term (i.e. just below the 80 years plus cut off), for which the existing lease value is £465,000.

New lease – premium computation

Date of valuation: 25 March 2010

Lease expiry date: 25 March 2089

<u>Diminution in value of landlord's interest</u>

Difference between the value before grant of the new lease

<u>Term</u>

Rent	£50 p.a.		
YP 79 years @ 8%	12.4714	£624	

<u>Reversion</u>

To 'share of freehold' with vacant possession value (new lease value – 99% FHVP)	£505,050		
Deferred 79 years @ 5%	0.0212	£10,707	£11,331

Flats: new lease claims: valuation issues

minus

and the value after the new lease is granted

<u>Term</u>

New lease at a peppercorn rent	£0	£0	

<u>Reversion</u>

To share of freehold with vacant possession value – as above	£505,050		
Deferred 169 years @ 5%	0.0003	£152	£152
Diminution in value of landlord's interest			£11,179

plus

<u>Landlord's share of marriage value</u>

Difference between the aggregate of values of interests <u>post</u> grant of the new lease

Landlord's interest	£152		
Tenant's proposed interest	£500,000	£500,152	

less

Aggregate of values of interests <u>prior</u> to grant of the new lease

Landlord's interest	£11,331		
Tenant's existing interest	£465,000	£476,331	
Marriage value		£23,821	
50% thereof		0.5	£11,911
plus diminution in value of landlord's interest (from above)			£11,179
New lease premium (excluding costs)			£23,090
		Say	£23,100

Compare this with the premium at Example 1 (£10,200 excluding costs); whereas there is an increase in the diminution in value of landlord's interest, the balance of the increase in premium is the landlord's 50 per cent share of marriage value, highlighting the importance to the tenant of the claim being made before the cut off point is reached.

113

Leasehold enfranchisement explained

To give a general idea as to the order of premium where the existing has 50 years unexpired, we look at a further example.

Example 4

New lease premium for a term of 50 years unexpired, for which the existing lease value is £375,000.

Date of valuation: 25 March 2010

Lease expiry date: 25 March 2060

<u>Diminution in value of landlord's interest</u>

Difference between the value before grant of the new lease

<u>Term</u>

Rent	£50 p.a.		
YP 50 years @ 8%	12.2335	£612	

Reversion

To 'share of freehold' with vacant possession value (new lease value – 99% FHVP)	£505,050		
Deferred 50 years @ 5%	0.0872	£44,040	£44,652

minus

and the value after the new lease is granted

<u>Term</u>

New lease at a peppercorn rent	£0	£0	

Reversion

To share of freehold with vacant possession value – as above	£505,050		
Deferred 140 years @ 5%	0.0011	£556	£556

Diminution in value of landlord's interest	£44,096

plus

<u>Landlord's share of marriage value</u>

Difference between the aggregate of values of interests <u>post</u> grant of the new lease

Landlord's interest	£556	
Tenant's proposed interest	£500,000	£500,556

Flats: new lease claims: valuation issues

less			
Aggregate of values of interests <u>prior</u> to grant of the new lease			
Landlord's interest	£44,652		
Tenant's existing interest	£375,000	£419,652	
Marriage value		£80,904	
50% thereof		0.5	£40,452
plus diminution in value of landlord's interest (from above)			£44,096
New lease premium (excluding costs)			£84,548
		Say	£84,550

In the next examples, we look at the effect on premium if the five per cent deferment rate is increased for a term of less than 20 years.

Example 5

Premium based on a short term lease – 15 years unexpired, for which the existing lease value is £177,500.

Date of valuation: 25 March 2010

Lease expiry date: 25 March 2025

<u>Diminution in value of landlord's interest</u>

Difference between the value before grant of the new lease

<u>Term</u>

Rent	£50 p.a.		
YP 15 years @ 8%	8.5595	£428	

<u>Reversion</u>

To 'share of freehold' with vacant possession value (new lease value – 99% FHVP)	£505,050		
Deferred 15 years @ 5%	0.4810	£242,929	£243,357

minus

and the value after the new lease is granted

115

Leasehold enfranchisement explained

<u>Term</u>			
New lease at a peppercorn rent	£0	£0	
<u>Reversion</u>			
To share of freehold with vacant possession value – as above	£505,050		
Deferred 105 years @ 5%	0.0060	£3,030	£3,030
Diminution in value of landlord's interest			£240,327
plus			
<u>Landlord's share of marriage value</u>			
Difference between aggregate of values of interests <u>post</u> grant of the new lease			
Landlord's interest	£3,030		
Tenant's proposed interest	£500,000	£503,030	
less			
Aggregate of values of interests <u>prior</u> to grant of the new lease			
Landlord's interest	£243,357		
Tenant's existing interest	£177,500	£420,857	
Marriage value		£82,173	
50% thereof		0.5	£41,087
plus diminution in value of landlord's interest (from above)			£240,327
New lease premium (excluding costs)			£281,414
		Say	£281,400

Flats: new lease claims: valuation issues

Example 6

Following on from Example 5, the deferment rate is increased to <u>5.5 per cent</u> in the 'before' computation to show the difference in premium.

Date of valuation: 25 March 2010

Lease expiry date: 25 March 2025

<u>Diminution in value of landlord's interest</u>

Difference between the value before grant of the new lease

<u>Term</u>

Rent	£50 p.a.		
YP 15 years @ 8%	8.5595	£428	

<u>Reversion</u>

To 'share of freehold' with vacant possession value (new lease value – 99% FHVP)	£505,050		
Deferred 15 years @ 5.5%	0.4479	£226,212	£226,640

minus

and the value after the new lease is granted

<u>Term</u>

New lease at a peppercorn rent	£0	£0	

<u>Reversion</u>

To share of freehold with vacant possession value – as above	£505,050		
Deferred 105 years @ 5%	0.0060	£3,030	£ 3,030

Diminution in value of landlord's interest	£223,610

plus

<u>Landlord's share of marriage value</u>

Difference between the aggregate of values of interests <u>post</u> grant of the new lease

Landlord's interest	£3,030	
Tenant's proposed interest	£500,000	£503,030

less

Aggregate of values of interests <u>prior</u> to grant of the new lease

Landlord's interest	£ 226,640	
Tenant's existing interest	£177,500	£404,140
Marriage value		£98,890
50% thereof	0.5	£49,445
plus diminution in value of landlord's interest (from above)		£223,610
New lease premium (excluding costs)		£273,055
	Say	£273,050

An increase of <u>0.5 per cent</u> to the deferment rate in the 'before' computation, results in a corresponding decrease of <u>£8,350</u> in the new lease premium.

In the calculation of the diminution in value of landlord's interest, the 'share of freehold' capital value is applied in calculating the two reversionary interests (before (i.e. the current value) and after grant of the new lease).

Where the unexpired term of the existing lease as at the date of valuation is 80 years or less, the values of the new lease and the existing lease are needed in the marriage value computation. Note the legislation is drafted to the effect that where the unexpired term of the existing lease at the relevant date <u>exceeds 80 years,</u> the marriage value shall be taken as nil (para. 4, s. (2A)).

In an ideal world, valuers in any one particular set of circumstances would have comparable sales evidence to assess the share of freehold and new lease values for the price computation. This is not always the case. Having said that, with the passage of time and more and more new leases having been granted, cases where there is no evidence of long lease sales are rare. As a result, it is often possible to use market evidence of sales of comparable flats.

Invariably, all comparables require some form of adjustment, even if it is only for the floor of a flat in the same block of flats.

Typically, valuers are required to make adjustments for the following, inter alia:

- time;
- lease length (relativity);
- improvements (condition);
- floor (including lateral);
- outside space, including a roof terrace, balcony, patio and garden;
- position; and if applicable
- the final adjustment for the benefit of the Act or Act rights.

In *The Earl Cadogan v Farrokh Faizapour & John Stephenson* [2010] UKUT 3 (LC), a collective enfranchisement of 54-56 Cadogan Square and 26-28 Clabon Mews, London SW1, the tribunal discusses adjustments of comparables, and provides a commentary on what it describes as non-physical factors and physical factors.

In this case, the valuers made adjustments to comparable sales for each of the following:

- time;
- relativity;
- condition;
- lateral flats;
- off-square and edge of square;
- floor level difference on second and third floors; and
- other.

At paragraph 32 of their decision, the tribunal say:

> 'The adjustments made by both parties in respect of relativity, location and for lateral layout are expressed as percentages. The adjustments made for condition are expressed as a figure per square foot. Applying percentage adjustments is commutative, i.e. it does not matter to the result in which order those adjustments are made. However, the deduction of a spot figure for condition is not commutative and the point at which that deduction is made will affect the result'.

The tribunal goes on to say that it prefers the approach which incorporates adjustments for non-physical factors (time and relativity) before making allowances for physical factors (condition, location and lateral layout).

Turning to the existing lease value, one of the statutory requirements within the marriage value computation is that there is no right to a new lease, so that the effect on value of the right to the new lease must be ignored. Existing lease sales, and in particular those of 80 years and less unexpired, take place in a wholly (in a sense) 'contaminated market' where leasehold reform rights exist. Accordingly, analysis of existing lease sales in the market may produce inconsistent results and prove unsatisfactory. This is because, unlike the position prior to 1993, the parties in the market bargain in the knowledge that the tenant has statutory rights. Having said that, it is the author's experience in PCL that tenant's will generally 'overpay' for leasehold interests. And this is not solely due to the effects of the legislation.

The exception is in those comparatively few cases where the original lease was less than 21 years, in which case, it is not a qualifying lease, section 5(3).

It is this contentious issue that has vexed all parties involved in leasehold reform valuations.

The question of relativity was first examined in detail in *Arrowdell Ltd v Coniston Court (North) Hove Ltd* [2007] RVR 39.

Paragraph 57:

> 'As we have said above, we have been acutely aware of the difficulty of reaching a satisfactory conclusion on relativity in the light of the inadequacy of the available evidence, and it is clear that this is a problem that is liable to confront LVTs in all such cases. The likelihood is that decisions will be varied and inconsistent, while if local perceptions of relativities are built up as the result of decisions and settlements, it is improbable that these will properly reflect no-Act values. Against this background, we consider that graphs of relativity are capable of providing the most useful guidance. While it may be that relativities will vary between one type of property and another and from area to area, we think that there is little doubt that the predominant factor is the length of the term. It ought, we believe, to be possible to produce standard graphs, distinguishing between mortgage-dependent markets and those that are not so dependent, on the basis of a survey of assessments made by experienced valuers addressing themselves properly to the hypothetical no-Act world. We express the hope that the Royal Institution of Chartered Surveyors may find itself able to carry out such an exercise

and to produce guidance in the form of standard graphs that can readily be applied by valuers in carrying out enfranchisement valuations. Such graphs could be used as evidence by LVTs, with the relativities shown being applied by them in the absence of evidence compelling the adoption of other figures.'

Pursuant to this, the President of RICS set up a Leasehold Reform Working Group to report on this issue.

The Leasehold Reform Working Group set up post *Arrowdell* has reported to the President of RICS; the report has now been published and can be found at http://www.rics.org/site/download

Relativity

What is relativity?

In *RICS Research, Leasehold Reform: Graphs of Relativity*, October 2009 'leasehold relativity' is defined as the value of a dwelling held on a lease at any given unexpired term, divided by the value of the same dwelling in possession to the freeholder, expressed as a percentage. Relativity is a method of calculating a capital value by reference to another, which in turn is to be adopted in the computation.

Whilst the Working Group was formulating its report, relativity was simultaneously being examined at length in the conjoined cases *Nailrile Limited v Earl Cadogan* [2008] LRA/114/2006 Lands Tr (*Lalvani v Earl Cadogan* – 6 flats at 62 Cadogan Square, London SW1). In their interim decisions, the members (at para. 228), reaffirm the comments in *Arrowdell*.

Paragraph 228:

> 'Looking at the evidence overall we agree with the comments of the tribunal in *Arrowdell*: "In such circumstances, in our view, it is necessary for the tribunal to do the best it can with any evidence of transactions that can usefully be applied, even though such transactions take place in the real world rather than the no-Act world. Regard can also be had to graphs of relativity..." In the absence of any better evidence, we think it is right to rely on such transactions and graphs in this instance'.

The members go on to say that in these cases the Gerald Eve graph for 44 years unexpired (the subject flats' existing lease unexpired terms) shows a relativity of 69.2 per cent (it is referred to as 'normal relativity'), before adjustment for onerous ground rent; and the graph of graphs produced by Beckett and Kay (2007, first revision) shows a corresponding range of relativities from 62.0 per cent to 76.5 per cent, with a mid-point of 69.25 per cent.

The tribunal determined a normal relativity of 71 per cent for the 44 years term, before adjustment for the onerous ground rent provisions.

Benefit of the Act or Act rights

There is reference in paragraph 228 to the adjustment for the 'benefit of the Act' or 'Act rights' as it is also known. When analysing comparable sales transactions in leasehold reform to reach the existing lease value in the marriage value computation, an adjustment is required, where the comparable property is subject to a qualifying lease, to strip out the increase in value the market reflects for the benefits in leasehold reform. The assumptions at paragraphs 4A and 4B to Schedule 13 corresponding to those to calculate the diminution in value of the landlord's interest under paragraph 3.

When assessing the value attributable to the benefit of the Act, the valuer must be aware that those rights extend beyond the fiscal benefit of the right to a new lease and to retain part of the marriage value. The non-fiscal points were first discussed by the Lands Tribunal in *Chelsea Properties Ltd v Earl Cadogan*, (LRA/69 2007, unreported), which concerned a new lease claim on a flat in Cadogan Square, London SW1. In their decision (para. 46), the members said the benefits include:

- the ability to acquire the new lease to be granted at a time of the tenant's choosing;
- at a price determined by the tribunal in default of agreement, based on values at a fixed date;
- the ability to offer the new lease for sale at a later date to a much wider market than one limited to those wishing to buy a very short lease; and
- the ability to defer indefinitely the terminal lease obligations, including in particular a schedule of dilapidations.

The benefits are discussed further in *Nailrile* (para. 216), where the above points are reiterated and further include:

- the price excludes the tenant's overbid whilst guaranteeing him 50 per cent of the marriage value;
- whereas there is a fixed valuation date, the tenant does not have to pay the purchase price immediately.

All of the above is to be contrasted with the no-Act world, where the landlord is in an overwhelmingly strong negotiating position and the leaseholder has no certainty of being granted a new lease.

The tribunal go on at paragraph 217 to say that these benefits will always lead to a higher price being paid for an existing leasehold interest in the Act world compared with the no-Act world. And whereas it is foreseeable that a purchaser may pay too much for the benefit of the Act (by which it is meant that the price paid for the existing leasehold when added to the reversionary freehold interest exceeds the value of the unencumbered freehold interest), there are no circumstances in which that is likely to happen in the no-Act world. It is not accepted that where there is no marriage value, there is no benefit of the Act. The approach of adopting a flat percentage of the existing leasehold value for the benefit of the Act is confirmed.

Assessing the percentage deduction for the benefit of the Act in any one set of circumstances is a matter of valuation judgment and opinion.

The author of this chapter was a member of the Working Group and was one of the expert witnesses in *Nailrile (Lalvani)*, and I would draw your attention to the following points:

- Such were the diverse opinions of the valuers in the Working Group, it was not possible to produce finite graphs on which all could agree, i.e. there is no single 'generic' graph for any one market or area.
- In some areas, there is a great deal of evidence to analyse – in others, comparatively little.
- The report includes various graphs produced by firms with experience in this field; with each graph is background information on its production. Accordingly, the valuer and practitioner in leasehold reform are in a position to select what they believe to be the most appropriate graph for the particular case, and can advise as to why it has been chosen in preference to any/all of the others. The valuer and practitioner may conclude that a combination of any two or more graphs is appropriate.
- The graphs show relativity to corresponding share of freehold value for varying unexpired terms, each on the basis of

ground rent and lease provisions, which would not otherwise affect value.

For further information on relativity including what the graphs are and how they are compiled, see the report.

It is not the case that graphs are to be used in isolation; valuers are to make the best use they can of any sales evidence. In addition to which, decisions of the tribunals and settlement analyses can also be used, but note the following.

In *Arbib*, the Summary paragraph 4, decisions of the LVT are not evidence per se, but if the full facts of the case can be analysed, assistance can be gained from them. Similarly, at paragraph 7, settlement analyses can assist where the valuers, on behalf of both the landlord and the tenant, have agreed the constituent parts.

Valuers are familiar with the concept of 'weight' to be attributed to evidence. When presented with any one particular case, the valuer and the practitioner are required to attribute what they believe to be the appropriate weight to the various types of evidence available to them. The Lands Tribunal in *Nailrile* attributed 'most weight upon the sale of the second floor flat at number 62' (in fact, one of the subject properties), paragraph 225; this being one comparable of over 100 listed in the schedules of sales transactions proposed.

In Examples 1–6 inclusive, the new lease value is £500,000 and the corresponding share of freehold value is £505,050. The relativity of the new lease value to corresponding share of freehold value equates to 99 per cent (£500,000 divided by £505,050, expressed as a percentage).

In the examples where there is a marriage value element (3–6 incl.), the existing lease values are: (a) 79 years unexpired – £465,000; (b) 50 years unexpired – £375,000; and (c) 15 years unexpired – £177,500.

The existing lease values within the respective marriage value computations represent the following relativities:

Example 3 – £465,000 divided by £505,050 = 92.07 per cent for the 79 years term.

Example 4 – £375,000 divided by £505,050 = 74.25 per cent for the 50 years term.

Examples 5 & 6 – £177,500 divided by £505,050 = 35.15 per cent for the 15 years terms.

Two further decisions of the UT/LT give guidance in this area.

In *Dependable Homes Limited v Mann & Mann* [2009] UKUT 171 (LC), the tribunal, at paragraph 34, highlights the no-Act world assumption to be taken into consideration; and refers to its own adjustment of 7.5 per cent for the benefit of the Act in *Nailrile*.

A relativity of 83 per cent (in this case to both the freehold and new lease values) is determined for the 54 years existing lease value.

In *Sarum Properties Limited v Webb, Webb & Webb* [2009] UKUT 188 (LC), the new and existing lease values in the tribunal's determination of the premium payable represent 99 per cent and 92 per cent of corresponding freehold value for the 167.7 years and 77.7 years terms, respectively.

Onerous ground rents

An 'onerous ground rent' is one that otherwise has an adverse effect on the capital value of the existing lease, that is to say, a purchaser will pay less for the interest when compared to the same property on a lease with nominal rent provisions. Typically, whereas a ground rent of (say) £50 per annum is regarded as 'nominal', a ground rent of £2,000 per annum (where the corresponding share of freehold value is (say) £500,000), would be regarded as onerous.

An onerous ground rent will increase the premium for a new lease for two main reasons:

- the diminution in value of landlord's interest will increase where the ground rent is £2,000 per annum as opposed to £50 per annum, as a higher sum (rent) is to be capitalised to compensate the landlord for the loss of rent once the new lease has been granted (the new lease being at a peppercorn rent); and
- the existing lease value, where required in the marriage value computation, is less valuable pro rata than its corresponding value of a lease with nominal ground rent provisions, by virtue of being adversely affected by the onerous ground rent provisions.

Onerous ground rents in the context of graphs of relativity are discussed at page 5 of the RICS research document referred to earlier.

The first case where an onerous ground rent was discussed is *Carl v Grosvenor Estate Belgravia* [2000] 38 EG 195 Lands Tr. Two points are of note:

- it is accepted that a high (onerous) ground rent can have an adverse effect on the existing lease value (para. 25); and
- the approach to assess the existing lease value where it is established that the lease is subject to an onerous ground rent (para. 28).

In *Carl*, the existing lease value was calculated by initially assessing what the value of the lease would be with nominal ground rent provisions (see later), and thereafter applying a multiplier of ten to the unpalatable ground rent, and deducting the resultant capital sum from the existing lease value with nominal provisions.

Following *Carl*, the valuer is to assess what the maximum palatable ground rent is for the existing lease. That is to say, the maximum ground rent that does not have an adverse effect on the existing lease value; i.e. a buyer in the open market would not lower his bid or purchase price for the lease to reflect the rent provisions (see later). This is generally either assessed as a fixed sum, say £500 per annum, or as a percentage of freehold with vacant possession value, say 0.1 per cent of freehold with vacant possession value.

In *Millard Investments Ltd v The Earl Cadogan* (unreported 2004, LVT), the tribunal determined the palatable ground rent at 0.1 per cent of freehold vacant possession value. To calculate the allowance (adjustment) for the high ground rent, the tribunal adopted a formulaic approach, by capitalising and deferring the excess sum, applying the same rates as those for calculating the value of the freeholder's interest.

We now look at an example to show this.

Flats: new lease claims: valuation issues

Example 7

In this example, the premium for a new lease is calculated based on a medium term lease – 50 years unexpired, for which the corresponding existing lease value with nominal ground rent provisions is £375,000 (as per Example 4), but there is an onerous ground rent of £2,000 per annum, fixed, which reduces the existing lease value to £354,400 (see later).

Date of valuation: 25 March 2010

Lease expiry date: 25 March 2060

Diminution in value of landlord's interest

Difference between the value before grant of the new lease

Term

Rent	£2,000 p.a.		
YP 50 years @ 7%		13.8007	£27,601

Reversion

To 'share of freehold' with vacant possession value (new lease value – 99% FHVP)	£505,050			
Deferred 50 years @ 5%		0.0872	£44,040	£71,641

minus

and the value after the new lease is granted

Term

New lease at a peppercorn rent	£0	£0

Reversion

To share of freehold with vacant possession value – as above	£505,050			
Deferred 140 years @ 5%		0.0011	£556	£556

Diminution in value of landlord's interest	£71,085

plus

Landlord's share of marriage value

Difference between the aggregate of values of interests <u>post</u> grant of the new lease

Landlord's interest	£556	
Tenant's proposed interest	£500,000	£500,556

127

Leasehold enfranchisement explained

less

Aggregate of values of interests <u>prior</u> to grant of the new lease

Landlord's interest	£71,641	
Tenant's existing interest (see later)	£354,400	£426,041

Marriage value		£74,515	
50% thereof		0.5	£37,258

plus diminution in value of landlord's interest (from above)	£71,085
New lease premium (excluding costs)	£108,343
Say	£108,350

Analysis of onerous ground rent provisions to establish existing lease value:

Share of freehold value (from above)	£505,050	
Palatable ground rent equates to (say) 0.1% of share of freehold value		£505 p.a.
Existing lease ground rent	£2,000 p.a.	
less 'palatable' ground rent	£505 p.a.	
Onerous (unpalatable) rent	£1,495 p.a.	
YP 50 years @ 7%	13.8007	£20,632
Adjustment for onerous ground rent (say)		£20,600

Existing lease value with nominal ground rent provisions (from above)	£375,000
less adjustment for onerous ground rent	£20,600
	£354,400

Equating to (£354,400 ÷ £505,050) 70.17% of share of freehold value.

The onerous ground rent has the effect of increasing the new lease premium in Example 4 of £84,550 to £108,350 – an increase of <u>£23,800</u>. So the premium is higher if the existing lease has onerous ground rent provisions.

Flats: new lease claims: valuation issues

It is for the valuer to choose the approach to calculate the adjustment for the onerous ground rent provisions. Initially, select the maximum annual rent for any given existing lease value, which does not have an adverse effect, either by way of a fixed sum or percentage of corresponding share of freehold value; and thereafter select the method to calculate the capital sum to adjust the corresponding existing lease value with nominal rent provisions. In practice, there is little evidence to show what the threshold for the palatable sum is; generally it is a matter of opinion, coupled with market experience. Following *Carl*, a fixed multiplier of ten is applied; an alternative approach is that adopted in *Millard* by capitalising the unpalatable sum at an appropriate rate. This latter approach is borne of capital sums paid by tenants to 'buy out' onerous provisions.

Where the review to an onerous ground rent is at a future date, the adjustment is deferred. A review which is, say, more than five years hence, might be disregarded, as purchasers in the market may treat the review as being too remote to affect the lease value; each case is to be taken on its merits.

In Example 7, the onerous ground rent is assessed as that above 0.1 per cent of corresponding share of freehold value (i.e. the maximum palatable rent is £505 p.a.), and the capitalisation rate adopted is seven per cent.

We now consider the new lease premium where the existing lease has a very short term unexpired, say less than five years.

Example 8

In this example, we calculate the premium based on a very short term lease – three years unexpired. For short term leases, three further valuation issues need to be considered.

- the tenant's right to hold over at the expiration of the term as an assured tenant (*Local Government and Housing Act* 1989 s.186 (2) (3));
- the prospect of the landlord seeking to enact section 61 (landlord's right to terminate new lease on grounds of redevelopment) within the last year of the existing lease term; and
- the approach to valuing the existing lease.

You are instructed to advise a lessee whose existing lease has a term of three years unexpired, with the ground rent fixed at £50 p.a. Further to your inspection, you value the new lease (93 years) at £350,000 and comparable flats in the vicinity are being let on assured shorthold tenancies in the region of £400 per week.

The valuation is as follows

Leasehold enfranchisement explained

Date of valuation: 25 March 2010

Lease expiry date: 25 March 2013

Diminution in value of landlord's interest

The rental value on an assured shorthold tenancy equates to £20,800 p.a. – which in turn is less than the £25,000 p.a. limit for the tenant to hold over as an assured tenant when the lease expires. Some valuers will argue that the landlord's interest is adversely affected by the prospect of the tenant holding over at the expiration of the term as an assured tenant. Accordingly, an adjustment to the reversionary interest is made; it is assessed at ten per cent here.

Difference between the value before grant of the new lease

Term

Rent	£50 p.a.		
YP 3 years at 8%	2.5771	£129	

Reversion

To 'share of freehold' with vacant possession value (new lease value – 97.5% FHVP)	£358,975		
less 10% (to reflect potential of tenant holding over)	£35,898		
	£323,077		
Deferred 3 years @ 5%	0.8638	£279,074	£279,203

minus

and the value after the new lease is granted

Term

New lease at a peppercorn rent	£0	£0	

Reversion

To share of freehold with vacant possession value – as above	£358,975		
Deferred 93 years @ 5%	0.0107	£3,841	£3,841

Diminution in value of landlord's interest £275,362

plus

Landlord's share of marriage value

With regard to the tenant's proposed interest, there is the prospect that the landlord will seek to enact section 61. Some valuers are of the opinion that

Flats: new lease claims: valuation issues

this adversely affects the value of the proposed interest. To highlight this, a deduction of five per cent is made from the new lease value in the marriage value computation.

In valuing the tenant's existing interest, the capitalisation approach can be applied, as opposed to either analysis of market sales, and/or use of graphs of relativity. Dual rate tables are adopted and the rental value of £400 per week, on an assured shorthold tenancy (AST), is adjusted downwards to reflect the full repairing and insuring (FRI) terms of the existing lease, when compared with the AST terms – a deduction of 25 per cent is made for this.

The marriage value computation is as follows

Difference between aggregate of values of interests <u>post</u> grant of the new lease

Landlord's interest		£3,841	
Tenant's proposed interest	£350,000		
Less 5%	£17,500		
		£332,500	£336,341

less

Aggregate of values of interests prior to grant of the new lease

Landlord's interest		£279,203	
Tenant's existing interest			
AST rental value	£400 per week		
Less 25% for FRI terms	£100 per week		
	£300 per week		
× 52 weeks	52		
	£15,600 p.a.		
YP 3 years @ 9% and 2.25%	2.4042		
		£37,506	£316,709
Marriage value			£19,632
50% thereof		0.5	£9,816
plus diminution in value of landlord's interest (from above)			£275,362
New lease premium (excluding costs)			£285,178
		Say	£285,200

131

Following on from Example 8, the valuer needs to be aware of the following:

(1) Lessee's right to remain in occupation

The *Local Government and Housing Act* 1989, section 186 and Schedule 10, provide for tenants of leases upon expiry (i.e. at term) to hold over as an assured tenant. The provisions, as originally drafted, were intended to phase out 'statutory tenancies' under the *Rent Act* 1977. Their effect extends into valuations under leasehold reform legislation.

An assured tenancy is one that provides security of tenure (as per the 1977 Act), but it is one where the rental value does not exceed £25,000 per annum (Sch. 1, para 2 of the 1988 Act as amended by the *Rating (Housing) Regulations* 1990).

The threshold for an assured tenancy is to be raised from £25,000 per annum to £100,000 per annum (£1,923 per week), with effect from 1 October 2010 (Assured Tenancies (Amendment) (England) Order 2010), and applying to England only. The immediate effect of this would be to extend rights to lessees of higher value properties to remain in occupation, albeit at a market rent.

Any increase in the rental value limit for an assured tenancy would extend rights to hold over to further lessees; as to whether those lessees take up those rights, only time will tell. From a lessee's perspective, he must have it in mind that any amending legislation will only extend rights in his favour, and that may in turn provide the opportunity to acquire a new lease at a lesser premium pro rata. Conversely, landlords must have it in mind that rights to lessees to hold over may be extended per se; and, if so, those extended rights will have to be borne in mind in leasehold reform valuations.

(2) Application to defeat tenant's claim where landlord intends to redevelop (s.47).

Where a landlord has given a counter-notice under section 45, he may apply to the court to declare that the right to the new lease is not exercisable on the grounds of his intention to redevelop, see chapter 1, 'Landlord intends to redevelop'.

Checklist for the tenant's valuer

Even at this relatively early stage, the valuer has had many things to consider, a number of which are discussed later in this chapter. Nevertheless, the following is a checklist of points to consider.

- Is the existing lease term in excess of 80 years? Time is of the essence.
- Have you been provided with the full lease documentation, including any licence to alter and deed of variation?
- Do you have details for access to inspect?
- Anticipate legal questions (typically an outline of the tenant's rights in leasehold reform, the sequence of events and timetable generally of a claim).
- The make-up of the computation for the new lease premium.
- Diminution in the landlord's interest, term and reversion.
- Landlord's 50 per cent share of marriage value.
- Relativity.
- The computation for the sum(s) to be included in the notice.
- Intermediate leasehold interests (ILIs); and
- Market conditions, timing of the claim.

Short unexpired terms:

- tenant's right to hold over as an assured tenant;
- landlord's right to terminate the new lease on grounds of redevelopment, (s.61); and
- method of valuation of the existing lease – capitalisation approach, as opposed to analysis of market sales and/or use of graphs of relativity.

The landlord's view

Any notice in leasehold reform is instigated by the tenant(s); accordingly, the timing of submission and the contents thereof are in his (the tenant's) hands.

From a landlord's perspective, his involvement in the statutory process starts in earnest on the receipt of notice of claim, unless he has had an early warning, having been served a notice under section 41 (right of qualifying tenant to obtain information about superior interests, etc.). Also, he may sometimes have had claims for other flats in the same block.

Although it is the landlord's advisers, both legal and valuation, who will in due course report on the claim including drafting, preparation and serving of the counter-notice, it is the landlord's responsibility to instruct his advisers at the earliest opportunity. One of the requirements of the notice is to include the date by which the counter-notice is to be served (s.42(5)); it is imperative that this date is met, see chapter 1, 'Landlord fails to serve a counter-notice'.

The landlord needs advice on the validity of the claim. Bearing in mind the strict timetable, the legal and valuation advice should be sought concurrently, with both advisers being instructed upon receipt of the notice. A quite common mistake is for the landlord to instruct his solicitor to report on the validity of the claim, which may take, say, two to three weeks, and then instruct the valuer to give his advice; this has the effect of eating into the time available to serve the counter-notice, so as and when the valuer is instructed, he may be obliged to work to an unreasonable deadline.

To recap, the first consideration for any landlord upon receipt of a notice is to instruct his advisers in good time, so that the report on claim and valuation advice can be sought. Solicitors will draft the counter-notice and seek to serve the same (generally), no later than two weeks prior to the date specified in the notice.

The valuer, upon receipt of instructions, will require access to inspect and be provided with the relevant lease documentation. The Act allows for access to carry out the inspection in reasonable time (s.44), and both the claimant's and solicitor's contact details are detailed in the notice.

The valuations follow the same principles as those for the tenant, save that for calculating the sum(s) for the counter-notice one would expect the valuer to assess the proposed sum(s) on the basis that the best reasonable outcome on each valuation point would fall in favour of the landlord.

Typically, in Example 1, a five per cent deferment rate would be adopted, but the proposed new lease value might be increased by ten per cent to £550,000, being within a reasonable margin of valuation tolerance.

Similarly, where there is a marriage value element, the existing lease value would represent a lower relativity. Having said that, where two experienced valuers in the same locality have common evidence available, their respective valuations to the new lease premium might be expected to be in line with one another.

Negotiations to reach settlement of the new lease premium do not (generally) start until after the counter-notice has been served.

Checklist for the landlord's valuer

This follows, generally, the checklist for the tenant's valuer, with these further considerations.

- The date by which the counter-notice is to be served.
- Do you have the details to make arrangements for access to inspect at the earliest opportunity?
- Aim to report in good time for service of the counter-notice, say at least two weeks prior; your report to include the premium for the new lease and proposed sum(s) for the counter-notice.

Intermediate landlords – intermediate leasehold interests (ILIs)

In some cases there will be an intermediate lease.

We now look at the statutory provisions with respect to intermediate leasehold interests. To highlight the requirements of the legislation, we use examples coupled with diagrammatic schedules in the examples for illustration.

First of all we look at the relevant paragraphs in Schedule 13.

Schedule 13, Part III

In accordance with Schedule 13, paragraph 1, an 'intermediate leasehold interest' means the interest of any person falling within section 40(4)(c), to the extent that it is an interest in the tenant's flat subsisting immediately before the grant of the new lease.

Amounts Payable to Owners of Intermediate Leasehold Interests

Amount payable to owner of intermediate interest (para. 6)

6. In connection with the grant of the new lease to the tenant there shall be payable by the tenant to the owner of any

intermediate leasehold interest an amount which is the aggregate of-
(a) the diminution in value of that interest as determined in accordance with paragraph 7; and
(b) any amount of compensation payable to him under paragraph 9.

Diminution in value of intermediate interest (para. 7)

7(1) The diminution in value of any intermediate leasehold interest is the difference between-
(a) the value of that interest prior to grant of the new lease; and
(b) the value of that interest once the new lease is granted.

(2) Each of those values shall be determined, as at the relevant date, in accordance with paragraph 8.

Value of intermediate interests (para. 8)

8 (1) Subject to sub-paragraph (2), paragraph 3(2) to (6) shall apply for determining the value of any intermediate leasehold interest for the purposes of any provision of this Schedule with such modifications as are appropriate to relate those provisions of paragraph 3 to a sale of the interest in question subject to the tenant's lease for the time being and to any leases intermediate between the interest in question and that lease.

(2) The value of an intermediate leasehold interest which is the interest of the tenant under a minor intermediate lease shall be calculated by applying the formula set out in sub-paragraph (6) instead of in accordance with sub-paragraph (1).

(3) "A minor intermediate lease" means a lease complying with the following requirements, namely-
(a) it must have an expectation of possession of not more than one month and
(b) the profit rent in respect of the lease must be not more than £5 per year.

(4) "Profit rent" means an amount equal to that of the rent payable under the lease on which the minor intermediate

lease is in immediate reversion, less that of the rent payable under the minor intermediate lease.

(5) Where the minor intermediate lease or that on which it is in immediate reversion comprises property other than the tenant's flat, then in sub-paragraph (4) the reference to the rent payable under it means so much of that rent as is apportioned to that flat.

(6) The formula is—

$$P = £\frac{R}{Y} - \frac{R}{Y(1+Y)^n}$$

where-

P = the price payable;

R = the profit rent;

Y = the yield (expressed as a decimal fraction) from 2.5 per cent. Consolidated Stock;

n = the period, expressed in years (taking any part of a year as a whole year), of the remainder of the term of the minor intermediate lease as at the relevant date.

(7) In calculating the yield from 2.5 per cent. Consolidated Stock, the price of that stock shall be taken to be the middle market price at the close of business on the last trading day in the week before the relevant date.

(8) For the purposes of this paragraph the expectation of possession carried by a lease is the expectation which it carries at the relevant date of possession after the tenant's lease, on the basis that—
  (a) (subject to sub-paragraph (9)) the tenant's lease terminates at the relevant date if its term date fell before then, or else it terminates on its term date; and
  (b) any other lease terminates on its term date.

(9) In a case where before the relevant date for the purposes of this Chapter the immediate landlord of the tenant had given notice to quit terminating the tenant's lease on a

Owners of intermediate interests entitled to part of marriage value (para. 10)

10(1) This paragraph applies in a case where–
    (a) the premium payable by the tenant in respect of the grant of the new lease includes an amount in respect of the landlord's share of the marriage value, and
    (b) there are any intermediate leasehold interests.

(2) The amount payable to the landlord in respect of his share of the marriage value shall be divided between the landlord and the owners of any such intermediate interests in proportion to the amounts by which the values of their respective interests in the flat will be diminished in consequence of the grant of the new lease.

(3) For the purposes of sub-paragraph (2)–
    (a) the amount by which the value of the landlord's interest in the flat will be so diminished is the diminution in value of that interest as determined for the purposes of paragraph 2(a); and
    (b) the amount by which the value of any intermediate leasehold interest will be so diminished is the diminution in value of that interest as determined for the purposes of paragraph 6(a).

(4) Where the owner of any intermediate leasehold interest is entitled in accordance with sub-paragraph (2) to any part of the amount payable to the landlord in respect of the landlord's share of the marriage value, the amount to which he is so entitled shall be payable to him by the landlord.

The Act is specific that in a leasehold reform computation, any leaseholder who has an interest that falls between the competent landlord and the qualifying tenant, is to be compensated for any loss that he suffers; even if the loss is nominal, say, £1 – reference thereto is required in the notice and must form part of the new lease premium; and also a share of marriage value, where applicable.

Intermediate leases are granted for two main areas, in effect: those that have been granted by landlords for the purposes of providing a legal vehicle for development (typically); and those that are primarily granted for management purposes (e.g. the modern tripartite arrangements).

The former are generally granted at a consideration in return of rights to develop a number of flats within a building, with varying types of ground rent provisions – which in some cases are onerous or have onerous reviews at a future date.

Those that are created for management purposes, which either provide a nominal profit rent or can be described as 'post boxes' – that is to say they are revenue neutral, with the aggregate of the existing lease rents being equal to the corresponding head lease rent to the landlord. There are cases where the tenants are the shareholders in the intermediate management company.

The area of valuation that has vexed practitioners in leasehold reform for some time is that whilst the new lease is at a peppercorn rent, the intermediate leaseholder is required to continue to pay his rent unabated. As a result, there is a net loss to the intermediate lease, and this affects its value.

These issues and various approaches to calculate the diminution in value of the intermediate interest in new lease claims were examined at length in *Nailrile*; and how this can affect a potential collective enfranchisement claim, including the purchase price payable under Schedule 6.

There is no short cut to the analysis of an ILI in any one particular claim; the principles of *Nailrile* need to be understood and the valuation approaches are best described in examples.

The valuer must bear it in mind that in assessing the diminution in value of an intermediate interest, the value of that interest once the new lease has been granted may be negative.

The interest to be valued

Whereas it is the intermediate leasehold interest in relation to the flat that is to be valued, it is to be valued as a component of a sale of the whole of that interest (*Nailrile*, paras. 31 and 32) (*Squarepoint*, para 19).

As with calculating the diminution in value of landlord's interest, two valuations of the interest are required: (1) prior to the new lease being granted; and (2) post the new lease being granted (para. 7, s. (1)(a) and (b) and (2)).

The diminution in value of the intermediate interest is the difference between the two.

In most cases, the value in the intermediate interest is based on the profit rent. Having said that, there are intermediate interests with significant reversionary interests; we consider leasehold reversionary interests later. Firstly, we shall examine those with either a nil or nominal reversionary interest; and where there is no other part of the interest which may be attributed value, such as the ability to collect a notional rent for a caretaker's flat through the service charge provisions.

Where the value in the intermediate lease is in the profit rent, the problem area hitherto has been the approach to valuing the ILI once the new lease has been granted, because of the loss of rent following the grant of the new lease. Generally, the valuation of the ILI prior to grant of the new lease is straightforward, as will be shown in the examples.

The valuer, in accordance with the principles in *Nailrile*, must establish the following:

- the profit rent of the intermediate lease before the new lease is granted, whether positive, negative or nil; and
- the profit rent of the intermediate lease after the new lease has been granted, similarly whether positive, negative or nil.

It follows in a new lease claim that there are five possibilities, which include the 'post box':

- the intermediate lease profit rent is positive both before and after;
- the intermediate lease profit rent is positive before and nil after;
- the intermediate lease profit rent is positive before and negative after;
- the intermediate lease profit rent is nil before and negative after (the post box being that where the intermediate lease is revenue neutral); and
- the intermediate lease profit rent is negative both before and after.

Flats: new lease claims: valuation issues

In *Nailrile* there was consensus amongst the valuers as to how to value the ILI before the new lease is granted, but not after. The tribunal addressed the latter issue; their decisions are as follows:

- where the profit rent of the intermediate lease is positive, the ILI is to be valued adopting either the capitalisation or total profit rent approaches (paras. 124, 140(a) and 229(m)); and
- where the profit rent of the intermediate lease is negative, the ILI is to be valued adopting the single rate approach (paras. 131, 140(b) and 229(o)).

These approaches are examined in detail later; we shall consider each of the possibilities by way of examples. For continuity, the following examples are based on a purpose built block of flats over basement, ground and first to fourth floors, as follows:

Basement – caretaker's flat, storerooms and ancillary space; and

Ground and First to Fourth floors – two flats per floor (all held on long leases).

The leases: the building is subject to an intermediate lease (head lease) for a term of 50 years unexpired at a current rent of £500 per annum with a fixed review to £1,000 per annum in 25 years; and the existing leases are for terms to the intermediate lease (less last three days), at varying ground rents with reviews coincidental with the intermediate lease rent reviews.

The valuer and solicitor are required to establish the lease structure including rent provisions. This is not necessarily a straightforward exercise, but with access to the Land Registry and provisions of section 41 (right of qualifying tenant to obtain information about superior interests, etc.), it is attainable. The office copy entries of the Land Registry will provide details of the landlord, any intermediate lease interest, and terms of respective leases. From the terms, the competent landlord and any intermediate interest can be ascertained. If not, the provisions of section 41 can be implemented.

Be aware in valuations with intermediate leases of the provisions of Schedule 11, paragraph 10 'deemed surrender and re-grant of leases of other landlords'.

Leasehold enfranchisement explained

Whereas the legislation allows for the new lease to be granted with different provisions and terms to the existing lease, albeit substantially in the same form, and is specific as to term and rent (sections 56 and 57); any intermediate lease is deemed to have been surrendered and re-granted on the same terms. Hence, the intermediate lease rent remains unabated post grant of the new lease, which in turn is subject to a peppercorn rent.

Set out below in diagrammatic form is the building, with the respective rent provisions.

Intermediate lease (head lease)

£500 p.a. rising to £1,000 p.a.

Fourth	**Flat 9** £150 p.a. rising to £300 p.a.	**Flat 10** £150 p.a. rising to £300 p.a.
Third	**Flat 7** £125 p.a. rising to £250 p.a.	**Flat 8** £125 p.a. rising to £250 p.a.
Second	**Flat 5** £100 p.a. rising to £200 p.a.	**Flat 6** £100 p a. rising to £200 p a.
First	**Flat 3** £75 p.a. rising to £150 p.a.	**Flat 4** £75 p.a. rising to £150 p.a.
Ground	**Flat 1** £50 p.a. rising to £100 p.a.	**Flat 2** £50 p.a. rising to £100 p.a.
Basement	Caretaker's flat, storerooms and ancillary space	

The total profit rent and capitalisation approaches

Where the intermediate lease profit rent is positive, either the total profit rent or capitalisation approaches apply. Each adopts dual rate tables as follows:

- the remunerative rate – to be assessed by the valuer from market evidence and/or opinion – but it is likely that the rate will be the same in both the before and after valuations; and
- the accumulative (asf) rate at 2.25 per cent (being the risk-free rate adopted in calculating the deferment rate in *Sportelli*, based on index linked gilts) for both the before and after valuations.

Valuers will be familiar with the basic principles of 'dual rate' tables:

1. the remunerative rate being the return (interest) on the investment (capital outlay); and

2. the accumulative (asf) rate being the sinking fund to replace the investment, bearing in mind it is a wasting asset.

The total profit rent approach (as the name suggests), is based on valuing the whole of the intermediate lease. Whereas the capitalisation approach is based on the requirement to value the ILI as a component part of the whole of the interest; this approach is shown in examples.

Turning to the situation where the intermediate lease profit rent is negative, the valuer is directed (by the Lands Tribunal), to adopt the single rate approach.

The single rate approach

Adopting the single rate approach, the rate of return depends on the circumstances, and as directed in *Nailrile*, is as follows:

- where the intermediate lease rent is either fixed or increases by fixed amounts, and is nominal throughout the term of the ILI, the rate is that of 2.5 per cent Consolidated Stock (Consols) rounded down; and
- where the intermediate lease rent is either currently a substantial amount, or is subject to review to a substantial unknown amount, based on either a capital or rental value of a notional leasehold or freehold interest, a lower rate is applied to reflect the increased risk – between the risk-free

Leasehold enfranchisement explained

rate of 2.25 per cent and that of 2.5 per cent Consolidated Stock (Consols).

At this juncture, it may be helpful to recap on all of the above and include those further points in a checklist.

Checklist

In addition to those points in the checklist on page 133, the valuer needs to consider the following, where there is an intermediate leaseholder to be compensated.

- The effect of an intermediate leaseholder's reversionary interest where it is substantial is discussed later.
- If there is an intermediate lease, is there more than one?
- How will you collate the information required to analyse the ILI including access to the Land Registry?
- The interest to be valued is the ILI, but as a component part of a sale of the whole of the intermediate lease (*Nailrile*, paras. 32 & 124).
- As with the diminution in value of landlord's interest, two valuations are required, 'before and after'.
- Before grant of the new lease, is the intermediate lease profit rent positive, nil or negative?
- After grant of the new lease, is the intermediate lease profit rent positive, nil or negative?
- Where either positive or nil, the total profit rent or capitalisation approaches apply.
- Where negative, the single rate approach applies; either the yield on 2.5 per cent Consolidated Stock or a yield between the risk-free rate of 2.25 per cent and the yield on 2.5 per cent Consolidated Stock (Consols), depending on the circumstances of the case and the rent provisions.

We now look at a series of examples with a view to considering the different situations the valuer may be confronted with.

Fundamentally, the principles follow those of calculating the diminution in value of the landlord's interest.

Flats: new lease claims: valuation issues

Example 9

The lessee at Flat 3 proposes submitting a claim for a new lease and you are asked to provide the valuation advice, which is to include the new lease premium and sum(s) to be proposed in the notice. Further to your inspection and enquiries, which include investigating the intermediate lease details, you value the new lease at £500,000 and the existing lease at £375,000.

Have it in mind that, whereas the new lease is at a peppercorn rent, the intermediate lease rent provisions remain unabated.

Analysis of the ILI

Flat No	Before Rent (£ p.a. prior to grant of the new lease)	After Rent (£ p.a. post grant of the new lease)	Review in 25 years
1	£50	£50	£100
2	£50	£50	£100
3	**£75**	**£0**	**£0**
4	£75	£75	£150
5	£100	£100	£200
6	£100	£100	£200
7	£125	£125	£250
8	£125	£125	£250
9	£150	£150	£300
10	£150	£150	£300
Totals	£1,000 p.a.	£925 p.a.	£1,850 p.a.
less Intermediate lease rent	£500 p.a.	£500 p.a.	£1,000 p.a.
Profit rent	£500 p.a.	£425 p.a.	£850 p.a.

In these circumstances, the intermediate lease profit rent is positive both prior to grant of the new lease and once the new lease has been granted.

Accordingly, the diminution in value of the intermediate interest is calculated either by the total profit rent or capitalisation approaches.

Having said that, to adopt the capitalisation approach, the intermediate lease rent needs to be 'apportioned' so that the diminution can be calculated. The reasons for this become apparent as and when further new leases have been granted.

145

Leasehold enfranchisement explained

It is unclear as to the method to apportion the intermediate lease rent in these circumstances; as there are ten flats in the building, the rent could be apportioned one tenth to each. Alternatively, the rent can be apportioned pro rata to the existing lease rent provisions.

Apportionment of the intermediate lease rent pro rata to the existing lease rent provisions.

Flat No	**Before** Rent (£ p.a. prior to grant of the new lease)	Proportion of aggregate of existing lease rents (£1,000 p.a.)	Corresponding proportion of intermediate lease rent (£500 p.a.)	**After** Rent (£ p.a. post grant of the new lease)	And review in 25 years
1	£50	5%	£25	£50	£100
2	£50	5%	£25	£50	£100
3	**£75**	**7.5%**	**£37.50**	**£0**	**£0**
4	£75	7.5%	£37.50	£75	£150
5	£100	10%	£50	£100	£200
6	£100	10%	£50	£100	£200
7	£125	12.5%	£67.50	£125	£250
8	£125	12.5%	£67.50	£125	£250
9	£150	15%	£75	£150	£300
10	£150	15%	£75	£150	£300
Totals	£1,000 p.a.	100%	£500 p.a.	£925 p.a.	£1,850 p.a.
less Intermediate lease rent	£500 p.a.			£500 p.a.	£1,000 p.a.
Profit rent	£500 p.a.			£425 p.a.	£850 p.a.

From the above, the intermediate lease profit rent is positive both before (£500 p.a.), and after (£425 p.a.), the new lease at Flat 3 has been granted.

In which case, either the total profit rent or capitalisation approaches apply.

We now consider the particular circumstances where the intermediate leasehold interest is a 'minor intermediate lease' (MILI), for which there is a formula to be applied.

A MILI is one that has a relatively nominal value. To avoid unnecessary costs being incurred in assessing its value, the statutory formula is applied to circumvent this.

A MILI is an interest which meets the following requirements:
- it must have an expectation of possession of not more than one month; and
- the intermediate lease profit rent must not be more than £5 per annum.

Flats: new lease claims: valuation issues

In addition to which, the profit rent requirement is to be met further to any rent review.

In *Nailrile* the MILI provisions were examined in detail, note the following:
- the interest to be valued can be a MILI in the 'before' valuation and not in the 'after' valuation;
- there must be an expectation of possession, but not for more than one month;
- the profit rent must be a positive sum; and
- does the MILI formula apply where there are rent reviews? This is unlikely to arise in practice other than exceptionally. The profit rent requirement is not satisfied where the post review profit rent attributable to the flat is or could be in excess of £5.

One can have a situation where the intermediate interest to be valued is a MILI in the before position, but it is not in the after.

In this example, the existing lease rent is £75 per annum, and the apportioned intermediate lease rent is £37.50 per annum – the intermediate lease profit rent equals £37.50 per annum, which in turn exceeds the £5 per annum limit – accordingly the MILI provisions do not apply.

In full, the computation is as follows

Date of valuation: 25 March 2010

Lease expiry date: 25 March 2060

<u>Diminution in value of landlord's interest</u>

Difference between the value before the grant of the new lease

<u>Term (1)</u>

Intermediate lease rent (from table)	£37.50 p.a.		
YP 25 years @ 8%		10.6748	£400

<u>Term (2)</u>

Intermediate lease rent (from table)	£75 p.a.		
YP 25 years @ 8%		10.6748	
Deferred 25 years @ 8%		0.1460	£117

<u>Reversion</u>

To 'share of freehold' with vacant possession value (new lease value – 99% FHVP)	£505,050			
Deferred 50 years @ 5%		0.0872	£44,040	£44,557

minus

Leasehold enfranchisement explained

and the value after the new lease is granted

Term (1)

Rent (from table)	£37.50 p.a.	
YP 25 years @ 8%	10.6748	£400

Term (2)

Rent (from table)	£75 p.a.	
YP 25 years @ 8%	10.6748	
Deferred 25 years @ 8%	0.1460	£117

Reversion

To 'share of freehold' with vacant possession value – as above	£505,050		
Deferred 139.99 years @ 5%	0.0011	£556	£1,073

Diminution in value of landlord's interest	£43,484

Diminution in value of intermediate interest (ILI)

Difference between the value before grant of the new lease

Term (1)

Existing lease rent	£75 p.a.

less

Proportion of intermediate lease rent (from table)	£37.50 p.a.	
Profit rent	£37.50 p.a.	
YP 25 years @ 9% and 2.25%	8.3170	£312

Term (2)

Existing lease rent	£150 p.a.

less

Proportion of intermediate lease rent (from table)	£75 p.a.		
Profit rent	£75 p.a.		
YP 24.99 years @ 9% and 2.25%	8.3159		
Deferred 25 years at 9%	0.1160	£72	£384

Flats: new lease claims: valuation issues

minus

and the value after the new lease is granted

<u>Term (1)</u>

New lease rent (at a peppercorn)	£0 p.a.	
less		
Proportion of intermediate lease rent	£37.50 p.a.	
Profit rent	−£37.50 p.a.	
YP 25 years @ 9% and 2.25%	8.3170	−£312

<u>Term (2)</u>

New lease rent (at a peppercorn)	£0 p.a.		
less			
Proportion of intermediate lease rent	£75 p.a.		
Profit rent	−£75 p.a.		
YP 24.99 years @ 9% and 2.25%	8.3159		
Deferred 25 years @ 9%	0.1160	−£72	−£384
Diminution in value of intermediate interest			£768

<u>Landlord's share of marriage value</u>

Difference between the aggregate of values of interests <u>post</u> grant of the new lease

Landlord's interest	£1,073	
Intermediate leaseholder's interest	−£384	
Tenant's proposed interest	£500,000	£500,689

less

Aggregate of values of interests <u>prior</u> to grant of the new lease

Landlord's interest	£44,557	
Intermediate leaseholder's interest	£384	
Tenant's existing interest	£375,000	£419,941

Leasehold enfranchisement explained

Marriage value			£80,748		
50% thereof			0.5	£40,374	
plus					
Diminution in value of landlord's interest				£43,484	
and					
Diminution in intermediate interest			£768		
New lease premium (excluding costs)				£84,626	
			Say	£84,600	

Apportioned as follows:

In accordance with Schedule 13, paragraph 10, marriage value is apportioned pro rata to the diminution in value of each interest

Landlord

$$£43,484 + \frac{(43,484)}{(43,484+768)} \times £40,374$$

$$£43,484 + £39,673 = £83,157$$

Say £83,150

Intermediate leaseholder

$$£768 + \frac{(768)}{(43,484+768)} \times £40,374$$

$$£768 + £701 = £1,469$$

Say £1,450

£84,600

The example is set out in full for illustrative purposes. The valuer may adopt either the total profit rent or the capitalisation approaches, but having said that, it is imperative to understand the provisions of Schedule 13, paragraphs 6, 7, 8 and 10.

Both approaches result in the same diminution in value of intermediate interest and correspondingly new lease premium.

Flats: new lease claims: valuation issues

The landlord's rent is apportioned pro rata to the aggregate of existing lease rents; a rate of return of eight per cent is applied to this. As the intermediate lease rent provisions remain unabated once the new lease is granted, the diminution in value of the landlord's interest is, in effect, the difference between the values of the before and after reversionary interests.

In calculating the diminution in value of the intermediate interest, a remunerative rate of nine per cent is adopted, being one per cent above the corresponding rate of return applied to calculating the diminution in value of the landlord's interest.

The accumulative rate of 2.25 per cent is taken from *Nailrile*, being the risk-free rate in *Sportelli*.

Now we consider the situation in our building five years later, where new leases have been granted at Flats 3, 6, 7 and 10.

Set out below, in diagrammatic form, is the building with the up to date rent provisions.

Intermediate lease (head lease)

£500 p.a. rising to £1,000 p.a.

Fourth	**Flat 9** £150 p.a. rising to £300 p.a.	**Flat 10** £0 p.a.
Third	**Flat 7** £0 p.a.	**Flat 8** £125 p.a. rising to £250 p.a.
Second	**Flat 5** £100 p.a. rising to £200 p.a.	**Flat 6** £0 p.a.
First	**Flat 3** £0 p.a.	**Flat 4** £75 p.a. rising to £150 p.a.
Ground	**Flat 1** £50 p.a. rising to £100 p.a.	**Flat 2** £50 p.a. rising to £100 p.a.
Basement	Caretaker's flat, storerooms and ancillary space	

Leasehold enfranchisement explained

Example 10

The lessee at Flat 9 proposes submitting a claim for a new lease and you are asked to provide the valuation advice, which is similar to that in Example 9. You value the new lease at £600,000 and the existing lease at £425,000.

Analysis of the ILI

Flat No	Before Rent (£ p.a. prior to grant of the new lease)	After Rent (£ p.a. post grant of the new lease)	Review in 20 years
1	£50	£50	£100
2	£50	£50	£100
3	£0	£0	£0
4	£75	£75	£150
5	£100	£100	£200
6	£0	£0	£0
7	£0	£0	£0
8	£125	£125	£250
9	**£150**	**£0**	**£0**
10	£0	£0	£0
Totals	£550 p.a.	£400 p.a.	£800 p.a.
less Intermediate lease rent	£500 p.a.	£500 p.a.	£1,000 p.a.
Profit rent	£50 p.a.	−£100 p.a.	−£200 p.a.

Now the intermediate lease profit rent is positive prior to grant of the new lease (£50 p.a.), but is negative (−£100 p.a.) once the new lease has been granted. Accordingly, the diminution in value of the intermediate interest is calculated adopting both the capitalisation and single rate approaches.

As previously, the intermediate interest is to be valued as a whole. The apportionment of the intermediate lease rent is as follows:

152

Flats: new lease claims: valuation issues

Flat No	Before Rent (£ p.a. prior to grant of the new lease)	Proportion of aggregate of existing lease rents (£550 p.a.)	Corresponding proportion of intermediate lease rent (£500 p.a.)	After Rent (£ p.a. post grant of the new lease)	And review in 20 years
1	£50	9.09%	£45.45	£50	£100
2	£50	9.09%	£45.45	£50	£100
3	£0	0%	£0	£0	£0
4	£75	13.64%	£68.20	£75	£150
5	£100	18.18%	£90.90	£100	£200
6	£0	0%	£0	£0	£0
7	£0	0%	£0	£0	£0
8	£125	22.73%	£113.65	£125	£250
9	£150	27.27%	£136.35	£0	£0
10	£0	0%	£0	£0	£0
Totals	£550 p.a.	100%	£500 p.a.	£400 p.a.	£800 p.a.
less Intermediate lease rent	£500 p.a.			£500 p.a.	£1,000 p.a.
Profit rent	£50 p.a.			−£100 p.a.	−£200 p.a.

As discussed, the intermediate lease profit rent is positive before the new lease is granted (£50 p.a.), but is negative once the new lease has been granted (− £100 p.a.).

The capitalisation and single rate approaches apply.

For the purposes of the single rate approach, as the ground rent provisions are not onerous for the duration of the term, and the review is at a finite date to a fixed sum, the rounded yield on 2.5 per cent Consolidated Stock (Consols) applies. At the time of publication, the yield is 4.6 per cent (or thereabouts).

In full, the computation is as follows

Date of valuation: 25 March 2015

Lease expiry date: 25 March 2060

<u>Diminution in value of landlord's interest</u>

Difference between the value before the grant of the new lease

<u>Term (1)</u>

Intermediate lease rent (from
  table above)   £136.35 p.a.
YP 20 years @ 8%   9.8181   £1,339

Leasehold enfranchisement explained

Term (2)

Intermediate lease rent (from table)	£272.70 p.a.		
YP 25 years @ 8%	10.6748		
Deferred 20 years @ 8%	0.2146	£625	

Reversion

To 'share of freehold' with vacant possession value	£606,061		
(new lease value – 99% FHVP)			
Deferred 45 years @ 5%	0.1113	£67,455	£69,419

minus

and the value after the new lease is granted

Term (1)

Rent (from table)	£136.35 p.a.		
YP 20 years @ 8%	9.8181	£1,339	

Term (2)

Rent (from table)	£272.70 p.a.		
YP 25 years @ 8%	10.6748		
Deferred 20 years @ 8%	0.2146	£625	

Reversion

To share of freehold with vacant possession value – as above	£606,061		
Deferred 134.99 years @ 5%	0.0014	£849	£2,813

Diminution in value of landlord's interest	£66,606

Diminution in value of intermediate interest (ILI)

Difference between the value before grant of the new lease

Term (1)

Existing lease rent	£150 p.a.

less

Proportion of intermediate lease rent (from table)	£136.35 p.a.

Flats: new lease claims: valuation issues

Profit rent	£13.65 p.a.		
YP 20 years @ 9% and 2.25%	7.6839	£105	

Term (2)

Existing lease rent	£300 p.a.		
less			
Proportion of intermediate lease rent (from table)	£272.70 p.a.		
Profit rent	£27.30 p.a.		
YP 24.99 years @ 9% and 2.25%	8.3159		
Deferred 20 years at 9%	0.1784	£41	£146

minus

and the value after the new lease is granted

Term (1)

New lease rent (at a peppercorn)	£0 p.a.		
less			
Proportion of intermediate lease rent	£136.35 p.a.		
Profit rent	−£136.35 p.a.		
YP 20 years @ 4.6%	12.8960	−£1,758	

Term (2)

New lease rent (at a peppercorn)	£0 p.a.		
less			
Proportion of intermediate lease rent	£272.70 p.a.		
Profit rent	−£272.70 p.a.		
YP 24.99 years @ 4.6%	14.6736		
Deferred 20 years @ 4.6%	0.4068	−£1,628	−£3,386
Diminution in value of intermediate interest			£3,532

Landlord's share of marriage value

Difference between the aggregate of values of interests <u>post</u> grant of the new lease

Landlord's interest	£2,813	
Intermediate leaseholder's interest	−£3,386	
Tenant's proposed interest	£600,000	£599,427

less

Aggregate of values of interests <u>prior</u> to grant of the new lease

Landlord's interest	£69,419	
Intermediate leaseholder's interest	£146	
Tenant's existing interest	£425,000	£494,565

Marriage value		£104,862
50% thereof	0.5	£52,431

plus

Diminution in value of landlord's interest £66,606

and

Diminution in value of intermediate interest £3,532

New lease premium (excluding costs) £122,569

Say £122,600

Apportioned as follows:

<u>Landlord</u>

£66,606 + (66,606) × £52,431
          ─────────────────────
             (66,606+3,532)

£66,606 + £49,791   = £116,397

                                  Say £116,400

<u>Intermediate leaseholder</u>

£3,532 + (3,532) × £52,431
         ──────────────────
            (66,606+3,532)

£3,532 + £2,640   = £6,172

                                  Say £6,200

                                       £122,600

Again the example is set out in full for illustrative purposes.

In the next example, we look at the valuation issues where the intermediate lease is negative after the new lease has been granted, and the rent is either currently substantial or will be subject to review to an unknown amount, based on either a capital or rental value of a notional leasehold or freehold interest. A lower rate of return is applied to reflect the increased risk, the rate to be between the risk-free rate of 2.25 per cent and that of 2.5 per cent. Consolidated Stock, at the time of publication, 4.6 per cent or thereabouts.

The rate adopted in *Nailrile (62 Cadogan Square, London SW1)* is 3.5 per cent; which is 0.75 per cent less than the yield on 2.5 Consols as at the date of valuation in *62 Cadogan Square, SW1*.

Example 11

The building is subject to an intermediate lease (head lease) for a term of 51 years unexpired, at a current rent of £500 per annum with reviews to one per cent of the aggregate of freehold vacant possession values in one year and 25 years thereafter.

The existing leases are for terms to the intermediate lease (less last three days), at ground rents to a fixed proportion of the intermediate lease rent, with coincidental reviews.

In the example, there is no further element to the intermediate lease to attribute value (i.e. the caretaker's flat).

Set out below, in diagrammatic form, is the building with the respective rent provisions.

Intermediate lease (head lease)

£500 p.a. with reviews

Fourth	**Flat 9** £50 p.a. with review to 10% of intermediate lease rent	**Flat 10** £50 p.a. with review to 10% of intermediate lease rent
Third	**Flat 7** £50 p.a. with review to 10% of intermediate lease rent	**Flat 8** £50 p.a. with review to 10% of intermediate lease rent
Second	**Flat 5** £50 p.a. with review to 10% of intermediate lease rent	**Flat 6** £50 p.a. with review to 10% of intermediate lease rent

Leasehold enfranchisement explained

First	**Flat 3** £50 p.a. with review to 10% of intermediate lease rent	**Flat 4** £50 p.a. with review to 10% of intermediate lease rent
Ground	**Flat 1** £50 p.a. with review to 10% of intermediate lease rent	**Flat 2** £50 p.a. with review to 10% of intermediate lease rent
Basement	Caretaker's flat, storerooms and ancillary space	

The lessee at Flat 9 proposes submitting a claim for a new lease and you are asked to provide the valuation advice.

Further to your inspection and enquiries, you value the new lease at £500,000, and the existing lease at £375,000 with nominal ground rent provisions.

From information provided, you ascertain the requirement to value each of the other flats on new leases to calculate the intermediate lease rent on review, and the subject flat's rent on review accordingly.

Fourth	**Flat 9** £500,000	**Flat 10** £500,000
Third	**Flat 7** £525,000	**Flat 8** £525,000
Second	**Flat 5** £550,000	**Flat 6** £550,000
First	**Flat 3** £575,000	**Flat 4** £575,000
Ground	**Flat 1** £550,000	**Flat 2** £550,000
Basement	Caretaker's flat, storerooms and ancillary space	

The existing lease rent provisions are coincidental with those of the intermediate lease rent. Flat 9 is apportioned ten per cent of the intermediate lease rent on review, which in turn is calculated as follows:

Aggregate of new lease values:

Flat 1	£550,000
Flat 2	£550,000
Flat 3	£575,000
Flat 4	£575,000
Flat 5	£550,000
Flat 6	£550,000
Flat 7	£525,000
Flat 8	£525,000

Flats: new lease claims: valuation issues

Flat 9	£500,000
Flat 10	£500,000
	£5,400,000 (representing, as previously, 99% of freehold vacant possession value)

Corresponding FHVP £5,454,545 with intermediate lease rent on review at 1% thereof = £54,545 p.a., say £54,500 p.a.

Flat 9 is apportioned 10% thereof – £5,450 p.a.

In these circumstances, the rent on review in one year of £5,450 per annum is assumed to be effective for the remainder of the term; having said that, have it in mind that there is a further review to an unknown sum which will be substantial.

Note the requirement to value all of the flats in the building, albeit that only one new lease claim is contemplated. This being a consequence of the requirements of Schedule 13.

Analysis of the ILI

Flat No	Before Rent (£ p.a. prior to grant of the new lease)	After Rent (£ p.a. post grant of the new lease)	Review in 1 year	Review in 26 years (say)
1	£50	£50	£5,450	£5,450
2	£50	£50	£5,450	£5,450
3	£50	£50	£5,450	£5,450
4	£50	£50	£5,450	£5,450
5	£50	£50	£5,450	£5,450
6	£50	£50	£5,450	£5,450
7	£50	£50	£5,450	£5,450
8	£50	£50	£5,450	£5,450
9	£50	£0	£0	£0
10	£50	£50	£5,450	£5,450
Totals less Intermediate lease rent	£500 p.a. £500 p.a.	£450 p.a. £500 p.a.	£49,050 p.a. £54,500 p.a.	£49,050 p.a. £54,500 p.a.
Profit rent	£0 p.a.	–£50 p.a.	–£5,450 p.a.	–£5,450 p.a.

Leasehold enfranchisement explained

The intermediate lease profit rent is 'nil' prior to grant of the new lease (£0 p.a.), but is negative once the new lease has been granted (−£50 p.a. rising to −£5,450 p.a.), and to a substantial sum.

At the outset, the intermediate lease was a post box, that is to say the aggregate of the existing lease rents equals the intermediate lease rent payable to the landlord.

In these circumstances, the diminution in value of the intermediate leasehold interest is calculated adopting the single rate approach, with the rate of return being between the risk-free rate in *Sportelli* (2.25 per cent) and the yield on 2.5 per cent Consols (at the time of publication 4.6 per cent or thereabouts).

The intermediate lease rent is apportioned pro rata to the existing lease rent provisions, as previously.

Flat No	Before Rent (£ p.a. prior to grant of the new lease)	Proportion of aggregate of existing lease rents (£500 p.a.)	Corresponding proportion of lease rent (£500 p.a.)	After Rent (£ p.a. post grant of new lease)	And reviews in 1 and 26 years
1	£50	10%	£50	£50	£5,450
2	£50	10%	£50	£50	£5,450
3	£50	10%	£50	£50	£5,450
4	£50	10%	£50	£50	£5,450
5	£50	10%	£50	£50	£5,450
6	£50	10%	£50	£50	£5,450
7	£50	10%	£50	£50	£5,450
8	£50	10%	£50	£50	£5,450
9	£50	10%	£50	£0	£0
10	£50	10%	£0	£50	£5,450
Totals	£500 p.a.	100%	£500 p.a.	£450 p.a.	£49,050 p.a.
less Intermediate lease rent	£500 p.a.			£500 p.a.	£54,500 p.a.
Profit rent	£0 p.a.			−£50 p.a.	−£5,450 p.a.

In full, the computation is as follows:

Date of valuation: 25 March 2010

Lease expiry date: 25 March 2061

<u>Diminution in value of landlord's interest</u>

Difference between the value before the grant of the new lease

Term (1)

Intermediate lease rent (from table)	£50 p.a.	
YP 1 year @ 4%	0.9615	£48

Term (2)

Intermediate lease rent (from table)	£5,450 p.a.	
YP 50 years @ 5%	18.2559	
Deferred 1 year @ 5%	0.9524	£94,759

Reversion

To 'share of freehold' with vacant possession value (new lease value – 99% FHVP)	£505,050		
Deferred 51 years @ 5%	0.0831	£41,970	£136,777

minus

and the value after the new lease is granted

Term (1)

Rent (from table)	£50 p.a.	
YP 1 year @ 4%	0.9615	£48

Term (2)

Rent (from table)	£5,450 p.a.	
YP 50 years @ 5%	18.2559	
Deferred 1 year @ 5%	0.9524	£94,759

Reversion

To share of freehold with vacant possession value – as above	£505,050		
Deferred 140.99 years @ 5%	0.0010	£505	£95,312

Diminution in value of landlord's interest	£41,465

Diminution in value of intermediate interest (ILI)

Difference between the value before grant of the new lease

Term (1)

Existing lease rent	£50 p.a.

less

Proportion of intermediate lease rent (from table)	£50 p.a.			
Profit rent	£0 p.a.			
YP n/a	n/a	£0		

Term (2)

Existing lease rent	£5,450 p.a.			
less				
Proportion of intermediate lease rent (from table)	£5,450 p.a.			
Profit rent	£0 p.a.			
YP n/a	n/a			
Deferred n/a	n/a	£0	£0	

minus

and the value after the new lease is granted

Term (1)

New lease rent (at a peppercorn)	£0 p.a.			
less				
Proportion of intermediate lease rent	£50 p.a.			
Profit rent	−£50 p.a.			
YP 1 year @ 3.5%	0.9662	−£48		

Term (2)

New lease rent (at a peppercorn)	£0 p.a.			
less				
Proportion of intermediate lease rent	£5,450 p.a.			
Profit rent	−£5,450 p.a.			
YP 49.99 years @ 3.5%	23.4539			
Deferred 1 year @ 3.5%	0.9662	−£123,503	−£123,551	
Diminution in value of intermediate interest			£123,551	

Flats: new lease claims: valuation issues

Landlord's share of marriage value

Difference between the aggregate of values of interests <u>post</u> grant of the new lease

Landlord's interest	£95,312	
Intermediate leaseholder's interest	−£123,551	
Tenant's proposed interest	£500,000	£471,761

less

Aggregate of values of interests <u>prior</u> to grant of the new lease

Landlord's interest	£136,777	
Intermediate leaseholder's interest	£0	
Tenant's existing interest (see below)	£328,000	£464,777

Marriage value		£6,984
50% thereof	0.5	£3,492

plus

Diminution in value of landlord's interest   £41,465

and

Diminution in value of intermediate interest   £123,551

New lease premium (excluding costs)   £168,508

                                            Say   £168,500

Apportioned as follows:

Landlord

£41,465   +   (41,465)   ×   £3,492
              ──────────
              (41,465+123,551)

£41,465   +   £878   =   £42,343
                                      Say £42,350

Intermediate leaseholder

£123,551 +   (123,551) ×   £3,492
              ──────────
              (41,465+123,551)

£123,551 +   £2,615   =   £126,166
                                      Say £126,150

                                          £168,500

> Analysis of the onerous ground rent provisions to establish the existing lease value:
>
> | | | |
> |---|---|---|
> | Share of freehold value (from above) | £505,050 | |
> | Palatable ground rent equates to, say, 0.1% of share of freehold value | | £505 p.a. |
> | Onerous ground rent on review | £5,450 p.a. | |
> | less palatable ground rent | £505 p.a. | |
> | Onerous (unpalatable) rent | £4,945 p.a. | |
> | Ten times thereof | 10 | |
> | Deferred 1 year at 5% | 0.9524 | |
> | | £47,096 | |
> | Adjustment for onerous ground rent, say | | £47,000 |
> | Existing lease value with nominal ground rent provisions (from above) | | £375,000 |
> | less onerous ground rent adjustment | | £47,000 |
> | | | £328,000 |
>
> Equating to (£328,000 ÷ £505,050) 64.94% of share of freehold value.
>
> In this example, as the adjustment for the onerous ground rent is calculated by applying a multiplier of ten as opposed to capitalising the sum over the term, it is deferred for one year to the review date.

Intermediate lease reversion

Where the intermediate lease has a reversion for a number of years, it is likely that not only will the value of the intermediate lease be positive before the new lease is granted, but also similarly positive once the new lease has completed; this being due to the value of the reversionary interest. In which case, dual rate tables would be applicable throughout. Having said that, there are valuers who will say that as the intermediate lease has a reversion of substantial value, single rate tables should apply.

We now look at an example where the intermediate lease has a reversion of 25 years.

Flats: new lease claims: valuation issues

Example 12

In this example, we review Example 9, but now the intermediate lease has a reversion of 25 years. The existing lease also has a term of 25 years, the valuation is as follows:

The lessee at Flat 4 proposes submitting a claim for a new lease and you are asked to provide the valuation advice. Further to your inspection and enquiries, you value the new lease at £500,000 and the existing lease at £252,525.

Analysis of the ILI

Flat No	Before Rent (£ p.a. prior to grant of new lease)	After Rent (£ p.a. post grant of new lease)	Review in 25 years
1	£50	£50	£100
2	£50	£50	£100
3	£0	£0	£0
4	**£75**	**£0**	n/a
5	£100	£100	£200
6	£100	£100	£200
7	£125	£125	£250
8	£125	£125	£250
9	£150	£150	£300
10	£150	£150	£300
Totals less Intermediate lease rent	£925 p.a. £500 p.a.	£850 p.a. £500 p.a.	£1,700 p.a. £1,000 p.a.
Profit rent	£425 p.a.	£350 p.a.	£700 p.a.

We know from Example 9 that the intermediate lease profit rent is positive both prior to and after grant of the new lease. In this example, the intermediate lease has a 25 years' reversion, which is of substantial value. It is unlikely, where the ground rent provisions are nominal, that the intermediate lease will be negative after grant of the new lease. Accordingly, in valuing the diminution of the intermediate interest, dual rate tables are applied to the profit rent element.

As previously, apportionment of the intermediate lease rent is pro rata to the existing lease rent provisions.

Leasehold enfranchisement explained

Flat No	Before Rent (£ p.a. prior to grant of the new lease)	Proportion of aggregate of existing lease rents (£925 p.a.)	Corresponding proportion of intermediate lease rent (£500 p.a.)	After Rent (£ p.a. post grant of the new lease)	And review in 25 years
1	£50	5.4%	£27	£50	£100
2	£50	5.4%	£27	£50	£100
3	£0	–	–	£0	£0
4	£75	8.2%	£41	£0	n/a
5	£100	10.8%	£54	£100	£200
6	£100	10.8%	£54	£100	£200
7	£125	13.5%	£67.50	£125	£250
8	£125	13.5%	£67.50	£125	£250
9	£150	16.2%	£81	£150	£300
10	£150	16.2%	£81	£150	£300
Totals	£925 p.a.	100%	£500 p.a.	£850 p.a.	£1,700 p.a.
less Intermediate lease rent	£500 p.a.			£500 p.a.	£1000 p.a.
Profit rent	£425 p.a.			£350 p.a.	£700 p.a.

The intermediate lease deferment rate

Whereas in Example 9 the landlord's deferment rate is five per cent (following the *Sportelli* rate), to a reversion of the share of freehold interest; the intermediate lease is to a reversion of a 25 years lease. The question is as to the appropriate deferment rate to be applied to the 25 years lease?

In *Nailrile*, paragraph 87, the tribunal determined a deferment rate of 5.5 per cent for a reversion to a 54 years lease. The increase of 0.5 per cent being an addition to the 4.5 per cent risk premium in the *Sportelli* generic deferment rate to reflect the fact that as the lease is a declining asset, there is a greater risk of receiving the reversion at a downturn in the market.

A deferment rate of 5.75 per cent is adopted here (reflecting an increase of 0.75 per cent to the *Sportelli* generic deferment rate risk premium) for the 25 years lease.

In full, the computation is as follows:

Date of valuation: 25 March 2010

Intermediate lease expiry date: 25 March 2060

Existing lease expiry date: 25 March 2035

Diminution in value of landlord's interest

Difference between the value before the grant of the new lease.

Flats: new lease claims: valuation issues

Term (1)
Intermediate lease rent (from table)	£41 p.a.		
YP 25 years @ 8%	10.6748	£438	

Term (2)
Intermediate lease rent (from table)	£82 p.a.		
YP 25 years @ 8%	10.6748		
Deferred 25 years @ 8%	0.1460	£128	

Reversion

To 'share of freehold' with vacant possession value (new lease value – 99% FHVP)	£505,050			
Deferred 50 years @ 5%	0.0872	£44,040	£44,606

minus

and the value after the new lease is granted

Term (1)
Rent (from table)	£41.p.a.		
YP 25 years @ 8%	10.6748	£438	

Term (2)
Rent (from table)	£82 p.a.		
YP 25 years @ 8%	10.6748		
Deferred 25 years @ 8%	0.1460	£128	

Reversion

To share of freehold with vacant possession value – as above	£505,050			
Deferred 115 years @ 5%	0.0037	£1,869	£2,435

Diminution in value of landlord's interest	£42,171

Diminution in value of intermediate interest (ILI)

Difference between the value before grant of the new lease

Term (1)
Existing lease rent	£75 p.a.

less

167

Leasehold enfranchisement explained

Proportion of intermediate lease rent (from table)	£41 p.a.		
Profit rent	£34 p.a.		
YP 25 years @ 9% and 2.25%	8.3170	£283	

Term (2)

Existing lease rent	£0 p.a.		
less			
Proportion of intermediate lease rent (from table)	£82 p.a.		
Profit rent	–£82 p.a.		
YP 25 years @ 9% and 2.25%	8.3170		
Deferred 25 years at 9%	0.1160	–£79	

Reversion

To 25 years lease with vacant possession value – at 50% of corresponding freehold with vacant possession value (£505,050)	£252,525		
Deferred 25 years @ 5.75%	0.2472	£62,424	£62,628

minus

and the value after the new lease is granted

Term (1)

New lease rent (at a peppercorn)	£0 p.a.		
less			
Proportion of intermediate lease rent	£41 p.a.		
Profit rent	–£41 p.a.		
YP 25 years @ 9% and 2.25%	8.3170	–£341	

Term (2)

New lease rent (at a peppercorn)	£0 p.a.
less	
Proportion of intermediate lease rent	£82 p.a.

Flats: new lease claims: valuation issues

Profit rent	−£82 p.a.		
YP 25 years @ 9% and 2.25%	8.3170		
Deferred 25 years @ 9%	0.1160	−£79	

Reversion

As the new lease is for a term beyond that of the intermediate lease, the reversionary interest is now 'nil'   £0   £0   −£420

Diminution in value of intermediate interest   £63,048

Landlord's share of marriage value

Difference between the aggregate of values of interests <u>post</u> grant of the new lease

Landlord's interest	£2,435	
Intermediate leaseholder's interest	−£420	
Tenant's proposed interest	£500,000	£502,015

less

Aggregate of values of interests <u>prior</u> to grant of the new lease

Landlord's interest	£44,606	
Intermediate leaseholder's interest	£63,048	
Tenant's existing interest (25 years)	£252,525	£360,179

Marriage value		£141,836	
50% thereof		0.5	£70,918

plus

Diminution in value of landlord's interest   £42,171

and

Diminution in value of intermediate interest   £63,048

New lease premium (excluding costs)   £176,137

Say   £176,150

Apportioned as follows:

Leasehold enfranchisement explained

```
Landlord
£42,171   +   (42,171)      ×   £70,918
              ─────────
              (42,171+63,048)
£42,171   +   £28,423                          =    £70,594
                                               Say  £70,600

Intermediate leaseholder
£63,048   +   (63,048)       ×   £70,918
              ─────────
              (42,171+63,048)
£63,048   +   £42,495                          =    £105,543
                                               Say  £105,550
                                                    ────────
                                                    £176,150
```

Checklist

In addition to those points listed above, where the intermediate lease has a reversion, the valuer needs to consider the following.

- The deferment rate to be applied, which following *Nailrile* will be based on an increase in the risk premium in *Sportelli*, because as the interest is a declining asset, there is a greater risk the reversion will be received at a downturn in the market. Following that reasoning, there is an argument that the adjustment to the risk premium will vary with the length of the reversion.
- As the intermediate lease is unlikely to become negative, dual rate tables would apply; but there are those that say single rate tables might be appropriate as there is a reversionary interest of substantial value.

Further valuation examples

Moving on from the above, there are two further areas where new lease claims can be made, and for which specific valuation issues arise.

Prior to *Howard de Walden Estates Ltd v Aggio* [2009] 1 AC 39, it was believed that a head lessee (intermediate leaseholder) was not a qualifying tenant within the meaning of the Act (see chapter 1, 'The qualifying tenant'). Post *Aggio*, where an intermediate leaseholder retains a flat within the interest, a notice for a new lease can be submitted. Typically, this might be applicable to a caretaker's flat (accommodation), flats occupied by statutory tenants (*Rent Act* 1977) or assured tenancies.

We now look at examples where the specific valuation issues arise for each.

Example 13

The caretaker's flat

In our building, the caretaker's flat is in the basement; new leases have been granted at Flats 3 and 4. To recap, the outline details are as follows.

Intermediate lease (head lease)

£500 p.a. rising to £1,000 p.a.

Fourth	**Flat 9** £150 p.a. rising to £300 p.a.	**Flat 10** £150 p.a. rising to £300 p.a.
Third	**Flat 7** £125 p.a. rising to £250 p.a.	**Flat 8** £125 p.a. rising to £250 p.a.
Second	**Flat 5** £100 p.a. rising to £200 p.a.	**Flat 6** £100 p.a. rising to £200 p.a.
First	**Flat 3** £0 p.a. rising to £0 p.a.	**Flat 4** £0 p.a. rising to £0 p.a.
Ground	**Flat 1** £50 p.a. rising to £100 p.a.	**Flat 2** £50 p.a. rising to £100 p.a.
Basement	Caretaker's flat, storerooms and ancillary space	

You are now approached by the intermediate leaseholder (head lessee) and asked to provide valuation advice on a potential claim for a new lease at the caretaker's flat.

Further to your inspection, you value the caretaker's flat 'share of freehold' with vacant possession at £400,000.

The caretaker's flat is included within the demise of the head lease; the head lease covenants include: only to use the flat as a basement caretaker's flat; to provide a full time caretaker; such caretaker to reside rent free on a service basis.

The existing leases (underleases) allow for the provision of the caretaker's flat at a market rent, the rent to be recovered from the underlessees within their respective service charge provisions. You value the flat at £250 per week (£13,000 p.a.).

Leasehold enfranchisement explained

As the existing leases include the provision for a caretaker, the new lease will reflect this also. Similarly, the intermediate lease and the new lease of the caretaker's flat are only to be assigned as one lot, so the provision of the caretaker under the new lease and the provisions under the existing underleases remain unaltered.

Analysis of the ILI

Flat No	Before Rent (£ p.a. prior to grant of the new lease)	After Rent (£ p.a. post grant of the new lease)	Review in 25 years
Caretaker's Flat	£13,000	£13,000	£13,000
1	£50	£50	£100
2	£50	£50	£100
3	£0	£0	£0
4	£0	£0	£0
5	£100	£100	£200
6	£100	£100	£200
7	£125	£125	£250
8	£125	£125	£250
9	£150	£150	£300
10	£150	£150	£300
Totals less	£13,850 p.a.	£13,850 p.a.	£14,700 p.a.
Intermediate lease rent	£500 p.a.	£500 p.a.	£1,000 p.a.
Profit rent	£13,350 p.a.	£13,350 p.a.	£13,700 p.a.

Following *Nailrile*, the intermediate lease is to be valued as a whole, with the caretaker's flat as a component part. The valuation is as follows.

Date of valuation: 25 March 2010

Intermediate lease expiry date: 25 March 2060

<u>Diminution in value of landlord's interest</u>

Difference between the value before the grant of the new lease

Term (1)

Intermediate lease rent	£500 p.a.	
YP 25 years @ 8%	10.6748	£5,337

Flats: new lease claims: valuation issues

Term (2)

Intermediate lease rent	£1,000 p.a.		
YP 25 years @ 8%	10.6748		
Deferred 25 years @ 8%	0.1460	£1,559	

Reversion

To 'share of freehold' with vacant possession value	£400,000		
Deferred 50 years @ 5%	0.0872	£34,880	£41,776

minus

and the value after the new lease is granted

Term (1)

Intermediate lease rent	£500 p.a.	
YP 25 years @ 8%	10.6748	£5,337

Term (2)

Intermediate lease rent	£1,000 p.a.		
YP 25 years @ 8%	10.6748		
Deferred 25 years @ 8%	0.1460	£1,559	

Reversion

To share of freehold with vacant possession value – as above	£400,000		
Deferred 140 years @ 5%	0.0011	£440	£7,336

Diminution in value of landlord's interest			£34,440

Landlord's share of marriage value

Value of new lease

Term (1)

Existing lease rent	£13,850 p.a.	
less		
Intermediate lease rent (from table)	£500 p.a.	
Profit rent	£13,350 p.a.	
YP 25 years @ 9%	9.8226	£131,132

Leasehold enfranchisement explained

Term (2)

Existing lease rent	£14,700 p.a.			
less				
Intermediate lease rent (from table)	£1,000 p.a.			
Profit rent	£13,700 p.a.			
YP 25 years @ 9%	9.8226			
Deferred 25 years at 9%	0.1160	£15,610		

Reversion

To value of 90 years lease – @ 97.5% of freehold vacant possession value - £390,000	£390,000			
Deferred 50 years @ 5.25%	0.0774	£30,186	£176,928	

Value of existing lease

Term (1)

Existing lease rent	£13,850 p.a.		
less			
Intermediate lease rent (from table)	£500 p.a.		
Profit rent	£13,350 p.a.		
YP 25 years @ 9% and 2.25%	8.3170	£111,032	

Term (2)

Existing lease rent	£14,700 p.a.		
less			
Intermediate lease rent (from table)	£1,000 p.a.		
Profit rent	£13,700 p.a.		
YP 25 years @ 9% and 2.25%	8.3170		
Deferred 25 years at 9%	0.1160	£13,217	£124,249

Thus marriage value:

Flats: new lease claims: valuation issues

Difference between the aggregate of values of interests <u>post</u> grant of the new lease			
Landlord's interest	£7,336		
Intermediate leaseholder's interest	£176,928	£184,264	
less			
Aggregate of values of interests <u>prior</u> to grant of the new lease			
Landlord's interest	£41,776		
Intermediate leaseholder's interest	£124,249	£166,025	
Marriage value		£18,239	
50% thereof		0.5	£9,120
plus			
Diminution in landlord's interest			£34,440
New lease premium (excluding costs)			£43,560
		Say	£43,550

Whereas dual rate tables are adopted to capitalise the profit rent to the existing lease, single rate tables are applied to value the new lease as the interest now includes a substantial reversion (90 years), albeit deferred 50 years.

A deferment rate of 5.25 per cent is applied to the 90 years leasehold reversion, as compared with the five per cent incorporated in the landlord's interest where the reversion is to share of freehold. This follows the principles in *Nailrile* post *Sportelli*, where an increase to the risk premium is made; as the leasehold is a declining asset, the risk of receiving the reversion at a downturn in the market is greater.

Lease terms: a typical term of a head lease would covenant against part assignment (alienation) of the interest; in which case, post *Aggio*, the question arises as to whether the terms of the new lease (in the example above, the caretaker's flat), allow for independent assignment from the head lease.

In *Cadogan v 26 Cadogan Square Limited* (unreported, 2009, LVT), the tribunal held that Cadogan's proposed restriction on assignment would have been fundamentally inconsistent with the separation of the flat from the rump of the head lease. The flat in this case was let on an AST at the date of valuation.

Conversely in *Cadogan Holdings Limited v Charles Carey-Morgan and Jonathan Money* (unreported, 2009, LVT), the tribunal did impose a covenant restricting independent assignment of the *Aggio* lease. This case concerns a basement caretaker's flat at 15 Tite Street, London SW3; and the decision reflected the head lease and underlease caretaking provisions. An appeal has been submitted by the claimants.

A flat occupied by a statutory tenant (Rent Act 1977)

We now consider the valuation issues where one of the flats in our building is occupied by a statutory tenant; Flat 2. All ten of the flats were originally subject to existing leases to the term of the intermediate lease less last three days.

Flats 3 and 4 are now subject to new leases.

The lessee of Flat 2 seeks your advice on a potential new lease, and explains that the flat is occupied by a statutory tenant. Further to your inspection, you value the new lease (in repair) of Flat 2 at £550,000 (as previously); similarly, the existing lease at £412,500. In addition to which, the statutory tenant is approximately 70 years old. From your local knowledge, you know that statutory tenanted properties with tenants of this age, and where the fair rent has been registered, achieve a corresponding 70 per cent of long leasehold/share of freehold with vacant possession value, equating to a 30 per cent discount.

Generally, statutory tenanted property is unmodernised and does not meet the minimum level of condition 'in repair' to be assumed in the statutory valuation.

Notwithstanding the condition of the flat, it is to be assumed to be in repair for the purposes of the new lease price computation, as the sale of the interest is subject to the relevant lease, which in turn has a covenant to repair (para 3, s. (2) (a)).

The valuation is as follows:

Flats: new lease claims: valuation issues

Example 14

Analysis of the ILI

Flat No	Before Rent (£ p.a. prior to grant of the new lease)	After Rent (£ p.a. post grant of the new lease)	Review in 25 years
1	£50	£50	£100
2	£50	£0	£0
3	£0	£0	£0
4	£0	£0	£0
5	£100	£100	£200
6	£100	£100	£200
7	£125	£125	£250
8	£125	£125	£250
9	£150	£150	£300
10	£150	£150	£300
Totals	£850 p.a.	£800 p.a.	£1,600 p.a.
less Intermediate lease rent	£500 p.a.	£500 p.a.	£1,000 p.a.
Profit rent	£350 p.a.	£300 p.a.	£600 p.a.

Apportionment of the intermediate lease rent pro rata to the existing lease rent provisions.

Flat No	Before Rent (£ p.a. prior to grant of the new lease)	Proportion of aggregate of existing lease rents (£850 p.a.)	Corresponding proportion of intermediate lease rent (£500 p.a.)	After Rent (£ p.a. post grant of the new lease)	And review in 25 years
1	£50	5.9%	£29.50	£50	£100
2	£50	5.9%	£29.50	£0	£0
3	£0	0%	£0	£0	£0
4	£0	0%	£0	£0	£0
5	£100	11.8%	£59	£100	£200
6	£100	11.8%	£59	£100	£200
7	£125	14.7%	£73.50	£125	£250
8	£125	14.7%	£73.50	£125	£250

Leasehold enfranchisement explained

9	£150	17.6%	£88	£150		£300
10	£150	17.6%	£88	£150		£300
Totals less	£850 p.a.	100%	£500 p.a.	£800 p.a.		£1,600 p.a.
Intermediate lease rent	£500 p.a.			£500 p.a.		£1,000 p.a.
Profit rent	£350 p.a.			£300 p.a.		£600 p.a.

Date of valuation: 25 March 2010

Existing lease expiry date: 22 March 2060

Diminution in value of landlord's interest

Difference between the value before the grant of the new lease

Term (1)

Intermediate lease rent (from table)	£29.50 p.a.	
YP 25 years @ 8%	10.6748	£315

Term (2)

Intermediate lease rent (from table)	£59 p.a.	
YP 25 years @ 8%	10.6748	
Deferred 25 years @ 8%	0.1460	£92

Reversion

To 'share of freehold' with vacant possession value (new lease value – 99% FHVP)	£555,555		
Deferred 50 years @ 5%	0.0872	£48,444	£48,851

minus

and the value after the new lease is granted

Term (1)

Rent (from table above)	£29.50 p.a.	
YP 25 years @ 8%	10.6748	£315

178

Flats: new lease claims: valuation issues

<u>Term (2)</u>

Rent (from table above)	£59 p.a.		
YP 25 years @ 8%	10.6748		
Deferred 25 years @ 8%	0.1460	£92	

Reversion

To share of freehold with vacant possession value – as above	£555,555		
Deferred 139.99 years @ 5%	0.0011	£611	£1,018

Diminution in value of landlord's interest		£47,833

<u>Diminution in value of intermediate interest (ILI)</u>

Difference between the value before grant of the new lease

<u>Term (1)</u>

Existing lease rent	£50 p.a.		
less			
Proportion of intermediate lease rent (from table)	£29.50 p.a.		
Profit rent	£20.50 p.a.		
YP 25 years @ 9% and 2.25%	8.3170	£171	

<u>Term (2)</u>

Existing lease rent	£100 p.a.		
less			
Proportion of intermediate lease rent (from table)	£59 p.a.		
Profit rent	£41 p.a.		
YP 24.99 years @ 9% and 2.25%	8.3159		
Deferred 25 years at 9%	0.1160	£40	£211

minus

and the value after the new lease is granted

<u>Term (1)</u>

New lease rent (at a peppercorn)	£0 p.a.	
less		

Leasehold enfranchisement explained

Proportion of intermediate lease rent	£29.50 p.a.			
Profit rent	−£29.50 p.a.			
YP 25 years @ 9% and 2.25%	8.3170	−£245		

Term (2)

New lease rent (at a peppercorn) £0 p.a.

less

Proportion of intermediate lease rent	£59 p.a.			
Profit rent	−£59 p.a.			
YP 24.99 years @ 9% and 2.25%	8.3159			
Deferred 25 years @ 9%	0.1160	−£57	−£302	
Diminution in value of intermediate interest				£513

Landlord's share of marriage value

Difference between the aggregate of values of interests <u>post</u> grant of the new lease

Landlord's interest		£1,018		
Intermediate leaseholder's interest		−£302		
Tenant's proposed interest	£550,000			
less 30% to reflect statutory tenant	£165,000	£385,000	£385,716	

less

Aggregate of values of interests <u>prior</u> to grant of the new lease

Landlord's interest		£48,851		
Intermediate leaseholder's interest		£211		
Tenant's existing interest	£412,500			
less 30% to reflect statutory tenant	£123,750	£288,750	£337,812	
Marriage value			£47,904	
50% thereof			0.5	£23,952

plus		
Diminution in value of landlord's interest		£47,833
Diminution in value of intermediate interest		£513
New lease premium (excluding costs)		£72,298
	Say	£72,300

Apportioned as follows:

<u>Landlord</u>

£47,833 + (47,833) × £23,952
⎯⎯⎯⎯⎯⎯⎯⎯⎯⎯
(47,833 + 513)

£47,833 + £23,698 = £71,531

Say £71,500

<u>Intermediate leaseholder</u>

£513 + (513) × £23,952
⎯⎯⎯⎯⎯⎯⎯⎯⎯⎯
(47,833 + 513)

£512 + £254 = £767

Say £800

£72,300

A flat occupied by an assured tenant (Housing Act 1988)

The valuation principles follow those of Example 14, save that the corresponding deductions for the tenant's right to remain in occupation would be lesser sums (say ten to 15 per cent, depending on market evidence). This is because whereas a statutory tenant has the same right to remain in occupation, his 'fair rent' within the meaning of the *Rent Act* 1977 is a market rent adjusted for 'scarcity', which typically in PCL might be a deduction of 20 per cent from the market rental value.

One of the statutory assumptions for fair rent under the 1977 Act is that, in effect, there are a similar number of properties to let as there are tenants seeking to rent. As demand generally exceeds supply, an adjustment is made to reflect scarcity.

On the other hand, there is no such assumption for rental value under an assured tenancy; this is reflected in the lesser adjustment downwards, from market evidence, as the landlord will be in receipt of a market rent unadjusted for scarcity, albeit the tenant has the right to remain in occupation.

Ultimately, if a lessee is a 'qualifying tenant' where the subject lease is subject to either a statutory or an assured tenant, the disadvantage of being unable to gain vacant possession may provide the opportunity to acquire a new lease, which in turn would be subject to the occupying tenant, at a more favourable, i.e. lower, premium.

Compensation

Compensation for loss arising out of grant of new lease

Schedule 13, paragraphs 5 and 9 for the landlord and owner of any intermediate leasehold interest. Paragraph 9, in effect, confirms that the provisions that apply to the landlord, similarly apply to the owner of any intermediate leasehold interest.

The provisions apply where the landlord will suffer as follows:

5.(1) Where the landlord will suffer any loss or damage to which this paragraph applies, there shall be payable to him such amount as is reasonable to compensate him for that loss or damage.

(2) This paragraph applies to-
 (a) any diminution in value of any interest of the landlord in any property other than the tenant's flat which results from the grant to the tenant of the new lease; and
 (b) any other loss or damage which results therefrom to the extent that it is referable to the landlord's ownership of any such interest.

(3) Without prejudice to the generality of paragraph (b) of sub-paragraph (2), the kinds of loss falling within that paragraph include loss of development value in relation to the tenant's flat to the extent that it is referable as mentioned in that paragraph.

(4) In sub-paragraph (3) 'development value', in relation to the tenant's flat, means any increase in the value of the landlord's interest in the flat which is attributable to the

possibility of demolishing, reconstructing, or carrying out substantial works of construction affecting the flat (whether together with any other premises or otherwise).

9. Paragraph 5 shall apply in relation to the owner of any intermediate leasehold interest as it applies in relation to the landlord.

At subsection 3, the kinds of loss falling within that paragraph include loss of development value in relation to the tenant's flat.

An example is a house which has been previously converted into a number of flats, and the building is now more valuable for reconversion back to a single family dwelling. Where one of the lessees seeks a new lease, the claim for compensation under paragraph 5 would reflect the difference between the value for reconversion as a house and the value as flats. Factors to be taken into consideration in cases such as this include:

- the landlord's ability to gain possession of each of the other flats; and
- section 61, the right of the landlord to terminate the lease.

Watton v The Trustees of the Ilchester Estates [2002] (unreported LT), concerned a new lease claim in a mid 19th century town house, converted into four flats, in London W14. It is helpful to know that the unexpired terms of the existing leases were approximately 40 years, and each of the remaining flats were held by the landlord and let on assured shorthold tenancies.

In *Watton*, it was common ground that the property was more valuable for reconversion to a house; the issues, inter alia, were the treatment of tenant's improvements, allowances (if any) for uncertainty and prospect of repossession under section 61.

Section 61, (landlord's right to terminate new lease), provides that the new lease can be terminated by the landlord for the purposes of redevelopment during the last 12 months of the existing lease, and during the last five years of the new term. There are practical and valuation implications for the short unexpired term which were discussed at Example 8.

The tribunal determined as follows:

(1) for the purposes of calculating the proportion of additional value attributable to the flat to the landlord's existing interest, tenant's improvements were not to be disregarded (para. 45);

(2) a deduction of 25 per cent is made from the additional value of the landlord's interest to reflect market perception of uncertainty and the relatively short window of opportunity for the necessary action to be taken by the landlord (para. 51);

(3) a deduction of ten per cent is made to the new lease value in the marriage value computation against risk of the landlord enacting section 61 at the original term date; and

(4) notwithstanding the likelihood of the landlord enacting section 61 at the original term date, the compensation for other loss attributable to the remaining flats is to be similarly discounted by 25 per cent.

Watton is a very good example of the treatment of other loss under Schedule 13, paragraph 5. The valuer should be aware of the approach to calculating the additional sums, and the allowances made for uncertainties and risks.

The two-stage enfranchisement:

In *Nailrile*, the Lands Tribunal determined that compensation could be payable where a negative interest is generated in the intermediate lease (in the particular case controlled by the existing lessees), which in turn would lessen the overall price for collective enfranchisement, in accordance with paragraph 14, Part V of Schedule 6: (valuation etc. of interests in specified premises with negative values).

The first stage is for the lessees to take new leases which will be at peppercorn rents. The effect of this is to create a negative profit rent, hence negative value in the intermediate lease. Where the existing lease rents are substantial, or will be pursuant to review, the corresponding negative interest of the intermediate lease will also be substantial.

The second stage, once the new leases have completed, is to submit a section 13 notice for collective enfranchisement, the purchase price payable for which is under Schedule 6.

Flats: new lease claims: valuation issues

Paragraph 14 provides:

(1) that any interest which has a negative value shall be nil (subsections (1)(a); and (b)); and

(2) where any intermediate interest is a negative amount, any superior interest shall be reduced in value.

In *Nailrile*, the tribunal accepted the landlord's argument that with the head lease rent provisions remaining unaltered post grant of the new lease, and thus the negative value created, the prospect of a collective enfranchisement would adversely affect the value of his reversion.

It held that the diminution in the value of the freeholder's interest constitutes a loss either within paragraph 5(2)(a) (to the extent it is a diminution in value of the other flats), or within paragraph 5(2)(b) (to the extent that it is a diminution in value of the subject flats); and accordingly there is no need to determine the extent to which it falls within either of these provisions. The tribunal went on to say they believe that the diminution in value falls wholly within paragraph 5(2)(b), paragraph 64.

At paragraph 62 the tribunal sets out its reasoning as to the application of paragraph 5(2)(b) taken in conjunction with paragraph 5(2)(a), as follows:

- it is not a diminution in value of the freeholder's interest in any property other than the tenant's flat;
- it results from the grant to the tenant of the new lease; and
- it is referable to the freeholder's ownership of his interest in the other flats because it is by reason of such ownership that he can be compelled, on a collective enfranchisement of those flats and the subject flat, to transfer his interest to a nominee purchaser at a price determined under the provisions of Schedule 6.

We shall look at the mechanics of these circumstances by way of an example, which follows on from Example 11 where the intermediate lease and existing leases (underleases) have onerous ground rent provisions.

The tenants have since completed the purchase of the freehold interest by negotiation, and therefore the decision as to quantum of compensation will not be published. Nevertheless, it is important for the valuer to understand the background and mechanics of the two stage process.

Leasehold enfranchisement explained

Nailrile overturns the LVT's decisions at Flats 3 and 5, 61 Great Cumberland Place, London W1 (LON/NL/4577/05, unreported), where similar arguments were raised. This property comprised five flats, with an intermediate lease. The intermediate lease and corresponding existing lease rent reviews provided for substantial uplift in three years. New leases had been granted previously at Flats 1, 2 and 4. The decisions were appealed, but terms for the sale of the freehold interest were agreed between the freeholder and the underlessees by negotiation.

Example

The two stage process

Stage 1 – a building is subject to an intermediate lease (head lease) for a term of 40 years unexpired at a ground rent which has been agreed at £50,000 per annum from 25 March 2010. The intermediate lease is in the control of the underlessees.

The existing leases are for terms to the intermediate lease (less last three days), at ground rents to a fixed proportion of the intermediate lease rent, with coincidental reviews.

Set out below, in diagrammatic form, is the building with the respective rent provisions

Intermediate lease (head lease)

£50,000 per annum from 25 March 2010

Fourth Floor	Flat 6, ground rent at 12.5% of intermediate lease rent – £6,250 per annum – new lease value £1,000,000
Third Floor	Flat 5, ground rent at 15% of intermediate lease rent – £7,500 per annum – new lease value £1,100,000
Second Floor	Flat 4, ground rent at 17.5% of intermediate lease rent – £8,750 per annum – new lease value £1,200,000
First Floor	Flat 3, ground rent at 25% of intermediate lease rent – £12,500 per annum – new lease value £1,500,000
Ground Floor	Flat 2, ground rent at 20% of intermediate lease rent – £10,000 per annum – new lease value £1,300,000
Basement Floor	Flat 1, ground rent at 10% of intermediate lease rent – £5,000 per annum – new lease value £750,000

The intermediate lease is a post box; the aggregate of the existing lease ground rents equals the intermediate lease rent.

Flats: new lease claims: valuation issues

Stage I

Each of the lessees serves a notice for a new lease. The purpose of this is to build up a negative value in the intermediate lease. To highlight this we look at the price computation for the new lease at Flat 3.

Date of valuation: 25 March 2010

Flat 3

Diminution in value of landlord's interest

Difference between the value before grant of the new lease

Term

Intermediate lease rent (from table)	£12,500 p.a.		
YP 40 years @ 6%	15.0463	£188,079	

Reversion

To 'share of freehold' with vacant possession value (new lease value – 99% FHVP)	£1,515,150			
Deferred 40 years @ 5%	0.1421	£215,303	£403,382

minus

and the value after the new lease is granted

Term

Intermediate lease rent (from table and as above)	£12,500 p.a.		
YP 40 years @ 6%	15.0463	£188,079	

Reversion

To 'share of freehold' with vacant possession value (new lease value – 99% FHVP)	£1,515,150			
Deferred 129.99 years @ 5%	0.0018	£2,727	£190,806

Diminution in value of landlord's interest	£212,576

Diminution in value of intermediate interest (ILI)

Difference between the value before grant of the new lease

Term

Existing lease rent	£12,500 p.a.

Leasehold enfranchisement explained

less

proportion of intermediate
lease rent (from the table)   £12,500 p.a.

Profit rent	£0 p.a.		
YP 39.99 years @ 3.5%	21.3526		£0

minus

and the value after the new lease is granted

Term

New lease rent (at a peppercorn)   £0 p.a.

Less proportion of intermediate
lease rent   £12,500 p.a.

Profit rent	−£12,500 p.a.		
YP 39.99 years @ 3.5%	21.3526	−£266,908	−£266,908

Diminution in value of intermediate interest   £266,908

Marriage value

The difference between the aggregate of values of interests <u>post</u> grant of the new lease

Landlord's interest	£190,806	
Intermediate leaseholder's interest	−£266,908	
Tenant's proposed interest	£1,500,000	£1,423,898

less

Aggregate of values of interests <u>prior</u> to grant of the new lease

Landlord's interest	£403,382	
Intermediate leaseholder's interest	£0	
Tenant's existing interest (see below)	£890,000	£1,293,382

Marriage value		£130,516
50% thereof	0.5	£65,258

plus

Diminution in value of landlord's interest   £212,576

and

Diminution in value of intermediate interest   £266,908

Flats: new lease claims: valuation issues

New lease premium (excluding costs)		£544,742
	Say	£544,750

Apportioned as follows:

<u>Landlord</u>

$$£212,576 + \frac{(212,576)}{(212,576 + 266,908)} \times £65,258$$

£212,576 +	£28,932	=	£241,508
		Say	£241,500

<u>Intermediate leaseholder</u>

$$£266,908 + \frac{(266,908)}{(266,908 + 212,576)} \times £65,258$$

£266,908 +	£36,326	=	£303,234
		Say	£303,250
			£544,750

<u>Analysis of the onerous ground rent provisions to establish the existing lease value</u>:

Share of freehold value (from above)	£1,515,150
Palatable ground rent per annum equates to (say) 0.1% of share of freehold value	£1,515
Ground rent (per annum)	£12,500
less palatable ground rent (per annum)	£1,515
Onerous (unpalatable) rent (per annum)	£10,985
Ten times thereof	10
	£109,850
Adjustment for onerous ground rent, say	£110,000
Existing lease value with nominal ground rent provisions at 66% of share of freehold value − £1,515,150 @ 66%	£1,000,000

less adjustment	£110,000
Existing lease value	£890,000

Pursuant to granting the new lease at Flat 3, a negative value of −£266,908 has been generated in the intermediate lease.

If all the lessees had served notices for new leases, the negative value would become:

Intermediate lease rent	£50,000		
YP 39.99 years @ 3.5%	21.3526		£1,067,630
		Say	£1,067,650

Stage 2

With the passage of time and the six new leases having completed, say two years later, a section 13 notice is served for collective enfranchisement, with all six lessees participating.

For these purposes the new lease values and corresponding share of freehold values remain unaltered.

The computation is in accordance with Schedule 6, as follows:

Fourth Floor	Flat 6, new lease value – £1,000,000
Third Floor	Flat 5, new lease value – £1,100,000
Second Floor	Flat 4, new lease value – £1,200,000
First Floor	Flat 3, new lease value – £1,500,000
Ground Floor	Flat 2, new lease value – £1,300,000
BasementFloor	Flat 1, new lease value – £750,000

Intermediate lease for a term of 38 years unexpired at a fixed ground rent of £50,000 per annum.

The enfranchisement price in accordance with Schedule 6:

Date of valuation: 25 March 2012

<u>Value of the freeholder's interest</u>

Participators – all lessees

Term

Intermediate lease rent	£50,000 p.a.	
YP 38 years @ 6%	14.8460	£742,300

<u>Reversions</u>

127.99 years unexpired leasehold interests – aggregate of 'share of freehold' with vacant possession values

Flat 6 –	£1,000,000	
Flat 5 –	£1,100,000	
Flat 4 –	£1,200,000	
Flat 3 –	£1,500,000	
Flat 2 –	£1,300,000	
Flat 1 –	£750,000	

£6,850,000 @ 99%	£6,919,190	
Deferred 127.99 years @ 5%	0.0019	£13,146
		£755,446
Deduct negative value of intermediate lease (para. 14 (2) see later)		£1,041,920
		–£286,474

Value of intermediate leasehold interest

Rent receivable from tenants	£0	
less rent to freeholder	£50,000 p.a.	
Profit rent	–£50,000 p.a.	
YP 37.99 years @ 3.5%	20.8384	–£1,041,920

Therefore in accordance with paragraph 14 (1)(b), assess at nil

Enfranchisement price

Freeholder's interest	–£286,474
plus	
Intermediate leaseholder's interest	£0
Total	–£286,474

Enfranchisement price negative amount, hence 'nil'.

The question remains as to the level of compensation in cases such as this. From the computation of the new lease premium at Flat 3, the landlord's proportion of premium reflects the 90 years further distant reversion and pro rata apportionment of marriage value.

In *Nailrile*, the tenants admitted that their intention was to operate the two stage process, and the Lands Tribunal decided that compensation be payable, but the quantum was not determined. Landlords may use the decision to seek compensation in each case as a precursor to negotiating a head rent reduction, which in practical terms is the preferred option, but not one provided for by the statute.

The basis of the claim for compensation is that, on a collective enfranchisement after the grant of the new lease, the price payable to the landlord would be less, by a greater amount than the price payable for the lease extension, than it would be if the new lease had not been granted (para. 60).

An approach to assess the amount of compensation payable is to calculate the difference between the price the freeholder receives from collective enfranchisement where there is no stage 1, and the aggregate of premiums received by him at stage 1 in the two stage process.

That approach is criticised and questioned as follows: (a) it does not necessarily reflect the market value of the reversion; (b) there is no separate analysis of compensation payable for each new lease claim; (c) should the head rent payable over the time for the two stage process be offset in any event; and (d) whether either any assumptions or disregards are to be applied?

It is no argument that the second stage collective enfranchisement claim might not be made. The tribunal did not feel that this lack of certainty precluded a claim for compensation as the value of the interest would depend on the view taken by the market of the possibility of future events occurring.

The amount of compensation would depend on the likelihood that the tenants would pursue a collective claim. If that prospect was low, the diminution in value of the freeholder's interest would be correspondingly small, hence so would the level of compensation.

In considering the 'likelihood and timing of a claim in any one particular case', the valuer will have in mind the intermediate lease rent provisions. In *61 Great Cumberland Place, London W1*, the rent review, which would have resulted in a substantial uplift, was three years hence; the likelihood was that a claim for collective enfranchisement would have been made once the new leases at Flats 3 and 5 had completed, such that completion of the freehold purchase took place prior to the effective date of the rent review.

In *Nailrile* the rent review effective date was approximately three months after the various dates of valuation for the new lease claims. How long pursuant to those new leases completing would the owners of the intermediate lease (the new leaseholders) continue to pay the substantial rent if, by way of submitting a claim for collective enfranchisement, the purchase price would be 'nil' and payment of that rent would at completion of the enfranchisement, cease? In both of these cases, the intermediate leaseholder and the underlessees were, effectively, one and the same; on that basis, and in the particular circumstances of each, this suggests that the prospect of an enfranchisement claim was both high and, as regards to timing, imminent. That is to be contrasted with circumstances where the intermediate lessee is unconnected with the underlessees; and whereas new lease claims may have already completed and other claims be pending, the prospect and timing of a collective enfranchisement claim are less certain and the timing for which is unknown. That is not to say compensation for diminution in value is not due, but its sum pro rata would be expected to be less.

Each case is to be handled on its merits, factors to be taken into consideration to assess the compensation may include: (1) the timing of the respective new lease claims; and (2) the perceived likelihood and timing of the section 13 notice.

One immediate consequence of the Lands Tribunal decisions in *Nailrile*, bearing in mind the loss is manifested when the new lease is granted, is that if compensation is to be sought, it is at the new lease stage and not at collective enfranchisement. Valuers advising tenants proposing to take new leases have to have it in mind that where there is an intermediate lease, which after a new lease has been granted, could in turn lead to the landlord suffering a loss at collective enfranchisement, compensation will be sought at the outset and be proposed within the section 45 counter-notice sums.

Evidence

In *Sportelli*, paragraphs 91 to 99, the Court of Appeal considers the 'precedent effect of the (Lands) Tribunal's decision'. To put it into context, the application of the generic deferment rate of 4.75 per cent for houses, with an increase for flats of 0.25 per cent, countrywide. Thereafter, further consideration is given to the particular circumstances of the cases, being properties within PCL, in relation to properties 'Outside the PCL', paragraphs 100 to 102.

It is long established that decisions on matters of fact or opinion by LVTs and the Lands Tribunal are not precedent for the tribunals (see *Cadogan Estates Limited v Hows* [1989] 2 EGLR 216), although a decision of the Lands Tribunal may be referred to where general guidance has been given on valuation principles or procedure (see *Clinker & Ash Limited v Southern Gas Board* (1967) 203 EG 735, *Arbib*, para 116.

The Lands Tribunal in *Sportelli* set out the 'General effect of conclusions' of their decisions in paragraphs 113 to 123.

At paragraph 117, the tribunal states that its function is:

> ...'to make decisions on points of law and on what may be called principles of practice to which regard should be had by the first-tier tribunals and by practitioners dealing with claims in any of the tribunal's original or appellate jurisdictions'.

It goes on to say at paragraph 121 that:

> 'The prospect of varying conclusions on the deferment rate in different cases reached on evidence that was less comprehensive than that before us can therefore be avoided by LVTs adopting the practice of following the guidance of this decision unless compelling evidence to the contrary is adduced'.

At paragraph 99 of its decision in *Sportelli*, the Court of Appeal confirms that it is an important role of the Lands Tribunal to promote consistent practice in land valuation matters; and unless legislature intervenes, to expect LVTs to follow generally that lead. The court goes on to consider properties outside the PCL, which were not subject to the appeals, and says there is an implicit distinction between the two. The consequences of this have been discussed earlier in this chapter on those subsequent cases before the tribunals where departure from the generic deferment rate of 4.75 per cent has been sought.

Ultimately, each case is to be determined on the basis of the evidence before it; that premise remains undisturbed. But such were the circumstances of the three Lands Tribunal hearings on the deferment rate issue (*Pockney, Arbib and Sportelli*), with the extensive expert valuation evidence before each (both land and latterly, financial), presented by leading counsel in the field, the court has confirmed that one of the tribunal's roles is to promote consistent practice; leastwise where the tribunal's decision has been reached after such detailed and considered examination.

A case in point on the question of decisions on points of law and principles of practice are the decisions of the Lands Tribunal in *Nailrile*. Both the LVTs and practitioners in leasehold reform now adopt the valuation approaches for assessing the diminution in value of the intermediate leaseholder's interest as part of the calculation of the new lease premium under Schedule 13; the directions as to the method of valuation result in consistent practice.

Summary

Valuations to calculate the premium for a new lease under Schedule 13 range from the comparatively straightforward to the exceedingly complicated and complex. From the tenant's and landlord's perspectives, assuming a valid claim, they will have but one question, 'how much?'

Until you have investigated the circumstances of any one particular case, how straightforward or otherwise the premium computation will be, will not be apparent. The valuation issues have been examined in detail in relation to Schedule 13, including marriage value, intermediate leasehold interests and compensation.

It is expected that the valuer will have a general understanding of the statutory provisions and the valuation principles. A detailed analysis of both *Sportelli* and *Nailrile* are included as it is fundamental the valuer understands the background and principles of each.

Whereas the *Sportelli* analyses are considered here, they have further relevance in chapters 4 and 7, collective enfranchisement and house claims under the 1993 and 1967 Acts.

3

Flats: collective enfranchisement

Introduction

Chapter I of Part I of the *Leasehold Reform, Housing and Urban Development Act* 1993 confers on certain tenants of flats the right to acquire the freehold of premises containing those flats known as 'the right to collective enfranchisement'. There seems to be a great deal of enthusiasm among tenants to purchase their freeholds and, indeed, flats with a 'share of freehold' are seen as a more attractive purchase than those without. However, careful consideration should be given to whether acquiring the freehold is really in the tenants' best interests.

Depending on the nature of the premises, managing freehold premises can be a time consuming and difficult job. There has been a great deal of statutory intervention in the field of residential landlord and tenant in recent years and even for the professional, there is plenty of scope for mistakes to be made. Whilst tenants may co-operate fully in seeking to acquire the freehold, leases get assigned and disagreements as to the management of the premises arise. It is often not easy, nor is it conducive to good neighbourly relations, to have to challenge one's neighbour directly over his choice of wooden flooring as opposed to relying on a third party landlord to enforce the covenants in his lease. Similarly, suing your neighbours because they fail to see the need to repair the roof, which is leaking above your top floor flat, is not only unlikely to win you many friends, but may ultimately prove fruitless if the freehold owning company has no assets other than the freehold itself.

It is, therefore, important to consider what the tenants actually want. If there are management issues with the landlord, then the tenants may be able to have a manager appointed under the

Landlord and Tenant Act 1987 or they could acquire the 'Right to Manage' under the *Commonhold and Leasehold Reform Act* 2002 without having to prove mismanagement. If the tenants want to be able to extend their leases, then consideration should be given to whether it may be preferable for the tenants to extend their leases individually.

If it is decided that buying the freehold is the appropriate course of action, then regard should be had to whether the landlord has recently sold or proposes to sell the freehold. The *Landlord and Tenant Act* 1987 confers on certain tenants a right of first refusal if the landlord proposes to dispose of property, and before such a disposal, the landlord must serve on the tenants a notice offering to dispose of the property to them. If such a notice has been served in relation to the freehold, then it is important to consider whether it would be cheaper for the tenants to accept the landlord's offer rather than exercise their right to collectively enfranchise. If no notice has been served, but the landlord has disposed of the freehold, then the tenants will have the right to have the freehold transferred to them on the terms of that disposal. If this is the case, regard should be had to whether requiring such a transfer would again be cheaper than collectively enfranchising.

If making a claim to collectively enfranchise is the most appropriate way forward, then consideration should be given to whether it is also appropriate to make claims for new leases at the same time. Collective enfranchisement requires co-operation amongst the tenants and a claim could easily fall apart before the freehold is acquired. A well drafted participation agreement is obviously a way to avoid this. However, where the leases are short or the unexpired terms of the leases are about to fall below 80 years, the point at which marriage value becomes payable and the premium payable for a new lease jumps up; a delay in making a claim for a new lease caused by an abortive claim to acquire the freehold could be costly for a tenant. One way to avoid this is to serve a tenant's notice to acquire a new lease at the same time as making a claim to collectively enfranchise. The collective enfranchisement claim has the effect of suspending the operation of the initial notice during the currency of that claim. However, if the collective enfranchisement claim fails, the suspension is lifted and the claim for a new lease continues with the valuation date being the date when the tenant's notice was given.

Leasehold enfranchisement explained

What can be acquired?

Freehold interests

The right to collective enfranchisement is the right of qualifying tenants of flats contained in premises, to which the Act applies, to have the freehold of those premises acquired on their behalf:

- by a person or persons appointed by them for the purposes, known as the 'nominee purchaser';
- at a price determined in accordance with the Act (s.1(1)).

Where the right to collective enfranchisement is exercised in relation to any such premises ('the relevant premises'), the qualifying tenants are also entitled, but not required, to acquire the freehold of any property if:

- it is appurtenant property, which is demised by the lease held by a qualifying tenant of a flat within the relevant premises; or
- it is property which any such tenant is entitled under the terms of the lease of his flat to use in common with the occupiers of other premises (whether those premises are within the relevant premises or not) (ss.1(2)(a) and (3)).

By virtue of section 1(7), 'appurtenant property' in relation to a flat means any garage, outhouse, garden, yard and appurtenances belonging to, or usually enjoyed with, the flat. This definition is almost identical to the meaning given to 'premises' in section 2(3) of the *Leasehold Reform Act* 1967 and also appears in section 62(2) in relation to new lease claims. Consequently, regard should be had to both chapters 1 and 5 where the meaning of 'premises' and 'qualifying flat' are discussed.

> *Example*
>
> The qualifying tenants are tenants of flats within a block of flats, which forms part of an estate consisting of four blocks of flats. The flats are let together with garages on the estate and under the terms of the lease, the tenants are entitled to use the garden grounds of the estate immediately in front of the block, in common not only with the other occupiers of their block, but with the occupiers of one of the other blocks.
>
> The tenants are entitled to acquire not only the block, being the 'relevant premises', but also the garages, being appurtenant property demised by the leases held by the qualifying tenants of flats within the relevant premises, and

Flats: collective enfranchisement

> the garden grounds immediately in front of the block, being property which the tenants are entitled, under the terms of the leases of their flats, to use in common with the occupiers of other premises.

Rather than conveying the freehold of property which the tenant is entitled to use in common with others, the freeholder can instead:

- grant permanent rights over that property or over any other property so that the tenant has nearly the same rights as those he presently enjoys; or
- transfer to the tenants the freehold of any other property, over which any such permanent rights may be granted (s.1(4)).

So long as the rights offered are equivalent, the LVT has no discretion to determine what is to be acquired: *Shortdean Place (Eastbourne) Resident's Association Limited v Lynari Properties Ltd* [2003] 3 EGLR 147. However, if the rights offered are not equivalent, section 1(4) is not satisfied: *Ulterra Ltd v Glenbarr (RTE) Co Ltd* [2008] 1 EGLR 103.

> *Example*
>
> In the previous example, rather than transferring the garden grounds immediately in front of the block to the tenants, the freeholder could grant permanent rights either over those garden grounds, or over other garden grounds on the estate, or could transfer other garden grounds to the tenants. However, if he were to offer to grant permanent rights over the garden grounds, but to reserve to himself a right to build on those grounds (there having been no such reservation previously), the rights offered would not be equivalent rights and section 1(4) would not be satisfied.

Leasehold interests

Where the right to collective enfranchisement is exercised in relation to the relevant premises, the participating qualifying tenants are also either required or entitled to acquire certain leasehold interests:

- any leasehold interest, which is superior to the lease held by a qualifying tenant of a flat within the relevant premises, must be acquired (ss.2(1)(a) and (2)); and

- the leasehold interest of any common parts of the relevant premises, or of property falling within section 1(2)(a) (i.e. appurtenant property or property used in common with others), can be acquired where the acquisition of that interest is reasonably necessary for the proper management or maintenance of those common parts or that property (ss.1(2)(b) and 2(1)).

If a lease demises not only common parts, for example, but other property, the leasehold interest of which the tenants are not entitled to acquire, then the tenants will not be entitled to acquire the leasehold interest of that other property (s.2(4)). Where flats are let under secure or introductory tenancies by public sector landlords, special provisions apply and regard should be had to sections 2(5) and (6).

> *Example*
>
> In the previous example, suppose that the flats only are subject to a head lease. So if the freeholder is A Ltd, A Ltd has granted a lease of all the flats on the estate to B Ltd, which in turn has granted long leases in respect of some of those flats and rents out the others on assured shorthold tenancies. Suppose also, that A Ltd has granted a head lease of the common parts of the blocks, the garden grounds of the estate and the garages to C Ltd.
>
> The participating qualifying tenants of one of the blocks, will have to acquire B Ltd's interest in every flat let to a qualifying tenant, but cannot acquire B Ltd's interest in any other flats. Further, the qualifying tenants may be entitled to acquire C Ltd's interest in the common parts of their block, any garages let with their flats and the garden grounds immediately in front of the block, where the acquisition of those interests is reasonably necessary for the proper management or maintenance of those common parts or that property, but not any other interest of C Ltd.

Other interests

The nominee purchaser, on behalf of the qualifying tenants, may be required to acquire further interests if an owner of any of the interests set out above has an interest in other property, and following the acquisition of his interest that other property would:

- for all practical purposes cease to be of use and benefit to him; or
- cease to be capable of being reasonably managed or maintained by him (s.21(4)).

Flats: collective enfranchisement

> *Example*
>
> In the previous example, suppose that between the block and the boundary of the estate is a small piece of land, which the tenants have no right to acquire, but which is only of practical use with the block. A Ltd could require the nominee purchaser to acquire this piece of land as well.

Leasebacks

It may be that the freeholder of the relevant premises owns flats or other units himself, which are not let to qualifying tenants. If this is the case, then on acquiring the freehold, the nominee purchaser would acquire those units and the freeholder would be left with nothing. Consequently, the Act provides for such units to be leased back to the freeholder (s.36).

If the freeholder is a public sector landlord or housing association, then it is likely that any flats which are let, other than on long leases, will be subject to a mandatory leaseback, i.e. the nominee purchaser must grant the freeholder a lease of those flats (Part II of Schedule 9).

Any other freeholder who owns a unit, which is not let to a person who is a qualifying tenant, can require the nominee purchaser to grant him a lease of that unit (Sch. 9, para.5). Further, if the freeholder is a resident landlord (as to which see below), then he can require the nominee purchaser to grant him a lease of the unit, which he occupies as a qualifying tenant (Sch. 9, para.6).

By virtue of section 38(1) a 'unit' means:

- a flat;
- any other separate set of premises which is constructed or adapted for use for the purposes of a dwelling; or
- a separate set of premises let, or intended for letting on a business lease.

Any lease granted by virtue of Schedule 9 is for a term of 999 years at a peppercorn rent and on such terms, which as far as possible, provide the freeholder with the rights he would have, if he were to own the freehold of the unit (Part IV of Schedule 9). Where the unit is already subject to a lease, then the lease back to the freeholder takes effect subject to that lease (s.36(3)).

201

> **Example**
>
> In the previous example, suppose that three of the flats in the block, which is the subject of a claim for collective enfranchisement, are not let on long leases. A Ltd can require a leaseback of those flats. However, the flats are subject to B Ltd's head lease. Consequently, A Ltd's lease takes effect subject to B Ltd's lease, i.e. A Ltd remains B Ltd's landlord and the nominee purchaser becomes A Ltd's landlord.
>
> (Note: B Ltd is on the face of it a qualifying tenant of the three flats which are not let on long leases: *Howard de Walden Estates Ltd v Aggio* [2009] 1 AC 39. However, by virtue of section 5(5), there is taken to be no qualifying tenant of those flats, as, apart from that subsection, the same tenant would be the qualifying tenant of at least three flats in the block.)

It is possible for the parties to agree to depart from the terms provided for in Part IV (Sch. 9, paras.4 and 7). In the case of a mandatory leaseback such a departure must be approved by an LVT. This is not necessary where the leaseback is not mandatory. However, the LVT in the case of non-mandatory leasebacks does have jurisdiction to direct that there should be a departure on the application of either party if it is reasonable in the circumstances.

Qualifying criteria

Qualifying premises

Premises qualify if:

- they consist of a self-contained building or part of a building;
- they contain two or more flats held by qualifying tenants; and
- the total number of flats held by such tenants is not less than two-thirds of the total number of flats contained in the premises (s.3(1)).

'Flat' is defined in section 101(1) as being a separate set of premises (whether or not on the same floor):

- which forms part of a building; and
- which is constructed or adapted for use for the purposes of a dwelling; and
- either the whole or a material part of which lies above or below some other part of the building.

Flats: collective enfranchisement

> *Example*
>
> A converted terraced house is divided into three flats. The ground floor flat is retained by the landlord and let on an assured shorthold tenancy. The remaining two flats are let to qualifying tenants.
>
> The premises contain two flats held by qualifying tenants, which constitute two-thirds of the total number of flats contained in the premises. Consequently, the premises qualify to be collectively enfranchised (the landlord could, of course, require a lease back of the flat retained by him).

Self-contained building or part of a building

By virtue of section 3(2), a building is self-contained if it is structurally detached and part of a building is self-contained if:

- it constitutes a vertical division of the building;
- the structure of the building is such that, that part could be redeveloped independently of the remainder of the building; and
- the relevant services for occupiers of that part are provided independently of the relevant services provided for occupiers of the remainder of the building; or
- could be so provided without involving significant interruption in the provision of any such services for occupiers of the remainder of the building.

'Relevant services' means services provided by means of pipes, cables or other fixed installations, for example, electricity, gas and water.

> *Example*
>
> In the previous example, the terraced house is not structurally detached and therefore cannot be a self-contained building. However, it is vertically divided from, could be redeveloped independently of, and the relevant services are independent of the relevant services for, the rest of the terrace. Consequently, the terraced house is a self-contained part of a building and as such qualifies to be collectively enfranchised.

Excluded premises

Mixed-use premises

Mixed-use premises, i.e. those used for both residential and non-residential purposes can be excluded from the right collectively to enfranchise depending on the extent of the non-residential use. If the floor area of the non-residential parts exceeds 25 per cent of the internal floor area of the premises as a whole (excluding the common parts), then the premises will be excluded (s.4(1)(b)).

For the purposes of section 4, residential parts include:

- any part or parts of the premises occupied for residential purposes (s.4(1)(a)(i));
- any part or parts of the premises used, or intended for use in conjunction with a particular dwelling, for example, a garage, parking space or storage area (s.4(2)); and
- common parts (s.4(1)(a)(ii)).

For the purposes of determining the internal floor area of the premises or a part of them:

- the floors of the premises are to be taken as extending (without interruption) throughout the whole of the interior of the premises or that part; and
- the common parts of the premises are to be excluded (s.4(3)).

> **Example**
> In the previous example, the landlord decides to convert the ground floor flat into a shop. The internal floor area of the shop is 450ft^2. The internal floor area of the two flats is 950ft^2 and the internal floor area of the common parts is 300ft^2. The internal area of the whole premises (excluding the common parts), is 1400ft^2 of which 450ft^2 or 32 per cent is used for non-residential purposes. The premises now do not qualify to be collectively enfranchised as the internal floor area of the non-residential parts exceeds 25 per cent of the internal floor area of the whole premises (excluding the common parts).

'Common parts' by virtue of section 101(1) include the structure and exterior of the building (or part of the building) and any common facilities within it.

Flats: collective enfranchisement

Split freehold

Where different persons own the freehold of different parts of the premises, the premises as a whole do not qualify to be collectively enfranchised if any of those parts is a self-contained part of a building (s.4(3A)).

> *Example*
>
> In the previous examples, the terrace consists of three houses. As house number one does not qualify to be collectively enfranchised since the landlord converted the ground floor flat, the tenants of house number one wish to acquire the freehold of the whole terrace together with the tenants of the other houses. Whilst the freeholds of houses one and two are owned by the same person, the freehold of house number three is owned by someone else. As house number three is a self-contained part of a building, the terrace as a whole cannot be collectively enfranchised. However, houses numbered one and two can together be collectively enfranchised as they are together (and individually), a self-contained part of a building, namely the terrace.

Resident landlords

Premises with resident landlords may not qualify to be collectively enfranchised by virtue of section 3(4). However, this provision is not as straight forward as it may otherwise seem. In order to be excluded, the following conditions must be satisfied:

- the premises must contain not more than four units (s.3(4));
- the premises must not be, or must not form part of, a purpose-built block of flats (s.10(1)(a));
- the same person must have owned the freehold of the premises since before the conversion of the premises into two or more flats or other units (s.10(1)(b)); and
- the freehold owner, or an adult member of his family, must have occupied a flat or other unit contained in the premises as his only or principal home for the previous 12 months (s.10(1)(c)).

Where the freehold of any premises is held on trust, regard should be had to section 10(4).

A 'purpose-built block of flats' means a building which, as constructed, contained two or more flats (s.10(6)). For the purposes of section 10(1)(c), an adult member of the freehold owner's family is:

205

- his spouse or civil partner;
- a son, daughter, son-in-law, daughter-in-law, stepson, stepdaughter, stepson-in-law or stepdaughter-in-law of either the freehold owner or his spouse or civil partner aged 18 or over; and
- the father or mother of the freehold owner or his spouse or civil partner (s.10(5)).

> *Example*
>
> In the previous examples, it will be remembered that house number one is a converted terraced house and therefore not a purpose-built block of flats. Further, it does not contain more than four units. Suppose the landlord owned the freehold of the house prior to its conversion into flats and that rather than converting the ground floor flat into a shop, the landlord let his stepdaughter reside in it as her only home. Once his stepdaughter has lived there for 12 months, and for so long as she continues to live there, the premises will be premises with a resident landlord within the meaning of section 3(4) and will not qualify to be collectively enfranchised.

Operational railways

Premises which include the track of an operational railway are excluded from the right to collective enfranchisement (s.3(5)). For the definitions of 'track', 'operational' and 'railway' see section 3(5).

Qualifying tenants

Pursuant to section 5(1), a tenant is a qualifying tenant of a flat if he is the tenant of the flat under a long lease. Where there are joint tenants, they are regarded as jointly constituting the qualifying tenant of the flat (s.5(4)(b)).

However, in relation to claims to collectively enfranchise, there are a number of situations where tenants, who would otherwise be qualifying tenants for the purposes of subsection 1, do not in fact qualify and these exceptions are more extensive than they are in relation to new lease claims. The exceptions are as follows:

- the tenant's lease falls within one of the exceptions contained in section 5(2), see chapter 1;
- there is also a qualifying tenant of an inferior lease (s.5(4)(a));

Flats: collective enfranchisement

> **Example**
>
> A grants B a lease of a flat for a term of 99 years. B grants C a sub-lease of the flat for a term of 90 years. C is a qualifying tenant and therefore B cannot also be a qualifying tenant by virtue of section 5(3) and 5(4)(a).

- the qualifying tenant is (or is among those constituting), the qualifying tenant of three or more flats within the same premises (s.5(5)); or

> **Example**
>
> A property is split into six flats. A is the tenant of Flat 2; A and his wife are the joint tenants of Flat 3 and A and his brother are the joint tenants of Flat 5. By virtue of section 5(5) there are no qualifying tenants of Flats 2, 3 and 5.

- the qualifying tenant is a body corporate and it, or an associated company of it, is (or is among those constituting), the qualifying tenant of three or more flats within the same premises (s.5(6)).

Qualifying leases

By virtue of section 7, 'long lease' has the same meaning in relation to a claim to collectively enfranchise as it does in relation to a claim for a new lease, and regard should be had to the relevant section of chapter 1.

Tenants unable to participate

There are a number of situations where a tenant, who is a qualifying tenant under a long lease, is prevented from participating in giving a notice claiming the right to collective enfranchisement or from subsequently electing to participate in the claim. These are as follows:

- there has been a prior notice by the tenant or the landlord terminating the lease (Sch. 3, paras. 1 and 2);
- an order for possession has been made or there are pending forfeiture proceedings (Sch. 3, para. 3); or
- compulsory purchase procedures have been instituted in respect of the whole or part of the tenant's flat (Sch. 3, para. 4).

Who is the landlord?

Before making a claim to collectively enfranchise, it is important to identify who the landlord is for the purposes of such a claim. This landlord is known as 'the reversioner' and he and any other landlords are known as 'relevant landlords'. In order to identify the reversioner, it is necessary to identify which one of three situations applies:

- situation one – one person owns all the interests which the tenants are seeking to acquire;
- situation two – the tenants are seeking to acquire interests of persons, other than the person who owns the freehold of the premises to which the claim relates; or
- situation three – the freehold of the premises to which the claim relates is owned by more than one person.

Situation one

This is the most straightforward situation: the reversioner is the person whose interests the tenants are seeking to acquire (s.9(1)).

Situation two

In this situation, the reversioner is the person who owns the freehold of the premises to which the claim relates (s.9(2) and Sch. 1, para. 1) unless:

- all the relevant landlords agree that another relevant landlord is to be the reversioner and apply to the court to have that person appointed as reversioner and the court so appoints that person (Sch. 1, para. 2);
- the person designated as reversioner is:
    - absent;
    - incapacitated;
    - unwilling to act as reversioner; or
    - there are special circumstances which require another relevant landlord to act as the reversioner and the court, on the application of any of the relevant landlords, appoints such other relevant landlord as it thinks fit to be the reversioner (Sch. 1, para. 3);
- on the application of any of the relevant landlords or the nominee purchaser, the court replaces the designated reversioner with another relevant landlord by reason of any

actual or apprehended delay or default on the part of the designated reversioner (Sch. 1, para. 4); or
- on the application of the qualifying tenants, where the designated reversioner cannot be found or his identity cannot be ascertained, the court makes an order appointing any other relevant landlord to be the reversioner (s.26(3)).

Situation three

In this situation, the tenants can effectively choose who is to be the reversioner. The tenants must specify in their initial notice, a person who owns a freehold interest in the premises or, if no such person can be found or his identity ascertained, a relevant landlord (s.13(2A)), and this person will be the reversioner (s.9(2A) and Sch. 1, para 5A) unless:

- all the relevant landlords agree that another relevant landlord is to be the reversioner and apply to the court to have that person appointed as reversioner, and the court so appoints that person (Sch. 1, para. 5B);
- The person designated as reversioner is:
  - absent;
  - incapacitated;
  - unwilling to act as reversioner; or
  - there are special circumstances which require another relevant landlord to act as the reversioner and the court, on the application of any of the relevant landlords, appoints such other relevant landlord as it thinks fit to be the reversioner (Sch. 1, para. 5C); or
- on the application of any of the relevant landlords or the nominee purchaser, the court replaces the designated reversioner with another relevant landlord by reason of any actual or apprehended delay or default on the part of the designated reversioner (Sch. 1, para. 5D).

Schedule 2 contains provisions relating to special categories of landlords, those categories being as follows:

- mortgagees in possession of the landlord's interest;
- custodian trustees in whom the landlord's interest is vested;
- landlords under a disability;
- landlords whose interest is held in trust;
- landlords whose interest is subject to a settlement;
- university and college landlords; and
- ecclesiastical landlords.

Leasehold enfranchisement explained

If the landlord falls into one of the above categories, then regard ought to be had to Schedule 2.

Finding the landlords

Having identified who is designated as reversioner, it is necessary to find out not only his, but any other relevant landlords' names and addresses. In order to do this, the first step will be to look at the Land Register. Unfortunately, many people do not keep their address on the Land Register up to date. Further, the Act does not provide that notices can be served on an address contained in the Land Register. Consequently, it is likely to be prudent to obtain such names and addresses by service of a notice under section 11. There are two notices which a qualifying tenant may give under this section in order to obtain such names and addresses; these are:

- a notice to the immediate landlord or any person receiving rent on behalf of the immediate landlord (s.11(1)); and
- a notice to any freeholder (s.11(3)).

A notice under section 11(1) may be served requiring the recipient to give the tenant within 28 days (so far as is known to the recipient), the name and address of every person who owns:

- a freehold interest in the relevant premises;
- the freehold of any property not contained in the relevant premises, which:
    - is demised by the tenant's lease; or
    - the tenant is entitled under the terms of his lease to use in common with other persons; and
- any leasehold interest in the relevant premises or in any such other property which is superior to that of any immediate landlord of the tenant (s.11(2)).

A notice under section 11(3) may be served requiring any freeholder to give the tenant within 28 days (so far as is known to him), the name and address of every person, apart from the tenant, who is:

- a tenant of the whole of the relevant premises;
- a tenant or licensee of any separate set of premises contained in the relevant premises; or
- a tenant or licensee of the whole or any part of common parts so contained, or of any property not so contained, which:
    - is demised by the tenant's lease; or

Flats: collective enfranchisement

- o the tenant is entitled under the terms of his lease to use in common with other persons.

Once the tenant has the relevant names and addresses, there may be information which the tenant reasonably requires to make a claim to collectively enfranchise. Such information can be obtained by serving a notice under section 11(4) on:

- any person who owns a freehold interest in the relevant premises;
- any person who owns a freehold interest in the whole or any part of common parts so contained, or of any property not so contained, which:
  - o is demised by the tenant's lease; or
  - o the tenant is entitled under the terms of his lease to use in common with other persons;
- a tenant of the whole of the relevant premises;
- a tenant or licensee of any separate set of premises contained in the relevant premises; and
- a tenant or licensee of the whole or any part of common parts so contained, or of any property not so contained, which:
  - o is demised by the tenant's lease; or
  - o the tenant is entitled under the terms of his lease to use in common with other persons.

The tenant can, by service of a notice under section 11(4), acquire:

- information relating to the recipient's interest (s.11(4)(i));
- (so far as is known by the recipient), information relating to any interest derived out of that interest (s.11(4)(ii);
- a right, on giving reasonable notice, to be provided with a list of documents:
  - o sight of which is reasonably required by the tenant;
  - o which, on a proposed sale the seller would be expected to make available to the buyer (ss.11(5)(a) and (6));
- a right to inspect, at a reasonable time and on giving reasonable notice, any such documents (s.11(5)(b));
- a right, on payment of a reasonable fee, to be provided with a copy of any documents, which are contained in any list or have been inspected (s.11(5)(c));
- information as to whether the recipient has received, in respect of any premises containing the tenant's flat:
  - o a notice under section 13 in the case of which the relevant claim is still current, or
  - o a copy of such a notice; and if so

- information as to the date on which the notice under section 13 was given and the name and address of the nominee purchaser in relation to that claim (ss.12(1)(a) and (2)); and
- information as to whether any property in which the tenant's flat is comprised is affected by the *Inheritance Tax Act* 1984 (ss.12(1)(b) and (3)).

Any information requested by a notice under section 11(4) must be provided within 28 days of the giving of notice and any person who is required to supply a list, permit inspection or supply a copy of any documents must do so within 28 days of being so required (s.11(7)). If, within six months of having received a notice under section 11(4), a person:

- disposes of his interest;
- acquires a relevant interest; or
- receives a section 13 notice or a copy of one, and the tenant who has given the notice under section 11(4) is not one of the qualifying tenants who has given the section 13 notice,

then he must notify the tenant of that disposal or acquisition, or the date of the notice and name of the nominee purchaser within 28 days (ss.11(8) and 12(5)).

If the recipient of a notice served under section 11 fails to provide the information sought, then it will be necessary to serve a default notice under section 92 and seek an order from the court requiring him to make good the default, if he has not done so within 14 days of the giving of the notice. For an example of a default notice, see chapter 1.

Missing landlords

Where one of several relevant landlords cannot be found or his identity cannot be ascertained, this will not necessarily cause a problem. If he is the reversioner, another relevant landlord can either be appointed (s.26(3)) or specified (s.13(2A)), as applicable, in his place. If he is one of the other relevant landlords, then the court can dispense with the need to serve a copy of an initial notice on him (s.26(2)) and give directions (Sch. 1, para. 6(3)). However, if there is only one relevant landlord (i.e. the reversioner), and he cannot be found or his identity cannot be ascertained, or there are more than one, but none of them can be found or their identities cannot be ascertained, the situation is more problematic. Section 26 provides that in those circumstances, the court can make a vesting order in favour of the qualifying tenants.

Sections 26 and 27 set out the nature of such an order and the requirements and procedure for obtaining one. These provisions are very similar to those in sections 50 and 51 relating to new lease claims, and regard should be had to that part of chapter 1, which discusses those provisions. However, in relation to a collective enfranchisement claim, there is, what ought to be, a quicker and cheaper way of acquiring the freehold where the landlord is missing without the need to rely on sections 26 and 27. The *Landlord and Tenant Act* 1987 provides for tenants to be able to acquire the freehold of the premises containing their flats where the landlord is in breach of any covenant relating to the repair, maintenance, insurance or management of the premises. Nearly all leases will contain such covenants, and if the landlord is missing, he is almost certain to be in breach of them, if only the covenant to insure the premises.

Under sections 26 and 27, the tenants will need to make an application to the County Court in the first instance, then have the LVT determine the terms of the vesting order before returning to the County Court to have a conveyance executed. Under the 1987 Act, the tenants could acquire the freehold following one application to the County Court for an order under section 33 of that Act. The price payable for the freehold under that section is such amount as a surveyor, selected by the President of the Lands Tribunal, certifies. In other words, there is no need to make an application to the LVT. Once the tenants pay that amount and any outstanding ground rent, etc. into court, then an order made under section 33 provides that the freehold is to vest in the tenants' nominee, without the need for any conveyance to be executed.

If any of the tenants' leases have terms of less than 80 years unexpired, then not only is the procedure under the 1987 Act likely to be cheaper, but they are likely to pay less for the freehold than they would under section 27. This is because the surveyor appointed is to determine the amount payable, on the assumption that none of the tenants are buying or seeking to buy the freehold. In other words, the amount determined will not include any marriage value.

Starting the claim

A claim to exercise the right to collectively enfranchise starts with the service of an initial notice, pursuant to section 13. The date the notice is given is known as the 'relevant date' and the qualification criteria must be met on that date (s.1(8)). Unless

Leasehold enfranchisement explained

the notice is delivered by hand, the date of the notice is unlikely to be the date the notice is 'given'.

Restrictions on serving an effective initial notice

A tenant's ability to serve an effective initial notice is restricted in the following circumstances:

- no notice may be given specifying the whole or part of any premises, which have been specified in a previous notice, so long as the earlier notice continues in force. (s.13(8));
- where any premises have been specified in a notice and that notice is withdrawn, deemed to have been withdrawn, or a landlord has successfully defeated the tenant's claim to a new lease on the ground that he intends to redevelop (i.e. he has obtained an order under section 23(1)), then no further notice can be given, which specifies the whole or part of those premises within the period of 12 months beginning with the date of withdrawal, deemed withdrawal or the order under section 23(1) becoming final (s.13(9));
- where a notice to treat has been served or a contract entered into for the purpose of compulsorily acquiring the whole or part of the specified premises (s.30(1)); and
- where the whole or part of the specified premises has been designated for inheritance tax purposes or is subject to an application for designation (s.31).

Requirements of an initial notice

There are no prescribed forms under the Act. However, legal stationers produce forms for notices and it is recommended that such a form is used. In any event, an initial notice must:

- be given to the reversioner (s.13(2)(a));
- be given by a number of qualifying tenants of flats, which is not less than half the total number of flats (s.13(2)(b)), and the tenants who give the notice are, at the time the notice is given, the 'participating tenants' (s.14(1)(a));

Example

A block contains ten flats, seven of which are let to qualifying tenants. At least five of those qualifying tenants must participate and serve the notice; five being half the total number of flats in the block.

- specify and be accompanied by a plan showing:
  - the premises of which the freehold is proposed to be acquired by virtue of section 1(1), i.e. the premises containing the flats (the 'specified premises') (s.13(3)(a)(i));
  - any property of which the freehold is proposed to be acquired by virtue of section 1(2)(a), i.e. appurtenant property and property used in common with others (s.13(3)(a)(ii)); and
  - any property over which it is proposed that rights (specified in the notice) should be granted in connection with the acquisition of the freehold of the specified premises or of any appurtenant property (s.13(3)(a)(iii));
- contain a statement of the grounds on which it is claimed that the specified premises are, on the relevant date, qualifying premises (s.13(3)(b)); and
- specify:
  - any leasehold interest proposed to be acquired (s.13(3)(c)(i)); and
  - any flats or other units contained in the specified premises which it is considered may be subject to a mandatory leaseback under Part II of Schedule 9, i.e. public sector and housing association tenancies, which are not long leases (s.13(3)(c)(ii)); and
- specify the proposed purchase price for each of the following, namely:
  - the freehold interest in the specified premises, or if the whole of the freehold is not owned by the same person, each of the freehold interests (s.13(3)(d)(i));
  - the freehold interest in any property which it is proposed should be acquired by virtue of section 1(2)(a), i.e. appurtenant property and property used in common with others (s.13(3)(d)(ii)); and
  - any leasehold interest (s.13(3)(d)(iii));
- state the full names of all the qualifying tenants of flats contained in the specified premises (not just those who are participating in the claim), and the addresses of their flats, and contain in relation to each of those tenants such particulars of his lease as are sufficient to identify it, including the date on which the lease was entered into, the term for which it was granted and the date of the commencement of the term (s.13(3)(e));
- state the full name or names of the person or persons appointed as the nominee purchaser for the purposes of section 15, and an address in England and Wales at which notices may be given to that person or those persons (s.13(3)(f));

- specify the date by which the reversioner must respond to the notice by giving a counter-notice under section 21 (s.13(3)(g)), which must be a date not less than two months after the initial notice is given (s.13(5));
- state whether copies of the initial notice are being given to anyone other than the recipient and, if so, to whom (Sch. 3, paras. 12(2) and 12A(2)); and
- be signed by each of the tenants by whom it is given (s.99(5)(a)).

Regard should be had to chapter 1 as to the signature of notices personally. However, it must be borne in mind that there are likely to be far more signatures required on an initial notice than are required on a tenant's notice claiming a new lease. Obtaining these signatures can be difficult and attaching signature sheets to the notice, which have been signed by the tenants prior to the notice being prepared, is not sufficient. The tenants must know what it is they are proposing in the notice and there must be a notice in existence for it to be signed: *Cascades and Quayside Ltd v Cascades Freehold Ltd* [2008] L&TR 23.

Example

Leasehold Reform, Housing and Urban Development Act 1993 ('the Act') Section 13

Initial notice by tenant

To: [*The reversioner's name and address*]
From: [*The full names and addresses of the qualifying tenants giving the notice*]

1. **The specified premises**
   The premises of which the freehold is proposed to be acquired by virtue of section 1(1) of the Act are shown edged red on the accompanying plan and known as: [*A brief description of the specified premises*] ('the specified premises').

2. **Additional freeholds**
   The property of which the freehold is proposed to be acquired by virtue of section 1(2)(a) of the Act are shown edged green on the accompanying plan and known as: [*A brief description*].

3. **Rights to be acquired**
   The rights which it is proposed should be granted under section 13(3)(a)(iii) of the Act are: [*A description of the rights*] over the property edged blue on the accompanying plan.

4. **Grounds of claim**
   The grounds upon which it is claimed that the specified premises are premises to which Part I Chapter I of the Act applies are:
   (a) they consist of a self-contained building or part of a building;
   (b) they contain at least two flats held by qualifying tenants; and
   (c) the total number of flats held by qualifying tenants is at least two-thirds of the total number of flats in the premises.

5. **Other leaseholds**
   The leasehold interest(s) proposed to be acquired under or by virtue of section 2(1)(a) or (b) of the Act [is][are]: [*the leasehold interest(s)*]

6. **Mandatory leaseback**
   The flats or other units contained in the specified premises in relation to which it is considered that requirements in Part II of Schedule 9 apply are: [*the flats or other units*].

7. **Price**
   The proposed purchase price is:
   1) £[*amount*] for the freehold interest in the specified premises;
   2) £[*amount*] for the property within paragraph 2 of this notice; and
   3) for the leasehold interest(s) within paragraph 6 of this notice: [*amounts for each one*].

8. **Qualifying tenants**
   The full names of all the qualifying tenants of flats in the specified premises, with the addresses of their flats and the particulars required by the Act, are set out on the accompanying tenant information sheet.

9. **Nominee purchaser**
   The full name(s) of the person(s) appointed to act as the nominee purchaser for the purposes of section 15 of the Act [is][are]: [*Names and addresses of all persons constituting the nominee purchaser*].

10. **Address for notices**
    The address in England and Wales at which notices may be given to the nominee purchaser under Part I Chapter I of the Act is: [*address in England and Wales at which notices may be given to the nominee purchaser*].

11. **Response date**
    The date by which you must respond to this notice by giving a counter-notice under section 21 is: [*a date at least two months after the notice is given*].

12. **Copies of the notice**
    Copies of this notice are being given to [*name of anyone other than the recipient to whom copies are being given*] in accordance with Schedule 3, paragraph [12][12A].

Date:

Signed: [*Each of the tenants' personal signatures and their names*]

The initial notice will not be invalid because of any inaccuracy in any of the 'particulars' required by section 13(3). Neither will it be invalid because of any misdescription of any of the property to which the claim extends (Sch. 3, para. 15(1)). Where the initial notice specifies any property which is not liable to be acquired or fails to specify any property which is liable to be acquired, the notice may be amended with the leave of the court (Sch. 3, para. 15(2)).

The initial notice is also not invalidated if any of the tenants by whom the notice is given are not qualifying tenants or are prohibited from participating in giving a notice, provided that the notice was given by a sufficient number of qualifying tenants who were not so prohibited (Sch. 3, para 16).

> **Example**
>
> A block contains ten flats, seven of which are let to qualifying tenants. Six tenants give an initial notice.
>
> **Situation one**: one of the participating tenants is not a qualifying tenant.
>
> The notice must be given by at least five qualifying tenants, five being half the total number of flats in the block. Five of the six tenants who have given the notice are qualifying tenants and therefore the notice is valid.
>
> **Situation two**: not only is one of the participating tenants not a qualifying tenant, one of them, who is a qualifying tenant, has had a claim for possession made against him on the ground that his lease is forfeit for non-payment of service charges, and that claim has yet to be determined.
>
> The tenant who is the subject of the possession claim is unable to participate in giving the notice. Consequently, only four of the participating tenants are qualifying tenants who are not prohibited from participating in giving a notice. As the notice must be given by at least five qualifying tenants, the notice is invalid.

Any other mistakes in the initial notice will not invalidate it if a reasonable recipient would nevertheless understand the notice (*Mannai Investment Co Ltd v Eagle Star Assurance Co. Ltd* [1997] AC. 749). For example, an obvious typographical error would not cause a problem. As to the consequences of serving an invalid notice, see the section on 'Receipt of an initial notice'.

How to serve the initial notice

The notice may be given to a landlord at an address provided pursuant to sections 47 or 48 of the *Landlord and Tenant Act*

1987 (s.99(3)), i.e. an address in England and Wales at which notices (including notices in proceedings) may be served on him by the tenant.

'Given' is not defined in the Act and therefore bears its ordinary and natural meaning. Further, unlike, for example, in the Civil Procedure Rules, which do not apply to a notice served under the Act, there is no deeming provision in the Act. In other words, the Act does not provide that if a notice is posted on a particular day it is deemed to have been given two days later, for example. However, by virtue of section 99(1)(b), the notice may be sent by post and pursuant to section 7 of the *Interpretation Act* 1978, service is deemed to be effected by properly addressing, pre-paying and posting a letter containing the notice, and unless the contrary is proved, to have been effected at the time at which the letter would be delivered in the ordinary course of post. Consequently, if the notice is posted and the reversioner does not subsequently prove that he did not receive it, then the notice is 'given' when it would be delivered in the ordinary course of post. Otherwise, when the notice is given will be a question of fact.

The lack of more detailed provisions as to service in the Act can cause significant problems. If a landlord does not in fact receive a notice, then proceedings may have reached an advanced stage before it is realised that the notice has not been validly served and the proceedings have to be abandoned (with the associated waste of costs). Consequently, and where possible, it is advisable to make contact with the landlord, his legal advisors or managing agents, prior to serving the notice and to ascertain from them, preferably in writing, where and how they will accept service of the notice.

Giving copies of the initial notice

Copies of the initial notice must be given to every other person known or believed to be a relevant landlord (Sch. 3, paras. 12(1) and 12A(1)). However, each recipient of an initial notice, or a copy of an initial notice, must give a copy to anyone they know or believe to be a relevant landlord, who is not stated in the notice or known by the recipient to have received a copy (Sch. 3, para. 13). The consequences of failing to comply with paragraphs 12 or 13 are set out in paragraph 14 of the Schedule.

Where it is not possible to give a copy of the notice to a relevant landlord because that person cannot be found, or his identity cannot be ascertained, then the court may make an order dispensing with the need to give a copy of the notice to that person (ss.26(2) and (3A)).

Registering the initial notice

The initial notice ought to be registered at the Land Registry once served; otherwise, it will be void against a purchaser of the freehold if the current freeholder sells. For guidance as to how to register the notice, see paragraph 6.4.1 of the Land Registry Practice Guide 27 available at www.landregistry.gov.uk

Effect of the initial notice

There are various effects of an initial notice, which are as follows:

- once an initial notice is given, no notice may be given specifying the whole or part of any premises, which have been specified in that notice so long as it continues in force (s.13(8));
- once the initial notice has been given, the nominee purchaser, any relevant landlord and any person authorised to act on their behalf, have rights of access to any part of any property specified in the notice (s.17);
- once the initial notice is registered, freeholders are prevented from disposing of their interests and they and any other relevant landlords are prevented from granting new leases (s.19(1)) and if a binding contract has already been entered into relating to a disposal, the operation of that contract is suspended whilst the initial notice continues in force (s.19(4));
- service of an initial notice restricts the landlord's and the tenant's ability to terminate the tenant's lease (see Sch. 3, paras. 5 to 7);
- the nominee purchaser becomes liable for the landlords' costs (s.33(1)), and this is likely to be so whether or not the notice is valid; and
- the operation of any tenant's notice served under section 42 is suspended (s.54(2)).

The costs in respect of which the nominee purchaser is liable are the reasonable costs that are incurred by the reversioner or any other relevant landlord in pursuance of the initial notice and are of and incidental to:

- any investigation reasonably undertaken:
  - as to whether the nominee purchaser is entitled to acquire the interests it is seeking to acquire, or
  - of any other question arising out of the initial notice;
- deducing, evidencing and verifying the title to any of those interests;
- making out and furnishing such abstracts and copies as the nominee purchaser may require;
- any valuation of those interests; and
- any conveyance of those interests.

A tenant is not liable under section 33 for any costs, which a party to any proceedings under the Act before a leasehold valuation tribunal incurs, in connection with those proceedings (s.33(5)). However, if a party behaves frivolously, vexatiously, abusively, disruptively or otherwise unreasonably in connection with the proceedings, then that party can be ordered to pay up to £500 in respect of the other side's costs (Sch. 12, para. 10(2) of the *Commonhold and Leasehold Reform Act* 2002).

'Reasonable' costs are such costs which the reversioner or other relevant landlord would incur if he were paying the costs himself, i.e. if the reversioner or relevant landlord increases the costs he incurs because the nominee purchaser is paying, such increase is not recoverable (s.33(2)).

The nominee purchaser

The nominee purchaser conducts all proceedings arising out of the initial notice (s.15(1)). Where there are a large number of participating tenants, it will often be easiest to form a company to act as the nominee purchaser. The Act contains provisions relating to 'Right to Enfranchise' (RTE) companies, which were covered in the introductory chapter. However, these provisions are not in force and may be repealed.

Where there are a small number of tenants, the tenants themselves, or one or more of them, may decide to act as nominee purchaser. Sections 15 and 16 of the Act deal with the situation where the nominee purchaser ceases to act, either because his appointment is terminated by the tenants or because he resigns or dies. Where a company acts as nominee purchaser, this is unlikely to occur, unless, for example, those behind the company allow it to be struck off the register. Otherwise, if a tenant dies, for example, this may necessitate the appointment of a new director, but it will not prevent the nominee purchaser company from acting. Where an individual or individuals are acting as nominee purchaser, then sections 15 and 16 are likely to be of greater relevance.

The nominee purchaser's appointment may be terminated by the participating tenants by giving notice to that effect to the nominee purchaser and the reversioner (ss.15(3) and (4)). A replacement must be found for that nominee purchaser unless there are two or more persons constituting the nominee purchaser, in which case the appointment of any (but not all of them), may be terminated and the person or persons remaining will be the nominee purchaser (s.15(8)). Copies of the notice must be given to any such remaining persons and to every relevant landlord who was given a copy of the initial notice (s.15(11)).

Any notice served under section 15(3) must:
- state that the nominee purchaser's appointment is to terminate on the date on which the notice is given (s.15(3));
- specify who the nominee purchaser will be from the date of giving the notice and an address in England and Wales at which notices may be given to that nominee purchaser (s.15(5)(a)); or
- state that the following information will be provided within 28 days:
  - the name of the nominee purchaser;
  - the date of appointment of that nominee purchaser; and
  - an address in England and Wales at which notices may be given to that nominee purchaser (s.15(5)(b)).

If the information is not provided within 28 days, then the initial notice will be deemed withdrawn at the end of those 28 days (s.15(10)).

The appointment of the nominee purchaser may also be terminated by the nominee purchaser himself. To terminate his appointment, the nominee purchaser must give a notice stating that he is resigning with effect from 21 days after the date of the notice to each of the participating tenants and the reversioner (ss.16(1) and (2)). Where the participating tenants have received such a notice or the person, or a person, constituting the nominee purchaser dies, they must by notice inform the reversioner of the resignation or death within 56 days. Any such notice must state:

- who will be the nominee purchaser;
- when that person will be appointed; and

Flats: collective enfranchisement

- an address in England and Wales at which notices may be given to that nominee purchaser (ss.16(3) and (5)).

If no notice is given within 56 days, then the initial notice will be deemed withdrawn at the end of those 56 days (s.16(8)).

Where two or more persons constitute the nominee purchaser and any (but not all of them), resign or die, the person or persons remaining will be the nominee purchaser (ss.15(8) and 16(4) and (6)). Copies of the notice given to the reversioner must be given to any such remaining persons and to every relevant landlord who was given a copy of the initial notice (s.16(9)).

The participating tenants

There is no statutory right to participate in a claim to collectively enfranchise and only the following qualifying tenants will be participating tenants for the purposes of a claim. They will remain participating tenants for so long as they remain qualifying tenants of flats within the specified premises (or in the case of personal representatives, for as long as the tenant's lease remains vested in them).

- Those by whom the initial notice is given (s.14(1)).
- From the date of assignment, the assignee of a lease of a participating tenant who has notified the nominee purchaser within 14 days of the assignment, of the assignment, and that he is electing to participate in the claim (s.14(2)).
- A qualifying tenant who, following service of the initial notice, elects to participate in the claim, with the agreement of the other participating tenants, from the date of that agreement (s.14(3)). Any tenant who was prohibited from participating in the service of the initial notice, cannot subsequently elect to become a participating tenant, and a tenant cannot elect to participate whilst forfeiture proceedings are pending without the leave of the court (Sch. 3, para. 8).
- The personal representatives of a participating tenant from the date of the tenant's death, unless within 56 days of the death, they notify the nominee purchaser that they are electing to withdraw from the claim (s.14(5)).

Where the identity of the participating tenants changes, then within 28 days of being notified of that change, the nominee purchaser must give a notice under section 14(8) to the reversioner and give a copy of that notice to every other relevant landlord (s.14(7)). Where applicable, the notice must state:

- the flat with respect to which the notice is given (s.14(9));
- the date of any assignment and the name and address of the assignee (s.14(8)(a)(i));
- whether the assignee has or has not become a participating tenant (s.14(8)(a)(ii)));
- whether he has become a participating tenant in place of his assignor (s.14(8)(a)(iii)) (it may be that the assignor owns another flat in the specified premises and therefore continues to be a qualifying and participating tenant);
- the name and address of any person who has elected to, and has become, a participating tenant (s.14(8)(b));
- the date of death of any deceased tenant (s.14(8)(c)(i));
- the names and addresses of the personal representatives of any deceased tenant (s.14(8)(c)(ii)); and
- whether the personal representatives are or are not to be regarded as a participating tenant (s.14(8)(c)(iii)).

Where the notice states that any person is to be regarded as a participating tenant, the notice must be signed by each of those persons (s.14(9)).

Withdrawing the initial notice

At any time before a binding contract is entered into in pursuance of the initial notice, the participating tenants may withdraw the notice, by giving 'a notice of withdrawal' under section 28(1). A notice of withdrawal must be given to:

- the nominee purchaser;
- the reversioner; and
- every other relevant landlord who is either acting independently, or requires sums due to him to be paid directly to him, as opposed to the reversioner (s.28(2)).

As set out above, if an initial notice is withdrawn, no further notice can be given, which specifies the whole or part of the premises specified in the original notice within the period of 12 months beginning with the date of withdrawal (s.13(9)). Further, if the notice is withdrawn, then both the participating tenants and any former participating tenants (other than those who have assigned their lease to a participating tenant (s.28(5))), are liable to the reversioner and every other relevant landlord in respect of any costs which would be recoverable in accordance with section 33 (s.28(4)).

Flats: collective enfranchisement

Whilst section 33 provides that the nominee purchaser is liable for the costs, section 28 provides that, if the initial notice is withdrawn, the nominee purchaser is not liable; the liability is a liability of the tenants. Further, this liability is a joint and several liability of all persons concerned (s.28(6)). Where a claim proceeds, the nominee purchaser will acquire a substantial asset and if the costs under section 33 are not paid prior to completion, the reversioner and other relevant landlords have a vendor's lien over that asset, which provides security for the payment of their costs (s.32(2)). However, where the claim is withdrawn, the nominee purchaser is likely to have no assets and there is no such security. Hence it is the tenants behind the claim who become liable for the costs incurred, thereby making it more likely that the reversioner and other relevant landlords will be able to recover those costs. This is also the case if the initial notice is deemed withdrawn (s.29(6)).

Receipt of an initial notice

In the first instance, anyone receiving an initial notice must:

- give a copy to anyone they know or believe to be a relevant landlord if that person is not stated in the notice or known by the recipient to have received a copy (Sch. 3, para. 13(1)); and
- if they do so, add to the notice the names of anyone they are giving copies of the notice to, or who are known to them to have received a copy, and notify the qualifying tenants of the names they have added (Sch. 3, para. 13(3)).

As soon as possible after having received the initial notice, any landlord must give a notice to any tenant who has served a tenant's notice under section 42, informing him that that notice has been suspended. In addition, the notice must inform the tenant of the date on which the initial notice was given and the name and address of the nominee purchaser (s.54(3)).

Relevant landlords

By virtue of section 9(3), the reversioner conducts all proceedings arising out of an initial notice on behalf of all the relevant landlords. Consequently, other than distributing copies of the notice as set out above, any other relevant landlord cannot take any independent steps in those proceedings prior to a counter-notice being served. It is the duty of any other relevant landlord, however, to give the reversioner all such information and assistance as he may reasonably require. If the relevant landlord fails to provide such information and assistance, he will be liable to indemnify the reversioner in respect of any loss so caused (Sch. 1, para. 8(1)). Further, other relevant landlords are required to contribute to the reversioner's costs so far as they are not recoverable or recovered from the nominee purchaser or any other person (Sch. 1, para. 8(2)).

As to the conduct of proceedings by the reversioner and the circumstances in which any other relevant landlord may act independently following service of a counter-notice, see below. Of course, any other relevant landlord may, in any event, want to investigate for himself whether his interest is liable to be acquired and/or obtain a valuation of his interest and, therefore, regard should be had to the following.

The reversioner

In the first instance the landlord will want to ascertain whether the notice is valid. In this regard, reference should be made to the paragraph above dealing with the contents of an initial notice and the validity thereof.

Even if the initial notice is believed to be invalid, it is often advisable to serve a counter-notice, but to serve such a notice without prejudice to the contention that the initial notice is invalid. This avoids a situation in which the initial notice is, in fact, found to be valid and terms of acquisition are then those stated in the initial notice, by virtue of the landlord having failed to serve a counter-notice, see the discussion of section 25(1) which follows.

The Act is silent as to the procedure to be followed where a tenant serves an invalid notice, i.e. a notice which does not comply with the requirements of section 13(3), as opposed to a notice served by tenants who are not entitled to exercise the right to collectively enfranchise. However, by virtue of section 90(2) the County Court has jurisdiction to determine the validity of a notice. Consequently, if the tenants refuse to accept the invalidity of their notice, an application ought to be made to the County Court for a declaration that the notice is invalid. However, where a tenant has served an invalid notice, he is not precluded from serving a further notice and does not have to wait 12 months before doing so (see *Sinclair Gardens Investments (Kensington) Ltd v Poets Chase Freehold Co Ltd*

[2008] 1 WLR 768). Consequently, the landlord may see little point in incurring the costs of a County Court application and may prefer to proceed as if the notice were valid.

If the notice is, on its face, valid, the next step is to check whether there is anything which would preclude service of an effective initial notice. In this regard, reference should be had to the 'Restrictions on serving an effective tenant's notice'.

Having ascertained that the notice is, on its face, valid and that the tenants are not precluded from serving it, it is necessary to check whether the interests which the tenants are seeking to acquire are in fact liable to be acquired (see 'What can be acquired?' above), and whether the premises, the tenants, and their leases, meet the qualification criteria set out above. In order to do this, the reversioner may require the nominee purchaser to deduce the title of any of the tenants by whom the initial notice was given within 21 days (ss.20(1) and (2)). If, in respect of any tenant, the nominee purchaser does not comply with the requirement and the initial notice would not have been valid, but for the inclusion of that tenant, then the initial notice will be deemed to have been withdrawn at the end of those 21 days (s.20(3)).

Having concluded that the tenants are entitled to acquire some, if not all, of the interests specified in the initial notice, a landlord will be keen to ascertain the price payable for his interest. To enable him to do this, whether he is the reversioner or another relevant landlord, he, and any person authorised to act on his behalf, has a right of access for the purposes of obtaining a valuation pursuant to section 17. The right is exercisable at any reasonable time and on giving not less than ten days' notice to the occupier of (or the person entitled to occupy), any premises to which access is sought. Further, the landlord's reasonable costs of, and incidental to, any such valuation are recoverable from the nominee purchaser by virtue of section 33(1)(d).

Reversioner's counter-notice

Any counter-notice is given under section 21 and must be given by the date specified in the initial notice. The counter-notice must:

- be given by the reversioner;
- comply with one of the three following requirements (s.21(2));

- - state that the reversioner admits that the participating tenants were, on the relevant date, entitled to exercise the right to collective enfranchisement in relation to the specified premises;
  - state that for such reasons as are specified in the counter-notice, the landlord does not admit that the participating tenants were so entitled; or
  - comply with either of the above two requirements but state that an application for an order under section 23(1) is to be made on the grounds that such landlord as is specified in the counter-notice, intends to redevelop the whole or a substantial part of the specified premises. For these purposes, the landlord wishing to make the application can be the reversioner or any other relevant landlord (Sch. 1, para. 9).
- If the counter-notice admits the claim:
  - state which (if any) of the proposals contained in the tenant's notice are accepted and which (if any) are not, and specify
    - in relation to each proposal, which is not accepted, the reversioner's counter-proposal (s.21(3)(a)(i)); and
    - any additional leaseback proposals by the reversioner (s.21(3)(a)(ii));
  - if, in a case where the nominee purchaser is seeking to acquire property which any tenant has a right to use in common with others, the freeholder of that property proposes to grant rights over that or other property, or to transfer other property, rather than transfer the specified property, specify
    - the nature of those rights and the property over which it is proposed to grant them; or
    - the other property, which the freeholder proposes to transfer (s.21(3)(b));
  - state which interests the nominee purchaser is to be required to acquire (s.21(3)(c));
  - state which rights, if any, any relevant landlord desires to retain (s.21(3)(d));
  - include a description of any provisions which the reversioner or any relevant landlord considers should be included in any conveyance to the nominee purchaser (s.21(3)(e));
- specify an address in England and Wales at which notices may be given to the landlord (s.21(6)); and
- contain a statement as to whether or not the specified premises are within the area of an estate management scheme under section 70 (The Leasehold Reform (Collective

Flats: collective enfranchisement

Enfranchisement) (Counter-notices) (England) Regulations 2002 and The Leasehold Reform (Collective Enfranchisement) (Counter-notices) (Wales) Regulations 2003).

Example

Leasehold Reform, Housing and Urban Development Act 1993
Section 21(2)(a)

Counter-notice admitting claim

Re: [*The specified premises*] ('the specified premises')

To: [*The name of the nominee purchaser*] (Company Registration Number [*number*]) ('the nominee purchaser') of [*The address of the nominee purchaser*]

And its solicitors, [*The name of the nominee purchaser's solicitors*]

From: [*The name of the reversioner*] ('the reversioner') of [*The address of the reversioner*]

TAKE NOTICE THAT:
1. The reversioner admits that the participating tenants were, on the relevant date, entitled to exercise the right to collective enfranchisement in relation to the specified premises.
2. The following proposals contained in the initial notice are accepted by the reversioner:
   (a) that the premises of which the freehold is proposed to be acquired by virtue of section 1(1) of the 1993 Act are the specified premises as shown edged red on the plan which accompanied the initial notice and known as [*address of specified premises*];
   (b) that there is no property of which the freehold is to be acquired under section 1(2)(a) of the 1993 Act;
   (c) that there is no property over which rights should be granted as mentioned in section 13(3)(a)(iii) of the 1993 Act;
   (d) that there are no leasehold interests to be acquired under section 2(1)(a) or (b) of the 1993 Act.
3. The following proposals contained in the initial notice are not accepted by the reversioner:
   (a) the proposed purchase price of £ [*amount*] for the freehold interest in the specified premises;
4. In relation to those proposals which are not accepted, the reversioner's counter-proposals are as follows:
   (a) that the purchase price for the freehold of the specified premises, subject to the leases-back referred to in paragraph 5 below, should be £ [*amount*]
5. The following are the reversioner's additional leaseback proposals:
   (a) Leases-back of [*proper description of each of the units*];
   (b) The terms of each leaseback to be:
      (i) the permitted user shall be either residential use or such other use as is the permitted use under planning control from time to time;

229

(ii) any covenant to comply with planning control shall be subject to a proviso that residential use shall not constitute a breach of that or any other covenant;
(iii) the terms set out in Schedule 9 paragraph 17 to the 1993 Act shall not be included;
(iv) save as aforesaid, the terms of the leases-back shall be in accordance with Part IV of Schedule 9 to the 1993 Act;
(v) so far as not inconsistent with the foregoing, the other terms of the leases-back shall be on the same terms as the existing long residential leases of flats in the specified premises with modifications appropriate for the situation of the units concerned.

6. The reversioner does not require the nominee purchaser to acquire any interests in accordance with section 21(4) of the 1993 Act.
7. The reversioner does not desire to retain any rights over the property which is included in the proposed acquisition by the nominee purchaser.
8. The reversioner considers that the conveyance to the nominee purchaser should contain an indemnity, indemnifying the reversioner against breaches by the nominee purchaser of the landlord's covenants under the leases in the specified premises.
9. The specified premises are not within the area of a scheme approved as an estate management scheme under section 70 of the 1993 Act.
10. The address in England and Wales at which notices may be given to the reversioner under Chapter I of Part I of the 1993 Act is [address in England and Wales at which notices may be given to the reversioner].

DATED [date]

Signed............................

[Name of person signing]

as solicitors and agents for and on behalf of [name of the reversioner]

Example

Leasehold Reform, Housing and Urban Development Act 1993 ('the Act') Section 21(2)(b)

Counter-notice not admitting claim

Re: [The specified premises] ('the specified premises')

To: [The name of the nominee purchaser] (Company Registration Number [number])

And its solicitors, [The name of the nominee purchaser's solicitors]

1. TAKE NOTICE that [name of the reversioner] does not admit that the participating tenants were on the relevant date entitled to exercise the right to collective enfranchisement in relation to the specified premises.

> 2. The reasons for not admitting the claim are as follows:
>   The specified premises do not qualify for collective enfranchisement:
>   (a) The specified premises are not a 'self-contained building' within the meaning of s.3(1)(a) of the Act as they are not structurally detached; and
>   (b) The specified premises are not a 'self-contained part of a building' within the meaning of s.3(1)(a) of the Act as they cannot be redeveloped independently of the remainder of the building.
> 3. The specified premises are not within the area of a scheme approved as an estate management scheme under section 70 of the Act.
> 4. The address in England and Wales at which notices may be given to the reversioner under Chapter I of Part I of the 1993 Act is [*address in England and Wales at which notices may be given to the reversioner*].
>
> Date:
>
> Signed:
> [*Solicitor's name and address*]
> Solicitors for [*reversioner's name*]

At the same time as the counter-notice is given or as soon as possible thereafter, the reversioner must give to the nominee purchaser copies of all tenant's notices (or copies thereof) received under section 42, either by him or any other relevant landlord, and copies of all counter-notices served pursuant to section 45 (Sch. 4, para. 1).

Checklist for landlords

In summary, upon receipt of an initial notice, a landlord ought to check the following.

- Is there anyone he knows or believes to be a relevant landlord and who is not stated in the notice or known by him to have received a copy?
- Is the notice, on its face, a valid notice? (See 'Requirements of an initial notice'.)
- Are there any restrictions on serving an initial notice? (See 'Restrictions on serving an effective initial notice'.)
- Do the participating tenants have the right to acquire the interests specified in the initial notice? (See 'What can be acquired?')

Conduct of proceedings by the reversioner

Save for any application under section 23(1), the reversioner conducts all proceedings arising out of an initial notice on behalf of all the relevant landlords; in particular:

- any notice given by or to the reversioner under Chapter II or section 74(3) following the giving of the initial notice, shall be given or received by him on behalf of all the relevant landlords (Sch. 1, para. 6(1)(a));
- the reversioner may, on behalf and in the name of, all or any of the relevant landlords:
  - deduce, evidence or verify the title to any property;
  - negotiate and agree with the nominee purchaser the terms of acquisition;
  - execute any conveyance for the purpose of transferring any interest to the nominee purchaser;
  - receive the price payable for the acquisition of any interest (for the circumstances in which that amount is not to be received by the reversioner see Sch. 1, para. 7(4));
  - take or defend any legal proceedings under Chapter I in respect of matters arising out of the initial notice (Sch. 1, para 6(1)(b)); and
- any determination of the court or LVT under Chapter I in proceedings between the reversioner and the nominee purchaser is binding on the other relevant landlords. However, in the event of a dispute, the reversioner may apply to the court for directions as to the manner in which the reversioner should act in the dispute (of Sch. 1, para. 6(2)).

If any of the other relevant landlords cannot be found, or their identity cannot be ascertained, the reversioner must apply to the court for directions as to how to proceed (Sch. 1, para. 6(3)). If the reversioner acts in good faith and with reasonable care and diligence, then he shall not be liable to any of the relevant landlords for any loss and damage caused by any act or omission of his (Sch. 11, para. 6(4)).

Relevant landlords acting independently

Following service of the counter-notice and by giving notice to both the reversioner and the nominee purchaser, any relevant landlord may:

- deal directly with the nominee purchaser in connection with:
  - deducing, evidencing or verifying the title to any property;

Flats: collective enfranchisement

- ○ negotiating and agreeing with the nominee purchaser the terms of acquisition; and
- ○ executing any conveyance for the purpose of transferring any interest to the nominee purchaser (Sch. 1, para. 7(1)(a));
- be separately represented in any legal proceedings in which his title to his property comes into question or in any legal proceedings relating to the terms of acquisition, so far as relating to the acquisition of any interest of his (Sch. 1, para 7(1)(b)); and
- require that any such amount shall be paid by the nominee purchaser to him or to a person authorised by him to receive it, instead of the reversioner (Sch. 1, para. 7(4)).

In any event, any relevant landlord may make an application under section 23(1) on the grounds that he intends to redevelop any premises in which the flat is contained (Sch. 1, para. 9(1)).

Preparing the conveyance

Once the counter-notice is served, there is usually a period of negotiation between the reversioner and the nominee purchaser as to the terms of the conveyance and the premium to be paid. Once these terms of acquisition have been agreed, or if it has not been possible to agree them, a leasehold valuation tribunal (LVT) has determined them, the conveyance can then be prepared. The timetable for preparing the conveyance is set out in paragraph 6 of Schedule 1 to the Leasehold Reform (Collective Enfranchisement and Lease Renewal) Regulations 1993 and is as follows:

- the reversioner must prepare the draft contract and give it to the nominee purchaser within 21 days of the terms of acquisition being agreed or determined by an LVT;
- the nominee purchaser must give the reversioner a statement of any proposals for amending the draft contract within 14 days of being given the draft contract, and if no statement is given by the nominee purchaser within 14 days, he is deemed to have approved the draft;
- the reversioner must give the nominee purchaser an answer, giving any objections to or comments on the proposals in the statement, within 14 days of being given the statement and if no answer is given within those 14 days, the reversioner is deemed to have approved the nominee purchaser's amendments to the draft lease.

Applications to the court or LVT

The procedures to be followed where the landlord is missing or the tenant serves an invalid notice, are set out above. What this section aims to deal with is the applications which follow from service of a valid notice.

It is unlikely that not only will the participating tenants' entitlement to exercise the right to collective enfranchisement be admitted, but that all the proposals contained in the initial notice will be accepted. It may be that the parties can come to a negotiated agreement. However, it is often the case that one or more applications will need to be made to the court or the LVT before the claim is finally determined.

Whilst the cost of proceedings before the court may be recoverable if an application succeeds, costs incurred in relation to any proceedings before the LVT are not recoverable, unless a party behaves frivolously, vexatiously, abusively, disruptively or otherwise unreasonably in connection with the proceedings, in which case costs are limited to £500 (Sch. 12, para. 10(2) of the *Commonhold and Leasehold Reform Act* 2002). Costs incurred in relation to proceedings before the LVT are not recoverable from a tenant under section 33 (s.33(5)).

There are numerous applications which can be made and careful attention must be paid to the deadlines for making each application. In most cases, the Act provides that if the deadline is missed, the initial notice is deemed withdrawn. If the initial notice is deemed to have been withdrawn, then no further notice can be given which specifies the whole or part of the premises specified in the previous notice, within the period of 12 months beginning with the date of the deemed withdrawal (s.13(9)).

The reversioner fails to serve a counter-notice

Where the reversioner has been properly served, but fails to serve a counter-notice, an application can be made to the court under section 25(1) for an order determining the terms on which the tenant is to acquire a new lease. Whilst section 25(1) states that:

> '...the court may, on the application of the nominee purchaser, make an order determining the terms on which he is to acquire, in accordance with the proposals contained in the initial notice, such interests and rights as are specified in it under section 13(3)' (emphasis added).

the court has no discretion and must make an order on the terms proposed in the initial notice: see *Willingdale v Globalrange Ltd* [2000] 2 EGLR 55. However, where any of the flats in the specified premises would be subject to a mandatory leaseback (see Part II of Schedule 9), the terms determined by the court must include terms which provide for the leasing back of those flats in accordance with section 36 and Schedule 9 (s.25(2)).

The requirements to be satisfied prior to an order being made are as follows:
- on the relevant date, the participating tenants were entitled to exercise the right to collective enfranchisement in relation to the specified premises (s.25(3)(a));
- if applicable, the requirements of Part II of Schedule 3 have been complied with as respects the giving of copies of the initial notice (s.25(3)(b)); and
- the application must be made not later than the end of the period of six months beginning with the date by which the counter-notice was required to be given (s.25(4)).

If no application is made within six months, then the initial notice will be deemed to have been withdrawn at the end of those six months (s.29(3)).

Example

To be inserted into a CPR Part 8 Claim Form, N208

Part 8 of the Civil Procedure Rules 1998 applies to this claim.

The Claimant, [*the nominee purchaser*], applies to the court for an order -
1) pursuant to section 25(1) of the Leasehold Reform Housing and Urban Development Act 1993 ('the Act'), determining the terms on which the Claimant is to acquire, in accordance with the proposals contained in the initial notice dated [*date*], such interests and rights as are specified in that notice; and
2) that the Defendants pay the costs of this application.

The grounds upon which the Claimant claims to be entitled to the order are the following:
1. The Defendants are the owners of the freehold reversion of premises situate and known as [*address*] ('the premises') registered with title absolute under title number [*title number*]. An office copy entry is annexed hereto at Schedule 1.
2. The premises consist of a self-contained building or part of a building; they contain two or more flats held by qualifying tenants and the total number of flats held by qualifying tenants, namely [*number of flats held by qualifying tenants*], is not less than two-thirds of the total number of flats contained in the premises, namely [*total number of flats*].

3. By a notice dated [*date*], [*names of tenants by whom notice was given*] as participating and qualifying tenants, served upon the Defendants an initial notice under section 13 of the Act proposing that they should acquire the freehold of the premises and appointing the Claimant to act as nominee purchaser for the purposes of section 15 of the Act. A copy of the notice together with office copy entries in relation to each of the leasehold titles held by the said participating and qualifying tenants and copies of their leases are annexed hereto at Schedule 2.
4. The date by which the Defendants were to serve a counter-notice under section 21 of the Act was [*date*] being in excess of two months after service of the initial notice.
5. No notice has been served pursuant to section 21 of the Act and the time for doing so has expired.
6. As permitted by CPR Part 8.5(7) the Claimant relies on the matters set out in this claim form as its evidence.

Once an order has been obtained under section 25(1), and if a binding contract has not been entered into within two months of the order becoming final or within such other period as may have been fixed by the court when making the order ('the appropriate period'), a further application can be made to the court under section 25(5). Upon such an application, the court can make any one of the following orders:

- an order providing for the interests to be acquired by the nominee purchaser to be vested in him on the terms determined by the court (s.25(6)(a));
- an order providing for those interests to be vested in him on those terms, but subject to such modifications as:
  o may have been determined by an LVT, on the application of either the nominee purchaser or the reversioner, to be required by reason of any change in circumstances since the time when the terms were determined by the court; and
  o are specified in the order (s.25(6)(b)); or
- an order providing for the initial notice to be deemed to have been withdrawn at the end of the appropriate period (s.25(6)(c)).

An order of the court becomes final if not appealed against on the expiry of the time for bringing an appeal (s.101(9)(a)). Pursuant to rule 52.4 of the Civil Procedure Rules, unless the lower court directs otherwise, an appellant must file an appellant's notice at the appeal court within 21 days after the date of the decision of the lower court.

As to the nature and operation of any vesting order made under sections 25(6)(a) or (b), see Schedule 5.

Any application under section 25(5) must be made not later than two months from the end of the appropriate period (s.25(7)). If no application is made within two months, then the initial notice will be deemed to have been withdrawn at the end of those two months (s.29(4)).

Timetable of required steps

It order to illustrate what steps are required to be taken when in circumstances where the reversioner fails to serve a counter-notice, the following assumes that the initial notice had been given on 1 January 2010.

Date	Time allowed	Steps, Significant Dates and Deadlines
1 January 2010		1. Service of the initial notice under section 13.
15 March 2010	At least two months after step 1.	2. Date specified in the initial notice by which the reversioner must respond to the notice by giving a counter-notice under section 21.
14 September 2010	Six months after date 2.	Deadline for an application under section 25(1) for an order determining the terms of acquisition.
9 November 2010		3. Decision of court.
Midnight 30 November – 1 December 2010	21 days after date 3.	4. Order under section 25(1) becomes final.
31 January 2011	Two months after date 4.	5. Appropriate period under section 25(8) ends. If a binding contract has not been entered into, an application can be made under section 25(5).
31 March 2011	Two months after date 5.	Deadline for an application under section 25(5).

The reversioner serves a non-admitting counter-notice

Section 22 is headed 'Proceedings relating to validity of initial notice'. This may be misleading as section 22 does not relate to proceedings to determine whether or not a notice does or does not comply with the requirements of an initial notice. Section 22 deals with the situation where the participating tenants have served an initial notice which is, on its face, a valid notice, but the reversioner disputes the tenants' entitlement to exercise the right to collective enfranchisement in relation to the specified premises.

Where the reversioner has served a counter-notice to that effect, an application can be made to the court by the nominee purchaser under section 22(1), for a declaration that the participating tenants were, on the relevant date, entitled to exercise the right to collective enfranchisement in relation to the specified premises. Any application under section 22(1) must be made within two months of the giving of the counter-notice to the nominee purchaser (s.22(2)). Pursuant to section 22, there are therefore three possible outcomes following the service of a non-admitting counter-notice.

No application is made

If no application is made under section 22(1) within the two months or an application is made but withdrawn, then the initial notice is deemed to have been withdrawn either at the end of those two months or on the date of the withdrawal of the application (s.29(1)).

A declaration is made under section 22(1)

If a declaration is made that the participating tenants were, on the relevant date, entitled to exercise the right to collective enfranchisement in relation to the specified premises, then the court must make an order:

- declaring that the reversioner's counter-notice shall be of no effect; and
- requiring the reversioner to give a further counter-notice to the nominee purchaser by such date as is specified in the order. This notice must admit the participating tenants' entitlement.

However, the above does not apply if the reversioner has stated in the counter-notice that a relevant landlord intends to make an application under section 23(1), on the grounds that he intends to redevelop the specified premises and an application for such an order has not been made or the period for doing so has not expired (s.22(4)).

If the reversioner is required to give a further counter-notice and does not do so by the date specified in the order, then section 25 applies (s.25(1)(b)).

An application under section 22(1) is dismissed

If an application under section 22(1) is dismissed, then the initial notice ceases to have effect on the order becoming final (s.22(6)).

Example

To be inserted into a CPR Part 8 Claim Form, N208

Part 8 of the Civil Procedure Rules 1998 applies to this claim

The Claimant, [*the nominee purchaser*], applies to the court for:
(1) An order pursuant to section 22 of the Leasehold Reform Housing and Urban Development Act 1993 ('the Act') declaring that the Claimants were, on the relevant date, entitled to exercise the right to collective enfranchisement in respect of premises situate and known as [*address*] registered with title absolute under title number [*title number*] ('the premises'); and
(2) in any event, an order that the Defendant pays the costs of this application.

The grounds upon which the Claimant claims to be entitled to the said order are:
1. The Defendant is the owner of the freehold reversion of the premises. An office copy entry is annexed hereto at Schedule 1.
2. By a notice dated [*date*] the [*names of tenants by whom the notice was given*] ('the tenants') as participating and qualifying tenants, served upon the Defendant an initial notice under section 13 of the Act, proposing that they should acquire the freehold of the premises and appointing [*nominee purchaser*] to act as nominee purchaser for the purposes of section 15 of the Act. A copy of the notice together with office copy entries in relation to each of the leasehold titles within the premises and copies of the tenants' leases are annexed hereto at Schedule 2.
3. The Defendant served a notice pursuant to section 21 of the Act dated [*date*], a copy of which is annexed hereto at Schedule 3.
4. The said notice did not admit that the tenants were entitled to exercise the right to collective enfranchisement in relation to the premises on the basis that 'the qualifying tenants were given notice of right of first refusal to purchase the appurtenant property which they did not accept and for which the deadline expired on 20 April 2007, at which time the reversioner became entitled to dispose of the appurtenant property on the open market'.

> 5. It is denied that service of a notice pursuant to section 5 of the Landlord and Tenant Act 1987 affects the tenants' right to collective enfranchisement in relation to the premises.
> 6. As permitted by CPR Part 8.5(7), the Claimants rely on the matters set out in this claim form as their evidence.

Timetable of required steps

In order to illustrate what steps are required to be taken when, in circumstances where the reversioner serves a counter-notice, which does not admit the participating tenants' entitlement to exercise the right to collective enfranchisement in relation to the specified premises, the following assumes that the initial notice has been given on 1 January 2010.

Date	Time allowed	Steps, Significant Dates and Deadlines
1 January 2010		Service of the initial notice under section 13.
1 March 2010		1. Reversioner serves a counter-notice under section 21.
30 April 2010	Two months after step 1.	Deadline for an application under section 22(1) for a declaration that the tenant had no right to acquire a new lease.

Landlord intends to redevelop

Any relevant landlord may apply to the court for an order pursuant to section 23(1), declaring that the right to collective enfranchisement shall not be exercisable in relation to the specified premises, by reason of that landlord's intention to redevelop the whole or a substantial part of those premises.

The prerequisites for an order under section 23(1) are as follows:

- the reversioner has given a counter-notice stating an application for an order under section 23(1) is to be made (s.23(1));
- not less than two-thirds of all the long leases on which flats contained in the specified premises are held are due

to terminate within the period of five years beginning with the relevant date, i.e. the date of service of the initial notice (s.23(2)(a));
- for the purposes of redevelopment, the landlord intends, once the leases in question have terminated, to:
  o demolish or reconstruct; or
  o carry out substantial works of construction on, the whole or a substantial part of the specified premises (s.23(2)(b));
- the landlord cannot reasonably carry out the proposed works without obtaining possession of the flats demised by those leases (s.23(2)(c)); and
- the application must be made within two months of giving the counter-notice (s.23(3)).

Whilst the application under section 23(1) must be made within two months of giving the counter-notice, where the reversioner has served a counter-notice which does not admit the tenants' entitlement to exercise the right to collective enfranchisement, the application cannot be proceeded with until such time (if any) as an order under section 22(1) becomes final (s.23(3)). Obviously, if the application under section 22 is dismissed, i.e. it is declared that the participating tenants are not entitled to exercise the right to collective enfranchisement, there will be no need to proceed with the application under section 23(1).

Pursuant to section 23, there are various possible outcomes following the service of a counter-notice which states that a landlord intends to redevelop.

No application is made

Where the reversioner gives a counter-notice stating that an application for an order under section 23(1) is to be made, but no application is made within two months of giving the counter-notice, then the reversioner can give a further counter-notice (s.23(6)). Any further counter-notice must be given within two months of the expiry of the deadline for making the application under section 23(1) (s.23(6) and (7)). The above does not apply where an application has been made under section 22, i.e. for an order declaring that the participating tenants are entitled to exercise the right to collective enfranchisement, so that the question of the tenants' entitlement can be determined in the first instance.

If the reversioner fails to give a further counter-notice within the time specified, then section 25 applies (s.25(1)(b)).

An application is made, but subsequently withdrawn

Where an application under section 23(1) is made, but subsequently withdrawn, the reversioner can give a further counter-notice. Such further counter-notice must be given within two months of the withdrawal of the application. This does not apply, however, where an application has been made under section 22, i.e. for an order declaring that the participating tenants are entitled to exercise the right to collective enfranchisement. If the reversioner fails to give a further counter-notice within the time specified, then section 25 applies (s.25(1)(b)).

An application succeeds

Where the application succeeds and the court makes the order sought, then the initial notice will cease to have effect upon that order becoming final (s.23(4)). In such circumstances, the tenant is not liable for any of the landlord's costs under section 33 (s.33(4)).

An application is dismissed

Where an application under section 23(1) is dismissed, the court must make an order:

- declaring that the reversioner's counter-notice shall be of no effect; and
- requiring the reversioner to give a further counter-notice to the tenant by such date as is specified in the order (s.23(5)).

If the landlord fails to give a further counter-notice within the time specified, then section 25 applies (s.25(1)(b)).

Timetable of required steps

In order to illustrate what steps are required to be taken when in circumstances where the landlord gives a counter-notice stating that an application for an order under section 23(1) is to be made, the following assumes that the initial notice has been given on 1 January 2010.

Flats: collective enfranchisement

Date	Time allowed	Steps, Significant Dates and Deadlines
1 January 2010		Service of the initial notice under section 13.
1 March 2010		**1.** Reversioner serves a counter-notice under section 21.
30 April 2010	Two months after step 1.	**2.** Deadline for application under section 23(1) for an order declaring that the right to collective enfranchisement shall not be exercisable by reason of a landlord's intention to redevelop.
15 May 2010		**3.** An application made under section 23(1) is withdrawn.
30 June 2010	Two months after date 2.	Date by which reversioner must serve a further counter-notice, where he has stated that an application for an order under section 23(1) is to be made, but no application has been made.
14 July 2010	Two months after date 3.	Date by which reversioner must serve a further counter-notice, where he has made an application under section 23(1), which he has subsequently withdrawn.

Application where terms are in dispute or there has been a failure to enter into a binding contract

Where the reversioner has given the tenant a counter-notice (or a further counter-notice pursuant to sections 22 or 23), admitting that the participating tenants were, on the relevant date, entitled to exercise the right to collective enfranchisement, but any of the terms of acquisition remain in dispute two months after that notice was given, either the nominee purchaser or the reversioner may apply to the LVT under section 24(1) for a determination of the matters in dispute. The LVT has jurisdiction to determine only the terms of the acquisition in dispute and this could include, for example, constituent elements of the purchase price where some, but not all, are agreed between the parties: *City of Westminster v CH2006 Ltd* [2009] UKUT 174 (CC).

Any such application must be made within six months of the counter-notice (or further counter-notice) being given (s.24(2)). If no application is made within six months, then the initial notice will be deemed to have been withdrawn at the end of those six months (s.29(3)). Consequently, the landlord may prefer not to make an application under section 24(1), but to wait to see if the nominee purchaser fails to do so.

'The terms of acquisition', by virtue of section 24(8), means the terms of the proposed acquisition by the nominee purchaser, whether relating to:

- the interests to be acquired;
- the extent of the property to which those interests relate or the rights to be granted over any property;
- the amounts payable as the purchase price for such interests;
- the apportionment of conditions or other matters in connection with the severance of any reversionary interest; or
- the provisions to be contained in any conveyance,

or otherwise, and includes any such terms in respect of any interest to be acquired in pursuance of section 1(4) or 21(4).

Where all the terms of acquisition have been agreed or determined by the LVT, but a binding contract has not been entered into within two months of the agreement or determination becoming final, or within a period fixed by the LVT known as 'the appropriate period', either the reversioner or the nominee purchaser may make an application to the court pursuant to section 24(3). Pursuant to section 101(9), a decision of the LVT is to be treated as becoming final if not appealed against on the expiry of the time for bringing an appeal. Pursuant to Regulation 20 of the Leasehold Valuation Tribunals (Procedure) (England) Regulations 2003, the expiry of the time for bringing an appeal is the end of the period of 21 days starting with the date the decision is sent to the parties.

Flats: collective enfranchisement

> *Example*
>
> To be inserted into a CPR Part 8 Claim Form, N208
>
> Part 8 of the Civil Procedure Rules 1998 applies to this claim
>
> The Claimant, [*the nominee purchaser*], applies to the court:
> (1) for an order pursuant to section 24(4) of the Leasehold Reform, Housing and Urban Development Act 1993 ('the Act') that the freehold interest in property situate and known as [*address*] registered with title absolute under title number [*title number*] ('the Property') should be vested in the Claimant upon the terms determined by the LVT and set out at paragraph 6 below; and
> (2) for an order that the Defendant do pay the costs of this application.
>
> The grounds upon which the Claimant claims to be entitled to the order are:
> 1. The Claimant is the nominee purchaser acting on behalf of the tenants of the Property.
> 2. The Defendant is the owner of the freehold reversion of the Property. An office copy entry is annexed hereto at Schedule 1.
> 3. By a notice dated [*date*] the qualifying tenants served upon the Defendant an initial notice under section 13 of the Act, proposing that they should acquire the freehold of the Property and appointing the Claimant to act as nominee purchaser for the purposes of section 15 of the Act. A copy of the said notice is annexed hereto at Schedule 2.
> 4. By counter-notice dated [*date*], the Defendant admitted that the Claimant was entitled to exercise the right to collective enfranchisement in relation to the property, but objected to the proposals contained in the initial notice in respect of the purchase price and the extent of the Property to be acquired. A copy of the said notice is annexed hereto at Schedule 3.
> 5. The terms of acquisition were not agreed and by application dated [*date*] the Claimant applied to the LVT for a determination of the terms of acquisition.
> 6. By a determination dated [*date*], the LVT decided that the freehold interest in the Property should be acquired on the following terms;
> [*Terms determined by the LVT*]
> A copy of the LVT's determination is annexed hereto at Schedule 4.
> 7. The appropriate period under section 24(6) of the Act ended on [*date*], but a binding contract incorporating the above terms has not been entered into.
> 8. As permitted by CPR Part 8.5(7) the Claimant relies on the matters set out in this claim form as its evidence.

Upon such an application, the court can make any one of the following orders:

- an order providing for the interests to be acquired by the nominee purchaser to be vested in him on the terms determined by the LVT (s.24(4)(a));

245

Leasehold enfranchisement explained

- an order providing for those interests to be vested in him on those terms, but subject to such modifications as:
  - may have been determined by an LVT, on the application of either the nominee purchaser or the reversioner, to be required by reason of any change in circumstances since the time when the terms were originally determined by the LVT, and
  - are specified in the order (s.24(4)(b)); or
- an order providing for the initial notice to be deemed to have been withdrawn at the end of the appropriate period (s.24(4)(c)).

As to the nature and operation of any vesting order made under sections 24(4)(a) or (b), see Schedule 5.

Any application under section 24(3) must be made not later than two months after the end of the appropriate period (s.24(5)). If no application is made within two months, then the initial notice will be deemed to have been withdrawn at the end of those two months (s.29(2)(b)).

Timetable of required steps

It order to illustrate what steps are required to be taken when, in circumstances where the reversioner has given the tenant a counter-notice admitting that the participating tenants were, on the relevant date, entitled to exercise the right to collective enfranchisement, but any of the terms of acquisition remain in dispute, the following assumes that the initial notice has been given on 1 January 2010.

Date	Time allowed	Steps, Significant Dates and Deadlines
1 January 2010		Service of the initial notice under section 13.
1 March 2010		1. Reversioner serves a counter-notice under section 21.
30 April 2010	Two months after step 1.	Date after which an application can be made to the LVT under section 24(1) for a determination of the matters in dispute.

30 September 2010	Six months after step 1.	Deadline for an application under section 24(1).
5 April 2011		**2.** Date of LVT decision determining the terms of acquisition under section 24(1) is sent to the parties.
Midnight 25/26 April 2011	21 days after date 2	**3.** LVT decision has not been appealed against and therefore becomes final.
25 June 2011	Two months after date 3.	**4.** The appropriate period under section 24(6) ends. If a binding contract has not been entered into, an application can be made under section 24(3).
25 August 2011	Two months after date 4.	Deadline for an application under section 24(3).

4

Flats: collective enfranchisement valuation issues

Introduction

As in the case of a claim for a new lease, the process is instigated by a group of tenants serving their notice. As this notice must specify the proposed price for each of the interests to be acquired, the valuation issues from the tenants' perspective are covered initially; thereafter the practical and valuation issues from the freeholder's viewpoint upon receipt of a notice are examined.

In collective enfranchisement, the nominee purchaser acquires the freehold interest outright with all interests in between from their existing leases. There are provisions for leasebacks (both mandatory and optional), however the nominee purchaser acquires the freehold interest in these also.

Whereas in a new lease claim the existing interest is extinguished (the process being a surrender and renewal in receipt of the new lease), in collective enfranchisement, unless the nominee purchaser otherwise chooses, the existing leases remain in situ, with all other interests being acquired. However, in practice, the participating leaseholders will be granted new 999 year leases at no premium.

Of the three areas in leasehold reform, collective enfranchisement of flats is the least common. A high proportion of house and new lease claims are coupled with a sale, thus taking advantage of the lessee's right to assign the benefit of a notice. On the other hand, collective enfranchisement is generally motivated by a group of lessees who wish to acquire the freehold interest as part of a longer term financial strategy and extended ownership.

Notwithstanding that, the lessee also has the right to assign his participation, (s.14 (2)).

In addition to the legal and valuation issues, there are the practicalities of mobilising and motivating a number of lessees to work together on a common aim over a period of time (generally, in practice, a minimum one year), negotiating the various legal and valuation issues, and finally completing the purchase as and when all the terms of the acquisition have been agreed.

Many of the valuation principles were covered in new lease claims. It is the author's view that collective enfranchisement valuations are generally more straightforward than new lease claims; typically, valuing intermediate leasehold interests is less cumbersome; so if the valuer has mastered the principles of a new lease claim, collective enfranchisement is a simpler exercise.

There are, however, further valuation issues to consider including 'hope value' (which is not a relevant factor in new lease or house claims), which will be discussed and explained in examples. Invariably, the further valuation issues are those that can be more problematic.

Similarly to new lease claims, it is intended to cover the spectrum of case examples, ranging from a two storey building with one flat per floor on existing leases in direct covenant with the freeholder, where the unexpired terms are over 80 years; through, typically, to a block of a number of flats with participators and non-participators, varying existing lease terms, caretaker's accommodation, garages, grounds and access roads.

Ultimately, if the principles are understood, the fundamental difference between advising a group of tenants contemplating an enfranchisement claim, as opposed to a tenant considering a new lease, is the time required to prepare the valuations and give your advice.

The valuation principles

The principles follow those in section 9(1C) of the *Leasehold Reform Act* 1967 as amended for houses (see chapter 7). The date of valuation is the 'relevant date', being the date that the notice of claim is given to the freeholder.

Leasehold enfranchisement explained

The tenants' enquiry

This follows the new lease enquiry, in addition to which there are the practical aspects to consider when advising a number of lessees ranging from a minimum of two, up to say 100 plus.

Where there are two lessees, the logistics are quite straightforward; on the other hand groups of tenants need to be 'managed' so that all of the information and any progress report is circulated in an orderly fashion. Typically, setting up a 'steering group' comprising two or three lessees, a solicitor and the valuer is the usual approach. With the advent of email, the passage of information is easier; however, from the valuer's point of view, where there are a number of lessees, you need to work to a single point of contact in conjunction with the solicitor, otherwise your time could be wholly taken up dealing with questions from various lessees on one case.

So from that initial enquiry, in addition to the valuation questions (i.e. unexpired terms 80 plus years?), the valuer needs to establish the ground rules and lines of communication as to how he can give his advice. In addition to which, it is useful to establish whether the group has a 'fighting fund' – typically £250 per participator to cover the costs of initial valuations, legal advice and maintaining a float generally. The establishment and progress of collecting the fighting fund is also a good barometer to gauge the willingness, desire and motivation of the group to proceed with the enfranchisement.

The valuer needs to bear in mind that he will almost certainly be required to 'apportion' each participator's contributory sum; and where there are non-participators, provide the sum for these also, so that whoever is covering this cost can be informed.

The valuation principles, generally, follow those of new lease claims; having said that, there is no two year ownership rule to participate – ownership per se allows a lessee to participate in collective enfranchisement. I reiterate this as there will come a time when all of those wishing to participate must confirm so.

Schedule 6

At Schedule 6 is the 'Purchase Price Payable by Nominee Purchaser', which comprises six Parts and 21 paragraphs.

The layout of the Schedule is similar to that of Schedule 13 for the premium payable for a new lease, albeit there are additional Parts and paragraphs.

Part I is General, comprising one paragraph which covers an intermediate leasehold interest and negative values, as follows:

PART I
GENERAL

Interpretation and operation of Schedule

1(1) In this Schedule–

'intermediate leasehold interest' means the interest of the tenant under a lease which is superior to the lease held by a qualifying tenant of a flat contained in the specified premises, to the extent that–

(a) any such interest is to be acquired by the nominee purchaser by virtue of section 2(1)(a), and
(b) it is an interest in the specified premises;

(2) Parts II to IV of this Schedule have effect subject to the provisions of Parts V and VI (which relate to interests with negative values).

Section 1 follows the corresponding section under Schedule 13. Section 2 says that Parts II to IV are subject to Parts V and VI.

Part II covers the freehold of the specified premises. It comprises four paragraphs setting out the price payable for the freehold of the specified premises (paragraph 2), briefly as follows:

- the value of the freeholder's interest (para. 3);
- the freeholder's share of marriage value (para. 4); and
- any compensation payable (para. 5).

PART II
FREEHOLD OF SPECIFIED PREMISES

Price payable for freehold of specified premises

2(1) Subject to the provisions of this paragraph, where the freehold of the whole of the specified premises is owned by the same person the price payable by the nominee purchaser for the freehold of those premises shall be the aggregate of–

(a) the value of the freeholder's interest in the premises as determined in accordance with paragraph 3,
(b) the freeholder's share of the marriage value as determined in accordance with paragraph 4, and
(c) any amount of compensation payable to the freeholder under paragraph 5.

(2) Where the amount arrived at in accordance with sub-paragraph (1) is a negative amount, the price payable by the nominee purchaser for the freehold shall be nil.

Value of freeholder's interest

3(1) Subject to the provisions of this paragraph, the value of the freeholder's interest in the specified premises is the amount which at the relevant date that interest might be expected to realise if sold on the open market by a willing seller (with no person who falls within sub-paragraph (1A) buying or seeking to buy) on the following assumptions—

(a) on the assumption that the vendor is selling for an estate in fee simple—
  (i) subject to any leases subject to which the freeholder's interest in the premises is to be acquired by the nominee purchaser, but
  (ii) subject also to any intermediate or other leasehold interests in the premises which are to be acquired by the nominee purchaser;
(b) on the assumption that this Chapter and Chapter II confer no right to acquire any interest in the specified premises or to acquire any new lease (except that this shall not preclude the taking into account of a notice given under section 42 with respect to a flat contained in the specified premises where it is given by a person other than a participating tenant);
(c) on the assumption that any increase in the value of any flat held by a participating tenant which is attributable to an improvement carried out at his own expense by the tenant or by any predecessor in title is to be disregarded; and
(d) on the assumption that (subject to paragraphs (a) and (b)) the vendor is selling with and subject to the rights and burdens with and subject to which the conveyance to the nominee purchaser of the freeholder's interest is to be made, and in particular with and subject to such permanent or extended rights and burdens as are to be created in order to give effect to Schedule 7.

Flats: collective enfranchisement valuation issues

(1A) A person falls within this sub-paragraph if he is–

    (a) the nominee purchaser, or
    (b) a tenant of premises contained in the specified premises, or
    (ba) an owner of an interest which the nominee purchaser is to acquire in pursuance of section 1(2)(a), or
    (c) an owner of an interest which the nominee purchaser is to acquire in pursuance of section 2(1)(b).

(2) It is hereby declared that the fact that sub-paragraph (1) requires assumptions to be made as to the matters specified in paragraphs (a) to (d) of that sub-paragraph does not preclude the making of assumptions as to other matters where those assumptions are appropriate for determining the amount which at the relevant date the freeholder's interest in the specified premises might be expected to realise if sold as mentioned in that sub-paragraph.

(3) In determining that amount there shall be made such deduction (if any) in respect of any defect in title as on a sale of the interest on the open market might be expected to be allowed between a willing seller and a willing buyer.

(4) Where a lease of any flat or other unit contained in the specified premises is to be granted to the freeholder in accordance with section 36 and Schedule 9, the value of his interest in those premises at the relevant date so far as relating to that flat or other unit shall be taken to be the difference as at that date between–

    (a) the value of his freehold interest in it, and
    (b) the value of his interest in it under that lease, assuming it to have been granted to him at that date;

and each of those values shall, so far as is appropriate, be determined in like manner as the value of the freeholder's interest in the whole of the specified premises is determined for the purposes of paragraph 2(1)(a).

(5) The value of the freeholder's interest in the specified premises shall not be increased by reason of–

    (a) any transaction which–
        (i) is entered into on or after the date, of the passing of this Act (otherwise than in pursuance of a contract entered into before that date), and

(ii) involves the creation or transfer of an interest superior to (whether or not preceding) any interest held by a qualifying tenant of a flat contained in the specified premises; or

(b) any alteration on or after that date of the terms on which any such superior interest is held.

(6) Sub-paragraph (5) shall not have the effect of preventing an increase in value of the freeholder's interest in the specified premises in a case where the increase is attributable to any such leasehold interest with a negative value as is mentioned in paragraph 14(2).

Fundamentally, the valuation of the freeholder's interest at paragraph 3 follows that of paragraph 3 of Schedule 13 for a new lease.

The assumptions correspond similarly save that of the no-Act world does not preclude taking into account a notice for a new lease under section 42 (subsection 1(b)); this is of particular importance when we consider 'hope value' later in the chapter.

In the first example we look at the purchase price payable by the nominee purchaser where the valuation is under paragraph 3 only.

In its simplest form, a collective enfranchisement claim can be submitted by two lessees where their existing leases have unexpired terms of over 80 years at the date of valuation, so that no marriage value is payable, (para. 4(2A)).

In these circumstances, both lessees have to participate (s.3(1)(c)).

Example 1

A two storey converted mid-terrace house with one flat per floor, with existing leases of 81 years unexpired from 25 March 2010, each at fixed ground rents of £100 p.a. Further to your inspections, you value the ground floor flat (Flat 1) at £225,000 on a share of freehold basis, and the first floor flat (Flat 2) at £200,000 on share of freehold also.

The date of valuation will be the date of receipt of claim, but for your initial advice and the examples in this chapter, we adopt 25 March 2010.

The valuation is in accordance with Schedule 6, paragraph 3.

Date of valuation: 25 March 2010.

Value of the freeholder's interest

Flats: collective enfranchisement valuation issues

Term		
Rent (two flats at £100 p.a. fixed)	£200 p.a.	
YP 81 years @ 8%	12.4755	£2,495
Reversion		
To aggregate of 'share of freehold' with vacant possession values –		
Flat 1 – £225,000		
Flat 2 – £200,000	£425,000	
Deferred 81 years @ 5%	0.0192	£8,160
Value of the freeholder's interest		£10,655 £10,655
plus		
Marriage value – as 81 years unexpired, if any, to be 'ignored' (CLRA 2002, s. 128 (3))		£0
Enfranchisement price (excluding costs)		£10,655
	Say	£10,650

For the purposes of the sum to be included in the notice, there is, arguably, little margin in these circumstances – the valuer may: (1) reduce the aggregate of share of freehold values to £375,000, (2) apply a higher capitalisation rate, and (3) adopt a higher deferment rate, all of which would lead to a lower enfranchisement price.

This is an example in its simplest form; two tenants submitting their claim where marriage value is nil (i.e. to be ignored).

The make up of the freeholder's interest was discussed under new lease claims (the landlord's interest), so it is not the intention to cover that ground in detail again (see chapter 2). We shall, however, discuss hope value when we look at non-participators in a further example.

It is, nevertheless, helpful to consider the valuation points in capitalisation and deferment rates under Schedule 6, as opposed to Schedule 13.

The capitalisation rate

Where the reversion is to a freehold interest, by convention, valuers apply single rate tables. For the 'undynamic but secure' ground rent provisions in Example 1, an eight per cent rate of return is applied.

If the asset is diminishing, typically an intermediate lease, dual rate tables are applied, which may incorporate an adjustment for tax. Each case is to be handled on its merits, and will depend on market evidence, where available, and the valuer's opinion.

The deferment rate

Similarly to the capitalisation rate, we analysed at length the question as to the appropriate deferment rate, its make up and the effect on price of the generic rate with adjustment for flats, in chapter 2. Five per cent is adopted here for flats. We now review the question of the appropriate rate in relation to Schedule 6.

At paragraphs 95 and 96 in *Sportelli*, the tribunal review their decision in *Arbib* (para. 163), as to their reasons for the increase of 0.25 per cent for flats to adjust the generic rate of 4.75 per cent to five per cent. The tribunal confirmed in *Sportelli* that the adjustment of 0.25 per cent is to reflect greater management problems for flats when compared with a house; and that those management problems are not necessarily greater or smaller for a single flat than a block of flats. To recap, bear in mind that all of the properties in *Sportelli* and *Arbib* are within PCL.

In chapter 2, various tribunal cases subsequent to *Sportelli* are discussed. Set out below, in brief, are the decisions under Schedule 6:

- *Sherwood Hall*, long term unexpired and outside PCL – five per cent.
- *10 Cheniston Gardens Limited*, long term unexpired – five per cent.
- *Nell Gwynn House*, long term unexpired – 6.5 per cent (LVT).
- *Hildron Finance Limited*, outside PCL – five per cent.
- *The Holt*, outside PCL, deterioration and obsolescence – five per cent.

At the time of publication, five appeals to the Upper Chamber of decisions of the LVT in collective enfranchisement are pending, for the deferment rate applicable for sub 20 years leases. The tribunals determined five per cent in each case, following *Sportelli*.

Flats: collective enfranchisement valuation issues

The properties (Nos. 23, 31, 37, 38 and 42, Cadogan Square, London SW1) are all in PCL, and the unexpired terms range from 17.31 years to 17.75 years.

Marriage value

We now look at Schedule 6, paragraph 4, the 'freeholder's share of marriage value':

Freeholder's share of marriage value

4(1) The marriage value is the amount referred to in sub-paragraph (2), and the freeholder's share of the marriage value is 50 per cent of that amount.

(2) Subject to sub-paragraph (2A), the marriage value is any increase in the aggregate value of the freehold and every intermediate leasehold interest in the specified premises, when regarded as being (in consequence of their being acquired by the nominee purchaser) interests under the control of the participating tenants, as compared with the aggregate value of those interests when held by the persons from whom they are to be so acquired, being an increase in value–

  (a) which is attributable to the potential ability of the participating tenants, once those interests have been so acquired, to have new leases granted to them without payment of any premium and without restriction as to length of term, and
  (b) which, if those interests were being sold to the nominee purchaser on the open market by willing sellers, the nominee purchaser would have to agree to share with the sellers in order to reach agreement as to price.

(2A) Where at the relevant date the unexpired term of the lease held by any of those participating members exceeds 80 years, any increase in the value of the freehold or any intermediate leasehold interest in the specified premises which is attributable to his potential ability to have a new lease granted to him as mentioned in sub-paragraph (2)(a) is to be ignored.

(3) For the purposes of sub-paragraph (2) the value of the freehold or any intermediate leasehold interest in the specified premises when held by the person from whom it

257

is to be acquired by the nominee purchaser and its value when acquired by the nominee purchaser-

   (a) shall be determined on the same basis as the value of the interest is determined for the purposes of paragraph 2(1)(a) or (as the case may be) paragraph 6(1)(b)(i); and
   (b) shall be so determined as at the relevant date.

(4) Accordingly, in so determining the value of an interest when acquired by the nominee purchaser–

   (a) the same assumptions shall be made under paragraph 3(1)(or, as the case may be, under paragraph 3(1) as applied by paragraph 7(1)) as are to be made under that provision in determining the value of the interest when held by the person from whom it is to be acquired by the nominee purchaser; and
   (b) any merger or other circumstances affecting the interest on its acquisition by the nominee purchaser shall be disregarded.

The first two valuation points to be aware of are:

   1) the freeholder's share of marriage value is 50 per cent (s.4(1)); and
   2) where the unexpired term of the participating member's lease exceeds 80 years, marriage value is to be ignored (s.4, subsection (2)(2A)).

The marriage value computation provides for the 'participating tenants' to grant themselves new leases at nil premiums, with no restriction as to length of term (it is generally assumed that the participating tenants will grant themselves 999 years leases/share of freehold interests at peppercorn rents).

As with new lease claims, it is a 'before and after' exercise. Marriage value being the difference in value of the aggregate of the various interests under the control of the participating tenants (assumed 999 years leases/share of freehold interests, as above, for the participators' flats), and the corresponding aggregate of values in the hands of the parties from whom they are to be acquired.

The valuer has to bear in mind that he is to attribute values to each of the interests before and after enfranchisement, which follows the approach to new lease claims. The main difference being that whereas in new lease claims the freeholder and any intermediate leaseholder may have a continuing, albeit less valuable, interest once the new lease has been granted, in collective enfranchisement any interest acquired outright by the nominee purchaser is of 'nil' value to the party from whom it has been acquired.

The definition is, arguably, cumbersome and convoluted; and at the time of drafting there is an appeal (dealt with in part) pending from a decision of the LT/UT to the Court of Appeal on its interpretation, *McHale v Earl Cadogan* [2008] PLSCS 298 LU/UT.

The questions on interpretation are with respect to the disregards, or otherwise, of tenant's improvements and the no-Act world (benefit of the Act or Act rights) in assessing the existing lease values of the participating tenants in the marriage value computation.

The marriage computation under Schedule 13, paragraph 4 (which is discussed in chapter 2), provides that in valuing the tenant's interest, the same assumptions to value the landlord's interest are to be applied (4A and 4B). Whereas the Act now makes it clear as to the assumptions to be applied to value the landlord's and tenant's interests (being the same), it is argued that their corresponding omission in Schedule 6 means that those assumptions do not apply; typically the disregard of tenant's improvements and the benefit of the Act.

In their decision at 42 Cadogan Square, London SW1 (*Ms Betul Erkman v Earl Cadogan*, LON/ENF/2008, 16 March 2007, unreported), the LVT determined that the disregards for tenant's improvements and the benefit of the Act did not apply as the Schedule omits the assumptions.

The counter argument to apply the same assumptions in valuing the participating tenants' existing leases, disregarding improvements and the benefit of the Act in the marriage value computation, follows the principles in *Norfolk v Trinity College, Cambridge* (1976) 32 P&CR 147. *Norfolk* was the first case to be heard at the Lands Tribunal under section 9(1A), where, unlike section 9(1), the tenant and members of his family are not to be excluded from the market.

The tribunal determined that the leasehold interest in the marriage value computation is to be valued disregarding tenant's improvements and without the right to acquire the freehold interest.

In *McHale*, at paragraphs 16, 17 and 18, the LT/UT determined that the same assumptions in valuing the freeholder's and any intermediate leaseholder's interests are to be applied in valuing the participating tenants' existing interests. The decision is being appealed.

Value of the participating tenants' existing interests

In the following examples, which include the marriage value computation, the participating tenants' existing interests are valued disregarding improvements and the benefit of the Act.

We now look at an example, again in its simplest form, where the freeholder's interest is acquired and there is no intermediate leasehold interest.

Example 2

Following on from Example 1, we now look at the valuation where the existing leases are 60 years unexpired, for which their values represent a relativity of 81 per cent of corresponding share of freehold value.

The price is made up of the freeholder's interest, plus 50 per cent of marriage value (para. 4(1)).

Date of valuation: 25 March 2010.

Value of the freeholder's interest

Term

Rent (two flats at £100 p.a.)	£200 p.a.	
YP 60 years @ 8%	12.3766	£2,475

Reversion

To aggregate of 'share of freehold' with vacant possession values—

Flat 1 – £225,000

Flat 2 – £200,000   £425,000

Deferred 60 years @ 5%	0.0535	£22,738
Value of the freeholder's interest		£25,213

Flats: collective enfranchisement valuation issues

plus			
<u>The freeholder's share of marriage value</u>			
Difference between the aggregate of values of interests under the control of the participating tenants:			
Freeholder's interest		£0	
Aggregate of participating tenants share of freehold values (para. 4(2)(a))		£425,000	£425,000
less			
Aggregate of values of interests prior to enfranchisement:			
Freeholder's interest (from above)	£25,213		
Aggregate of participating tenants existing lease values –			
Representing 81% of share of freehold value			
Flat 1 – £225,000 at 81% £182,250			
Flat 2 – £200,000 at 81% £162,000	£344,250	£369,463	
Marriage value		£55,537	
50% thereof (freeholder's share)		0.5	£27,769
plus value of the freeholder's interest (from above)			£25,213
Enfranchisement price (excluding costs)			£52,982
		Say	£53,000

Note the following with respect to the marriage value computation.

- Freeholder's interest – £0, the freeholder has had his interest acquired, accordingly £0.
- Aggregate of participating tenants share of freehold values – £425,000; once the participating tenants have acquired the freeholder's interest, they are at liberty to grant themselves interests with the optimum value for their flats, i.e. on the basis of share of freehold/999 years lease (para. 4, s.(2)(a)).
- Freeholder's interest (from above) – £25,213, this is the value of the interest in the hands of the freeholder.
- Aggregate of participating tenants existing lease values – £344,250, on the bases of disregard of tenant's improvements and the benefit of the Act.

261

Participators and non-participators

In an enfranchisement claim, there are likely to be non-participators – save where there are only two flats, both lessees under those circumstances are required to participate (s.3(1)).

Where there are both participators and non-participators, it is advisable to set out the price computation in tabular form, so that each element can be isolated and more readily understood by you, your clients and their legal advisers. The valuer will be required to isolate each participator's apportionment of the price, and will in any event be required to isolate the non-participators' element.

Ultimately, the participators will (as members of the nominee purchaser company), become the new landlord of the non-participators and will receive the premiums for any new leases subsequently granted. There will be circumstances where participators do not wish to contribute towards the apportionment of enfranchisement price to the non-participators, in which case those participators would not be due a share of any future receipts.

Where there are non-participators, the participators need to know the proportion of price to be met to cover the shortfall. Depending on the circumstances and the various participators' means, the shortfall could either be met by the participators (or a number of them), or a third party investor ('White Knight', to coin a phrase).

Be aware that non-participators flats are to be valued 'as seen' unless in disrepair in the freeholder's interest. The statutory disregard of 'tenant's improvements' does not apply to non-participators. If a non-participator's flat has been substantially improved, it is to be valued in its improved condition. For this reason, it is necessary for the valuer to inspect all of the non-participators' flats in collective enfranchisement.

We now look at two further issues in collective enfranchisement:

1) 'hope value'; and
2) 'hope value' in relation to a section 42 notice.

Hope value

Pursuant to the decisions of the House of Lords in *Sportelli*, hope value may be payable where there are non-participators in a collective enfranchisement claim.

The decisions of the House of Lords and the Lands Tribunal that the valuer must be aware of, and their respective reasons are as follows:

1) *Earl Cadogan v Sportelli & Others*, [2008] UKHL 71: at paragraph 115 of the decision, their Lordships confirm that hope value can be taken into account under paragraph 3 of Schedule 6, in so far as it is attributable to the possibility of non-participating tenants wishing to obtain new leases of their flats in the open market (and not pursuant to Schedule 13); and in addition at paragraph 69, convincingly conclude that pursuant to the Lands Tribunal decisions in *Sportelli*, hope value is to be assessed as a percentage of the marriage value.
2) In paragraphs 109 to 112 of *Sportelli*, the 'treatment in valuation' of hope value is considered. Two different approaches were put forward to assess hope value in those cases: (1) adjustment to the deferment rate; and (2) adding a lump sum. The tribunal concludes (para. 112) that adding a lump sum to the value of the reversion prior to the statutory marriage value apportionment is appropriate.
3) *Culley v Daejan Properties Limited* [2009] UKUT 168 (LC) is the first decision of the Upper Tribunal where hope value is assessed post *Sportelli*.

From the above we have: (1) the authority that hope value can be taken into account where there are non-participators in collective enfranchisement, and confirmation as to how it is to be assessed; (2) commentary and conclusion as to the Lands Tribunal's approach to assess hope value; and (3) a decision of the Upper Tribunal post points 1 and 2, showing the application of the decisions.

What is 'hope value'?

Schedule 6 does not include a definition of hope value, however at paragraph 66 of the decision in *Sportelli*, their Lordships say:

> 'However, where the landlord is selling his interest when the tenant is not in the market, a potential purchaser may well think that, in addition to its investment value, the freehold interest carries with it the potential benefit of a possible future sale of the freehold to the present tenant or a successor in title (or indeed the acquisition of the leasehold interest), thereby enabling a release of the marriage value in the future. In such a case, therefore, it can be said that, even though the tenant is not in the market at the time of the sale, the value of the freehold subject to the lease is greater than the aggregate of the capitalised rental stream and the deferred right to possession at the end of the term, and that something should be added for the possibility of a purchaser benefiting from a release of the marriage value. That additional sum is known as "hope value"'.

So hope value is the additional value attributable to the prospect of early release of marriage value, as a result of the freeholder selling a new lease or share of freehold (or buying in the leasehold interest), further to arms length negotiations to one or more of the lessees, i.e. not under the Act.

It is the third constituent part in the make up of the freeholder's interest when the 'term and reversion' method of valuation is used.

As marriage value is only payable in a collective enfranchisement claim with respect to 'participators'; where there are non-participators, with existing lease terms 80 years or less, the hope value calculation is required.

How is hope value to be calculated?

Example 3 below shows how hope value is calculated; before looking at that, the valuer should be aware what the tribunal members say in *Culley*.

Culley concerned the collective enfranchisement of a block of four flats in Hillingdon, West London. Two tenants of the four participated (the minimum required), and the existing leases had approximately 65 years unexpired.

At paragraph 51, the tribunal refers to its own decision in *Blendcrown Limited v The Church Commissioners for England* [2004] 1 EGLR 143 (para. 77) where they say:

'...hope value is by its nature speculative, uncertain and incapable of precise assessment. It is the value now of the chance of a future payment'.

In *Blendcrown*, a collective enfranchisement of a block of 80 flats with 15 non-participators (representing 17.2 per cent of the aggregate value), hope value was determined at five per cent of marriage value; the unexpired terms being 46.5 years.

At paragraph 63 of *Culley* the tribunal go on to say:

'There are in our judgment two particular valuation matters to be borne in mind in the determination of hope value. Firstly, it is likely to be greater if a proportion of non-participating flats is relatively large. Secondly, it will be lower if the unexpired terms are particularly long. In the present case the unexpired terms of the leases are 65.37 years and 50 per cent of the lessees are non-participators. Taking all matters into account, and bearing in mind the essentially speculative nature of hope value, we conclude that hope value in this case may be expressed as ten per cent of marriage value'.

We now look at the two particular valuation matters referred to in *Culley*:

- the unexpired term of the lease; and
- the number of non-participators compared to the number of participators.

The unexpired term of the lease – the shorter the unexpired term, the greater the pressure on the tenant to seek a new lease. In leasehold reform valuations, the marriage value released is at its greatest where the existing lease terms are in the region of 30–40 years unexpired. Where the unexpired term is, say, 60 years unexpired, there is less pressure on the tenant to seek a new lease for the reasons that the unexpired term is comparatively long and the marriage value to be released is not at its greatest. Having said that, it may be argued that as some lenders will only offer mortgage finance on 60 years plus, even at this relatively long term unexpired, there is a degree of urgency.

Where the unexpired term is, say, 20 years, the pressure on the tenant is increasing annually, albeit that the quantum of marriage value is decreasing pro rata. It must also be borne in mind that where the existing lease is 20 years unexpired, the order of premium may well be prohibitive to the tenant in any event.

The number of non-participators compared to the number of participators – in a block of four flats each with 60 years unexpired on the existing leases and one non-participator, the percentage of marriage value attributed to hope value would be less than that in a block of, say, 20 flats, each with 30 years unexpired on the existing leases and six non-participators.

It is not just the percentage number of non-participators which is the factor; one also has to consider the percentage of value of the non-participators in the building. Typically, this would be pertinent in a collective enfranchisement of a late Victorian/Edwardian house now converted into flats. In these circumstances, the flats' capital values can vary greatly; the first floor flat being considerably more valuable than, say, the basement caretaker's flat. The participators may represent 50 per cent of the total number of flats, but their percentage of aggregate of value could be 40 per cent.

Bearing in mind in *Culley* that the number of participants was the minimum required, and its location in a predominantly mortgage-dependent market, the ten per cent of marriage value for hope value appears, at first glance, low, and thus reflects the speculative nature of hope value described in *Blendcrown*.

A calculation for hope value will form part of the price computation where there is a non-participator with an existing lease of 80 years or less; it may, in any event, be valued at nil. Having said that, as hope value is additional value released pursuant to negotiations outside the Act, theoretically a sum for it could be included for a lease with more than 80 years unexpired; but bearing in mind *Culley*, under such circumstances its sum would most probably be nominal.

We now look at the calculation of hope value following the approach in *Culley*.

Flats: collective enfranchisement valuation issues

Example 3

A four storey converted terrace house with one flat per floor, each with existing leases of 60 years unexpired, at fixed ground rents of £100 p.a. Further to your inspections, you value the four flats as follows:

Flat no.	Floor	Ground rent	Participator/ non-participator	Existing lease value £	Share of freehold value £	Comments
1	Ground	£100 p.a.	P	£182,250	£225,000	Garden
2	First	£100 p.a.	P	£162,000	£200,000	
3	Second	£100 p.a.	Non-P	£153,900	£190,000	'as is' – in repair
4	Third	£100 p.a.	P	£145,800	£180,000	

The price is made up of the freeholder's interest, which now includes hope value, plus 50 per cent of marriage value.

Date of valuation: 25 March 2010.

<u>Value of the freeholder's interest</u>

Participators

Term

Rent (three flats at £100 p.a.)	£300 p.a.	
YP 60 years @ 8%	12.3766	£3,713

Reversion

To aggregate of 'share of freehold' with vacant possession values –

Flat 1 – £225,000
Flat 2 – £200,000
Flat 4 – £180,000

	£605,000	
Deferred 60 years @ 5%	0.0535	£32,368
		£36,081

plus

<u>Hope value</u>

See computation below	£1,235	£37,316

<u>Non-participator</u>

Term

Rent (one flat at £100 p.a.)	£100 p.a.	
YP 60 years @ 8%	12.3766	£1,238

267

Reversion

To 'share of freehold' with vacant possession value –

Flat 3 – £190,000	£190,000		
Deferred 60 years @ 5%	0.0535	£10,165	£11,403
Value of the freeholder's interest			£48,719

Hope value with respect to flat 3, non-participator

Hope value is calculated as a percentage of marriage value.

Marriage value

Difference between the aggregate of values of interests under the control of the non-participating tenant

Value of the freeholder's interest	£0	
Share of freehold value –		
Flat 3 – £190,000	£190,000	£190,000

less

Aggregate of values of interests prior to enfranchisement

Value of the freeholder's interest (from above)	£11,403	
Non-participating tenant's existing lease value –		
Flat 3 – £153,900 (see table)	£153,900	£165,303
Marriage value		£24,697
Hope value at 5% thereof	0.05	£1,235

Note that hope value is calculated as a percentage of 100 per cent of the marriage value.

Plus the freeholder's share of marriage value

Note the marriage value computation includes participators only.

Difference between the aggregate of values of interests under the control of the participating tenants

Value of the freeholder's interest	£0	
Aggregate of participating tenants share of freehold values –		
Flat 1 – £225,000		
Flat 2 – £200,000		
Flat 4 – £180,000	£605,000	£605,000

Flats: collective enfranchisement valuation issues

less			
Aggregate of values of interests prior to enfranchisement			
Value of the freeholder's interest (from above)	£36,081		
Aggregate of participating tenants existing lease values (see table)			
Flat 1 – £182,250			
Flat 2 – £162,000			
Flat 4 – £145,800	£490,050	£526,131	
Marriage value		£78,869	
50% thereof		0.5	£39,435
Enfranchisement price:			
Value of the freeholder's interest (from above)			
Participators			£37,316
Non-participator			£11,403
plus			
Freeholder's 50% apportionment of marriage value			£39,435
Enfranchisement price (excluding costs)			£88,154
		Say	£88,150

Hope value is assessed at five per cent of the non-participator's (Flat 3) marriage value; the non-participator represents 25 per cent of the total number of flats, and the unexpired term is 60 years. In *Culley*, the non-participators represented 50 per cent of the total number of flats, and the unexpired terms were 65.37 years – on that basis, five per cent of marriage value is attributed.

Hope value in relation to a section 42 notice

Paragraph 3(1)(b) of Schedule 6 is as follows:

> on the assumption that this Chapter and Chapter II confer no right to acquire any interest in the specified premises or to acquire any new lease (except that this shall not preclude the taking into account of a notice given under section 42 with respect to a flat contained in the specified premises where it is given by a person other than a participating tenant);

Leasehold enfranchisement explained

The question is how to take this into consideration in the assessment of hope value.

At paragraph 107 of the House of Lords decision in *Sportelli*, Lord Neuberger says with respect to paragraph 3(1)(b):

> 'There are two reasons why, in my opinion, the bracketed words in para 3(1)(b) are significant for present purposes. First, all that the service of a section 42 notice does is to give the tenant a right to acquire a new lease: he can pull out at any time – see section 52. Accordingly, para 3(1) permits some hope value attributable to non-participating tenants' flats to be included on any view. Secondly, the bracketed words in para 3(1)(b) require one to take into account the "notice", not the rights and obligations which accrue pursuant to it. That suggests to me that the purpose of sub-para (b) is to entitle the landlord to argue that the section 42 notice is evidence that the tenant concerned is interested in acquiring a new lease of his flat. Where a non-participating tenant has served such a notice, the hope value attributable to his flat may well be increased because he has made it clear that he is interested in acquiring a new lease of his flat. In other words, by serving a section 42 notice, a non-participating tenant has, in my view, assisted any contention that he would be in the market, because he has evinced a desire to acquire a new lease of his flat at market value, which is what Schedule 13 effectively means that he would have to pay'.

From the above, albeit at the time of publication the author is unaware of an Upper Tribunal decision confirming this, what Lord Neuberger says is that where a section 42 notice has been served, and the tenant is a non-participator, the hope value (pro rata) attributable to this flat would be higher than for a flat where no such notice has been served. So in the assessment of hope value, there would two separate computations: (1) for those non-participators where no notice has been served; and (2) where a notice has been served. To the latter, a higher percentage of marriage value would be assessed as hope value.

This approach is shown in Example 4 to follow.

An alternative approach to assess hope value where a section 42 notice has been served, and one that has been adopted by valuers and the LVT hitherto (*Erkman* and *Earl Cadogan* at

Nos. 42 and 38 Cadogan Square, London SW1, respectively), is to apply an appropriate percentage to the anticipated new lease premium calculated under Schedule 13. What Lord Neuberger says in *Sportelli* suggests this might not be the correct approach, 'the notice being that what is to be taken into account, not the rights and obligations which accrue pursuant to it'; the latter would include the premium computation under Schedule 13.

On the face of it, the approach in *Culley* is to be adopted where a section 42 notice has been served.

Tenant's hope value

A further issue is raised by Lord Neuberger in *Sportelli*. Regarding tenant's hope value; at paragraph 93 he says:

> 'There is a potential complicating factor I should mention. In a case where the marriage value is shared equally, just as the landlord's interest should be valued excluding hope value, so, I am inclined to think, should the tenant's leasehold interest. In some cases, the valuation of the tenant's interest may include hope value, as the President in *Pitts* [2007] 3 EGLR 86, para 16, where he said that "hope value does not necessarily exclusively reside in the landlord's interest". It may well be unfair on the landlord if he is precluded from seeking hope value in circumstances where, for the purpose of assessing the marriage value, the tenant's leasehold interest is valued including hope value. So, while as a matter of principle, it appears to me that, under section 9(1A) [note the case in question referred to an enfranchisement claim of a house under section 9(1A) of the 1967 Act], the valuation of the landlord's interest should not include hope value, if it could be shown that the valuation of the tenant's interest included hope value and that this was illogical and unfair on the landlord, then an adjustment would have to be made'.

In *Chelsea Properties Limited v Earl Cadogan and Cadogan Estates Limited* (unreported, 2007), the Lands Tribunal determined that for the purposes of Schedule 13, paragraph 4A, 'hope value (i.e. the value representing the possibility of a deal being done between landlord and tenant), must be disregarded so far as concerns valuing the tenant's existing underlease', (para. 19).

Coming from an Estate Agency background and with a number of years' experience of selling flats on various unexpired terms in PCL, prior to the provisions of the 1993 Act being enacted, the author can confirm that tenant's hope value undoubtedly exists in the 'no-Act World'. Purchasers paying sums for leasehold interests otherwise reflecting that at some future date the freeholder would be willing to treat at arms length for a sale of an extended lease.

Whereas in the with-Act (real) world the timing of release of marriage value is in the tenant's hands, in the no-Act world, where the landlord is not compelled to grant a new lease or sell his freehold interest, it is he who has the final say in the timing of release of marriage value. That is not to say a freeholder in the no-Act world will only sit and wait for an approach from the tenant to treat; it was not uncommon for freeholders to approach tenants pre 1993 to seek to release marriage value. The same continues in the with-Act world, albeit to a lesser degree.

If tenant's hope value is to be disregarded in the marriage value computation, assessment of its quantum in the now wholly contaminated with-Act world is probably going to be on a hypothetical basis, unless there is historical data to analyse.

It is arguable that by making an adjustment for the benefit of the Act (Act rights), one removes tenant's hope value in any event. In which case, an analysis as to its quantum is redundant.

Further valuation issues

In addition to the various points raised in new lease claims, there are a number of specific issues that arise in collective enfranchisement. Save for relatively straightforward cases, typically Examples 1 and 2, any two collective enfranchisement claims are unlikely to be the same, with differing issues arising. These may include any number of the following, which also serves as a checklist.

- Caretaker's flat – the first question is to establish whether the nominee purchaser has a legal right to acquire the interest in any event; if so, the freehold interest is acquired. Having said that, the freeholder may be in a position to take an optional leaseback of the 'unit' if the provisions of Schedule 9, paragraph 5(1) are met, which include that the unit is not let to a qualifying tenant.

Where the tenants are in direct covenant with the freeholder, and the flat is to be acquired, the minimum price that the nominee purchaser might expect to pay is the freeholder's reversionary interest, i.e. the freehold with vacant possession value deferred over the term.

The lease documentation may allow for recovery of 'rent' through the service charge provisions from the lessees for the accommodation provided. There will probably be further argument as to whether the accommodation remains for use for caretaking services once the enfranchisement has completed. If not, the argument runs, the accommodation could be sold on the open market on a long lease with vacant possession, thus resulting in an early profit to the nominee purchaser. The counter arguments are that: (a) the participators will require the continuing services of the caretaker, in accordance with the respective lease covenants and obligations; and (b) the non-participators have similar covenants in their leases providing for caretaking services, thus preventing an open market sale. Each case is to be handled on its merits.

- Garages, outhouse, garden, yard – are appurtenant property and thus the freehold can be acquired where the property is demised by the lease held by a qualifying tenant. There are circumstances in collective enfranchisement where a number of garages are appurtenant property, but others forming part of the same terrace are not (see chapter 3).
- Grounds, private access road, drive, gardens and lightwells, etc. – where lessees have rights over grounds, etc. these are known as 'common use areas'. The freehold of these can be acquired in the collective enfranchisement, but the freeholder is entitled to retain the same and may choose to grant permanent 'equivalent rights' in lieu. In the balance of cases, there will be common use areas beyond the demise of the flats and common parts to be acquired as part of the enfranchisement. Each of these requires a value to be attributed, which in turn will be included in the notice. Assessing value is a matter of opinion; in the various cases that the author has handled, typical sums proposed in section 13 notices and section 21 counter-notices for lightwells have been £1, and for small communal gardens, £100.
- Leasebacks – there are provisions for mandatory and optional leasebacks. Optional leasebacks fall into two categories: (1) a

unit not let to a qualifying tenant; and (2) a unit occupied by the freeholder.

Typically, a shop unit is one on which the freeholder can seek an optional leaseback on the basis of a 999 years lease. This has the effect of removing the shop from the price computation, which in turn may suit both parties. Having said that, the landlord can oblige the nominee purchaser to acquire the shop, which depending on the circumstances, may make the enfranchisement price prohibitive.

This is particularly important with the amendment to section 4(1)(b) increasing the allowable non-residential part to 25 per cent, whereby many more buildings now qualify for collective enfranchisement.

In addition, this can include flats let on sub-21 years' leases, which in turn could be occupied by statutory tenants under the *Rent Act* 1977 or assured tenants under the *Housing Act* 1988. It is the author's experience, where a collective enfranchisement claim is made and there are flats occupied by either *Rent Act* protected statutory tenants or assured tenancies, that optional leasebacks will be taken – but this is not necessarily always going to be the case. This is one of those situations where 'alternative' proposals can be made in the notice and counter-notice.

Checklist for the tenants' valuer

Initial meeting:

- steering group/single point of contact;
- float (typically to cover initial valuation and legal costs);
- participators/non-participators;
- copy lease documentation;
- access arrangements for inspections; and
- likely timetable to service of notice.

Inspections:

- cross section or all of participating tenants' flats;
- all non-participating tenants' flats (improvements?);
- common parts;
- any caretaker's accommodation;
- underground car parking and garages;
- communal gardens and access routes; and
- any neighbouring property in same freehold ownership.

Valuation issues:

The freeholder's (and any intermediate leaseholder's) interest:

- general principles follow new lease claims;
- participators and non-participators;
- hope value;
- section 42 notice.

Marriage value:

- participators only;
- improvements and benefit of the Act?
- apportionment between interests.

Compensation:

- development value.

Price:

- individual sums for participators;
- prices for all interests to be acquired;
- apportionment attributable to non-participators including funding the same.

It will have become apparent that the more problematic issues in valuation in collective enfranchisement are not generally with respect to the participators, but the non-participators, where there is a caretaker's flat and any suspended section 42 notices (s.54(2)), inter alia.

We now look at intermediate leasehold interests.

Part III of Schedule 6 covers intermediate leasehold interests. It comprises four paragraphs, briefly as follows:

- price payable for intermediate leasehold interests (para. 6);
- value of intermediate leasehold interests (para. 7);
- compensation for loss on acquisition of interest (para. 8); and
- owners of intermediate interests entitled to part of marriage value (para. 9).

Paragraph 6, section 1 (a) and (b) says a separate price shall be payable for each interest; and the price shall be the aggregate of the value of the interest and any amount of compensation. This follows the corresponding paragraph in Schedule 13.

Paragraph 7 sets out the basis of valuing the intermediate interest and the assumptions to be applied; this follows Schedule 13, paragraph 8, including the provisions for valuing a minor intermediate lease. As the interest is to be acquired outright, there is no corresponding definition to that in Schedule 13, paragraph 7, 'diminution in value of intermediate interest'.

Paragraph 8, compensation for loss on acquisition of interest, follows Schedule 13, paragraph 9.

Paragraph 9, owners of intermediate interests entitled to part of marriage value, similarly follows Schedule 13, paragraph 10. The 50 per cent landlords' share of marriage value is to be apportioned pro rata to the value of the respective interests (see chapter 2).

Part III is as follows:

PART III
INTERMEDIATE LEASEHOLD INTERESTS

Price payable for intermediate leasehold interests

6(1) Where the nominee purchaser is to acquire one or more intermediate leasehold interests–

    (a) a separate price shall be payable for each of those interests; and
    (b) (subject to the provisions of this paragraph) that price shall be the aggregate of–
        (i) the value of the interest as determined in accordance with paragraph 7, and
        (ii) any amount of compensation payable to the owner of that interest in accordance with paragraph 8.

(2) Where in the case of any intermediate leasehold interest the amount arrived at in accordance with sub-paragraph (1)(b) is a negative amount, the price payable by the nominee purchaser for the interest shall be nil.

Value of intermediate leasehold interests

7(1) Subject to sub-paragraph (2), paragraph 3 shall apply for determining the value of any intermediate leasehold interest for the purposes of paragraph 6(1)(b)(i) with such modifications as are appropriate to relate that paragraph to a sale of the interest in question subject (where applicable) to any leases intermediate between that interest and any lease held by a qualifying tenant of a flat contained in the specified premises.

(1A) In its application in accordance with sub-paragraph (1), 3(1A) shall have effect with the addition after paragraph (a) of–

'(aa) an owner of a freehold interest in the specified premises, or'.

(2) The value of an intermediate leasehold interest which is the interest of the tenant under a minor intermediate lease shall be calculated by applying the formula set out in sub-paragraph (7) instead of in accordance with sub-paragraph (1).

(3) "A minor intermediate lease" means a lease complying with the following requirements, namely–

(a) it must have an expectation of possession of not more than one month, and
(b) the profit rent in respect of the lease must be not more than £5 per year; and, in the case of a lease which is in immediate reversion on two or more leases, those requirements must be complied with in connection with each of the sub-leases.

(4) Where a minor intermediate lease is in immediate reversion on two or more leases–

(a) the formula set out in sub-paragraph (7) shall be applied in relation to each of those sub-leases (and sub-paragraphs (5) and (6) shall also so apply); and
(b) the value of the interest of the tenant under the minor intermediate lease shall accordingly be the aggregate of the amounts calculated by so applying the formula.

(5) "Profit rent" means an amount equal to that of the rent payable under the lease on which the minor intermediate lease is in immediate reversion, less that of the rent payable under the minor intermediate lease.

(6) Where the minor intermediate lease or that on which it is in immediate reversion comprises property other than a flat held by a qualifying tenant, then in sub-paragraph (5) the reference to the rent payable under it means so much of that rent as is apportioned to any such flat.

(7) The formula is—

$$P = £\, \frac{R}{Y} - \frac{R}{Y(1+Y)^n}$$

where—

P = the price payable;

R = the profit rent;

Y = the yield (expressed as a decimal fraction) from 2½ per cent. Consolidated Stock;

n = the period, expressed in years (taking any part of a year as a whole year), of the remainder of the term of the minor intermediate lease as at the relevant date.

(8) In calculating the yield from 2½ per cent Consolidated Stock, the price of that stock shall be taken to be the middle market price at the close of business on the last trading day in the week before the relevant date.

(9) For the purposes of this paragraph the expectation of possession carried by a lease in relation to a lease ("the sub-lease") on which it is in immediate reversion is the expectation of possession which it carries at the relevant date after the sub-lease, on the basis that—

(a) (subject to sub-paragraph (10)) where the sub-lease is a lease held by a qualifying tenant of a flat contained in the specified premises, it terminates at the relevant date if its term date fell before then, or else it terminates on its term date; and

(b) in any other case, the sub-lease terminates on its term date.

(10) In a case where before the relevant date for the purposes of this Chapter the landlord of any such qualifying tenant as is mentioned in sub-paragraph (9)(a) had given notice to quit terminating the tenant's sub-lease on a date earlier than that date, the date specified in the notice to quit shall be substituted for the date specified in that provision.

Compensation for loss on acquisition of interest

8(1) Where the owner of the intermediate interest will suffer any loss or damage to which this paragraph applies, there shall be payable to him such amount as is reasonable to compensate him for that loss or damage.

(2) This paragraph applies to–

(a) any diminution in value of any interest of the owner of the intermediate leasehold interest in other property resulting from the acquisition of his interest in the specified premises; and
(b) any other loss or damage which results therefrom to the extent that it is referable to his ownership of any interest in other property.

(3) Without prejudice to the generality of paragraph (b) of sub-paragraph (2), the kinds of loss falling within that paragraph include loss of development value in relation to the specified premises to the extent that it is referable as mentioned in that paragraph.

(4) In sub-paragraph (3) "development value", in relation to the specified premises, means any increase in the value of the interest in the premises of the owner of the intermediate leasehold interest which is attributable to the possibility of demolishing, reconstructing or carrying out substantial works of construction on, the whole or a substantial part of the premises.

Owners of intermediate interests entitled to part of marriage value

9(1) This paragraph applies where paragraph 2 applies and–

(a) the price payable for the freehold of the specified premises includes an amount in respect of the freeholder's share of the marriage value, and
(b) the nominee purchaser is to acquire any intermediate leasehold interests.

(2) The amount payable to the freeholder in respect of his share of the marriage value shall be divided between the freeholder and the owners of the intermediate leasehold interests in proportion to the value of their respective interests in the specified premises (as determined for the purposes of paragraph 2(1)(a) or paragraph 6(1)(b)(i), as the case may be).

(3) Where the owner of an intermediate leasehold interest is entitled in accordance with sub-paragraph (2) to any part of the amount payable to the freeholder in respect of the freeholder's share of the marriage value, the amount to which he is so entitled shall be payable to him by the freeholder.

Further points on hope value

Two further points require discussion with respect to hope value:

1) treatment of tenant's improvements; and
2) an intermediate leaseholder's share of hope value, if any.

Whereas at the time of drafting, there has been a decision of the Upper Tribunal on the subject of hope value (*Culley*); the facts of that case did not address the questions of: (1) how a non-participator's flat which has been 'improved' is to be treated; and (2) whether an intermediate leasehold interest is entitled to a share of hope value.

Treatment of tenant's improvements – it is the author's view and following the House of Lords decision in *Sportelli*, that tenant's improvements are not to be disregarded in the hope value computation, principally as follows: (1) there is no disregard in paragraph 3 for improvements in valuing the non-participators' flats; and (2) the hope value computation takes place in the no-Act world where the freeholder's and the tenants' interests would be valued 'as seen', save as to any disrepair. Accordingly, in the next example, where a non-participator's flat is improved, the improved value is taken into the hope value computation.

Where there is an intermediate leasehold interest, with either a nominal or substantial reversion, is the intermediate lessee due a share of hope value in any event – it is the author's view that the intermediate lessee is due a share of hope value, apportioned following the marriage value sharing provisions, for the following reasons:

- If an intermediate leasehold interest has a substantial reversion, he would receive a share of hope value.
- Where the intermediate landlord has a nominal reversion, it is argued that when an extended lease is granted to the tenant, it is the freeholder who provides (surrenders) the lion's share of the reversion, and therefore the intermediate lessee should not receive any share of the premium.

    However, in the no-Act world where a freeholder and a tenant strike a bargain for an extended lease and there is an intermediate leasehold interest, the likelihood is that the intermediate lessee would receive an apportionment of the price paid (which may be a small proportion), if only to facilitate the problems circumvented in the legislation of the deemed surrender and re-grant of the intermediate lease in accordance with Schedule 11, paragraph 10.
- In addition, it is argued that the freeholder may grant an overriding 'reversionary lease' to bypass the intermediate landlord; that may be so in some cases, but on balance a share of the premium is more likely and being so, a share of hope value is due.
- The author does not believe that the intermediate leaseholder's entitlement to a share of marriage value provided in paragraph 9 is relevant for these purposes, as the hope value calculation is one in the no-Act world.

On the basis of each of the above, in the following example, tenant's improvements are not disregarded in the hope value computation, and the intermediate leaseholder is apportioned a share of the same. It is anticipated that future decisions of the Upper Tribunal will give guidance on these two issues.

We now look at an example which covers a number of the valuation issues that can arise in a collective enfranchisement claim. As long as the valuer follows the principles that have been discussed to this point, even the most daunting of price computations, with its associated complications, can be mastered.

Leasehold enfranchisement explained

> *Example 4*
>
> You are invited to advise a group of tenants on their potential collective enfranchisement claim on a block of flats in PCL. You have had your initial meeting, received confirmation of your instructions, have carried out your inspections, and have established the following.
>
> The building is a freehold purpose built block of 40 flats over basement, ground and first to tenth floors. The basement and areas immediately surrounding the building provide 40 single lock-up garages, a caretaker's flat, communal gardens, and a private roadway.
>
> From the legal documentation provided, there is a head lease in place for an original term of 99 years, with 45 years unexpired (as at the assumed date of valuation), at an initial rent of £2,000 per annum, doubling every 33 years.
>
> The underleases are for terms to the head lease at initial ground rents of £150 per annum, doubling every 33 years. A number of the flats are now subject to new leases pursuant to claims under the 1993 Act.
>
> The head lease user covenant provides for a caretaker's flat (Flat A); further covenants include: only to use the flat as a basement caretaker's flat; to provide a full time caretaker; such caretaker to reside rent free on a service basis.
>
> The existing underleases and new leases allow for the caretaker's flat to be provided at a market rent, the rent and associated costs to be recovered from the lessees within their respective service charge provisions. You value the flat at £200 per week (£10,400 per annum) on FRI terms.
>
> You, in conjunction with the solicitor advising the group, establish that the participators and non-participators are as follows, with their respective lease ground rent provisions and capital values (which include one lock-up garage per flat). 'In repair' each flat per floor has equal value.
>
> The tenant at Flat 20 has submitted a section 42 notice for a new lease; for which a section 45 counter-notice admitting the claim has been served. The tenant is a non-participator.
>
> The valuation issues in this collective enfranchisement include, inter alia, the following:
>
> - an intermediate lease;
> - varying years unexpired lease terms;
> - participators and non-participators (including the head lessee);
> - flats that are both 'in repair' and 'improved';
> - hope value;
> - the non-participators include the tenant at Flat 20 who has served a section 42 notice, which in turn has been admitted;

Flats: collective enfranchisement valuation issues

- a caretaker's flat;
- 40 lock-up garages, which in this case are all demised with the individual flats, thus are appurtenant property; and
- communal gardens and private roadway – common use areas.

The valuation is as follows:

Participators

Share of freehold, new and existing lease vacant possession values 'in repair' with any value attributable to improvements disregarded.

Flat No. & Garage	Floor	Unexpired Term Years	Current Ground Rent (£ p.a.)	Ground Rent on Review (£ p.a.)	Existing Lease Value £	Share of Freehold Value £	Comments
1	Gd	45	£300	£600	£315,000	£450,000	
2	Gd	135	£0	£0	n/a	£450,000	MV nil
4	Gd	45	£300	£600	£315,000	£450,000	
6	1st	135	£0	£0	n/a	£475,000	MV nil
7	1st	45	£300	£600	£332,500	£475,000	
8	1st	45	£300	£600	£332,500	£475,000	
9	2nd	135	£0	£0	n/a	£490,000	MV nil
10	2nd	45	£300	£600	£343,000	£490,000	
12a	3rd	45	£300	£600	£350,000	£500,000	
15	3rd	45	£300	£600	£350,000	£500,000	
16	3rd	135	£0	£0	n/a	£500,000	MV nil
17	4th	45	£300	£600	£353,500	£505,000	
21	5th	45	£300	£600	£357,000	£510,000	
22	5th	45	£300	£600	£357,000	£510,000	
26	6th	45	£300	£600	£360,500	£515,000	
28	6th	135	£0	£0	n/a	£515,000	MV nil
29	7th	45	£300	£600	£364,000	£520,000	
30	7th	45	£300	£600	£364,000	£520,000	
31	7th	45	£300	£600	£364,000	£520,000	
33	8th	45	£300	£600	£367,500	£525,000	
34	8th	45	£300	£600	£367,500	£525,000	
36	8th	135	£0	£0	n/a	£525,000	MV nil
38	9th/10th	45	£300	£600	£560,000	£800,000	
40	9th/10th	45	£300	£600	£560,000	£800,000	
TOTALS		135 yrs	£0	£0	n/a	£2,955,000	
		45 yrs	£5,400	£10,800	£6,713,000	£9,590,000	

Leasehold enfranchisement explained

Non-Participators

Share of freehold, new and existing lease vacant possession values 'as is' save where in disrepair, in which case valued 'in repair' – any value attributable to improvements is not disregarded.

Typically, to highlight this point, Flat 3 on the ground floor is valued share of freehold at £475,000 compared with £450,000 for Flats 1, 2 and 4 – £25,000 being the value of improvements.

The head lessee is a non-participator, accordingly the caretaker's flat share of freehold value is listed here.

Flat No. & Garage	Floor	Unexpired Term Years	Current Ground Rent (£ p.a.)	Ground Rent on Review (£ p.a.)	Existing Lease Value £	Share of Freehold Value £	Comments
A	B	45	£10,400	£10,400	n/a	£200,000	
3	Gd	45	£300	£600	£332,500	£475,000	
5	1st	45	£300	£600	£332,500	£475,000	
11	2nd	45	£300	£600	£343,000	£490,000	
12	2nd	45	£300	£600	£343,000	£490,000	
14	3rd	45	£300	£600	£357,000	£510,000	
18	4th	135	£0	£0	n/a	£505,000	HV-nominal
19	4th	45	£300	£600	£353,500	£505,000	
20	4th	45	£300	£600	£374,500	£535,000	s.42 notice, admitted
23	5th	135	£0	£0	n/a	£550,000	HV-nominal
24	5th	45	£300	£600	£357,000	£510,000	
25	6th	45	£300	£600	£360,500	£515,000	
27	6th	45	£300	£600	£385,000	£550,000	
32	7th	45	£300	£600	£364,000	£520,000	
35	8th	45	£300	£600	£367,500	£525,000	
37	9th/10th	45	£300	£600	£612,500	£875,000	
39	9th/10th	135	£0	£0	n/a	£800,000	HV–nominal
TOTALS		135 yrs	£0	£0	n/a	£1,855,000	
		45 yrs	£3,600	£7,200	£4,508,000	£6,440,000	excluding Flat 20
		Caretaker's Flat	£10,400	£10,400	n/a	£200,000	
		Flat 20	£300	£600	£374,500	£535,000	

The price is made up of the freeholder's interest, which includes hope value, the intermediate leaseholder's interest, plus 50 per cent of marriage value.

Date of valuation: 25 March 2010

Lease expiry dates – 25 March 2055
                     25 March 2055
                     25 March 2145

Value of the freeholder's interest

Participators

Term

Leases to March 2055

Head lease initial rent at £2,000 per annum doubling every 33 years, current rent £4,000 per annum, with review up to £8,000 per annum in 12 years. Twenty-four underlessees of 40 participating, apportion head rent to participators at 24/40ths – 60 per cent.

Term (1)

Rent (60% of £4,000 p.a.)	£2,400 p.a.	
YP 12 years @ 6%	8.3838	£20,121

Term (2)

Rent (60% of £8,000 p.a.)	£4,800 p.a.	
YP 33 years @ 6%	14.2302	
Deferred 12 years @ 6%	0.4970	£33,948

Reversions

March 2055

45 years lease interests – aggregate of 'share of freehold' vacant possession values	£9,590,000	
Deferred 45 years @ 5%	0.1113	£1,067,367
		£1,121,436

March 2145

135 years lease interests – aggregate of 'share of freehold' vacant possession values	£2,955,000	
Deferred 135 years @ 5%	0.0014	£4,137

plus

Hope value

See computations below:

Non-participators (excluding Flat 20)		£136,590	
Flat 20		£23,170	£1,285,333

Non-participators

Term

Leases to March 2055

Head lease initial rent at £2,000 per annum doubling every 33 years, current rent £4,000 per annum, with review up to £8,000 per annum in 12 years. Sixteen underlessees of 40 non-participating, apportion head rent to non-participators at 16/40ths – 40 per cent (including Flat 20, see later).

Term (1)

Rent (40% of £4,000 p.a.)	£1,600 p.a.	
YP 12 years @ 6%	8.3838	£13,414

Term (2)

Rent (40% of £8,000 p.a.)	£3,200 p.a.	
YP 33 years @ 6%	14.2302	
Deferred 12 years @ 6%	0.4970	£22,632

Reversions

March 2055

45 years lease interests – aggregate of 'share of freehold' vacant possession values (including Flat 20)	£6,975,000	
Deferred 45 years @ 5%	0.1113	£776,318
		£812,364

March 2145

135 years lease interests – aggregate of 'share of freehold' vacant possession values	£1,855,000		
Deferred 135 years @ 5%	0.0014	£2,597	
Caretaker's flat – 'share of freehold' vacant possession value	£200,000		
Deferred 45 years @ 5%	0.1113	£22,260	£837,221

Value of intermediate leaseholder's interest

Participators

Flats: collective enfranchisement valuation issues

Term

Head lease rent apportioned as above.

Term (1)

Rent receivable from underlessees	£5,400 p.a.	
Less rent to freeholder	£2,400 p.a.	
Profit rent	£3,000 p.a.	
YP 12 years @ 7% and 2.25%	6.9678	£20,903

Term (2)

Rent receivable from underlessees	£10,800 p.a.	
Less rent to freeholder	£4,800 p.a.	
Profit rent	£6,000 p.a.	
YP 33 years @ 7% and 2.25%	11.0184	
Deferred 12 years @ 7%	0.4440	£29,353
Reversion – nominal		£0
		£50,256

plus

Hope value

See computations below:

Non-participators (excluding Flat 20)	£6,574	
Flat 20	£903	£57,733

Non- participators

Term

Head lease rent apportioned as above.

Term (1)

Rent receivable from underlessees	£3,900 p.a.	
Less rent to freeholder	£1,600 p.a.	
Profit rent	£2,300 p.a.	
YP 12 years @ 7% and 2.25%	6.9678	£16,026

Term (2)

Rent receivable from underlessees	£7,800 p.a.	
Less rent to freeholder	£3,200 p.a.	

Profit rent	£4,600 p.a.		
YP 33 years @ 7% and 2.25%	11.0184		
Deferred 12 years @ 7%	0.4440	£22,504	
Reversion – nominal		£0	
		£38,530	

The caretaker's flat

Term

Rent receivable from underlessees £10,400 p.a.

YP 45 years @ 8% and 2.25%	10.7448	£111,746	£150,276

Hope value

Hope value is assessed as a percentage of marriage value of the non-participating tenants' flats; a separate computation is carried out for Flat 20, as a section 42 notice has been admitted. Flats with new leases of 135 years' terms are excluded, as hope value attributable to those would be 'nominal'.

Marriage value computation for non-participators, excluding Flat 20:

The difference between the aggregate of values of interests under the control of the non-participating tenants...

Freeholder's interest	£0	
Intermediate leaseholder's interest	£0	
Non-participating tenants' aggregate share of freehold vacant possession values (see table)	£6,440,000	£6,440,000

less

Aggregate of values of interests prior to enfranchisement

Freeholder's interest –	£ 750,565	
Intermediate leaseholder's interest –	£36,122	
Aggregate of non-participating tenants' existing lease values –	£4,508,000	£5,294,687
Marriage value		£1,145,313
Hope value at 12.5% thereof	0.125	£143,164

Hope value apportioned as follows:

Following approach in Schedule 6, paragraph 9, hope value is apportioned pro rata to the value of each interest.

Flats: collective enfranchisement valuation issues

Freeholder

$$\frac{(750,565)}{(750,565 + 36,122)} \times £143,164 = £136,590$$

Intermediate leaseholder

$$\frac{(36,122)}{(36,122 + 750,565)} \times £143,164 = £6,574$$

Marriage value computation for non-participator, Flat 20:

The difference between the aggregate of values of interests under the control of the non-participating tenant ...

Freeholder's interest	£0	
Intermediate leaseholder's interest	£0	
Non-participating tenant's share of freehold vacant possession value (see table)	£535,000	£535,000

less

Aggregate of values of interests prior to enfranchisement

Freeholder's interest –	£61,799	
Intermediate leaseholder's interest –	£2,408	
Non-participating tenant's existing lease value –	£374,500	£438,707
Marriage value		£96,293
Hope value at 25% thereof	0.25	£24,073

Hope value apportioned as above:

Freeholder

$$\frac{(61,799)}{(61,799 + 2,408)} \times £24,073 = £23,170$$

Intermediate leaseholder

$$\frac{(2,408)}{(2,408 + 61,799)} \times £24,073 = £903$$

Marriage value

Note the marriage value computation includes participators only.

The difference between the aggregate of values of interests under the control of the participating tenants ...

Freeholder's interest	£0
Intermediate leaseholder's interest	£0

289

Leasehold enfranchisement explained

Participating tenants' aggregate share of freehold with vacant possession values (see table)	£9,590,000	£9,590,000

less

Aggregate of values of interests prior to enfranchisement

Freeholder's interest – (from above)	£1,121,436
Intermediate leaseholder's interest – (from above)	£50,256
Aggregate of participating tenants' existing lease values – (from above)	£6,713,000 £7,884,692
Marriage value	£1,705,308
50% thereof	0.5 £852,654

Apportionment of marriage value:

<u>Freeholder</u>

$$\frac{(1,121,436)}{(1,121,436 + 50,256)} \times £852,654 = £816,082$$

<u>Intermediate leaseholder</u>

$$\frac{(50,256)}{(50,256 + 1,121,436)} \times £852,654 = £36,572$$

Enfranchisement price (excluding costs): £3,183,315

Made up of as follows:

<u>Freeholder's apportionment</u>

Participators including hope value	£1,285,333	
Non-participators including caretaker's flat	£837,221	
Marriage value	£816,082	
Communal gardens and private roadway, say	£100	£2,938,736
	Say	£2,938,735

<u>Intermediate leaseholder's apportionment</u>

Participators including hope value	£57,733
Non-participators including caretaker's flat	£150,276

290

Flats: collective enfranchisement valuation issues

Marriage value	£36,572	
Communal gardens and private roadway, say	£1	£244,582
	Say	£244,580

The computation is set out in full to highlight all of the valuation issues; note the following:

- single rate tables are applied to the freeholder's rental stream (six per cent), to calculate the value of the 'term'; on review, by convention, the deferment rate applied for the numbers of years to uplift is the same as the capitalisation rate. The deferment rate in these circumstances is not to be confused with that applied to the vacant possession value in calculating the value of the freeholder's reversion;
- dual rate tables are applied to calculate the value of the intermediate lease, similarly by convention;
- a deferment rate of five per cent is adopted to calculate the value of the freeholder's reversion, following *Sportelli*;
- in the hope value calculation, tenants' improvements are not disregarded, and the intermediate leaseholder is apportioned a pro rata share, for the reasons stated;
- forty per cent of the tenants are non-participators, for which the unexpired terms of the existing leases are 45 years; hope value is assessed at 12.5 per cent of the marriage value;
- a section 42 notice has been served and admitted at Flat 20; hope value is assessed at 25 per cent of marriage value in this case, being double that for the remainder of the non-participating flats, to reflect the fact that the tenant has made it clear he is interested in taking a new lease; and
- comparatively nominal prices are proposed for the communal gardens and the private roadway, but be aware sums are required nonetheless.

Checklist for the freeholder's valuer

In the main, as with new lease claims, this follows the checklist for the tenant's valuer. There are, however, a number of specific valuation issues and practical points to be addressed and to be aware of when advising a freeholder in an enfranchisement claim.

- The date by which the counter-notice is to be served, bearing in mind that if the timetable follows that for new lease claims,

there will be a greater workload to be undertaken, which in some cases will be far greater.
- The solicitor and the valuer are to work in tandem. Whereas for most new lease claims, the solicitor will probably not inspect the flat, in collective enfranchisement it is probable he will want to accompany the valuer on a cross section of inspections of the various flats. More importantly, he will want to inspect the outside of the premises, particularly where there are grounds, a private access road, and garages, etc.
- There will be, in most cases, questions as to whether the freeholder admits the nominee purchaser's claim to acquire the freehold interest in common use areas, typically, as opposed to granting permanent equivalent rights thereto. Accordingly, there will be questions up to the date of the service of the counter-notice as to the constituent parts that are claimed by the nominee purchaser, and which are contended for by the freeholder. It is advisable to value the various constituent parts on 'either/or' bases from the outset; by doing so, the chances of having to prepare valuations at short notice are minimised and the client is made aware of the various valuation issues at the earliest opportunity.
- Intermediate leasehold interest – whereas in a new lease claim the intermediate lease effectively continues in its present form; in collective enfranchisement, it is acquired outright. In which case, the intermediate leaseholder may take a more pro-active role prior to the counter-notice being served.
- Participators and non-participators – bear in mind the proportion of participators to non-participators (including aggregate value), and the unexpired terms of the existing leases in assessing the percentage of marriage value to be taken as hope value.
- Appurtenant property – it is for the solicitor to advise whether property is appurtenant within the meaning of the Act; however, he may require information, advice and assistance from the valuer's inspections.
- Leasebacks, mandatory and optional – have in mind the effect on price of commercial premises; and for property where an optional leaseback can be taken, advice will be required on either/or bases.

Further valuation considerations:

A porter's flat

In *Hildron Finance Limited*, the Lands Tribunal discounted the agreed long leasehold vacant possession value of the porter's flat of £300,000 to £200,000, on the basis that a sale of the flat was not prohibited within the lease provisions (the lessor being obliged to maintain the services of a porter, but not a resident porter). The discount reflected the fact that pursuant to a sale, the lessor (the hypothetical purchaser), would still have the problem of providing the portering services; and in any event, if the flat was retained, the lease provisions resulted in a shortfall in the collection of the notional rent.

Telecommunications masts

With the advent of mobile telephone technology, and its accompanying ever-increasing demand for 'mast sites', roof tops of blocks of flats provide an opportunity for telecommunication providers to extend and improve their coverage. Typically, agreements are reached with freeholders to site a mast for a number of years for the payment of an annual rent; such agreements have value.

From a tenant's perspective, mast sites are generally unwelcome. There is the continuing argument on health issues (parents being particularly vociferous); they are usually unsightly, and in collective enfranchisement have an effect on the price. The freeholder will seek a sum to recompense him for loss of income through the agreement. Conversely, it is to be anticipated that the participating tenants will argue that upon completion of the enfranchisement, such are the potential concerns to health; any agreement is to be terminated. Each case is to handled on its merits; it is the author's experience that the LVT is reluctant to attribute a value for telecommunications masts to the enfranchisement price, least of all where there is no planning consent.

In the LVT's decision in *Buckley House (Freehold) Limited v Copper Smith Corporation* (LON/ENF/836/03 dated 14 September 2004, unreported), no value was attributed for a potential telecommunications mast on the roof where there was no planning consent for the same at the date of valuation.

Compensation

Paragraph 5 follows that in Schedule 13:

Compensation for loss resulting from enfranchisement

5(1) Where the freeholder will suffer any loss or damage to which this paragraph applies, there shall be payable to him such amount as is reasonable to compensate him for that loss or damage.

(2) This paragraph applies to–

   (a) any diminution in value of any interest of the freeholder in other property resulting from the acquisition of his interest in the specified premises; and
   (b) any other loss or damage which results therefrom to the extent that it is referable to his ownership of any interest in other property.

(3) Without prejudice to the generality of paragraph (b) of sub-paragraph (2), the kinds of loss falling within that paragraph include loss of development value in relation to the specified premises to the extent that it is referable as mentioned in that paragraph.

(4) In sub-paragraph (3) "development value", in relation to the specified premises, means any increase in the value of the freeholder's interest in the premises which is attributable to the possibility of demolishing, reconstructing, or carrying out substantial works of construction on, the whole or a substantial part of the premises.

(5) Where the freeholder will suffer loss or damage to which this paragraph applies, then in determining the amount of compensation payable to him under this paragraph, it shall not be material that–

   (a) the loss or damage could to any extent be avoided or reduced by the grant to him, in accordance with section 36 and Schedule 9, of a lease granted in pursuance of Part III of that Schedule, and
   (b) he is not requiring the nominee purchaser to grant any such lease.

Note that compensation pursuant to the 'two stage' collective enfranchisement is collected at stage one and not stage two (*Nailrile* paras. 60 to 65); once stage two is reached, it is too late.

Development value

Where a block of flats has the potential for further development, typically a penthouse flat on the roof, the freeholder is strongly advised to seek planning consent for this before a collective enfranchisement claim is made. Firstly, any discount for uncertainty in gaining consent to the site value is removed, bearing in mind the relevant date is the date the notice is given; and secondly, a freeholder's dealings in his interest are restricted under section 19 where the initial notice of collective enfranchisement has been registered.

In *Sherwood Hall*, the Upper Tribunal reduced the LVT's sum for development value in the enfranchisement price from £50,000 to £10,000. In this case, planning consent was granted on appeal eight months post the date of valuation; the initial application for consent having been made four months after the collective enfranchisement claim was given.

In *Arrowdell*, the Lands Tribunal, having assumed an unrestricted site value for roof space with planning consent of £300,000, accepted the valuer on behalf of the landlord's deduction of 50 per cent for uncertainty, and made a further deduction of £10,000 to reflect a covenant.

In *Earl Cadogan v 2 Herbert Crescent Freehold Limited* (LRA/91/2007 dated 15 May 2009), an appeal of the decision of the LVT in the collective enfranchisement of a building where its value for redevelopment into a single house was considerably more than that as flats, the Lands Tribunal in their valuation of the freeholder's interest, assuming conversion to a single house, made deductions from the freehold vacant possession value for the following:

- planning risk, although it is understood this was minimal;
- to buy out a tenant who would have had a statutory right to hold over as an assured tenant, albeit Schedule 10 of the 1989 Act provides for suitable alternative accommodation and thus to give vacant possession;
- the uncertainty of the operation of the provisions of section 61 and Schedule 14 to terminate the new lease on the grounds of redevelopment of another flat; and
- in accordance with the above, the compensation payable under section 61.

The unexpired terms of the existing leases were 4.12 years.

In the Upper Tribunal's decision in *Forty-Five Holdings Limited v Grosvenor (Mayfair) Estate*, (2010) PLSCS 2 it was held that in valuing the freehold when acquired by the nominee purchaser, Schedule 6, paragraphs 4(3) and (4) are to be construed on the basis of enquiring what is the value of the freehold in the hands of the nominee purchaser, rather than the value which the nominee purchaser could obtain by immediately reselling the freehold in the market (para. 23), and any merger of the freehold and leasehold interests is to be disregarded under paragraph 4(4)(b) (para. 25).

This was an appeal from a decision of the LVT by the nominee purchaser (*Forty-Five Holdings Ltd*), who was also a participating tenant. The question being, whether in calculating marriage value, the potential to release development value was to be taken into account. The Upper Chamber dismissed the appeal and held that development value should be included in the marriage value computation.

Part IV is 'other interests to be acquired' and comprises four paragraphs, 10 to 13, which in turn follow paragraphs 2 to 5.

PART IV
OTHER INTERESTS TO BE ACQUIRED

Price payable for other interests

10(1) Where the nominee purchaser is to acquire any freehold interest in pursuance of section 1(2)(a) or (4) or section 21(4), then (subject to sub-paragraph (3) below) the price payable for that interest shall be the aggregate of–

   (a) the value of the interest as determined in accordance with paragraph 11,
   (b) any share of the marriage value to which the owner of the interest is entitled under paragraph 12, and
   (c) any amount of compensation payable to the owner of the interest in accordance with paragraph 13.

(2) Where the nominee purchaser is to acquire any leasehold interest by virtue of section 2(1) other than an intermediate leasehold interest, or he is to acquire any leasehold interest in pursuance of section 21(4), then (subject to sub-paragraph (3) below) the price payable for that interest shall be the aggregate of–

(a) the value of the interest as determined in accordance with paragraph 11, and
(b) any amount of compensation payable to the owner of the interest in accordance with paragraph 13.

(3) Where in the case of any interest the amount arrived at in accordance with sub-paragraph (1) or (2) is a negative amount, the price payable by the nominee purchaser for the interest shall be nil.

Value of other interests

11(1) In the case of any such freehold interest as is mentioned in paragraph 10(1), paragraph 3 shall apply for determining the value of the interest with such modifications as are appropriate to relate it to a sale of the interest subject (where applicable) to any leases intermediate between that interest and any lease held by a qualifying tenant of a flat contained in the specified premises.

(2) In the case of any such leasehold interest as is mentioned in paragraph 10(2), then–

(a) (unless paragraph (b) below applies) paragraph 3 shall apply as mentioned in sub-paragraph (1) above;
(b) if it is the interest of the tenant under a minor intermediate lease within the meaning of paragraph 7, sub-paragraphs (2) to (10) of that paragraph shall apply with such modifications as are appropriate for determining the value of the interest.

(3) In its application in accordance with sub-paragraph (1) or (2) above, paragraph 3(6) shall have effect as if the reference to paragraph 14(2) were a reference to paragraph 18(2).

(4) In its application in accordance with sub-paragraph (2) above, paragraph 3(1A) shall have effect with the addition after paragraph (a) of–

"(aa) an owner of a freehold interest in the specified premises or".

Marriage value

12(1) Where any such freehold interest as is mentioned in paragraph 10(1) is an interest in any such property as is mentioned in section 1(3)(a)–

    (a) sub-paragraphs (2) to (4) of paragraph 4 shall apply with such modifications as are appropriate for determining the marriage value in connection with the acquisition by the nominee purchaser of that interest; and

    (b) sub-paragraph (1) of that paragraph shall apply with such modifications as are appropriate for determining the share of the marriage value to which the owner of that interest is entitled.

(2) Where–

    (a) the owner of any such freehold interest is entitled to any share of the marriage value in respect of any such property, and

    (b) the nominee purchaser is to acquire any leasehold interests in that property superior to any lease held by a participating tenant,

the amount payable to the owner of the freehold interest in respect of his share of the marriage value in respect of that property shall be divided between the owner of that interest and the owners of the leasehold interests in proportion to the value of their respective interests in that property (as determined for the purposes of paragraph 10(1) or (2), as the case may be).

(3) Where the owner of any such leasehold interest ("the intermediate landlord") is entitled in accordance with sub-paragraph (2) to any part of the amount payable to the owner of any freehold interest in respect of his share of the marriage value in respect of any property, the amount to which the intermediate landlord is so entitled shall be payable to him by the owner of that freehold interest.

Compensation for loss on acquisition of interest

13(1) Where the owner of any such freehold or leasehold interest as is mentioned in paragraph 10(1) or (2) ("relevant interest") will suffer any loss or damage to which this paragraph applies, there shall be payable to him such amount as is reasonable to compensate him for that loss or damage.

(2) This paragraph applies to–

    (a) any diminution in value of any interest in other property belonging to the owner of a relevant interest, being diminution resulting from the acquisition of the property in which the relevant interest subsists; and

    (b) any other loss or damage which results therefrom to the extent that it is referable to his ownership of any interest in other property.

(3) Without prejudice to the generality of paragraph (b) of sub-paragraph (2), the kinds of loss falling within that paragraph include loss of development value in relation to the property in which the relevant interest subsists to the extent that it is referable to his ownership of any interest in other property.

(4) In sub-paragraph (3) "development value", in relation to the property in which the relevant interest subsists, means any increase in the value of the relevant interest which is attributable to the possibility of demolishing, reconstructing or carrying out substantial works of construction on, the whole or a substantial part of the property.

Part V is 'valuation etc. of interests in specified premises with negative values', and comprises four paragraphs, 14 to 17.

Negative value interests – where an interest has a negative value, typically an intermediate lease where the profit rent is negative pursuant to a number of new leases having been granted under Schedule 13, in Schedule 6, paragraph 14, s(1)(a) and (b), the negative amount 'for those purposes shall be nil'.

In addition, where an intermediate lease has a negative amount, 'any interest superior to the negative interest, and having a positive value, shall be reduced in value' (s.2).

This is the basis of the unfairness highlighted in *Nailrile* in the two stage enfranchisement process discussed in chapter 2, for which the Lands Tribunal determined that compensation may be payable under Schedule 13, paragraph 5.

Nailrile raises the question as to whether the freeholder should seek compensation under paragraph 5 pursuant to all section 42 notices where there is an intermediate lease. Even where the profit rent to the intermediate leaseholder is a relatively small amount, if a pro rata head rent reduction is not taken by agreement when each new lease is granted (the legislation does not allow for this), at some future date, as and when a notice of collective enfranchisement claim is given, the negative value of the intermediate lease will be offset against any positive value of a superior interest, which includes the interest of the freeholder. The counter argument to compensation being payable on a piecemeal basis is the uncertainty of an enfranchisement claim being undertaken (if at all) in the future.

Paragraph 14:

PART V
VALUATION, ETC. OF INTERESTS IN SPECIFIED PREMISES WITH NEGATIVE VALUES

Valuation of freehold and intermediate leasehold interests

14(1) Where–

    (a) the value of a freeholder's interest in the specified premises (as determined for the relevant purposes), or

    (b) the value of any intermediate leasehold interest (as determined for the relevant purposes),

is a negative amount, the value of the interest for those purposes shall be nil.

(2) Where sub-paragraph (1) applies to any intermediate leasehold interest whose value is a negative amount ("the negative interest"), then for the relevant purposes any interests in the specified premises superior to the negative interest and having a positive value shall be reduced in value–

(a) beginning with the interest which is immediately superior to the negative interest and continuing (if necessary) with any such other superior interests in order of proximity to the negative interest;
(b) until the aggregate amount of the reduction is equal to the negative amount in question; and
(c) without reducing the value of any interest to less than nil.

(3) In a case where sub-paragraph (1) applies to two or more intermediate leasehold interests whose values are negative amounts, sub-paragraph (2) shall apply separately in relation to each of those interests–

(a) beginning with the interest which is inferior to every other of those interests and then in order of proximity to that interest; and
(b) with any reduction in the value of any interest for the relevant purposes by virtue of any prior application of sub-paragraph (2) being taken into account.

(3A) Where sub-paragraph (2) applies–

(a) for the purposes of paragraph 5A(2)(a), and
(b) in relation to an intermediate leasehold interest in relation to which there is more than one immediately superior interest,

any reduction in value made under that sub-paragraph shall be apportioned between the immediately superior interests.

(4) For the purposes of sub-paragraph (2) an interest has a positive value if (apart from that sub-paragraph) its value for the relevant purposes is a positive amount.

(5) In this Part of this Schedule "the relevant purposes"–

(a) as respects a freeholder's interest in the specified premises, means the purposes of paragraph 2(1)(a) or, as the case may be, 5A(2)(a); and
(b) as respects any intermediate leasehold interest, means the purposes of paragraph 6(1)(b)(i).

Paragraphs 15 and 16 cover calculation and apportionment of marriage value. Paragraph 17 covers adjustment of compensation.

Part VI comprises four paragraphs, numbers 18 to 21 and covers valuation of other interests with negative values. It follows the corresponding four paragraphs in Part V.

Paragraph 18:

PART VI
VALUATION, ETC. OF OTHER INTERESTS WITH NEGATIVE VALUES

Valuation of freehold and leasehold interests

18(1) Where–

    (a) the value of any freehold interest (as determined in accordance with paragraph 11(1)), or

    (b) the value of any leasehold interest (as determined in accordance with paragraph 11(2)),

is a negative amount, the value of the interest for the relevant purposes shall be nil.

(2) Where, in the case of any property, sub-paragraph (1) applies to any leasehold interest in the property whose value is a negative amount ("the negative interest"), then for the relevant purposes any interests in the property superior to the negative interest and having a positive value shall, if they are interests which are to be acquired by the nominee purchaser, be reduced in value–

    (a) beginning with the interest which is nearest to the negative interest and continuing (if necessary) with any such other superior interests in order of proximity to the negative interest;

    (b) until the aggregate amount of the reduction is equal to the negative amount in question; and

    (c) without reducing the value of any interest to less than nil.

(3) In a case where sub-paragraph (1) applies to two or more leasehold interests in any property whose values are negative amounts, sub-paragraph (2) shall apply separately in relation to each of those interests–

    (a) beginning with the interest which is inferior to every other of those interests and then in order of proximity to that interest; and

(b) with any reduction in the value of any interest for the relevant purposes by virtue of any prior application of sub-paragraph (2) being taken into account.

(4) For the purposes of sub-paragraph (2) an interest has a positive value if (apart from that sub-paragraph) its value for the relevant purposes is a positive amount.

(5) In this Part of this Schedule "the relevant purposes"–

(a) as respects any freehold interest, means the purposes of paragraph 10(1)(a); and
(b) as respects any leasehold interest, means the purposes of paragraph 10(2)(a).

Summary

As with claims for new leases, valuations to calculate the collective enfranchisement price under Schedule 6 range from the comparatively straightforward to the exceedingly complicated and complex. A number of the principles do, however, follow those of Schedule 13.

The valuation issues affecting 'participators' are relatively straightforward; there are further complications when one considers non-participators, hence hope value (including cases where a section 42 notice has been served); appurtenant property; common use areas, leasebacks, both mandatory and optional; porter's and caretaker's accommodation; development value; and negative interests, inter alia.

The appeal of the Lands Tribunal decision in *McHale* on the question of whether tenants' improvements and the benefit of the Act are to be disregarded in the marriage value computation is pending; this decision will have an impact on all collective enfranchisement claims where the marriage value computation is required.

The decision of the House of Lords confirming that hope value can be payable where there are non-participators, coupled with the Upper Chamber's decision in *Culley*, give the valuer guidance on this issue, but questions remain as to whether tenants' improvements are to be disregarded in the calculation and if an intermediate leaseholder is due a share of hope value.

There are the day to day practical aspects to consider in 'case management'. With particular regard to lines of communication and passage of information; the valuer needs to be organised, otherwise any one instruction could take up an inordinate amount of time. Where the premises have a large number of flats, the valuations will take time, and will include a number of issues.

5

Houses: the right of a tenant to acquire the freehold

Introduction

Part I of the *Leasehold Reform Act* 1967 confers on tenants of leasehold houses the right to acquire on fair terms the freehold of the house and premises. The background to this legislation and the various amendments it has undergone are set out in the introductory chapter. What this part of the book aims to focus on is the position at present and the various issues to be considered when advising the tenant of a house, who is considering purchasing his freehold, or indeed the landlord of such a tenant.

What is a house?

By virtue of section 2(1) a 'house' is a building, which:

- is designed or adapted for living in;
- can reasonably be called a house;
- does not have to be detached;
- may be divided horizontally into flats or maisonettes; and
- is not divided vertically.

The definition is far wider than might be supposed as is illustrated below.

Designed or adapted for living in

The building does not have to be solely designed or adapted for living in and therefore mixed use premises can be a 'house' within the meaning of the Act, for example, a shop with a flat above it.

In ascertaining whether a building is 'designed or adapted for living in', firstly, it is necessary to consider the building as initially built and the purpose for which it was originally designed. Secondly, it is necessary to consider whether work has subsequently been done to the building so that the original design has been changed. In considering each of these matters, the ultimate concern is to decide whether the purpose for which the building was designed or adapted was 'for living in'. There is no requirement that the building actually be in such a physical state that it could be lived in (*Boss Holdings Ltd v Grosvenor West End Properties Ltd* [2008] 1 WLR 289), but 'living in' requires some degree of permanence (*Hosebay Ltd v Day* (Unreported, 2009, Central London County Court).

> *Examples*
>
> A terraced property was built in the eighteenth century as a single private residence and comprised six floors. Up until 1942, the property was used as a single residence but thereafter, the three upper floors were retained for residential use while the lower floors were occupied for business use. By the time the tenant sought to acquire the freehold, both the commercial and residential uses had ceased and the property was vacant. The rooms on the three upper floors had been stripped back to their basic structure. Plaster had been hacked off the walls and some ceilings and floorboards had been removed. The fact that the property had not been occupied for a number of years and had become internally dilapidated and incapable of beneficial occupation, did not detract from the fact that it had been designed for living in when it was first built and was therefore a house within the meaning of the Act: *Boss Holdings Ltd v Grosvenor West End Properties Ltd*.
>
> Victorian terraced houses were being used to provide short-term accommodation to tourists and other visitors to London in 'rooms with self-catering facilities'. As such, they were not 'lived in'. However, the houses were plainly, originally, buildings 'designed or adapted for living in' as large Victorian family houses and notwithstanding the changes made to the fabric of each building, and notwithstanding the use to which each building was actually being put, they were, either by origin or by their adaptation, 'designed or adapted for living in' within the meaning of the Act. *Hosebay Ltd v Day*.

Reasonably called a 'house'

If a building can reasonably be called a 'house', it does not matter that it can reasonably be called something else: *Lake v Bennett* [1970] QB 663.

> *Examples*
>
> **Buildings which <u>can</u> reasonably be called 'houses'**
>
> A terraced dwelling-house consisting of a ground floor and basement with two floors above. The ground floor was converted and sublet for use as a betting shop whilst the other parts were used for dwelling purposes. The building could reasonably be called a house and therefore was a house within the meaning of the Act, notwithstanding that it could also be called a shop with an upper part and a basement: *Lake v Bennett*.
>
> A building consisting of a shop with living accommodation above, which was one of a row of four similar buildings forming a shopping parade: *Tandon v Trustees of Spurgeons Homes* [1982] AC 755.
>
> A building located within a parade of buildings with shops on the ground floor and purpose built, self contained maisonettes arranged on two floors above. The maisonette was let on an assured shorthold tenancy and the tenant was not resident in either the commercial or residential parts of the building. The property was a 'house' as any manifestation of the reasonable man would have concluded that the property was a house: *Hareford Ltd v Barnet London Borough Council* [2005] 2 EGLR 72.
>
> Two adjoining houses separately let under two leases to the same tenant who ran the two houses together as one guest house. There was an opening between the two houses on the first floor. As each house was structurally separate with a separate lease, one of them could reasonably be called a house: *Wolf v Crutchley* [1971] 1 WLR 99.
>
> Victorian terraced houses used to provide short-term accommodation for tourists and other visitors to London in 'rooms with self-catering facilities'. *Hosebay Ltd v Day*.

> *Examples*
>
> **Buildings which <u>cannot</u> reasonably be called 'houses'**
>
> The Ritz Hotel: *Lake v Bennett* per Salmon LJ at 672C.
>
> A block of flats: *Lake v Bennett* per Salmon LJ at 672C.
>
> A building built as a residential house and part of a Victorian terrace. Its essential structure remained unchanged and it still looked like a house at the relevant date. The tenant held a long lease of the building which stipulated that 88.5 per cent of the building was to be used as offices and 11.5 per cent or one storey was to be used as a residential flat. The appearance of a dwelling house was to be maintained and any indication of the professional use of the building was prohibited. The terms of the lease, the uses of the building and the proportions of the uses at the relevant date meant that it was no longer reasonable to call the building a 'house' within the meaning of the Act: *Grosvenor Estates Ltd v Prospect Estates Ltd* [2009] 1 WLR 1313.

Divided buildings

If the building is divided horizontally, then the flats or other units into which it is divided are not 'houses', but the building as a whole may be a 'house' (s.2(1)(a)). Conversely, if a building is divided vertically, the building as whole is not a 'house', but any of the units into which it is divided may be 'houses' (s.2(1)(b)).

Example

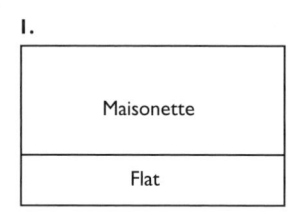

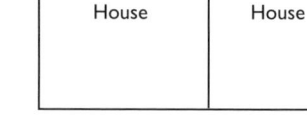

1.

Maisonette
Flat

The whole building may be a 'house'

2.

House	House

The whole building cannot be a 'house'

In either case, the line of separation does not need to be an unbroken line, i.e. it does not need to lie in a single plane.

> *Example*
>
> A house and a mews flat physically linked by a basement, which extended under both properties but which was used by only the house, and by a door between the two at ground floor level. The two properties were not together a 'house' as they were vertically divided, albeit not in an unbroken vertical line: *Malekshad v Howard de Walden Estates Ltd* [2003] 1 AC 1013.
>
> Two neighbouring properties were originally separate properties. The first consisted of a garage and living accommodation on the ground floor and living accommodation on the first floor. The other had garages on the ground floor with a flat above. In 1977, a communicating door was made through the party wall giving access from the patio of the first property to a utility room at the back of the ground floor in the second property, and from there to the garages in that property. There was one head lease of both properties, which required them to be used as a single private dwelling house, but permitted the flat on the first floor of the second property to be sublet, as it was. Both properties were together one 'house' within the meaning of the Act as they were not divided vertically in the manner contemplated by section 2(1)(b). There was no vertical division down the party wall because the utility room and garage of the second property were part of the first, both in practice, and by design of both the landlord and tenant. *Collins v Howard de Walden Estates Ltd* [2003] HLR 70.

Non-detached buildings

If a building is not structurally detached and a material part of it lies above or below a part of the structure not comprised in the building, the premises cannot be a house for the purposes of Part I (s.2(2)).

> **Examples**
>
> Two adjoining properties with shops on the ground floor and residential accommodation above separately let under two leases to the same tenant. A hole had been made in the wall between the two shops, which were used by the tenant as one shop. Each property was still one building with a hole knocked through into the next building and therefore it could not be said that a material part of one building lay below a part of the structure not comprised in the building: *Peck v Anicar Properties Ltd* [1971] 1 All ER 517.
>
> Two semi-detached houses, Nos. 5 and 6, with an opening in the dividing wall giving access from No. 6 to the front room of No. 5, which was used as a storeroom; the doorway of that room to the rest of No. 5 having been bricked up. By the time of the claim, the tenant had in fact filled in the opening between the two houses and re-opened the doorway. It was held that whether or not the opening existed, No. 6 did not include the front room of No. 5 and could reasonably be called a house. Consequently, no part of No. 6 lay above or below a part of No. 5. However, if the front room had formed part of No. 6, it would have been considered a material part: *Gaidowski v Gonville & Caius College, Cambridge* [1975] 1 WLR 1066.
>
> A terraced house, on one side of which was a passageway at ground floor level, which was not part of the demise. The first and second floors of the house extended over the passageway. Whilst a material part of the house lay above something which was not included in the demise, namely the land included in the passageway, no part of the house lay above a structure not comprised in the house: *Cresswell v Duke of Westminster* [1985] 2 EGLR 151.
>
> In *Malekshad* the basement was not a 'material part' of the house and therefore the fact that it lay beneath the mews flat did not preclude the house from being a 'house' for the purposes of the Act.

The extent of the freehold to be acquired

The right to acquire the freehold extends to 'the house and premises' and the meaning of 'premises' is considered below. The right does not extend to any underlying minerals comprised in the tenancy, if the landlord requires that the minerals be excepted and if proper provision is made for the support of the house and premises as they have been enjoyed during the tenancy and in accordance with its terms (s.2(6)). If, as a result, the freehold of part of the property demised to the tenant is excluded from being acquired, then the transfer of the freehold operates as a surrender of the tenancy in respect of that property. This is unless the landlord and the tenant agree otherwise, or the court for the protection of either of them from hardship or inconvenience, orders otherwise (s.2(7)).

As a general rule, and by virtue of section 2(3), 'premises' is to be taken as referring to any garage, outhouse, garden, yard and appurtenances which are let to the tenant with the house. Further, an 'appurtenance' must be within the curtilage of the house.

> *Examples*
>
> The demised premises included a cultivated garden and a paddock divided by a fence. Whilst the cultivated garden could be acquired, the paddock was not a 'garden'. Neither was it an 'appurtenance', as being separated from the garden by a fence, it was not within the curtilage of the house: *Methuen-Campbell v Walters* [1979] 1 QB 525.
>
> The tenant held a lease of a five storey house and, to the rear, a mews house consisting of a garage and flat above. It was held that the flat above the garage could not be regarded as an outhouse or appurtenance: *Dugan-Chapman v Grosvenor Estates* [1997] 1 EGLR 96.

For premises to be 'let with' a house there must be a reasonably close connection between the transactions of letting the house and letting the premises.

> *Example*
>
> A tenant held both a lease of two semi-detached houses and a lease of an additional piece of land at the end of the garden of one of the houses ('the garden strip'). The lease of the garden strip was an underlease carved out of a head lease, which was originally held by the tenant of neighbouring property. The freehold owner of both the semi-detached houses and the garden strip acquired the head lease by assignment, so that at the date of the tenant's claim, the landlord and the tenant of the houses were also the landlord and tenant of the garden strip. It was held that there was not sufficient connection between the transactions leading to the grant of the leases for it to be said that the garden strip was 'let with' the house and therefore the garden strip could not be acquired: *Gaidowski v Gonville & Caius College, Cambridge* [1975] 1 WLR 1066.

Houses: the right of a tenant to acquire the freehold

There are two exceptions to the general rule outlined.

Exception 1

There are other premises let with the house and premises, but which are not let to the same tenant.

> *Example*
>
> A house is originally let with a garage, i.e. both the house and the garage are demised by the same lease. The tenant's interest in the garage only is assigned to a third party, known as a severance of the term. Whilst the house and garage are let together, i.e. they are both demised by the same lease, following the assignment, they are not let to the same tenant.

Where premises are let with the house and premises and not let to the same tenant, but let by the same landlord, then the landlord can give the tenant notice objecting to the freehold of the house and premises being acquired without the freehold of the additional premises also being acquired. If, following service of such a notice, the tenant agrees to acquire the freehold of the additional premises or the court is satisfied that it would be unreasonable to require the landlord to retain them without the house and premises, then those additional premises are treated as included in the 'house and premises' (s.2(4)). If, by virtue of section 2(4), additional premises are to be included, then the Act applies as if the tenant held a tenancy of those premises on terms identical to the actual tenancy and as if the actual tenant were a sub-tenant (s.2(7)).

> *Example*
>
> If, in the example above, the reversion of the original lease is vested in the same person, i.e. the landlord of the house is also the landlord of the garage, then that landlord can serve on the tenant of the house a notice objecting to the tenant acquiring the freehold of the house without acquiring the freehold of the garage. If, following service of such a notice, the tenant agrees to acquire the freehold of the garage or a court is satisfied that it would be unreasonable to require the landlord to retain the freehold of the garage without the freehold of the house, then the tenant will have the right to acquire the freehold of both the house and the garage. For this purpose, the tenant will be treated as holding a tenancy of the garage on the terms on which the garage is let and the actual tenant of the garage will be treated as being his sub-tenant.

Exception 2

Part of the house or premises lies above or below other premises, which the landlord owns (s.2(5)).

> **Example**
>
> In *Malekshad*, the basement of the house extended under the adjoining mews flat and there fore lay below other premises, which the landlord owned.

In such a situation, the landlord may give the tenant notice objecting to him acquiring the freehold of that part of the house and premises, which lies above or below the other premises. That part will not be acquired if, following service of such a notice, the tenant agrees not to acquire it or a court makes a determination in the landlord's favour. In order to make such a determination, a court must weigh the interests of the tenant against the interests of those interested in the other premises. The court must consider what hardship or inconvenience is likely to result to the tenant from the exclusion of the particular part of the house and premises, taking into account anything that can be done to mitigate its effects and any undertaking of the landlord to take steps to mitigate them. As against such hardship or inconvenience, the court must consider the difficulties involved in severing that part of the house and premises from the landlord's other premises, and any hardship or inconvenience likely to result from that severance to anyone with an interest in the other premises. Only if the difficulties, hardship or inconvenience of severance outweigh the hardship or inconvenience to the tenant, will the court make an order in the landlord's favour.

If the freehold of part of the property demised to the tenant is excluded from being acquired by virtue of section 2(5), then the transfer of the freehold operates as a surrender of the tenancy in respect of that property. This is unless the landlord and the tenant agree otherwise or the court for the protection of either of them from hardship or inconvenience orders otherwise (s.2(7)).

Qualification criteria

Due to the various amendments, the right to acquire the freehold can arise under one of a number of sections of the Act and which section the right arises under will depend on which of a number of financial limits the property falls within. Whilst the section the right to acquire the freehold arises under is relevant for the purpose of determining the price payable for the freehold, it is not relevant when considering whether the tenant does, in the first instance, have the right. Consequently, the general qualification criteria are considered here and the criteria for each particular section are considered as follows, when looking at the different bases of valuation.

In order to have the right to acquire the freehold of the house and premises, the following criteria must be met.

- The tenant must be the tenant of the whole house unless he is already the freeholder of those parts of the house of which he is not a tenant: *Peck v Anicar Properties Ltd* [1971] 1 All ER 517, per Lord Denning M.R. at 519c. However, as section 1(1) confers the right on '*a tenant of a leasehold house*', the tenant need not also be the tenant of the 'premises'.
- The tenancy must be a long tenancy (s.1(1)(a)).
- At the relevant time, the tenant must have been the tenant for the last two years (s.1(1)(b)), i.e. the tenant must have been the registered proprietor for the last two years.

Trustees holding a tenancy in their capacity as trustees can have the right to acquire the freehold, as can a beneficiary entitled or permitted to occupy a house pursuant to a trust, as to which, regard should be had to section 6. The personal representatives of a deceased tenant who had the right to acquire the freehold immediately before his death can exercise that right whilst the tenancy is vested in them (s.6A(1)). However, they cannot give notice of their desire to acquire the freehold more than two years after the grant of probate or letters of administration (s.6A(2)).

Exceptions

A tenant may have the right to acquire the freehold where he has not been the tenant for the last two years, if he has succeeded to the tenancy on the death of a family member and has been resident in the house. If this is the case, regard should be had to section 7.

There are also a number of situations where tenants who would otherwise have the right to acquire the freehold, in fact do not. These can be summarised as follows.

- **More than one tenancy** – where a house is let under more than one tenancy, then only the tenant with the lowest interest has the right to acquire the freehold (s.1(1ZA)).

> *Example*
>
> A grants B a lease of a house for a term of 99 years. B grants C a sub-lease of the house for a term of 90 years. C is a qualifying tenant and therefore B cannot also be a qualifying tenant by virtue of section 1(1ZA).

- **Houses containing a flat** – where part of the house is a flat, which is let to a qualifying tenant under the *Leasehold Reform Housing and Urban Development Act* 1993, the tenant of the house does not have the right to acquire the freehold of the house unless, at the relevant time, he has been occupying the house, or any part of it, as his only or main residence (whether or not he has been using it for other purposes) for the last two years or for periods amounting to two years in the last ten years (s.1(1ZB)).
- **Business tenancies** – as a general rule, business tenants within the meaning of Part II of the *Landlord and Tenant Act* 1954 do not have a right to acquire the freehold. There are exceptions to this and regard should be had to sections 1(1ZC) and (1ZD) where those exceptions are set out in full. However, in short, if the business tenancy is for a term of more than 35 years, either by the grant of a fixed term of more than 35 years or otherwise, and, at the relevant time, the tenant has been occupying the house, or any part of it, as his only or main residence (whether or not he has been using it for other purposes), for the last two years or for periods amounting to two years in the last ten years, then the tenant will have the right to acquire the freehold (ss.1(1ZC) and (1B)).

It is important to note that whilst a house may consist of business premises, for example, a house which is a shop with a flat above, the lease of the house will not necessarily be a business tenancy. If the tenant sub-lets the business premises, then he is not occupying them for the purposes of a business carried on by him and therefore the lease does not fall within Part II of the *Landlord and Tenant Act* 1954. As such, sub-letting is a useful means by which a business tenant may become entitled to acquire the freehold and this is something which a landlord ought to be alive to when considering any request to sub-let.

> *Example*
>
> The tenant under each of three leases of houses was Hosebay Ltd. Hosebay occupied the houses for the purposes of a business, 'Astons Apartments', which provided short term accommodation for tourists and other visitors to London. Upon legal advice, and for the purposes of making a claim to acquire the freehold of the houses, Hosebay sub-let the houses to Hindmill Ltd, an associated company, and thereafter Hindmill Ltd ran 'Astons Apartments'.
>
> Prior to the sub-letting, Hosebay's leases of the houses would have fallen within Part II of the *Landlord and Tenant Act* 1954. However, following the sub-letting, Hosebay was no longer occupying the houses for the purpose of a business carried on by it as Hindmill was occupying the houses and carrying on the business. Consequently, Part II no longer applied to Hosebay's leases and Hosebay was able to make a claim under the Act.
>
> The underleases were not shams as they took effect absolutely according to their purported terms and there was no pretence or secrecy about them. Further, whilst the underleases were artificial transactions in the sense that they were only entered into for a particular artificial purpose that did not prevent their being effective. *Hosebay Ltd v Day* (2009) PLSCS 318, CC.

- **Shared ownership leases** –tenants under certain shared ownership leases do not have the right to acquire the freehold of their house. In respect of leases granted before 11 December 1987, regard should be had to section 140 of the *Housing Act* 1980 and in respect of leases granted after that date, regard should be had to Schedule 4A of the Act (see also the introductory chapter).
- **The house is ancillary to other land and premises** – where a house is let to the tenant with other land or premises and the house is ancillary to that land or premises, the tenant does not have a right to acquire the freehold of the house (s.1(3)(a)).

> *Example*
>
> A lease demises an industrial estate on which is situated a house for use by a resident manager/caretaker/security guard. The house is ancillary to the land and premises constituting the industrial estate. Consequently, the tenant under the lease does not have a right to acquire the freehold of the house.

- **Agricultural property** – a tenant does not have the right to acquire the freehold of a house which is:
  - comprised in an agricultural holding within the meaning of the *Agricultural Holdings Act* 1986;
  - held under a tenancy in relation to which the *Agricultural Holdings Act* 1986 applies; or

- comprised in the holding held under a farm business tenancy within the meaning of the *Agricultural Tenancies Act* 1995 (s.1(3)(b)).
- **Housing provided for charitable purposes** – where section 1(3A) of the Act applies, a tenant does not have the right to acquire the freehold of a house at any time when the tenant's immediate landlord is a charitable housing trust and the house forms part of the housing accommodation provided by the trust in the pursuit of its charitable purposes (s.1(3)).
- **Sub-tenancies** – where a tenancy has been granted by a sub-demise out of a superior tenancy, which is not a long tenancy at a low rent and the grant was made in breach of the terms of the superior tenancy and there has been no waiver of the breach by the superior landlord (s.5(4)).

What is a long tenancy?

The first question to consider is whether the tenancy is a 'tenancy' within the meaning of the Act. The following types of tenancies are 'tenancies' within the meaning of the Act:

- an immediate tenancy;
- a sub-tenancy (s.5(4));
- a tenancy granted to a secure tenant pursuant to the 'right to buy' provisions in Part V of the *Housing Act* 1985 (s.118(1)(b) of the *Housing Act* 1985);
- a tenancy at law (s.37(1)(f)); and
- a tenancy in equity (s.37(1)(f)).

And the following types of tenancies are not 'tenancies' within the meaning of the Act:

- a tenancy at will (s.37(1)(f));
- a tenancy created by way of security, i.e. a mortgage term, and liable to termination by the exercise of any right of redemption or otherwise (s.37(1)(f));
- a tenancy created by way of trust under a settlement (s.37(1)(f)).

The next question to consider is whether the tenancy is a 'long tenancy'. This is, in short, a tenancy for a fixed term of more than 21 years (s.3(1)). To establish this it is necessary to ascertain:
- What is the length of the term specified in the lease?
- When did the term commence? This will be the later of the date of the tenancy and the date specified in the tenancy as

being the commencement of the term: see *Roberts v Church Commissioners for England* [1972] 1 QB 278.

Example

(1) A tenancy is dated 6 September 1990 and stated to be for a term of 22 years, commencing on 29 September 1990.

The term commences on 29 September 1990 and expires on 28 September 2012 and is therefore more than 21 years. Consequently, the tenancy is a 'long tenancy' within the meaning of the Act.

(2) A tenancy is dated 30 September 1991 and stated to be for a term of 22 years, commencing on 29 September 1990.

The term commences on 30 September 1991 and expires on 28 September 2012 and is therefore less than 21 years. Consequently, the tenancy is not a 'long tenancy' within the meaning of the Act.

Particular types of tenancy

Tenancies terminable before the end of the term – A tenancy may be for a fixed term of more than 21 years, but capable of earlier termination, for example, if it contains a break clause. Indeed, most tenancies will be capable of early termination by forfeiture. The fact that a tenancy is terminable before the end of the term does not exclude it from being a tenancy for a fixed term of more than 21 years and therefore a 'long tenancy' within the meaning of the Act (s.3(1)).

Tenancies terminable on or after death, marriage or the formation of a civil partnership – Such tenancies fall into two categories:

- those which determine automatically on death, etc. either because the tenancy is granted for a person's lifetime or because it is granted for a term of years, but is stated to determine on death, etc.; and
- those which are terminable by notice after death, etc.

Where a tenancy falls into the first category, by virtue of section 149(6) of the *Law of Property Act* 1925, it is deemed to be for a term of 99 years determinable after the death or marriage by notice and is a 'long tenancy' (s.3(1)).

Where a tenancy falls within the second category, it is capable of being a 'long tenancy', unless the following conditions are fulfilled:

- the notice is capable of being given at any time after the death or marriage of, or the formation of a civil partnership by, the tenant;
- the length of the notice is not more than three months; and
- the terms of the lease preclude both:
  - its assignment otherwise than by virtue of section 92 of the *Housing Act* 1985 (assignments by way of exchange); and
  - the sub-letting of the whole of the premises comprised in it (s.3(1)).

Consecutive tenancies – If, on the coming to an end of one tenancy, a tenant continues as the tenant of a house under a further tenancy and, in consequence, is the tenant of the house for more than 21 years, the tenant is not a tenant under a 'long tenancy' if neither tenancy is for a fixed term of more than 21 years: *Roberts v Church Commissioners for England* (previous page).

However, where the tenant was a tenant of any property under a long tenancy (i.e. a tenancy for a fixed term of more than 21 years), at a low rent and on the coming to an end of that tenancy became the tenant of the property, or any part of it, under a subsequent tenancy (whether by express grant or implication of law), then by virtue of section 3(2), that tenancy is deemed to be a long tenancy irrespective of its terms. As to what is a tenancy at a 'low rent', see the section dealing with the correct basis of valuation to follow.

Where one long tenancy (i.e. a tenancy for a fixed term of more than 21 years), follows on from another, then the Act applies as if there was a single tenancy, which began at the commencement of the first tenancy and ends at the expiry of the second (s.3(3)).

Renewable tenancies – a tenancy for a term fixed by law under a grant with a covenant or obligation for perpetual renewal is a 'long tenancy' unless it is a sub-tenancy and the superior tenancy is not a long tenancy (s.3(1)).

If a tenancy has not been granted for a fixed term of more than 21 years, but contains a covenant or obligation for renewal without payment of a premium (but not for perpetual renewal), and is or has been renewed so as to bring to more than 21 years the total of the terms granted, then the tenancy will be treated, by virtue of section 3(4), as having been granted for a fixed term of more than 21 years.

> **Example**
>
> A tenancy is granted for a fixed term of 15 years with a covenant that the tenancy will be renewed for a further 15 years at the request of the tenant, and without the tenant having to pay any premium upon such renewal. The tenancy is renewed at the tenant's request so that the total of the terms granted is 30 years. As such, the tenancy is, by virtue of section 3(4), treated as having been granted for a fixed term of more than 21 years and is therefore a 'long tenancy'.

Tenancies continued under statute – a tenancy may also have continued or be continuing under statute, for example, under Part I of the *Landlord and Tenant Act* 1954 or Schedule 10 to the *Local Government and Housing Act* 1989. Where this is the case, any period during which the tenancy is so continuing is included within the meaning of a long tenancy by virtue of section 3(5).

Periodical continuation tenancies – if a tenancy is granted to continue as a periodical tenancy after the expiration of a fixed term, then, in ascertaining whether it is for a fixed term of more than 21 years, it is to be treated as if there were two tenancies (1) granted to expire at the earliest time at which the tenancy could be brought to an end, by notice to quit given by the landlord; and (2) the other granted to commence at the expiration of the first (s.37(4)).

> **Example**
>
> A tenancy is granted for a fixed term of 20 years and a day, commencing on 29 September 1990 and from year to year thereafter. It is terminable upon 12 months notice given by the landlord no earlier than the expiry of the fixed term.
>
> The fixed term expires on 29 September 2010. The earliest date on which the landlord can serve notice to quit is 30 September 2010 and the earliest date on which the tenancy can be brought to an end by virtue of that notice is 29 September 2011. Consequently, the first tenancy is treated as a tenancy granted from 29 September 1990 to 29 September 2011 and therefore for a term exceeding 21 years.
>
> If the first tenancy is a tenancy at a low rent, then the second tenancy will also be a long tenancy by virtue of section 3(2).

Multiple concurrent tenancies – where parts of a house and premises are let under separate long tenancies with the same landlord and tenant, then the Act applies as if there were a single long tenancy. The commencement date of that tenancy is the earliest commencement date of any tenancy comprising the house and the term date is the earliest term date of any tenancy comprising the house (s.3(6)).

Right to buy tenancies – a tenancy granted pursuant to the 'right to buy' provisions of Part V of the *Housing Act* 1985 is a 'long tenancy' notwithstanding that it is granted for a term of 21 years or less (s.174 of the *Housing Act* 1985). However, it is unlikely that a tenancy so granted would be granted for less than 125 years.

Shared ownership leases – a tenancy created by the grant of a 'shared ownership' lease pursuant to Part V of the *Housing Act* 1985 is a 'long tenancy' notwithstanding that it is granted for a term of 21 years or less (s. 174 of the *Housing Act* 1985). However, certain such tenancies are excluded from the operation of the Act, as to which, in respect of leases granted before 11 December 1987, regard should be had to section 140 of the *Housing Act* 1980 and in respect of leases granted after that date, regard should be had to Schedule 4A of the Act.

Basis of valuation

Having established that the tenant has the right to acquire the freehold, the next step is to ascertain the correct basis for calculating the price payable for the house and premises. There are different bases of valuation depending on which section of the Act the tenant's right to acquire the freehold arises under. These various bases are set out in section 9 and are as follows.

Section 9(1A) – the price payable is to be ascertained in accordance with this subsection if:

- on 31 March 1990, the rateable value of the house and premises was above £1,000 in Greater London and £500 elsewhere; or
- the house and premises had no rateable value on 31 March 1990 and R exceeded £16,333 where

    $$R = \frac{0.06 \times \text{the premium payable on the grant of the tenancy}}{1 - (1.06)^{-\text{term of the tenancy}}}$$

    and
- the right to acquire the freehold arises under section 1 of the Act.

Section 9(1) – the price payable is to be ascertained in accordance with this subsection if:

- on 31 March 1990, the rateable value of the house and premises was not above £1,000 in Greater London or £500 elsewhere; or
- R did not exceed £16,333 (applying the formula), if there was no rateable value on 31 March 1990; and
- the right to acquire the freehold arises under section 1 of the Act.

Section 9(1) is the most favourable basis of valuation as far as the tenant is concerned as it does not provide for marriage value to be included.

Greater London is the area comprising the London boroughs, the City of London and the Inner and Middle Temples (s. 2 *London Government Act* 1963).

Section 9(1C) – the price payable is to be ascertained in accordance with this subsection if;

- the right to acquire the freehold arises by virtue of sections 1A or 1AA (whilst section 9(1C) refers to the right to acquire the freehold arising by virtue of section 1B, the right cannot arise by virtue of this section and this appears to be a drafting error).

Checklist

In order to determine the correct basis of valuation, it is necessary to ascertain in the first instance under which section of the Act the right to enfranchise arises. If it arises under sections 1A or 1AA, then the price payable is to be ascertained in accordance with section 9(1C). If it arises under section 1, then one must go on to consider each of the following questions in turn.

- Are the house and premises located in Greater London or elsewhere?
- What was the rateable value of the house and premises on 31 March 1990?
- If the house and premises are in Greater London, was the rateable value on 31 March 1990 above £1,000 or if there is no rateable value, does R exceed £16,333 applying the formula?
- If the house and premises are not in Greater London, was the rateable value on 31 March 1990 above £500 or if there is no rateable value, does R exceed £16,333 applying the formula?

If the answer to either of the last two questions is 'yes', then the price payable is to be ascertained in accordance with section 9(1A). Otherwise, it is to be ascertained in accordance with section 9(1).

Basis of qualification

The Checklist illustrates the point made earlier that the section the right to acquire the freehold arises under is relevant for the purpose of determining the price payable for the freehold, and it is therefore necessary to consider each of these sections. In what follows, the 'appropriate day' is 23 March 1965 unless the house had no rateable value at that date, in which case the appropriate date is the date on which a rateable value is first shown.

Section 1 – the right to acquire the freehold arises under this section in the following circumstances:

- if the tenancy was granted prior to 7 September 2009 (or it arises from a written agreement for the grant of that tenancy made before 7 September 2009), it is at a low rent at the relevant time and was at a low rent during the whole of the tenant's two-year qualifying ownership period;
- if the tenancy was entered into before 1 April 1990, the rateable value of the house and premises on the appropriate day was not more than £200, or £400 if they are in Greater London (this qualification criteria also applies if the tenancy was entered into after 1 April 1990 in pursuance of a contract made before that date, and the house and premises had a rateable value at the date of commencement of the tenancy or else at any time before 1 April 1990); or
- if the appropriate day falls on or after 1 April 1973 and the tenancy was created on or before 18 February 1966; the rateable value of the house and premises on the appropriate day was not more than £750, or £1,500 if they are in Greater London (s.1(5)(a)); or
- if the appropriate day falls on or after 1 April 1973 and the tenancy was created after 18 February 1966; the rateable value of the house and premises on the appropriate day was not more than £500, or £1,000 if they are in Greater London (s.1(5)(b)); or
- if the tenancy does not fall within the above criteria and it was created on or before 18 February 1966 and the appropriate day falls before 1 April 1973; the rateable value of the house and premises on 1 April 1973 was not more than £750, or £1,500 if they are in Greater London (s.1(6)); or

- if the tenancy does not fall within any of the above criteria, then on the date the contract for the grant of the tenancy was made or, if there was no such contract, on the date the tenancy was entered into R must not exceed £25,000 where:

$$R = \frac{0.06 \times \text{The premium payable on the grant of the tenancy}}{1 - (1.06)^{-\text{term of the tenancy}}}$$

The various financial limits are set out in the following flow chart (page 324), which assumes that the tenancy is either a tenancy at a low rent or a tenancy granted after 7 September 2009, in which case there is no requirement that it be at a low rent.

Section 1A – the right to acquire the freehold arises under this section if:

- the above financial limits are exceeded; and
- if the tenancy was granted prior to 7 September 2009 (or it arises from a written agreement for the grant of that tenancy made before 7 September 2009);
  o the tenancy is at a low rent; or
  o the tenancy falls within section 4A(1), i.e. it passes the alternative low rent test.

Section 1AA – the right to acquire the freehold arises under this section if:

- the tenancy was granted prior to 7 September 2009 (or it arises from a written agreement for the grant of that tenancy made before 7 September 2009);
- the above financial limits are not exceeded;
- the tenancy is not at a low rent; and
- the tenancy is not an excluded tenancy. Such tenancies are of houses in designated rural areas. Consequently, when dealing with a house in such an area, regard ought to be had to section 1AA(3).

Low rent

The low rent test is contained in section 4(1) of the Act. As a qualification criteria, it has now been abolished as regards tenancies granted after 7 September 2009 (s.300, *Housing and Regeneration Act* 2008). However, if a tenant is relying on section 3(2), i.e. he has a tenancy which is a long tenancy by virtue of

Leasehold enfrachisement explained

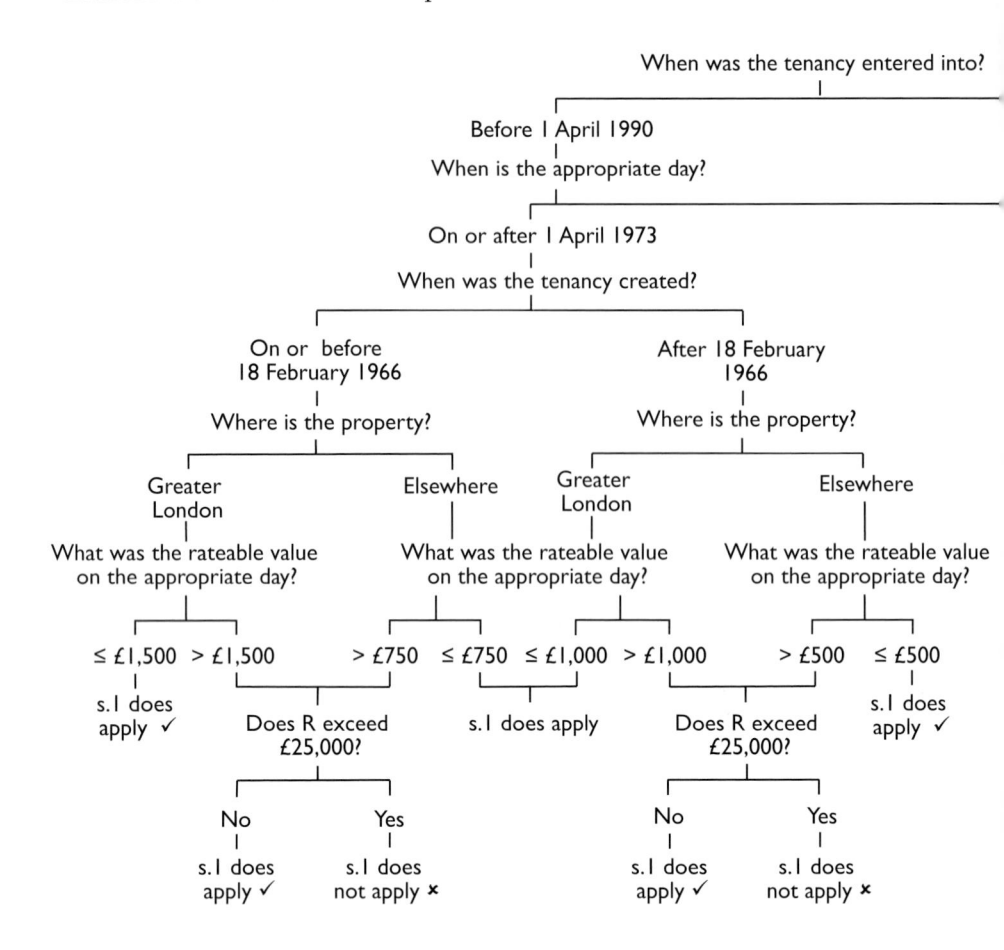

```
                                          When was the tenancy entered into?
                                                        │
                                      ┌─────────────────┴──────────────────
                                  Before 1 April 1990
                                          │
                                  When is the appropriate day?
                                          │
                              ┌───────────┴────────────────────────────────
                          On or after 1 April 1973
                                          │
                                  When was the tenancy created?
                                          │
                          ┌───────────────┴───────────────┐
                  On or before                        After 18 February
                  18 February 1966                         1966
                          │                                   │
                  Where is the property?              Where is the property?
                          │                                   │
              ┌───────────┴─────────┐           ┌─────────────┴─────────┐
          Greater                Elsewhere   Greater                 Elsewhere
          London                             London
             │                       │          │                        │
   What was the rateable value   What was the rateable value   What was the rateable value
   on the appropriate day?       on the appropriate day?        on the appropriate day?
```

≤ £1,500	> £1,500	> £750	≤ £750	≤ £1,000	> £1,000	> £500	≤ £500
s.1 does apply ✓	Does R exceed £25,000?		s.1 does apply		Does R exceed £25,000?		s.1 does apply ✓

	No	Yes			No	Yes	
	s.1 does apply ✓	s.1 does not apply ✗			s.1 does apply ✓	s.1 does not apply ✗	

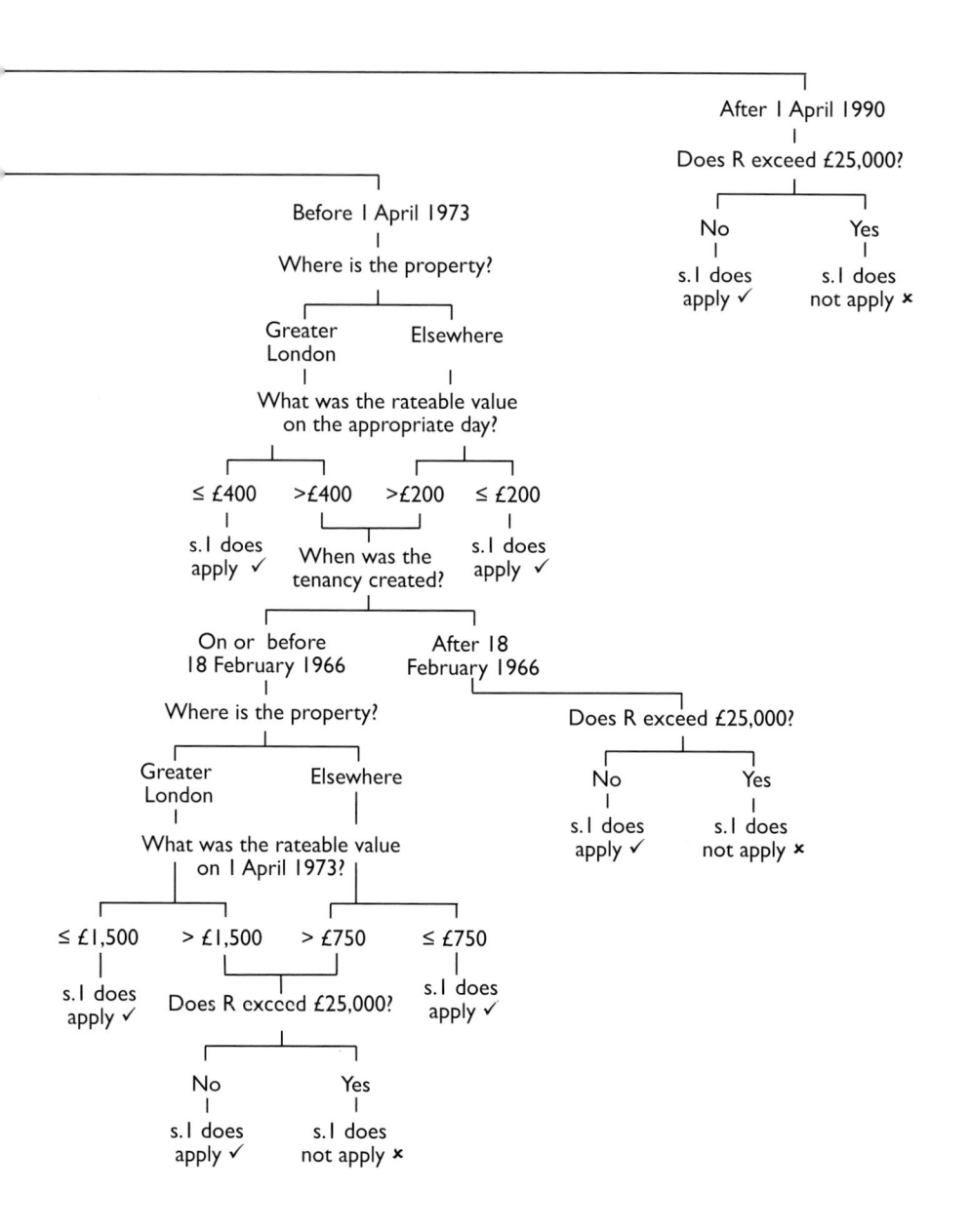

Houses: the right of a tenant to acquire the freehold

```
                                                                    After 1 April 1990
                                                                            |
                                                                    Does R exceed £25,000?
                                                                    ┌───────┴───────┐
                        Before 1 April 1973                        No             Yes
                                |                                   |               |
                        Where is the property?                   s.1 does       s.1 does
                        ┌───────┴───────┐                        apply ✓        not apply ✗
                    Greater          Elsewhere
                    London              |
                        |       What was the rateable value
                        |         on the appropriate day?
                ┌───────┴───────┐   ┌───────┴───────┐
              ≤ £400        > £400  > £200        ≤ £200
                |              └───┬───┘             |
             s.1 does        When was the        s.1 does
             apply ✓         tenancy created?    apply ✓
                            ┌───────┴───────┐
                      On or before        After 18
                     18 February 1966    February 1966
                            |                  |
                    Where is the property?     |
                    ┌───────┴───────┐          |
                Greater         Elsewhere      |
                London              |          |
                    |       What was the rateable value
                    |         on 1 April 1973?           Does R exceed £25,000?
          ┌─────┬───┴───┬─────┐    ┌───┴───┐             ┌───────┴───────┐
       ≤ £1,500  > £1,500  > £750  ≤ £750                No             Yes
          |        └───┬───┘         |                    |               |
       s.1 does    Does R exceed £25,000?  s.1 does    s.1 does       s.1 does
       apply ✓                              apply ✓    apply ✓        not apply ✗
                  ┌───────┴───────┐
                 No             Yes
                  |               |
               s.1 does       s.1 does
               apply ✓        not apply ✗
```

325

the fact that it follows on from a long tenancy at a low rent, the low rent test applies.

For a tenancy to be at a low rent pursuant to section 4(1)(i), the following conditions must be satisfied:

- the tenancy must have been entered into before 1 April 1990 (or in pursuance of a contract made before 1 April 1990);
- the property must have had a rateable value other than nil at the date of the commencement of the tenancy or else at any time before 1 April 1990; and
- the yearly rent must be less than two-thirds of the rateable value on the appropriate day or, if later, the first day of the term.

If the tenancy does not fall within section 4(1)(i), then it will be at a low rent pursuant to section 4(1)(ii) if the yearly rent payable is not more than £1,000 if the property is in Greater London and £250 if the property is elsewhere.

There is an exception relating to tenancies granted between 1 September 1939 and 31 March 1963 inclusive, and granted otherwise than by way of building lease. If at the commencement of the tenancy, the rent payable under it exceeded two-thirds of the letting value of the property, then the tenancy is not to be regarded as a tenancy at a low rent. However, by virtue of section 4(5) it is presumed that this exception does not apply until the contrary is shown. A building lease means a lease granted in pursuance or in consideration of an agreement for the erection or the substantial re-building or reconstruction of the whole or part of the house in question or a building comprising it (s.4(1)(d)).

For the purposes of section 4(1) and 4A(1) 'rent' means rent reserved as such. Any part of the rent which is payable in respect of services, repairs, maintenance, or insurance is to be disregarded. For example, where service charges are reserved as rent, those charges are not to be taken into account in determining the rent payable for the purpose of section 4(1) (s.4(1)(b)). Further, if as is commonly the case, the rent is to be suspended or reduced in the event of damage to the demised property, or the rent is to be increased in the event of a breach of covenant, this is also to be disregarded for the purposes of section 4(1) (s.4(1)(c)).

The alternative rent limits

As set out above, the right to acquire the freehold can arise under section 1A if the tenancy passes the alternative low rent test contained in section 4A(1). For the purposes of this test, one has to consider the rent payable in the 12 months following the commencement of the tenancy, known as 'the initial year'. If no rent was payable during this time, then the tenancy falls within section 4A(1). If rent was payable, then whether the tenancy falls within section 4A(1) depends on the amount payable and the date the tenancy was entered into.

For the tenancy to fall within section 4A(1)(a), the following criteria must be satisfied:

- the tenancy must have been entered into before 1 April 1963; and
- the total rent payable during the initial year must have been not more than two-thirds of the letting value of the property on the date of commencement of the tenancy.

For the tenancy to fall within section 4A(1)(b), the following criteria must be satisfied:

- the tenancy must have been entered into on or after 1 April 1963 but before 1 April 1990 (or pursuant to a contract made before that date);
- the property must have had a rateable value other than nil at the date of commencement of the tenancy or else at any time before 1 April 1990; and
- the total rent payable during the initial year must have been not more than two-thirds of the rateable value of the property on the relevant date.

The 'relevant date' is the date of the commencement of the tenancy or, if the property did not have a rateable value, or had a rateable value of nil on that date, the date on which it first had a rateable value other than nil (s.4A(2)(b)).

If the tenancy does not fall within either section 4A(1)(a) or (b), then it will fall within section 4A(1)(c), if the total rent payable during the initial year is not more than £1,000 if the property is in Greater London or £250 if it is elsewhere (see flowchart on page 328).

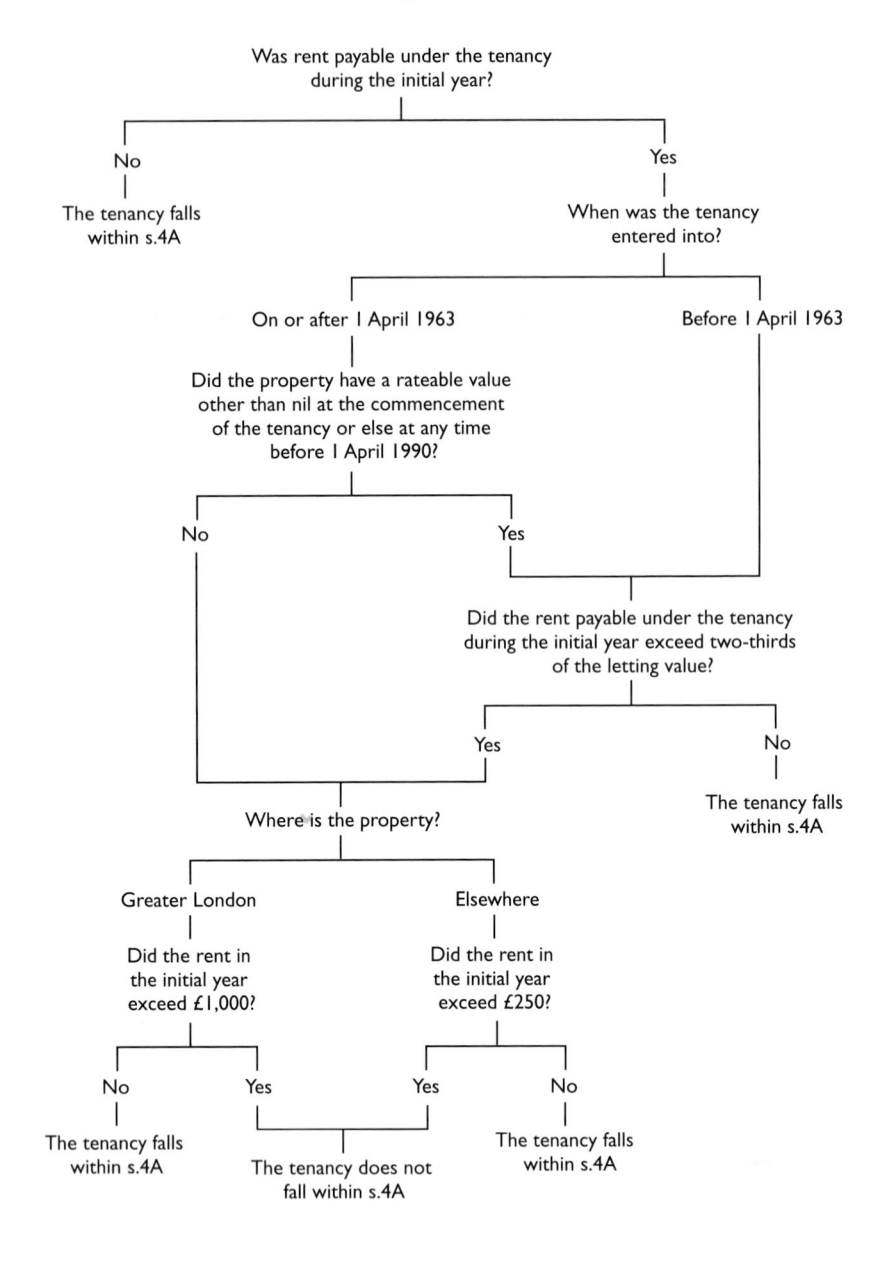

Leasehold enfranchisement explained

```
                Was rent payable under the tenancy
                   during the initial year?
          ┌──────────────────┴──────────────────┐
         No                                    Yes
          │                                     │
  The tenancy falls                     When was the tenancy
    within s.4A                             entered into?
                              ┌──────────────────┴──────────────────┐
                       On or after 1 April 1963              Before 1 April 1963
                              │
                    Did the property have a rateable value
                    other than nil at the commencement
                    of the tenancy or else at any time
                         before 1 April 1990?
                    ┌──────────┴──────────┐
                   No                    Yes
                    │                     │
                    │        Did the rent payable under the tenancy
                    │        during the initial year exceed two-thirds
                    │               of the letting value?
                    │            ┌──────────┴──────────┐
                    │           Yes                   No
                    │            │                     │
                    │            │             The tenancy falls
                    │            │                within s.4A
                    └──────┬─────┘
                    Where is the property?
           ┌───────────────┴───────────────┐
       Greater London                  Elsewhere
           │                               │
     Did the rent in                 Did the rent in
     the initial year                the initial year
     exceed £1,000?                  exceed £250?
      ┌────┴────┐                    ┌────┴────┐
     No        Yes                  Yes       No
      │         │                    │         │
 The tenancy   └─────────┬───────────┘   The tenancy falls
 falls within            │                  within s.4A
   s.4A          The tenancy does not
                  fall within s.4A
```

Starting the claim

A claim is started by serving a notice known as a notice of tenant's claim. Schedule 3 paragraph 6(1) to the Act and the Leasehold Reform (Notices) Regulations 1997 (SI 1997/640) as amended by the Leasehold Reform (Notices) (Amendment) (England) Regulations 2002 (SI 2002/1715) (or in Wales, the Leasehold

Reform (Notices) (Amendment) (Wales) Regulations 2002 (SI 2002/3187)) provide that the notice must be in a prescribed form or a form substantially to the same effect. The relevant form is Form 1 in the schedule to the 2002 Regulations, (see below). Form 1 is also the correct form to use if claiming an extended lease and one of the alternatives at paragraph 2 must be deleted according to which claim is being made: a claim cannot be made in the alternative and if it is, the notice is of no effect (*Byrnlea Property Investments Ltd v Ramsey* [1969] 2 QB 253).

The particulars, which are required to be inserted in the schedule to the notice, include those required by Schedule 3, paragraphs 6(1) and (2). Paragraph 6(3) of Schedule 3 provides that the notice shall not be invalidated by any inaccuracy in those particulars. In short, the particulars required are those which identify:

- the extent of the claim;
- that the tenant has the right to acquire the freehold;
- the section under which that right arises; and
- the section under which the house and premises fall to be valued.

Paragraph 6(3) also provides that the notice shall not be invalidated by any misdescription of the property to which the claim extends, and where the claim is stated in the notice to extend to property not properly included in the house and premises, or is not stated to extend to property which ought to be included, the notice may be amended so as to include or exclude such property with the leave of the court and on such terms as the court may see fit to impose.

Whilst the prescribed form provides for the notice to be signed by the tenant personally, it can be signed by a duly authorised agent. If there are joint tenants, then the notice must be given by all of them and signed either by each of them personally or by one or more persons duly authorised to sign on their behalf.

Leasehold Reform Act 1967

Notice of tenant's claim to acquire the freehold or an extended lease

To *[Name and address of person on whom this notice is served]* **(see Note I below)** [and]

To: *[Name and address of any recipient of a copy of this notice*]* **(see Note I below. In addition, your attention is drawn to paragraphs 8 to 10 of this notice)** *(*Delete if paragraphs 5 to 10 are deleted)*

1. I am the tenant of the house and premises of which particulars are given in the Schedule to this notice.

2. In exercise of my rights under Part I of the Leasehold Reform Act 1967, I give you notice of my desire –

[to have the freehold of the house and premises.]*

[to have an extended lease of the house and premises.]*

(*Delete whichever is inapplicable.)

3. The particulars on which I rely are set out in the Schedule to this notice.

4. If you are both my immediate landlord and the freeholder, you must give me, within two months of the service of this notice, a notice in reply in Form 3 set out in the Schedule to the Leasehold Reform (Notices) Regulations 1997 (or in a form substantially to the same effect), stating whether or not you admit my right [to have the freehold of the house and premises]* [to have an extended lease of the house and premises]* (*delete whichever is inapplicable) (subject to any question as to the correctness of the particulars of the house and premises) and, if you do not admit my right, stating the grounds on which you do not admit it. **(see Note 2 below)**

(The remaining paragraphs of this form should be deleted where the claimant's immediate landlord is known to be the freeholder of the house and premises.)

5. If you are not my immediate landlord, or if you are my immediate landlord but not the freeholder, you must comply with the requirements of paragraphs 7 and 8, but you need only give me the notice mentioned in paragraph 4 if you are the person designated as 'the reversioner' in accordance with Schedule 1 paragraph 2 to the Act. If you are the reversioner, you must give the notice mentioned in paragraph 4 within two months of the first service of this notice on any landlord. **(see Note 3 below)**

6. I have served a copy of this notice on the following person[s] whom I know or believe to have an interest in the house and premises superior to my tenancy – [insert name and address of each person on whom a copy of the notice has been served].

7. You must now serve a copy of this notice on any other person whom you know or believe to have an interest in the house and premises superior to my tenancy, and you must record on that copy the date on which you received this notice. If you serve a copy on any person you must add his name and, if you know it, his address to the list at the end of paragraph 6, and give me written notice of the name, and address (if known).

8. If you know who is, or believe yourself or another person to be, the reversioner, you must give me written notice stating the name and address (if known) of the person who you think is the reversioner, and serve copies of it on every person whom you know or believe to have an interest superior to my tenancy, stating on each copy the date on which you received this notice.

9. Anyone who receives a copy of this notice must, without delay, serve a further copy of it on any person whom he knows or believes to have an

interest in the house and premises superior to my tenancy but who is not named in the notice, unless he knows that that person has already received a copy of it, and he must also record on each further copy the date on which he received this notice. For each further copy served, you must add the name of the person served and, if you know it, his address to the list at the end of paragraph 6, and give me written notice of the name and (if known) the address of that person.

10. Anyone who receives a copy of this notice and who knows who is, or believes himself to be, the reversioner, must notify me in writing of the name and (if known) the address of the person known or believed by him to be the reversioner, and serve a copy of this notification on every person whom he knows or believes to have an interest superior to my tenancy.

[*Insert date.*]
Signed

(Tenant)
of [*insert address*]

[The name and address of my solicitor or agent, to whom further communications may be sent is]*   (*Delete if inapplicable.)

The Schedule

Particulars supporting tenant's claim

1. The address of the house.

2. Particulars of the house and premises sufficient to identify the property to which your claim extends. **(see Note 4 below)**

3. Particulars of the tenancy of the house and premises sufficient to identify the instrument creating the tenancy and to show that the tenancy is and has at the material times been a long tenancy or treated as a long tenancy. **(see Note 5 below)**

4. Particulars sufficient to show the date on which you acquired the tenancy. **(see Note 6 below)**

5.

(a) Particulars of the tenancy of the house and premises sufficient to show that the tenancy is and has at the material times been a tenancy at a low rent or treated as a tenancy at a low rent. **(see Note 7 below)**

OR

(b) If your claim is based on section 1AA (additional right to enfranchisement only in case of houses whose rent exceeds applicable limit under section 4), particulars of the tenancy sufficient to show that the tenancy is one in relation to which section 1AA has effect to confer a right to acquire the freehold of the house and premises. **(see Note 8 below)**

6. Particulars of any other long tenancy of the house or a flat forming part of the house held by any tenant. **(see Note 9 below)**

7. Where either –

(a) a flat forming part of the house is let to a person who is a qualifying tenant of a flat for the purposes of Chapter 1 or 2 of Part 1 of the Leasehold Reform, Housing and Urban Development Act 1993; or

(b) your tenancy is a business tenancy,

the following particulars:

   (i) the periods for which in the last ten years, and since acquiring the tenancy, you have and have not occupied the house as your residence; and

   (ii) during those periods what parts (if any) of the house have not been in your own occupation and for what periods, and

   (iii) what other residence (if any) you have had and for what periods, and which was your main residence. **(see Note 10 below)**

8. Additional particulars sufficient to show that the value of the house and premises does not exceed the applicable financial limit specified in section 1(1)(a)(i) or (ii), (5) or (6) of the Act. (These are not required where the right to have the freehold is claimed in reliance on any one or more of the provisions in section 1A, 1AA or 1B of the Act, or where the tenancy of the house and premises has been extended under section 14 and the notice under section 8(1) was given (whether by a tenant or a sub-tenant) after the original term date of the tenancy). **(see Note 11 below)**

9. Additional particulars sufficient to show whether the house and premises are to be valued in accordance with section 9(1) or section 9(1A) of the Act. (These are not required where the right to have the freehold is claimed in reliance on any one or more of the provisions in section 1A, 1AA or 1B of the Act, or where the tenancy of the house and premises has been extended under section 14 and the notice under section 8(1) was given (whether by a tenant or a sub-tenant) after the original term date of the tenancy).

10. Additional particulars where you rely on section 6 (rights of trustees), 6A (rights of personal representatives) or 7 (rights of members of family succeeding to tenancy on death) of the Act. **(see Note 12 below)**

Notes

1.

(a) Where the tenant's immediate landlord is not the freeholder, the claim may, in accordance with the Leasehold Reform Act 1967, as amended, be served on him or any superior landlord, and copies of the notice must be served by the tenant on anyone else known or believed by him to have an interest superior to his own (Sch. 3, para 8(1)).

(b) Where the landlord's interest is subject to a mortgage or other charge and the mortgagee or person entitled to the benefit of the charge is in possession of that interest, or a receiver appointed by him or by the court is in receipt of the rents and profits, the notice may be served either on the landlord or on the person in possession or the receiver (Sch. 3, para 9(1)).

(c) Any landlord whose interest is subject to a mortgage or other charge (not being a rent-charge) to secure the payment of money must (subject to special provisions applicable to debenture-holders' charges), on receipt of the claim inform the mortgagee or person entitled to the benefit of the charge (Sch. 3, para 9(2)).

2. The landlord must (unless note 3 applies) serve a notice in reply in Form 3 set out in the Schedule to the Leasehold Reform (Notices) Regulations 1997 (or in substantially the same form), within two months of the service on him of this notice. If he does not admit the tenant's right to have the freehold or an extended lease, the notice in reply must state the grounds on which the right is not admitted. If the landlord intends to apply to the court for possession of the house and premises in order to redevelop it (section 17) or to occupy it (section 18), his notice must say so. If he does not so intend, but he objects under subsection (4) or (5) of section 2 to the inclusion in the claim of a part of the house and premises which projects into other property, or to the exclusion from the claim of property let with the house and premises but not occupied with and used for the purposes of the house by any occupant of it, he must give notice of his objection with or before his notice in reply; unless in his notice in reply he reserves the right to give it later, in which case it must still be given within two months of the service on him of the tenant's notice. If the landlord admits the claim, the admission is binding on him, unless he shows that he was misled by misrepresentation or concealment of material facts, but it does not conclude any question of the correctness of the particulars of the house and premises as set out in the claim (Sch. 3, para. 7).

3. Where the tenant's immediate landlord is not the freeholder, any proceedings arising out of the tenant's notice, whether for resisting or for giving effect to the claim, must be conducted by the person who is designated as 'the reversioner' in accordance with Schedule 1 paragraph 2 to the Act and he must give the notice in reply. The reversioner is the landlord whose tenancy carries an expectation of possession of the house and premises of 30 years or more after the expiration of all inferior tenancies and, if there is more than one such landlord, it means the landlord whose tenancy is nearest to that of the tenant; if there is no such landlord, it means the owner of the freehold. The tenant will be informed in the notice in reply if it is given by a landlord acting as the reversioner.

4. 'Premises' to be included with the house in the claim are any garage, outhouse, garden, yard and appurtenances which at the time of the notice are let to the tenant with the house.

5. In respect of a house, 'long tenancy' has the meaning given by section 3 of the Act. (Special provisions apply in relation to business tenancies - see section 1(1ZC) of the Act inserted by section 140 of the Commonhold and Leasehold Reform Act 2002). Where there have been successive tenancies, particulars should be given of each tenancy. In the case of a lease already extended under the Act, the date of the extension and the original term date should be given. In addition to section 3 of the Act, section 174(a) of the Housing Act 1985 provides for certain tenancies granted pursuant to the right to buy to be treated as long tenancies. Section 1B of the Act also provides for certain tenancies terminable on death or marriage to be long tenancies for the limited right described in note 11. Under Schedule 4A to the Act, certain shared ownership leases granted by public authorities, housing associations and registered social landlords, carry neither the right to enfranchise nor the right to obtain an extended lease.

6. The claimant must have owned the lease for two years prior to the date of the application for enfranchisement or lease extension (section 1(1)(b) of the Act, as amended by sections 138 and 139 of the Commonhold and Leasehold Reform Act 2002).

7. In addition to the provision of section 4 of the Act (meaning of 'low rent'), section 1A(2) of the Act provides for tenancies falling within section 4A(1) of the Act to be treated as tenancies at a low rent for the limited right described in note 11.

8. Section 1AA confers a limited right to enfranchisement (described in note 11) in the case of leases which would qualify but for the fact that the tenancy is not a tenancy at a low rent, with two exceptions. The first is where the lease is excluded from the right under section 1AA(3), i.e. where the house is in an area designated as a rural area, the freehold of the house is owned together with adjoining land which is not occupied for residential purposes, and the tenancy was either granted on or before 1 April 1997 or was granted after that date but before the coming into force of section 141 of the Commonhold and Leasehold Reform Act 2002, for a term of 35 years or less. Information as to the location of designated rural areas is held at the offices of leasehold valuation tribunals. The second exception applies to any shared ownership lease (as defined by section 622 of the Housing Act 1985) originally granted by a housing association or a registered social landlord.

9. Section 1(1ZA) of the Act (inserted by section 138(2) of the Commonhold and Leasehold Reform Act 2002) provides that head lessees do not have rights to enfranchise, or a lease extension, where there exist inferior tenancies which confer on the tenant the right to enfranchise and a lease extension under the Act. Under section 1(1ZB) of the Act, where there exists an inferior long tenancy (as defined under section 7 of the Leasehold Reform, Housing and Urban Development Act 1993) of a flat which confers on the tenant the right to enfranchise or a new lease under that Act, the head lessee only has the right to enfranchise or a lease extension under the Act where he meets the residence requirement (see note 10 below). It is, therefore, necessary to provide details of any other long tenancies.

10. Particulars of residence and occupation are required in relation to those cases specified in paragraph 7 of the Schedule to this notice (see section 1(1ZB) and (1B) of the Act as inserted, respectively, by sections 138 and 139 of the Commonhold and Leasehold Reform Act 2002). The residence requirement in these specified cases is that the tenant has lived in the property as his only or main residence for the last two years or for periods amounting to two years in the last ten years.

11. A claimant who relies on any one or more of the provisions in section 1A, 1AA or 1B of the Act, (or where the tenancy of the house and premises has been extended under section 14 and the notice under section 8(1) was

given (whether by a tenant or a sub-tenant) after the original term date of the tenancy), has the right to have the freehold at a price determined in accordance with section 9(1C) of the Act, but not the right to have an extended lease.

Section 1A(1) applies to a tenancy of a house and premises, the value of which exceeds the applicable financial limit. Sections 1A(2) and 1B are described in notes 7 and 5, respectively. Section 1AA (described in note 8) applies to certain cases where the long lease fails the low rent test.

12.

(a) Where the claimant is giving the notice by virtue of section 6, 6A or 7 he is required (Sch. 3, para. 6(2)) to adapt the notice and show under paragraphs 4 and 7 of the Schedule to the notice the particulars that bring the claim within section 6, 6A or, as the case may be, section 7.

(b) Where the tenancy is or was vested in trustees the claimant should, for the purposes of a claim made in reliance on section 6, state the date when the tenancy was acquired by the trustees, and, where the case falls within paragraphs 7(a) or (b) of the Schedule to the notice, the date when the beneficiary occupied the house by virtue of his interest under the trust, and the particulars of any period of occupation by the beneficiary which are relied upon as bringing the case within section 6.

(c) Section 6A of the Act (inserted by section 142 of the Commonhold and Leasehold Reform Act 2002) provides that where a tenant dies and immediately before his death he qualified for the right to enfranchise or a lease extension, those rights can be exercised (up to two years after the date of probate or letters of administration) by his personal representatives. Where the tenancy is vested in personal representatives, they should, for the purposes of making a claim under section 6A, provide evidence that the deceased tenant qualified for the relevant right immediately before his death, state the date when the tenancy became vested in them, and provide evidence to show that probate or letters of administration have been granted no more than two years before the date of the claim for extension of the lease or enfranchisement.

(d) Where the claimant was a member of the previous tenant's family and became the tenant on the latter's death, for the purposes of a claim made in reliance upon section 7, the claimant should state the date on which the previous tenant acquired the tenancy, particulars of his relationship to the previous tenant and his succession to the tenancy, and particulars in respect of any period of occupation by himself on which the claimant relies as bringing the case within section 7.

Serving the notice of tenant's claim

Who to serve

The notice of tenant's claim is regarded as served on the landlord if it is served on any of the persons having an interest in the house and premises superior to the tenant and the 'relevant time' is the time of such service (Sch. 3, para. 8(1)(a)). Copies of the notice must also be served on any other person known or believed by the tenant to have such an interest and the notice must state whether copies are being served on anyone other than the recipient and, if so, whom (Sch. 3, paras. 8(1)(b) and (c)). The notice of tenant's claim will also be duly served if it is served on a mortgagee in possession or a receiver appointed by a mortgagee or the court (Sch. 3, para. 9(1)).

How to serve

Section 22(5) of the Act provides that section 66 of the *Landlord and Tenant Act* 1954 is to apply to the service of notices. Section 66(4) of the *Landlord and Tenant Act* 1954 provides that section 23 of the *Landlord and Tenant Act* 1927 is to apply for the purposes of that Act. Section 23(1) of the *Landlord and Tenant Act* 1927 takes effect subject to the *Recorded Delivery Service Act* 1962, and has been the subject of judicial interpretation in *Stylo Shoes Ltd v Prices Tailors Ltd* [1960] Ch. 396. Pursuant to these various statutory provisions and the case law, the notice of tenant's claim may be served by any one of the following methods:

- personal service;
- by leaving it for the landlord at his last known place of abode in England and Wales or place of business if the landlord is a limited company;
- by sending it through the post in a registered or recorded letter addressed to the landlord at his last known place of abode in England and Wales or place of business if the landlord is a limited company;
- in the case of a local or public authority or a statutory or a public utility company, by serving it on the secretary or other proper officer at the principal office of such authority or company;
- by serving it on any agent of the landlord duly authorised to receive it; or
- by serving it by any other method or at any other address, if it can be proved that the landlord did in fact receive the notice.

Sections 47(1) and 48(1) of the *Landlord and Tenant Act* 1987 contain provisions requiring a landlord to provide an address in England and Wales at which notices may be served on him. Further, section 23(2) of the *Landlord and Tenant Act* 1927 provides that a landlord is deemed served if the tenant serves on the former landlord and has not been notified of the change of landlord.

Pursuant to section 7 of the *Interpretation Act* 1978, service is deemed to be effected by properly addressing, pre-paying and posting a letter containing the notice, and unless the contrary is proved, to have been effected at the time at which the letter would be delivered in the ordinary course of post. In the case of service by any other method, there is no deeming provision and when the notice is served will be a question of fact.

Bars to serving

The tenant is not entitled to serve an effective notice of tenant's claim in the following circumstances:

- if a notice to treat has been served or a contract entered into for the purpose of compulsorily acquiring the whole or part of the house and premises (s.5(6)(a));
- if, in the previous 12 months, the tenant has given notice to his landlord withdrawing a previous notice of tenant's claim in respect of the house or any part of it (s.9(3)(b));
- if the landlord has made an application under section 17 on the ground that he proposes to redevelop the house and an order has been made on that application fixing the date for termination of the tenancy, or the tenant served a notice of his desire to have an extended lease within the 12 months preceding the landlord's application (s.17(6)(a));
- if the tenant has already given notice terminating the tenancy and that notice has not been superseded by the express or implied grant of a new tenancy (Sch. 3, para. 1(1));
- if there is an agreement for a future tenancy to which section 28 of the *Landlord and Tenant* Act 1954 or Schedule 10, paragraph 17 to the *Local Government and Housing Act* 1989 applies (Sch. 3, para. 1(1));
- if the landlord has given notice terminating the tenancy under section 4 or 25 of the *Landlord and Tenant Act* 1954 or Schedule 10 paragraph 4(1) to the *Local Government and Housing Act* 1989 and the notice of tenant's claim is served more than two months after the service of the landlord's notice unless:
    - the tenant applies to the court under section 24(1) of the *Landlord and Tenant Act* 1954 for an order for the grant of a new tenancy within two months of the service of the

landlord's notice, in which case the notice of tenant's claim will be effective if it is served within two months of making that application; or
- o the landlord gives his written consent to the notice of tenant's claim being served out of time (Sch. 3, para. 2); and
- if the tenant has previously given notice under section 16(2) of, or Schedule 5, paragraph 9(2), to the *Landlord and Tenant Act* 1954 (Sch. 3, paras. 4(4) and (5)).

Registering the notice of tenant's claim

The notice of tenant's claim ought to be registered at the Land Registry once served, otherwise it will be void against a purchaser of the freehold for value. Section 5(5) provides that the notice is registrable under the *Land Charges Act* 1972 or may be the subject of a notice under the *Land Registration Act* 2002 as if it were an estate contract. For guidance as to how to register the notice, see paragraph 5.2 of the Land Registry Practice Guide 27, available at www.landregistry.gov.uk

Effect of serving the notice of tenant's claim

Upon the tenant serving notice of tenant's claim, the landlord is bound to make to the tenant and the tenant is bound to accept a grant of the house and premises (s.8(1)), and pursuant to section 5(1), the rights and obligations of the landlord and tenant arising from the notice are enforceable as rights and obligations arising under a contract. As such, those rights and obligations can pass to any executor, administrator or assignee of the landlord and tenant and in the event of any default by the landlord or the tenant in carrying out their obligations, section 5(3) specifically provides that the other has the usual remedies for breach of contract available to them, i.e. specific performance, rescission and damages. The parties can also agree to terminate the contract at any time (s.23(2)(b)). The terms of the contract, follow.

As well as creating a contract, service of a notice of tenant's claim has various other effects:

- the tenant becomes liable to pay the landlord's costs regardless of whether the notice is or is not valid (s.9(4));
- if the landlord has made an application under section 17 on the ground that he proposes to redevelop the house, no order or further order may be made on that application except as regards costs (s.17(6)(b));

- any contract the landlord has entered into for the sale of the freehold to a third party is discharged unless certain conditions are met (s.5(7));
- during the currency of the claim and for three months thereafter, the tenancy will not terminate either by effluxion of time, the service of a notice to quit by the landlord or the termination of a superior tenancy. If the claim is not effective and the tenancy would, but for the claim, have terminated, then it will terminate upon the expiry of the three months (Sch. 3, para. 3(1));
- a landlord's notice terminating a tenancy under section 4 or 25 of the *Landlord and Tenant Act* 1954 or under Schedule 10 paragraph 4(1) to the *Local Government and Housing Act* 1989 is of no effect if served during the currency of the claim to acquire the freehold and ceases to have effect on the making of such claim (provided the notice of tenant's claim is served within two months of service of the landlord's notice) (Sch. 3, para. 2(2));
- similarly, a tenant's notice terminating the tenancy of any property is of no effect if given during the currency of the claim (Sch. 3, para. 1(2));
- if the tenancy is a business tenancy and the landlord has commenced proceedings under Part 2 of the *Landlord and Tenant Act* 1954 and the tenant serves a notice of tenant's claim in time, then no further steps can be taken in those proceedings otherwise than for their dismissal and the making of any consequential order (Sch. 3, para. 2A);
- during the currency of the claim, no proceedings to enforce any right of re-entry or forfeiture terminating the tenancy can be brought without the leave of the court, and leave will not be granted unless the court is satisfied that the claim was not made in good faith. If, for example, a notice of tenant's claim is served simply to avoid forfeiture, then it is likely to be found that the claim was not made in good faith and leave given to the landlord to issue forfeiture proceedings. If leave is given, the claim ceases to have effect (Sch. 3, para. 4(1));
- where forfeiture proceedings have already been commenced prior to the service of the notice of tenant's claim, the court in which the proceedings were brought may set aside or vary such order to such extent and on such terms as appear to be appropriate. If it appears to the court that the claim to acquire the freehold has not been made in good faith or there has been unreasonable delay in making the claim, then the court must order that the tenancy has terminated and the claim is invalid (Sch. 3, para. 4(2));

As regards those effects which are provided for by Schedule 3, they result not only from the service of a valid notice of tenant's claim, but also if the tenant making the claim is not entitled to acquire the freehold or the claim is made by a person who is not the tenant (Sch. 3, para. 5). The currency of the claim means the period between giving the notice and acquiring the freehold or the notice ceasing to have effect, being set aside by the court or being withdrawn or when the notice would cease to have effect, if valid (Sch. 3, para. 5(c)).

Assigning the notice of tenant's claim

As stated, the notice of tenant's claim can be assigned and the assignee of a notice can thereby acquire the freehold without having to wait two years. Section 5(2) provides that the rights and obligations of the tenant arising from the notice are not capable of subsisting apart from the tenancy of the entire house and premises. This means that (1) the notice can only be assigned upon the assignment of the tenancy; and (2) completion of the assignment of the notice must take place upon completion of the assignment of the tenancy. If the tenancy is assigned without the benefit of the notice or if the tenancy of one part of the house and premises is assigned to, or vests in, any person without the tenancy of another part, then the notice ceases to have effect. Further, the tenant is liable to compensate the landlord for any loss caused.

Missing landlords

If one of several landlords is missing, this does not cause a problem as one of the other landlords will be able to conduct the claim on behalf of that missing landlord. However, where there is only one landlord and that landlord is either missing, or his identity cannot be ascertained, it is obviously not possible to serve a notice of tenant's claim and thus start a claim. In such circumstances, the court is able to make an order vesting the freehold in the tenant upon him paying into court 'the appropriate sum' (s.27).

In order to obtain such a vesting order, the tenant must prove that:

- he is entitled to acquire the freehold; and
- he is prevented from giving notice because the landlord cannot be found, or his identity cannot be ascertained.

As regards the second requirement, the court may require the tenant to take such further steps by way of advertisement or otherwise as the court thinks proper for the purpose of tracing the landlord before it makes a vesting order (s.27(2)). For suggested steps, which could be taken to try and trace a missing landlord, see the section relating to missing landlords in chapter 1.

By virtue of section 27(5), the appropriate sum is the aggregate of:

- an amount determined by the Leasehold Valuation Tribunal (LVT) (or the Lands Tribunal on appeal) to be the price payable for the freehold in accordance with section 9; and
- the amount or estimated amount of any rent payable in respect of the house and premises up to the date of the conveyance, which has not previously been paid.

It may be that the landlord has been missing for some time, in which case no rent will have been paid for a number of years. Given that section 19 of the *Limitation Act* 1980 provides that no action to recover rent shall be brought after six years, it will not be necessary to pay more than six years' worth of rent into court.

In practice, the procedure is as follows:

- an application is made to the court (see the following example);
- the court may order that further steps be taken to trace the landlord;
- once the court is satisfied that the tenant is entitled to acquire the freehold and the landlord cannot be found, or his identity cannot be ascertained, the court will make an order and transfer the matter to the LVT;
- the LVT will determine the appropriate sum;
- the tenant pays into court the appropriate sum; and
- such person as the court designates will execute a conveyance in a form approved by the court.

The tenant is likely to incur significant costs in relation to the proceedings, both before the court and the LVT, through no fault of anyone other than the landlord who has neglected his property interests; whilst the appropriate sum will languish in the court's funds and can be claimed by the landlord at any time. It seems only fair, therefore, that the tenant should be able to recover his costs from the money in court. It is not possible to deduct the costs from the appropriate sum and pay the difference into court as the Act requires 'the appropriate sum' and not some lesser amount to be paid into court as a condition of the conveyance being executed. However, it is possible to obtain an order from the court, which provides that having paid the appropriate sum into court, the tenant is then entitled to have paid out to him his costs as assessed by the court.

Example

To be inserted into a CPR Part 8 Claim Form, N208

Details of Claim

1. The Claimants are qualifying tenants of a house and premises ('the premises') known as [*address of the premises*] under a lease dated [*date*].

2. The lease is a long tenancy at a low rent within the meaning of the Leasehold Reform Act 1967 ('the Act').

3. The Claimants wish to exercise their right to acquire the freehold of the premises at a price to be determined in accordance with the Act.

4. The Claimants are prevented from giving notice of their desire to have the freehold because the person to be served with the notice, namely the freehold owner of the premises, cannot be found and/or his identity cannot be ascertained. The Claimants have made all relevant enquiries including enquiries at the Land Registry, but have been unable to ascertain the identity of the person who owns the freehold.

5. The court is requested to make the following orders under section 27 of the Act:

   1) The Claimants shall take such further steps whether by way of advertisement or otherwise as the court thinks proper for the purpose of tracing the landlord.

   2) The rights and obligations of all parties shall be determined as if the Claimants had, at the date of the application, duly given notice of their desire to have the freehold under the Act.

   3) The price payable shall be determined by a leasehold valuation tribunal in accordance with section 27 of Act.

   4) Approval of the form of the conveyance in accordance with section 27(3) of the Act.

   5) That the house and premises shall be vested in the Claimants for the like estate and on the like terms (so far as circumstances permit), as if they had at the date of this application to the court given notice of their desire to have the freehold.

Houses: the right of a tenant to acquire the freehold

> 6) Such other directions as to the steps to be taken for giving effect to the Claimants' rights and obligations, including directions modifying or dispensing with any of the requirements of the Act or of regulations made under the Act.
>
> 7) That the landlord shall pay the Claimants' costs of the application to be subject to a summary assessment, such sum to be paid out of the appropriate sum paid into court under section 27(3) of the Act.
>
> 6. Part 8 of the Civil Procedure Rules applies to this claim.
> 7. This claim is made under section 27 of the Leasehold Reform Act 1967.
> 8. The Claimants have not complied with sections III or IV of the Practice Direction (Pre-Action Conduct).
> 9. The Claimants rely on the witness statement of [name] attached.

Receipt of a notice of tenant's claim

Anyone receiving a notice of tenant's claim, other than a person with no interest in the house and premises, must:

- serve a copy on anyone they know or believe to be a landlord if that person is not stated in the notice or known by the recipient to have received a copy (Sch. 3, para. 8(1)(d));
- if they do so, add to the notice the names of anyone they are giving copies of the notice to or who are known to them to have received a copy and notify the tenant of the names they have added (Sch. 3, paras. 8(1)(e) and 2(a));
- if they know, or they believe themselves to be, the reversioner, they must give a notice to the tenant stating who is thought by them to be reversioner (Sch. 3, para. 8(2)(b));
- if their interest is subject to a mortgage, they must inform the mortgagee that the notice has been given and give the mortgagee such further information as may from time to time be reasonably required (Sch. 3, para. 9(2)); and
- if the mortgagee is in possession or a receiver has been appointed, then they must send a copy of the notice to the mortgagee (Sch. 3, para. 9(1)).

In most cases, there will only be one landlord, namely the freeholder, and he will take all further steps. However, where there is more than one landlord, any further steps will be taken by 'the reversioner' (Sch. 1, para. 1(1)(b)). The 'reversioner' is any person who has a tenancy of the house carrying an expectation of possession of 30 years or more and, if there is more than one such person, the one with the lowest interest (Sch. 1, para. 2(a)). If there is no such tenancy, then the freeholder is the reversioner (Sch. 1, para. 2(b)). All other landlords are referred to as 'other landlords'.

> *Example 1*
>
> A grants B a tenancy of a house for a term of 125 years from 14 November 1945. B grants C a tenancy of the house for a term of 90 years from 15 October 1946. C grants D a tenancy of the house for a term of 75 years from 25 March 1947. D serves a notice of tenant's claim.
>
> Whilst there are two tenancies of the house superior to D's, only B has a tenancy which carries an expectation of possession of 30 years or more and, therefore, B is 'the reversioner'.

> *Example 2*
>
> A grants B a tenancy of a house for a term of 125 years from 14 November 1945. B grants C a tenancy of the house for a term of 90 years from 15 October 1946. C grants D a tenancy of the house for a term of 50 years from 25 March 1947. D serves a notice of tenant's claim.
>
> Both B and C have tenancies carrying an expectation of possession of 30 years or more. However, C's interest is the lowest interest and therefore C is 'the reversioner'.

> *Example 3*
>
> A grants B a tenancy of a house for a term of 99 years from 14 November 1945. B grants C a tenancy of the house for a term of 90 years from 15 October 1946. C grants D a tenancy of the house for a term of 75 years from 25 March 1947. D serves a Notice of Tenant's Claim.
>
> Whilst there are two tenancies of the house superior to D's, neither carry an expectation of possession of 30 years or more. Consequently, A as freeholder, is 'the reversioner'.

Save for any application under either section 17 or 18, the reversioner conducts all proceedings arising out of the notice of tenant's claim on behalf of the other landlords (Sch. 1, para. 1(1)(b) and 6(1)). In particular, the reversioner may, on behalf and in the name of, the other landlords:

- execute any conveyance of the freehold (Sch. 1, para. 4(1)(a)); and

- take or defend any legal proceedings in respect of matters arising out of the notice of tenant's claim (Sch. 1, para. 4(1)(b)).

However, in certain circumstances, the reversioner can, by court order, be replaced by one of the other landlords (Sch. 1, para. 3). The reversioner's acts are binding on the other landlords. However, in the event of a dispute, either the reversioner or any of the other landlords can apply to the court for directions as to the manner in which the reversioner should act on the matter in dispute (Sch. 1, para. 4(2)).

If any of the other landlords cannot be found, or his identity cannot be ascertained, the reversioner must apply to the court for directions as to how to proceed (paragraph 4(3) of Schedule 1). If the reversioner acts in good faith and with reasonable care and diligence, then he shall not be liable to any of the other landlords for any loss and damage caused by any act or omission of his (Sch. 1, para. 4(4)).

Any of the other landlords may:

- be separately represented in any legal proceedings in which his title to any property comes into question or in any legal proceedings relating to the price payable for the house and premises (Sch. 1, para. 5(1));
- deal directly with the tenant for the purpose of deducing, evidencing or verifying his title to any property if he objects to disclosing his title to the reversioner and gives written notice to both the reversioner and the tenant. Further, an other landlord must deal directly with the tenant, if the tenant, by written notice, requires him to do so (paragraph 5(2) of Sch. 1, para. 5(2));
- deal directly with the tenant for the purpose of agreeing the price payable for his interest if he gives written notice to both the reversioner and the tenant (Sch. 1, para. 5(3));
- require the reversioner to apply to an LVT for the price to be determined (Sch. 1, para. 5(3)); and
- require that any amount payable to him shall be paid by the tenant to him, or to a person authorised by him to receive it, instead of the reversioner (Sch. 1, para. 5(4)).

In any event, an other landlord may make an application under section 17 or 18 on the grounds that he intends to redevelop or occupy the house (Sch. 1, para. 6(1)).

It is the duty of an other landlord to give the reversioner all such information and assistance as he may reasonably require (Sch. 1, para. 5(5)(a)). If the other landlord fails to provide such information and assistance, he will be liable to indemnify the reversioner against any liability incurred by the reversioner in consequence of that failure (Sch. 1, para. 5(5)). Further, and so far as may be just, an other landlord will be required to contribute to the reversioner's costs so far as they are not recoverable or recovered from the tenant (Sch. 1, para. 5(6)).

Landlord's notice in reply

Within two months of the service of a notice of tenant's claim, the reversioner must give the tenant a notice in reply, stating whether or not the reversioner admits the tenant's right to acquire the freehold. If the reversioner does not admit the right, the notice must state the grounds on which it is not admitted (Sch. 3, para. 7(1)).

Schedule 3 paragraph 7(1) and the Leasehold Reform (Notices) Regulations 1997 provide that the notice must be in a prescribed form or a form substantially to the same effect. In England, the relevant form is Form 3 in the schedule to the Leasehold Reform (Notices) (Amendment) (No. 2) (England) Regulations 2002 (SI 2002/3209), which is set out below. In Wales, the appropriate form is Form 3 in the schedule to the Leasehold Reform (Notices) (Amendment) (Wales) Regulations 2003 (SI 2003/991). Form 3 is also the correct form to use if replying to a claim for an extended lease.

The prescribed form provides for the information required by paragraph 7 to be included in the notice and reference should be made to the notes included in the prescribed form in that regard.

Whilst the requirement to serve a notice in reply is in mandatory terms, there are very few consequences of failing to serve a notice, failing to serve a notice in the prescribed form or failing to provide the information required by paragraph 7. Perhaps the only consequence is that a tenant cannot commence court proceedings to enforce his right to acquire the freehold until he has received a notice in reply or, if he does not do so, two months have elapsed since the tenant gave his notice (paragraph 7(5) of Schedule 3). If the reversioner has failed to serve notice he may well be ordered to pay the tenant's costs of such proceedings, on the basis that they were incurred as a result of the reversioner's failure to reply.

Leasehold Reform Act 1967
Notice in reply to tenant's claim

To: [*Name and address of Claimant*]

1. I have received [a copy of]* your notice dated *(insert date)* claiming the right to have [the freehold]* [an extended lease]* *(*delete as appropriate)* of the house and premises described in your notice. (**see Note 1 below**)

2. [I admit your right (subject to any question as to the correctness of the particulars given in your notice of the house and premises).]* *(*delete if inapplicable)* (**see Note 2 below**)

3. [I do not admit your right on the following grounds: *(state grounds on which the tenant's right is not admitted)*]* *(*delete if inapplicable)*

4. [The house and premises are within an area of a scheme approved under [section 19 of the Act]* [section 70 of the Leasehold Reform, Housing and Urban Development Act 1993]*]* *(*delete as appropriate or delete entire paragraph if paragraph 2 has been deleted)* (**see Note 3 below**)

5. [In my opinion, the house should be valued in accordance with section [9(1)]*, [9(1A)]*, [9(1C)]* of the Act.]* *(*delete as appropriate or delete the entire paragraph if paragraph 2 has been deleted)* (**see Note 4 below**)

6. [I intend]* [(*name of person who intends*) intends]* to apply to the court for possession of the house and premises under [section 17]* [section 18]* of the Act.]* *(*delete the entire paragraph, if inapplicable, or delete whichever of the first alternatives does not apply and the reference to section 17 or section 18 as the circumstances require)* (**see Note 5 below**)

7. [I reserve the right to give notice under section 2 of the Act of my objection to the exclusion from the house and premises claimed by you of property let with the house and premises but which is not subject to a tenancy vested in you, or to the continued inclusion in the house and premises of parts lying above or below other premises in which I have an interest.]* *(*delete the entire paragraph if inapplicable)* (**see note 6 below**)

8. [This notice is given by me as the person designated by Schedule 1 paragraph 2 to the Act as the reversioner of the house and premises.]* *(*delete the entire paragraph, if you are the claimant's immediate landlord and also the freeholder)* (**see note 7 below**)

(Signature)

(Date)

[The name and address of my solicitor or agent, to whom further communications may be sent is]* *(*delete if inapplicable.)*

Notes

(References in this Form and these Notes to 'the Act' are references to the Leasehold Reform Act 1967.)

1. This notice must be given within two months of the service of the notice of the tenant's claim. Where there is a chain of landlords, the time limit runs from the date of the first service of the claimant's notice on any landlord (Sch. 3, paras. 7(1) and 8(1)(a) to the Act).

2. If the landlord admits the claim he will not later be able to dispute the claimant's right to have the freehold or an extended lease, unless he shows that he was misled by misrepresentation or concealment of material facts, but the admission does not conclude any question as to the correctness of the particulars of the house and premises as set out in the claim (Sch. 3, para. 7(4) to the Act).

3. Schemes approved under section 19 of the Act (retention of management powers for general benefit of neighbourhood) and section 70 of the Leasehold Reform, Housing and Urban Development Act 1993 (approval by leasehold valuation tribunal of estate management scheme) provide that within a specified area the landlord will retain powers of management and rights against leasehold houses and premises in the event of the tenants acquiring the freehold.

4. Where section 9(1) of the Act applies, the purchase price and cost of enfranchisement is determined on the basis of the value of the land and there is no element of marriage value.

Where section 9(1A) of the Act applies, the purchase price and cost of enfranchisement is determined on the basis of the land and the house including 50 per cent of any marriage value (see new section 9(1D) of the Act inserted by section 145 of the Commonhold and Leasehold Reform Act 2002). No marriage value is payable if the unexpired term of the lease exceeds eighty years (see new section 9(1E) of the Act inserted by section 146 of the Commonhold and Leasehold Reform Act 2002). The fact that the tenant has security of tenure will be taken into account in determining the price.

Where section 9(1C) of the Act applies, the purchase price and cost of enfranchisement is determined on the same basis as that under section 9(1A) of the Act, except that there is no security of tenure at the end of the lease, and additional compensation may be payable if the sale of the freehold results in the diminution of value of or any other loss or damage in relation to any interest of the landlord in any other property.

5. If the landlord (on the assumption, where this is not admitted, that the claimant has the right claimed) intends to apply to the court for an order for possession of the premises for redevelopment under section 17 or use as a residence under section 18 of the Act, the notice must say so (Sch. 3, para. 7(3) to the Act). (Where a claim is to have a freehold, only certain public authorities or bodies can resist it on the grounds of an intention to redevelop the property).

6. If the landlord intends to object (under subsection (4) or (5) of section 2 of the Act) to the exclusion from the claim of property let with the house and premises to the tenant but not at the relevant time subject to a tenancy vested in him (see amendment to section 2(4) made by section 138(4) of the Commonhold and Leasehold Reform Act 2002), or to the inclusion of part of the house and premises which projects into other property of the landlord's, notice of his objection must be given before or with this notice, unless the right to give it later is reserved by this notice (Sch. 3, para. 7(2) to the Act). In any case, notice of the objection must be given within two months of the service of the claimant's notice.

7. Where there is a chain of landlords, this notice must be given by the landlord who is designated as 'the reversioner' (see Sch. 1, paras. 1 and 2 to the Act). For this purpose, the reversioner is either the landlord whose tenancy carries an expectation of possession of the house and premises of 30 years or more after the expiration of all the inferior tenancies (or, if there is more than one such landlord, the one whose tenancy is nearest to that of the tenant) or, if there is no such landlord, the freeholder.

The landlord intends to apply for possession

There are two grounds upon which a landlord may apply for possession:

- for the purposes of redevelopment (s.17); and
- for use as a residence (s.18).

As set out in the notes to the prescribed form, most landlords are unable to resist the tenant's claim on the basis that they intend to redevelop and this ground is of greater importance where the tenant is claiming an extended lease. Consequently, section 17 is dealt with more fully in chapter 6 of this book.

The landlord may at any time before effect is given to a notice of tenant's claim, apply to the court for an order that he may resume possession of the property, on the ground that it, or part of it, is or will be, reasonably required by him for occupation as the only or main residence of the landlord or a person who is at the time of the application an adult member of the landlord's family (s.18(1)). However, a landlord is only so entitled if his interest in the house was purchased or created on or before 18

February 1966 (s.18(2)). Consequently, section 18 is of limited application, but if it does apply, reference should be made to the section itself and Schedule 2.

Terms of acquisition

The terms of the contract created by the service of a notice of tenant's claim are governed by the Leasehold Reform (Enfranchisement and Extension) Regulations 1967 (SI 1967/1879) as amended by the Leasehold Reform (Enfranchisement and Extension) (Amendment) (England) Regulations 2003 (SI 2003/1989) in England and the Leasehold Reform (Enfranchisement and Extension) (Amendment) (Wales) Regulations 2004 (SI 2004/699) in Wales. The regulations provide for the incorporation of Conditions of Sale contained in Part I of the Schedule to the Regulations, except insofar as the landlord and tenant agree otherwise. Those conditions include the following.

- The landlord can, by written notice, require that the tenant pay a deposit on account of the price payable for the freehold, which is the greater of three times the annual rent for the property or £25, and the tenant must pay the deposit within 14 days of the giving of the notice (condition 1).
- The tenant can be required by notice in writing to deduce title to his tenancy and, if he is relying on any period of occupation, to provide a statutory declaration detailing that occupation. Such information must be provided within 21 days of the landlord giving the notice (condition 2).
- If the landlord does not serve a notice in reply, or admits the tenant's claim, or a court order establishes the tenant's right, the tenant can require the landlord to prove his title (condition 3).
- The landlord and, if he is entitled to require the landlord to prove his title, the tenant, can require the other to state what rights of way and provisions concerning restrictive covenants the other requires to be included in the conveyance and in the event of either party failing to state their requirements, they are deemed not to have any (condition 5).
- One month after the price payable for the freehold has been determined by agreement, or otherwise, either the landlord or the tenant may give the other notice in writing requiring him to complete the conveyance and if such a notice is given, completion is to take place four weeks from the giving of the notice (condition 6).
- The tenant is to pay rent up to the date of completion and all outgoings thereafter. On completion, any rent or other

outgoings are to be apportioned and the tenant reimbursed, if necessary (condition 7).
- If completion is delayed, rent is payable up to the date of completion. However, if the delay has not been caused by the landlord, the landlord can choose instead to receive interest on the price payable for the freehold (or the balance, if a deposit has been paid) at the rate of two per cent above base and if the delay has not been caused solely by the tenant, the tenant can choose to deposit the price payable (or the balance) in a bank account, in which case the landlord is bound to accept the interest (condition 8).
- The conveyance is to be prepared by the tenant and a draft conveyance is to be delivered to the landlord's solicitor at least 14 days before the date for completion, and an engrossment for execution delivered at a reasonable time before that date (condition 9).
- If either the landlord or the tenant fails to perform any obligation arising out of the notice or the conditions, then the other may serve on him a notice specifying the default and requiring him to remedy it within two months. If the tenant does not comply with such a notice, then the parties are discharged from any further obligations other than the obligation to pay the landlord's costs and any deposit is forfeited to the landlord. If the landlord fails to comply with such a notice, then the parties are discharged from any further obligations and the tenant can have the deposit returned to him and does not have to pay the landlord's costs under section 9 (condition 10).
- The aforementioned time limits may be extended if:
    o the claimant is a sub-tenant and the reversioner, by notice, requires that any period of time stipulated in the conditions for the performance of any act by the landlord (other than in condition 10) should be doubled;
    o there are any court or tribunal proceedings, in which case any period during which those proceedings are pending is to be disregarded; and
    o a party dies or becomes incapable of managing his affairs, in which case the time limits can be extended for such period as may be reasonable in all the circumstances (condition 13).

The purchase price

The most important term of acquisition from the parties' point of view will be the price payable. The calculation of this price is dealt with in chapter 7. The price will either be agreed between the parties or, if it is not possible to reach agreement, be determined by an LVT (s.21(1)) or the Lands Tribunal on appeal.

Costs

Not so much a term of acquisition as a statutory obligation; the tenant is liable to pay the landlord's reasonable costs incurred in pursuance of the notice (s.9(4)). Such costs are limited to those, which are of or incidental to, the following matters:

- any investigation by the landlord of the tenant's right to acquire the freehold (s.9(4)(a));
- any conveyance or assurance of the house and premises, or any part thereof, or of any outstanding estate or interest therein (s.9(4)(b));
- deducing, evidencing and verifying the title to the house and premises or any estate or interest therein (s.9(4)(c));
- making out and furnishing such abstracts and copies as the tenant may require (s.9(4)(d)); and
- any valuation of the house and premises (s.9(4)(e)).

Such costs do not include costs incurred in relation to any application to an LVT (s.9(4A)).

As a statutory obligation, as opposed to a term of acquisition, the tenant is liable to pay the above costs even if he does not in fact complete the purchase of the freehold unless:

- the landlord successfully resists the notice of tenant's claim on the ground of his own occupation (s.18(6)(b));
- the tenant withdraws the notice of tenant's claim after the grant of a minister's certificate under section 19 (or where an application for a certificate is pending), (s.19(14)(b));
- the landlord fails to comply with a notice given by the tenant under condition 10 of the conditions (condition 10(3)); and
- the tenant withdraws the notice of tenant's claim and the notice was given before the making of a scheme application or the request for consent under Chapter IV Part I of the *Leasehold Reform Housing and Urban Development Act* 1993 (s.74(4) of that Act).

Withdrawal

Given the contract which is created by the service of a notice of tenant's claim, upon service of the notice, the tenant is bound to purchase the freehold, notwithstanding the fact that the purchase price has not been determined. Consequently, provision is made in the Act for the tenant to be able to withdraw from the claim once the purchase price has been determined (s.9(3)).

In order to withdraw within one month of the purchase price being ascertained or agreed, the tenant must serve on the landlord, written notice that he is unable or unwilling to acquire the house and premises at the price he must pay. Service of such a notice has the following effects:

- the notice of tenant's claim ceases to have effect;
- the tenant is liable to compensate the landlord in respect of any loss he has suffered as a result of being unable to dispose or deal with the house and premises or any neighbouring property (s.9(3)(a)); and
- the tenant is prevented from giving any further notice of tenant's claim with respect to the house or any part of it for 12 months (s.9(3)(b)).

Applications to the court or LVT

By virtue of section 20, the following proceedings are to be brought in the County Court:

- proceedings for determining whether a person is entitled to acquire the freehold of a house and premises or to what property his right extends;
- proceedings for determining what provisions ought to be contained in a conveyance;
- any proceedings relating to the performance or discharge of obligations arising out of a notice of tenant's claim, including proceedings for the recovery of damages or compensation in the event of the obligations not being performed;
- any proceedings for determining the amount of a sub-tenant's share under Schedule 2 of compensation payable to a tenant under section 17 or 18, or for establishing or giving effect to the sub-tenant's right to it; and
- proceedings to determine any question of apportionment of rent.

By virtue of section 21(1), the following matters, in default of agreement, are to be determined by an LVT;

- the price payable for the house and premises;
- the amount of costs payable;

Leasehold enfranchisement explained

- the amount of compensation payable to a tenant under section 17 or 18 for the loss of a house and premises;
- where the landlord is missing, the appropriate sum to be paid into court; and
- the amount of compensation payable where the termination of the tenancy is postponed by reason of the tenant serving a notice of tenant's claim and the claim is ultimately ineffective.

In addition, the LVT has jurisdiction to determine the following matters by agreement between the parties or where an application is made to the LVT in respect of one of the aforementioned matters:

- the provisions to be contained in a conveyance;
- any question of apportionment of rent; and
- the amount of a sub-tenant's share under Schedule 2 of compensation payable to a tenant under section 17 or 18 (s. 21(2)).

Perhaps the most common application is an application to the LVT to determine the price payable. Such an application cannot be made unless the landlord has told the tenant the price he is asking for or two months have passed since the service of the notice of tenant's claim and the landlord has not done so.

6

Houses: the right of a tenant to acquire an extended lease

Introduction

As well as conferring on tenants of leasehold houses the right to acquire the freehold, Part I of the *Leasehold Reform Act* 1967 also confers on such tenants the right to acquire on fair terms an extended lease of the house and premises. Such a lease will be of the 'house and premises' in substitution for the existing tenancy and for a term expiring 50 years after the 'term date' of that tenancy. No premium is payable upon the grant of the extended lease and this may be the only reason why a tenant wants to acquire an extended lease as opposed to the freehold of the house. In practice, few, if any, tenants claim an extended lease as opposed to the freehold as not only is the interest acquired less desirable, it is also more difficult to acquire, in that the qualification criteria are stricter. Consequently, this part of the book is deliberately brief.

Meaning of terms used

Regard should be had to chapter 5 as to what is a 'house' and what are 'premises' for the purposes of Part I and as to the meaning of the various other terms used in Part I.

As can be appreciated, one additional term, which is of particular importance when considering an extended lease, is the expression 'term date'. By section 37(1)(g) this is defined as being, in relation to a tenancy granted for a term of years certain, the date of expiry of that term. 'Extended term date' and 'original term date' mean respectively the term date of a tenancy with and without an extension under the Act.

Where a tenancy is continuing under section 19(2) of the *Landlord and Tenant Act* 1954 or Schedule 10 paragraph 16(2) to the *Local Government and Housing Act* 1988, the term date is the first day on which, apart from the said Acts, the tenancy could have been brought to an end by notice to quit (s.37(2)).

As is set out in chapter 5, where the tenant was a tenant of any property under a long tenancy (i.e. a tenancy for a fixed term of more than 21 years), at a low rent and on the coming to an end of that tenancy became the tenant of the property, or any part of it, under a subsequent tenancy (whether by express grant or implication of law), then by virtue of section 3(2), that tenancy is deemed to be a long tenancy irrespective of its terms. Where section 3(2) applies to a periodical tenancy, the term date is either:

- where the landlord has given notice to quit prior to the tenant serving a notice of tenant's claim, the date at which the tenancy is due to terminate by virtue of that notice; and
- where no notice to quit has been served, the earliest date at which the tenancy could be brought to an end by a notice to quit, ignoring any statute (s.37(3)).

Qualification criteria

As set out in chapter 5, the right to acquire the freehold can arise under one of a number of sections of the Act. However, the right to acquire an extended lease can only arise under section 1 of the Act. Consequently, whilst the general qualification criteria are the same for acquiring an extended lease as they are for acquiring the freehold, in order to acquire an extended lease, the tenancy must be at a low rent and the property must also fall within certain rateable values or other financial limits.

The general qualification criteria are set out in chapter 5 and can be summarised as follows.

- The tenant must be the tenant of whole house unless he is already the freeholder of those parts of the house of which he is not a tenant. However, the tenant need not also be the tenant of the 'premises'.
- The tenancy must be a long tenancy (s.1(1)(a)).
- At the relevant time, the tenant must have been the tenant for the last two years (s.1(1)(b)), i.e. the tenant must have been the registered proprietor for the last two years.

The meaning of 'long tenancy' and the exceptional cases are set out in chapter 5 and reference should be made to that part as if references to acquiring the freehold are references to acquiring an extended lease.

As is set out in chapter 5, a tenancy terminable by notice after death, marriage or the formation of a civil partnership is capable of being a 'long tenancy', unless three conditions are fulfilled. However, if that tenancy was granted before 18 April 1980 or in pursuance of a contract entered into before that date, then whilst the tenant may be able to acquire the freehold, he cannot acquire an extended lease (s.1B).

The meaning of 'low rent' is also considered in chapter 5 and reference should be made to that section. However, it ought to be noted that whilst section 300 of the *Housing and Regeneration Act* 2008 has (by amendments to the 1967 Act), abolished the low rent test as a qualification criteria for acquiring the freehold as regards tenancies granted after 7 September 2009, the test has not been abolished as a qualification criteria for acquiring an extended lease. Further, as it is not possible to acquire an extended lease by virtue of section 1A, the alternative low rent test cannot be used when seeking to do so.

As to the rateable values or other financial limits which a property must come within, reference should be made to that part of chapter 5 which deals with section 1, including the flow chart referred to therein.

Starting the claim

A claim is started in the same way as a claim to acquire the freehold and using the same prescribed from. The form is set out in chapter 5 and as is stated therein, one of the alternatives at paragraph 2 must be deleted according to which claim is being made: a claim cannot be made in the alternative and if it is, the notice is of no effect (*Byrnlea Property Investments Ltd v Ramsey* [1969] 2 QB 253). However, if a tenant gives notice of a desire to acquire the freehold and subsequently withdraws that notice under section 9(3), then he can at the time he serves a notice under section 9(3) serve a notice of his desire to have an extended lease (Sch. 3, para. 2(1E)). Further, if the tenant serves notice of a desire to acquire an extended lease, he can subsequently serve a notice of his desire to acquire the freehold, at which point the first notice will cease to have effect (s.5(8)).

A notice of tenant's claim is served in the same way and on the same persons whether the tenant is making a claim to acquire the freehold or an extended lease, and regard should be had to the relevant part of chapter 5.

The bars to serving an effective notice of tenant's claim are the same whether the tenant is making a claim to acquire the freehold or an extended lease, with the exception that the withdrawal of a notice to acquire the freehold does not prevent service of a notice to acquire an extended lease as set out above. As to the interrelationship between a notice of tenant's claim to acquire an extended lease and a landlord's application to terminate the tenancy on the grounds of redevelopment, see the following.

As with a notice to acquire the freehold, a notice to acquire an extended lease ought to be registered.

Where the tenant has a right to an extended lease and gives to the landlord a notice of tenant's claim of his desire to have it, the landlord is bound to grant and the tenant is bound to accept, in substitution for the existing tenancy, a new tenancy of the house and premises for a term expiring 50 years after the term date of the existing tenancy (s.14(1)). As with a notice to acquire the freehold and pursuant to section 5(1), the rights and obligations of the landlord and tenant arising from the notice of tenant's claim are enforceable as rights and obligations arising under a contract. As such, those rights and obligations can pass to any executor, administrator or assignee of the landlord and tenant and can be assigned. Of course, the terms of the contract differ depending on whether the tenant is acquiring the freehold or an extended lease. However, otherwise and save as regards any application by the landlord to terminate the tenancy on the grounds of redevelopment, the effects of serving a notice of tenant's claim are the same regardless of the claim being made.

If one of several landlords is missing, this does not cause a problem as one of the other landlords will be able to conduct the claim on behalf of that missing landlord. However, where there is only one landlord and that landlord is either missing, or his identity cannot be ascertained, it is obviously not possible to serve a notice of tenant's claim and thus start a claim. Whilst, in such circumstances, the court is able to make a vesting order if the tenant is seeking to acquire the freehold (s.27), there is no similar provision if the tenant is seeking an extended lease. Consequently, the tenant of a missing landlord is unable to acquire an extended lease.

Receipt of notice of tenant's claim

The position is the same whether the notice of tenant's claim is served in respect of a claim to acquire the freehold or an extended lease and regard should be had to the relevant part of chapter 5. Whilst the reversioner may not have sufficient interest in the house and premises to grant the new lease, he is able to execute the new lease on behalf of the other landlords.

The landlord's notice in reply must be in the prescribed form and that form is the same whether the claim is to acquire the freehold or an extended lease. The relevant prescribed form is set out in chapter 5.

Redevelopment rights

As touched upon in chapter 5, section 17 enables a landlord to terminate an extended tenancy on the ground that, for the purposes of redevelopment, he proposes to demolish or reconstruct the whole or a substantial part of the house and premises. Such a right is exercisable if either the tenancy has been extended (s.17(1)) or the tenant has given notice of his desire to have an extended tenancy (s.17(4)). If the landlord wishes to exercise the right, then he must apply to the court for an order that he may resume possession and such application cannot be made earlier than 12 months before the original term date.

If the landlord succeeds in his application, the tenancy determines and the tenant is entitled to be paid compensation by the landlord for the loss of the house and premises (s.17(2)). Further, the tenant does not have to make any payment to the landlord in respect of costs incurred by reason of any notice of tenant's claim (s.17(4)(b)).

Terms of acquisition

As with a claim to acquire the freehold, the terms of the contract created by the service of a notice of tenant's claim are governed by the Leasehold Reform (Enfranchisement and Extension) Regulations 1967 (SI 1967/1879) as amended by the Leasehold Reform (Enfranchisement and Extension) (Amendment) (England) Regulations 2003 (SI 2003/1989) in England and the Leasehold Reform (Enfranchisement and Extension) (Amendment) (Wales) Regulations 2004 (SI 2004/699) in Wales. The regulations provide for the incorporation of different

Conditions of Sale depending on whether the tenant is acquiring the freehold or an extended lease. As regards an extended lease, the conditions to be incorporated are those contained in Part 2 of the Schedule to the regulations, except insofar as the landlord and tenant agree otherwise. Those conditions include the following:

- The tenant can be required by notice in writing to deduce title to his tenancy and, if he is relying on any period of occupation, to provide a statutory declaration detailing that occupation. Such information must be provided within 21 days of the landlord giving the notice (condition 1).
- If the landlord does not serve a notice in reply or admits the tenant's claim or a court order establishes the tenant's right, the tenant can require the landlord, within four weeks, to state what modifications in the terms of the existing tenancy, and what further provisions, other than as to payment of rent, are to be made by the terms of the new tenancy (condition 2(1)).
- If the landlord does serve a notice in reply and admits the tenant's claim or a court order establishes the tenant's right, the landlord can require the tenant, within four weeks, to state what modifications in the terms of the existing tenancy, and what further provisions, other than as to payment of rent are to be made by the terms of the new tenancy (condition 2(2)).
- Any notice given under condition 2 must state the modifications in the terms of the existing tenancy and the further provisions to be made by the terms of the new tenancy required by the person giving the notice and in the event of either party failing to state their requirements, they are deemed not to have any (condition 2(3) and (4)).
- Within eight weeks after the giving of a notice by either party under condition 2, a draft of the lease shall be submitted by the landlord to the tenant for approval and the tenant shall approve the draft in writing, with or without amendments, within 21 days thereafter. If the tenant does not comply with this time limit, he is deemed to have approved the draft (condition 3).
- The lease, and as many counterparts as the landlord may reasonably require, shall be prepared by the landlord and the counterparts are to be delivered to the tenant a reasonable time before the completion date. On completion, the tenant is to deliver to the landlord the counterparts duly executed and the landlord is to deliver to the tenant, the lease duly executed (condition 3(3)).

Houses: the right of a tenant to acquire an extended lease

- After the expiration of the time for approval of the draft lease by the tenant, either the landlord or the tenant may give the other notice in writing requiring him to complete the grant of the lease and if such a notice is given, completion is to take place four weeks from the giving of the notice (condition 4).
- If either the landlord or the tenant fails to perform any obligation arising out of the notice or the conditions, then the other may serve on him a notice specifying the default and requiring him to remedy it within two months. If the tenant does not comply with such a notice, then the parties are discharged from any further obligations other than the obligation to pay the landlord's costs. If the landlord fails to comply with such a notice, then the parties are discharged from any further obligations and the tenant does not have to pay the landlord's costs under section 14 (condition 5).
- The time limits above may be extended if:
  - the claimant is a sub-tenant and the reversioner, by notice, requires that any period of time stipulated in the conditions for the performance of any act by the landlord (other than in condition 5) should be doubled;
  - there are any court or tribunal proceedings, in which case any period during which those proceedings are pending is to be disregarded; and
  - a party dies or becomes incapable of managing his affairs, in which case the time limits can be extended for such period as may be reasonable in all the circumstances (condition 8).

Costs

As with the purchase of the freehold, costs are not so much a term of acquisition as a statutory obligation. The tenant is liable to pay the landlord's reasonable costs incurred in pursuance of a notice of tenant's claim (s.14(2)). Such costs are limited to those, which are of, or incidental, to the following matters:

- any investigation by the landlord of the tenant's right to an extended lease (s.14(2)(a));
- any lease granting the new tenancy (s.14(2)(b)); and
- any valuation of the house and premises obtained by the landlord before the grant of the new tenancy for the purpose of fixing the rent payable under it (s.14(2)(c)).

Such costs do not include costs incurred in relation to any application to an LVT (s.14(2A)).

As a statutory obligation, as opposed to a term of acquisition, the tenant is liable to pay the above costs even if he does not in fact complete an extended lease unless:

- the landlord successfully resists the notice of tenant's claim on the ground of redevelopment (s.17(4)(b));
- the landlord successfully resists the notice of tenant's claim on the ground of his own occupation (s.18(6)(b)); or
- the landlord fails to comply with a notice given by the tenant under condition 5 of the conditions (condition 5(3)).

Execution of the new lease

A tenant is not entitled to require the execution of the new lease until he has tendered the following:

- any sums payable by way of rent or recoverable as rent in respect of the house and premises up to the date of tender;
- any costs he is required to pay as set out; and
- any other sums due and payable by the tenant to the landlord under or in respect of the existing tenancy or any collateral agreement.

If the amount of any of the above sums has not, or cannot be, fully ascertained, then the tenant may tender reasonable security for those sums instead (s.14(3)).

Terms of the new lease

Whilst the landlord and tenant are free to agree the terms of the new tenancy (s.15(7)), in default of agreement, the freedom of the parties to dictate such terms is severely limited. The new tenancy is to be a tenancy on the same terms as the existing tenancy as those terms apply at the date of service of the notice of tenant's claim, but with such modifications as may be required or appropriate to take account:

- of the omission from the new tenancy of property comprised in the existing tenancy (for example, under section 2(5));or
- of alterations made to the property demised since the grant of the existing tenancy; or
- in a case where the existing tenancy derives from two or more separate tenancies (see section 3(6)), of their combined effect and of the differences (if any) in their terms.

Further, provision is also to be made for the following:

- Where, under the new tenancy, the landlord will be liable to provide any services or to repair, maintain or insure the house and premises, but the existing tenancy does not provide for the tenant to make any payment to the landlord in respect of the cost thereof or only provides that a fixed amount is payable; the new tenancy will make provision for such payment as from the date when the new rent becomes payable. Further, such payments are to be reserved as rent (s.15(3)).
- Where there is an agreement collateral to the existing tenancy, provision is to be made for that to continue with any suitable adaptations (s.15(4)).
- Where in the existing tenancy or any collateral agreement there is a term which:
  - provides for or relates to the renewal of the tenancy,
  - confers any option to purchase or right of pre-emption in relation to the house and premises; or
  - provides for the termination of the existing tenancy before its term date otherwise than in the event of a breach of its terms;
  - such terms are to be excluded (s.15(5)).
- Where the new tenancy is granted after the term date of the existing tenancy, then the rent under the new tenancy is payable from the date of service of the notice of tenant's claim or the original term date, whichever is the later (s.15(6)).
- Where changes occurring since the date of commencement of the existing tenancy affect the suitability of the provisions of that tenancy, either the landlord or the tenant may require such provisions to be excluded or modified (s.15(7)).
- The new tenancy is to provide that any sub-tenancy is not to confer on the sub-tenant any right under the Act, as against the tenant's landlord, to an extended lease (ss.15(8) and 16(4)).
- The new tenancy is to reserve to the landlord the right to resume possession in accordance with section 17, i.e. on grounds of redevelopment (s.15(8)).

Rent

As to the calculation of the rent payable under the new lease, see chapter 7.

Rights under the new lease

The following rights are excluded following a lease extension under the Act:

- there is no right to extend the lease further (s.16(1)(b));
- the extended lease is not entitled to the protection of Part I or Part II of the *Landlord and Tenant Act* 1954 (s.16(1)(c));
- the *Rent Act* 1977 does not apply (s.16(1A)); and
- any sub-tenant is not entitled to the protection of Part I or Part II of the *Landlord and Tenant Act* 1954, the *Rent (Agriculture) Act* 1976 or the *Rent Act* 1977 (s.16(1)(d)).

The tenant under an extended lease does retain the right to acquire the freehold, however, and Schedule 10 to the *Local Government and Housing Act* 1989 continues to apply to the extended lease (s.16(1B)).

It is important to note that if a tenant does want to acquire the freehold having extended the lease, and the notice of tenant's claim to acquire the freehold is served after the original term date of the tenancy, then the price payable for the freehold is to be determined in accordance with section 9(1C). If, prior to the lease extension, the tenant would have been entitled to have the price determined in accordance with section 9(1), the tenant could end up paying more for the freehold following an extension than he would have before.

Applications to the court or LVT

By virtue of section 20, the following proceedings are to be brought in the County Court:

- proceedings for determining whether a person is entitled to acquire an extended lease of a house and premises, or to what property his right extends;
- proceedings for determining what provisions ought to be contained in a lease granting a new tenancy;
- any proceedings relating to the performance or discharge of obligations arising out of a notice of tenant's claim, including proceedings for the recovery of damages or compensation in the event of the obligations not being performed;
- any proceedings for determining the amount of a sub-tenant's share under Schedule 2 of compensation payable to a tenant under section 17 or 18, or for establishing or giving effect to the sub-tenant's right to it; and

- proceedings to determine any question of apportionment of rent.

By virtue of section 21(1), the following matters, in default of agreement, are to be determined by an LVT:

- the amount of rent to be payable for a house and premises;
- the amount of costs payable;
- the amount of compensation payable to a tenant under section 17 or 18 for the loss of a house and premises; and
- the amount of compensation payable where the termination of the tenancy is postponed by reason of the tenant serving a notice of tenant's claim and the claim is ultimately ineffective.

In addition, the LVT has jurisdiction to determine the following matters by agreement between the parties or where an application is made to the LVT in respect of one of the above matters:

- the provisions to be contained in a lease granting a new tenancy;
- any question of apportionment of rent; and
- the amount of a sub-tenant's share under Schedule 2 of compensation payable to a tenant under section 17 or 18 (s.21(2)).

7

Houses: extended leases and enfranchisement valuation issues

Introduction

The fundamental political premise to the *Leasehold Reform Act 1967* was to safeguard occupying owners of low value houses, subject to long leases at low rents. Those rights have since been extended to high value properties including owners of flats (new leases and collective enfranchisement). Since 1993, almost all houses qualify whatever their value. However, as the upper value limits have been relaxed, the valuation approach has also changed allowing, in particular, landlords to share marriage value (see also, the commentary in the introductory chapter).

The principle of assessing the price for enfranchisement was that although the land belongs in equity to the freeholder, the house belongs to the tenant.

The Act (as amended) provides for the tenant to either:

- take a new tenancy for a term expiring 50 years after the term date of the existing lease; at what is known as a 'modern ground rent' commencing at the original term date, subject to review after 25 years (s.14 – extended lease, s.15 terms of tenancy ... including rent); or to
- purchase the freeholder's (and any intermediate leaseholder's) interest.

We shall look at all of the valuation issues in turn, starting with the extended lease; and then consider each of the three bases of valuation for acquiring the freehold. Briefly the legislation provides for the following:

An extended lease

The qualifying criteria for this are discussed in chapter 6, which includes that the tenancy must be at a low rent, and the property must fall within certain rateable value limits (although the low rent test has been virtually repealed, it remains a qualifying condition for lease extensions). Accordingly, we shall consider:

- assessment of letting value for the purposes of the low rent test;
- how to seek a notional reduction in rateable value to meet the limits; and
- calculation of modern ground rent (section 15 rent), which includes establishing site value:
  (1) the 'cleared site' approach;
  (2) the 'standing house' approach; and
  (3) the 'new for old' approach.

Acquiring the freehold

The qualification criteria for the right to acquire the freehold arise under one of a number of sections of the Act, see chapter 5. There are three bases of valuation which have evolved from the passing of the 1967 legislation, briefly as follows:

- Section 9(1), the original basis and the most favourable from a tenant's perspective with the price principally comprising:
  (1) the capitalised value of the existing lease ground rent;
  (2) the capitalised value of the 'modern ground rent'; and
  (3) the value of the freeholder's reversion at the expiry of the new extended lease.
- Section 9(1A) (amendments to the 1967 Act by the *Housing Act 1974*) and applies, in effect, to higher value houses than those under section 9(1). The freehold price includes a sum for marriage value, as the valuation assumptions do not exclude the tenant and members of his family from the market to purchase, (s.1A (a)); the price is principally comprised:
  (1) the capitalised value of the existing lease ground rent;
  (2) the value of the freeholder's reversion to vacant possession deferred over the unexpired term; and
  (3) the freeholder's share of marriage value.
- Section 9(1C), where, in effect, a house qualifies for enfranchisement pursuant to the 1993 Act amendments, this basis will apply. It follows, broadly, section 9(1A) and allows for the payment of compensation under section 9A; accordingly the price is now principally comprised:

(1) the capitalised value of the existing lease ground rent;
(2) the value of the freeholder's reversion to vacant possession deferred over the unexpired term;
(3) the freeholder's share of marriage value; and
(4) compensation under section 9A.

An extended lease

The valuation issues in an extended lease claim are considered first. At the outset, the valuer should be aware that the issues with respect to: (a) letting value; (b) notional reduction in rateable value; and (c) calculation of modern ground rent (section 15 rent), are relevant for the purposes of the freehold price computation (where applicable), which are discussed later.

A tenant seeking to enfranchise now would generally be advised to acquire their freehold interest as opposed to an extended lease. The valuation loophole of first taking an extended lease and then submitting a claim for the freehold has been closed (see *Mosley v Hickman*).

Acquiring the freehold where an extended lease has been claimed

One fundamental valuation issue that advisers need to be aware of is the basis of price computation for the freehold interest where initially an extended lease has been taken, and the original term date has passed. The price payable for the freehold interest where the claim is submitted post the original term date is section 9(1C). If prior to taking the extended lease, the basis of valuation to acquire the freehold was section 9(1), the tenant could pay considerably more if the original term date is passed, and the basis is section 9(1C), section 1(1AA)(b).

The *Commonhold and Leasehold Reform Act* 2002, s.143(4) amends section 9(1A) of the 1967 Act as follows:

(1AA) Where, in a case in which the price payable for a house and premises is to be determined in accordance with subsection (1A) above, the tenancy has been extended under this Part of this Act–

(a) if the relevant time is on or before the original term date, the assumptions set out in that subsection apply as if the tenancy is to terminate on the original term date; and

(b) if the relevant time is after the original term date, the assumptions set out in paragraphs (a), (c) and (e) of that subsection apply as if the tenancy had terminated on the original term date and the assumption set out in paragraph (b) of that subsection applies as if the words "at the end of the tenancy" were omitted.

The effect of the above is that where an extended lease has been taken and the original term date has passed, the basis of valuation for the freehold price is section 9(1C), subject to disregarding tenant's improvements, and taking into account the tenant's rights (if any) to an assured tenancy under Schedule 10 of the *Local Government and Housing Act* 1989.

Section 1, 'tenants entitled to enfranchisement or extension'

Although section 1 of the 1967 Act has been amended considerably, as the right to acquire an extended lease can only arise under this section, the requirements that the tenancy be at a 'low rent' and within certain 'rateable value limits' remain. We now look at each in turn.

Section 4, 'meaning of low rent'

A low rent is one where the rent payable per annum under the tenancy is less than two-thirds of the rateable value on the appropriate day. The appropriate day being 23 March 1965; unless the house had no rateable value at that date, in which case the appropriate day is the date on which the rateable value is first shown (s.1(4)).

Where the tenancy has been granted between 1 September 1939 and 31 March 1963, a tenancy shall not be regarded as one at a low rent if at the commencement of the tenancy, the rent payable exceeded two-thirds of the 'letting value', (s.4(1)). We now consider letting value, albeit with the passage of time, it is the author's experience that cases where an understanding of this provision are required, are rare.

Letting value

There is no definition in the 1967 Act of 'letting value'; there is, however, direction from case law where the meaning and make up of letting value has been considered.

In *Johnston v Duke of Westminster* [1986] HL AC 839.

> 'A premium is manifestly part of the value that the landlord receives for letting the premises unless it can be attributed to other benefits such as furniture and so forth and I can see no reason why it should be excluded from the letting value of the premises.
>
> 'In my view, letting value should be construed as the best annual return attainable in the open market for the grant of a long lease on the same terms, whether this is achieved by letting at a rack rent or letting at a lower rent plus the payment of a premium. ...Unless there is any reason to suppose that the bargain between landlord and tenant was not made at arm's length, the combination of rent and premium will be very strong prima facie evidence of the open market letting value of that particular house let on those terms at that date, in which case, the only calculation that has to be made to see if the tenant is entitled to the freehold is to apply a mathematical formula based upon actuarial principles to convert the premium into an annual sum. On the other hand, if the rack rent has to be determined for a letting that occurred many years ago, much expensive and time consuming research will often be involved in seeking out sufficient truly comparable lettings to give a fair basis upon which to assess a rack rent (rack rent is a term known to valuers, being the maximum annual rent payable under a tenancy with its associated rights and obligations, at nil premium); an exercise designed to promote disagreement rather than agreement between expert witnesses, and a fruitful source for litigation'.

To reach the letting value, the premium paid is decapitalised over the term of the tenancy, to establish the annual equivalent; and in turn, this is added to the annual rent.

In *Gidlow-Jackson v Middlegate Properties Limited* [1974] QB 361, it was held that the letting value could not exceed the amount lawfully recoverable under the Rent Acts and the courts rejected the tenant's argument that the letting value should be assessed at the hypothetical annual rent attainable in the absence of rent controls.

In *Manson v Duke of Westminster* [1981] QB 323, 335, doubts about the correctness of the decision in *Gidlow-Jackson* were expressed; subsequently leave to appeal was refused in that case. In *Johnston* their Lordships concur with the decision in *Gidlow-Jackson*, saying that if the tenant's argument had been accepted, it would have worked most harshly against the landlords for not only would the landlord have been restricted to an artificially low rent for the term of the lease and for the indefinite period thereafter during the currency of the statutory tenancy, but would, in addition, have been faced with the prospect of having to sell his property to a tenant at an artificially low price.

We now look at an example of assessing letting value.

Example 1

A two storey mews in central London subject to a lease dated 10 June 1957 for a term of 52.75 years at a fixed ground rent of £50 per annum. The premium paid in consideration of the lease was £2,000. Is the rent payable less than two-thirds of the letting value, thus satisfying the low rent test?

Assessment of letting value:

Annual rent	£50 p.a.
plus	
Decapitalised premium paid over the term of the lease	
Premium paid	£2,000
divided by	
52.75 years purchase at 6%	15.8958
Annual equivalent	£125.82 p.a.
say	£125 p.a.
plus (from above)	£50 p.a.
Letting value	£175 p.a.
Two-thirds thereof	0.67
	£117 p.a.

£50 p.a. is less than two-thirds of the letting value assessed at £117 p.a. and the house, therefore, satisfies the low rent test.

Rateable value

Section 118 of the *Housing Act* 1974 not only introduced amendments to the rateable value limits to extend enfranchisement rights to higher value houses (s.9(1A)), but also provided that a notional reduction in rateable value could be sought (s.1 (4A)), under Schedule 8. Where certain rateable value limits are to be met, achieving a reduction to reflect tenant's improvements is important for two reasons:

- to bring houses beyond the higher rateable value limits into them, thereby qualifying the house for enfranchisement per se; and
- to move a house that might otherwise fall to be valued under a set of valuation assumptions which lead to a higher price, to a basis of valuation where a different set of assumptions applies, and thus lower price; typically moving a house from the section 9(1A) basis of valuation to section 9(1).

Schedule 8 provides as follows:

Paragraph 1 (1) says that where the tenant or any previous tenant has made or contributed to the cost of an improvement, he can serve on the landlord a notice in the prescribed form requiring him to agree a reduction in rateable value for the purposes of section 1(1) of the 1967 Act.

Subsection (2) says 'this schedule applies to any improvement made by the execution of works amounting to structural alteration, extension or addition'.

The Form, in outline, is as follows:

'Notice by Tenant to Landlord of Tenant's Improvements affecting Rateable Value'

It is to be dated, and state both the landlord and the house address.

1. Details of the tenant or any predecessor in title who have contributed to the costs of the improvements set out in the First Schedule.

2. The request to agree a reduction in the rateable value for the purposes of the 1967 Act.

3. The sum proposed that the rateable value is to be reduced to (£...).

4. If the reduction is not agreed to, do you agree the following?

(a) the improvements meet the requirements of the legislation;
(b) works set out in the Second Schedule were involved in the making of the improvements;
(c) either the tenant or any previous tenant contributed to the cost of those improvements; and
(d) the proportion of the cost borne by the tenant or any predecessor in title is £…

The Form is to be signed by the tenant.

There are two schedules: first, description of improvements; and second, description of works.

If the proposed reduction in rateable value is agreed to, the freeholder and tenant sign to the effect and for the purposes of the 1967 Act, the notional rateable value replaces the value in the list (para. 2(1)).

Where, after six weeks from the service of the notice under paragraph 1, the freeholder has not agreed to any of the proposals, the tenant applies to the County Court to have those matters determined; any such determination is final and conclusive (para. 2(2)). This application must be made within six weeks (or such longer time the court may allow) from the expiration of the initial six weeks post service of the notice to agree the matters proposed (para. 2(3)).

There is no prescribed form for the application to the County Court; ultimately the application seeks a declaration that the works constitute the tenant's improvements within the meaning of the legislation, such that the next stage can be moved to.

Whether the parties agree, or the County Court determines any of the points at issue, the parties (if applicable), then have a further two weeks to agree the notional reduction in rateable value.

Where there is failure to agree in writing the notional reduction in rateable value, the tenant has a further four weeks in which to make an application in the prescribed form (para. 3(3)): 'Application by Tenant to Valuation Officer for Certificate as to Reduction for the purposes of the *Leasehold Reform Act 1967* in the Rateable Value of Premises on account of Tenant's Improvements' (para. 3(1)(a) and (b)).

On receipt of the application, the valuation officer is required to certify whether or not the improvement has affected the rateable value as prescribed, and if so, by what amount (para. 3(2)(a) and (b)).

Paragraph 3(4) provides that where a reduction is to be made, it is to be proportioned where not all of the cost was contributed by the tenant or a previous tenant under the tenancy.

A flow chart shows the sequence of events (four stages) and mandatory time limits.

The valuation officer thereafter issues his certificate as required, for which there is no appeal. The certificate can only be challenged for judicial review, *R v Valuation Officer for Westminster, Ex. p. Rendall*, [1986] 1 EGLR 163 CA.

It is the author's experience that, not only are these cases rare, but also only occur where the legal and valuation arguments are not clear cut. It does not make commercial sense for the freeholder to contest the proposal to reduce the rateable value from, say, £1,100 to £850, if he believes the notional rateable value to be in the region of £900; save if he wants to rely on the tenant's failure to keep to the mandatory timetable. On the other hand, if the particular circumstances of the case are such that it is unclear that the tenant will be successful, it is likely that the provisions, including application to the County Court and ultimately to the valuation officer, will be required to be implemented.

Tenant's improvements are not defined in the 1974 Act; however, at paragraph 1(2) it says that the schedule applies to 'any improvement made by the execution of works amounting to structural alteration, extension or addition'.

In *Rendall*, the County Court determined that the following constituted improvements under Schedule 8:

- the addition of a room on the ground floor;
- the creation of a patio area on the mezzanine floor;
- the conversion of a bedroom on the third floor into a bathroom; and
- the installation of a gas boiler in place of a coke boiler.

In *Manley v Trustees of the Duke of Westminster* [1984], the County Court determined that the following were improvements:

- back extension works;
- new windows;
- some demolition and re-building; and
- insertion of a damp-proof course and provision of a solid floor.

When presented with one of these cases, the valuer and solicitor will work in tandem, being ever mindful of the statutory provisions including the mandatory time scales. The valuer will require, at least, a broad understanding of the finite facts to the make up of the rateable value in the list, including the analysis to support this. Bearing in mind that there is no appeal to the valuation officer's certificate, once it has been issued, it is essential for the valuer and solicitor to get both the procedure and the valuation issues right from the outset.

Either a meeting or informal discussions on the telephone with the valuation officer may provide the necessary information; if not, a formal proposal may be required to establish the basis and make up of the rateable value in the list.

Where the subject property forms part of a terrace or mews and there are other similar properties abutting or near neighbouring, the valuation issues may be resolved by the comparable method. In any event, the practical and short cut approach of direct comparison could give the valuer a general idea as to whether, in the particular circumstances of the case, it is worthwhile seeking a notional reduction in rateable value.

We now look at an example of adjustment to rateable value pursuant to tenant's improvements, to illustrate the issues.

Example 2

You are contacted by a local firm of solicitors who are advising a tenant on his potential claim for the freehold interest on his house. The tenant has provided his solicitor with a copy of the lease and details of works carried out to the house. You are provided with the same and are asked for your advice.

From the information provided and further to your inspection, you ascertain the following:

The property is a two storey mews house in central London subject to a lease dated 9 May 1956, for a term of 99 years from 25 December 1952, at a fixed ground rent of £125 p.a.

The lease plan shows the accommodation as originally designed to comprise briefly as follows:

Ground floor –   Coach house and stable;

First floor –   Reception room, kitchen, three bedrooms and one bathroom/WC.

Leasehold enfranchisement explained

At your inspection, you note the accommodation to comprise briefly as follows:

Ground floor – Reception room, two bedrooms with bathrooms/WCs ensuite and garage;

First floor – Reception room, kitchen, three further bedrooms and one bathroom/WC.

The lease documentation includes two Licenses for Alterations confirming briefly as follows:

Mid 1960s – conversion of the premises to provide two separate dwellings as follows:

Ground floor (part) –flat; and

Ground floor (part); and first floor – ground floor living accommodation and garage, and first floor living accommodation;

and further works in the early 1970s to put the property back to a single family dwelling

From your enquiries to the valuation officer you establish the following:

(A) <u>Revaluation in June 1975 'classed as one unit' as follows:</u>

102.1 sq m (living accommodation)	£1,050
(equating to £10.28 psm)	
Garage at £200	£200
Gross value	£1,250
Rateable value	£1,013

(B) <u>The 1973 list</u>

Flat – ground floor (part) 32.7 sq m (living accommodation) (equates to £13.00 psm)	£425
Maisonette, ground floor part, Garage and first floor comprising	£875
First floor (living accommodation) 71.0 sq m – @ £9.50 psm and	£675
Garage @ £200 (26.1 sq m – £7.66 psm)	£200
Gross value	£1,300
Rateable value	£1,027

From the above, you are able to calculate the notional adjustment to the rateable value for these tenant's improvements, as follows:

Ground floor:

(stable – now garage)		£200
(as above, 26.1 sq m equating to £7.66 psm)		
Coach house (garage)		
(area at 32.7 sq m @ 7.66 psm from garage analysis)	7.66	
	32.7	£250
First floor – 71.0 sq m @ £9.50 psm		
(as above)		£675
Gross value		£1,125
Rateable value		£908

From the information provided and your enquiries, you calculate that with the notional adjustment for the tenant's improvements, the rateable value is reduced to £908, thus moving the basis of valuation from section 9(1A) to section 9(1), which favours the tenant as he pays 'site' value and no marriage value.

Leasehold enfranchisement explained

Flow chart for sequence of events pursuant to tenant operating Schedule 8 to the *Housing Act* 1974, for adjustment to rateable value.

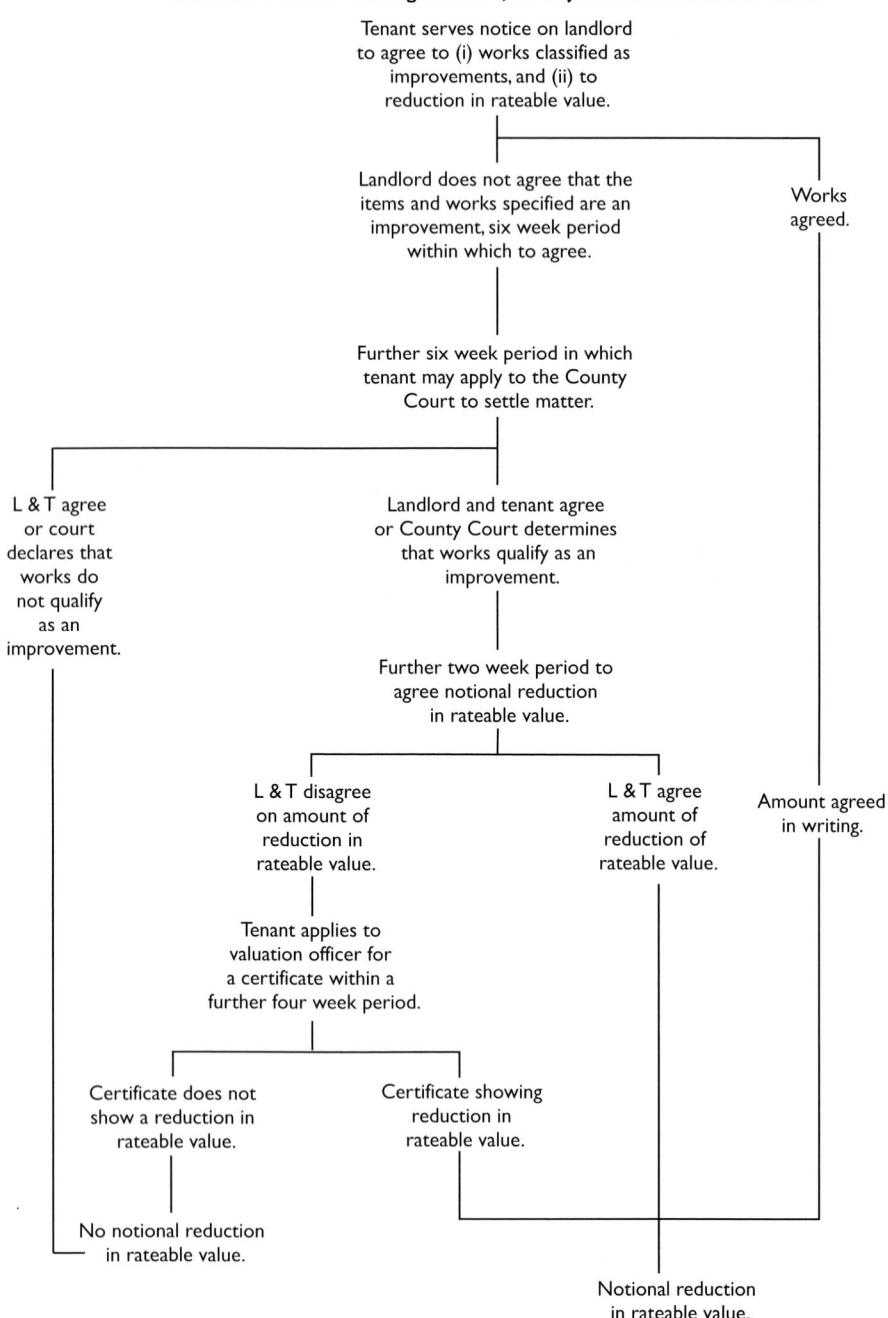

Tenant serves notice on landlord to agree to (i) works classified as improvements, and (ii) to reduction in rateable value.

↓

Landlord does not agree that the items and works specified are an improvement, six week period within which to agree. → Works agreed.

↓

Further six week period in which tenant may apply to the County Court to settle matter.

↓

L & T agree or court declares that works do not qualify as an improvement. | Landlord and tenant agree or County Court determines that works qualify as an improvement.

↓

Further two week period to agree notional reduction in rateable value.

↓

L & T disagree on amount of reduction in rateable value. | L & T agree amount of reduction of rateable value. → Amount agreed in writing.

↓

Tenant applies to valuation officer for a certificate within a further four week period.

↓

Certificate does not show a reduction in rateable value. | Certificate showing reduction in rateable value.

↓

No notional reduction in rateable value.

Notional reduction in rateable value.

378

Having considered assessment of letting value and notional reduction in rateable value with respect to the requirements of section 1 of the 1967 Act, we now look at calculation of the modern ground rent (section 15 rent), effective from the term date of the original tenancy. To recap, where a tenant takes an extended lease under section 14, he will receive a new tenancy for a term expiring 50 years after the original term date. The rent provisions of the original tenancy continue until that term date is reached. No premium is payable.

Arguably, the only benefit to the tenant of taking an extended lease was to secure a further 50 years right to remain in occupation, without payment of premium, albeit with provisions for rent review at some future date. Conversely, the tenant would have had statutory rights either to remain in occupation as a protected or an assured tenant at the expiration of the lease in any event. As a result of the amendments made by s.143(1)(a) of the CLRA 2002, where a tenancy has been extended under section 14, Schedule 10 to the LGHA 1989 now applies, thus giving rights of occupation not granted in the original legislation. In other words, there is now the right to an assured tenancy at the end of the extended term and the tenant can now enfranchise during the currency of the additional 50 year term.

It is to be assumed in valuations under section 9(1) (see later) for the calculation of the freehold price, that the tenant has taken a 50 years extended lease. The extended lease is at a modern ground rent with provisions for review at 25 years. So, on that basis, one has to assume that the current lease has an extra 50 years in valuing the freeholder's interest. In addition, the valuation issues are common to both an extended lease and section 9(1) computations.

The general principle is that the new tenancy shall be on the same terms as the existing tenancy, with such modifications as may be required or appropriate (s.15(1)).

The section 15 rent

Section 15 (2) provides:

(a) the rent shall be a ground rent in the sense that it shall represent the letting value of the site (without including anything for the value of buildings on the site) for the uses to which the house and premises have been put since the commencement of the existing tenancy, other than uses by which the terms of the new tenancy are not permitted or are permitted only with the landlord's consent;

(b) the letting value for this purpose shall be in the first instance the letting value at the date from which the rent based on it is to commence, but as from the expiration of twenty-five years from the original term date the letting value at the expiration of those twenty-five years shall be substituted, if the landlord so requires, and a revised rent become payable accordingly;

(c) the letting value at either of the times mentioned shall be determined not earlier than twelve months before that time (the reasonable cost of obtaining a valuation for the purpose being borne by the tenant), and there shall be no revision of the rent as provided by paragraph (b) above unless in the last of the twenty-five years there mentioned the landlord gives the tenant written notice claiming a revision.

Calculating this rent is not without difficulties. Sites are not let generally in the open market for 50 years' terms with provision for one rent review at 25 years, accordingly there is no comparable evidence of sites let to which the valuer can refer to reach the rental value. So what valuers do is to firstly calculate what the capital vale of the site was; and secondly to assess the return an investor would seek for the site on the bases of the statutory assumptions.

The established approach that evolved to calculating the section 15 rent is a two stage process, as follows:

- establish the site value; and
- decapitalise the site value at an appropriate percentage to reach the section 15 rent.

We consider each in turn.

Methods of valuing the site

There are three established methods for valuing the site as follows:

- the cleared site approach;
- the standing house approach; and
- the new for old approach.

The 'cleared site' approach

The most common method of valuation known to valuers is by reference to comparable transactions, the comparable method; the cleared site approach follows this.

In *Farr v Millersons Investments Limited* [1971] the Lands Tribunal set out the preferred methods of valuation to reach site value, depending on the circumstances. However, such is the hypothetical nature of the valuation to be carried out, it is normal practice to calculate the site value by more than one method, and then check the values against each other.

In *Farr*, the tribunal decided that the cleared site approach is suitable for those cases where the house is near the end of its economic life. It is 'the derivation of site value by reference to the price of sites sold for development or redevelopment for comparable uses'.

Land values in sales of development sites are generally referred to on a 'pounds per hectare/acre' basis; similarly, adopting the cleared site approach, values are referred to on a 'pounds per sq m/sq ft' basis.

Assessment on the basis of area is open to criticism and is to be used with caution. The statutory valuation requires the single house plot to be valued. Sales in the market are generally of sites with any number of plots, and analysis by direct proportion (i.e. dividing the sale price of a large site by the number of plots thereon), will not necessarily result in the correct order of value for a single plot. Plots with large gardens also need to be treated with care; depending on the circumstances, a large area of garden could be considerably less valuable pro rata than the area upon which the building stands.

A further approach is to apply an appropriate rate to the frontage of the house, with an allowance for its depth, if applicable.

In *Nash v Castell-y-Mynach Estate* (1975) 234 EG 293, the Lands Tribunal determined the site value to represent 50 per cent of the entirety value. The entirety value (that is the freehold vacant possession value of the house developed to its best advantage), was reached by reference to comparable house sales in the district, with a deduction made for the installation of water supply. Notwithstanding the short term unexpired (one and a half years), the tribunal were critical of the landlord's valuer whose evidence included reference to single house plot sales in the vicinity, saying that as the house still had an indeterminate future life, the cleared site approach was inappropriate.

In *Cadogan Estates Limited v Hows and another* [1989] 2 EGLR 216 and [1989] 48 EG 167, the Lands Tribunal also determined the site value to represent 50 per cent of the entirety value. The decision was based on settlement analyses on the Estate, supported by a comparable sale in the vicinity of a site for development. This case concerned a freehold claim of a two storey mews house in Cadogan Lane, London SW1 for which the price was to be under section 9(1).

More recently, in *Tsiapkinis v Cadogan* [2008] L&TR 21, the Lands Tribunal upheld the LVT's decision of site value, which represented 55 per cent of entirety value (albeit the sums in the valuation represent 58 per cent). In this case, a claim for the freehold interest under section 9(1) of a two storey Victorian terrace mews house in London SW1, the tribunal heard evidence to value the site adopting both the cleared site and the standing house approaches; and attributed values of £1,023,000 and £946,000 on each respectively. The unexpired term was just under 19 years. On the basis of the evidence before them, the tribunal attributed more weight to the cleared site approach, as in the circumstances the comparable analyses required less adjustment than that of the standing house approach and reflected some useful direct evidence of site value.

The 'standing house' approach

Generally, houses within the scope of the 1967 Act are in areas that are fully developed. In addition, a premise of the legislation per se is that occupiers are to remain in residence beyond the original terms of their leases. Giving guidance in their decision in *Farr*, the Lands Tribunal said that the standing house approach is to be adopted in cases 'where the house is likely to remain standing for the foreseeable future'.

The site value is reached by:

- firstly, establishing the freehold with vacant possession value of the house (referred to as its 'entirety value'); the house to be assumed to be modernised, in good condition and there is no disregard of tenant's improvements; and
- secondly, to apply a proportion (generally a percentage) to the entirety value to reach the site value.

The tribunal has stated that site element may range from 25 per cent to 40 per cent of entirety value, depending on the land market and the attributes of the site.

In *Lewis v James* (1981) 258 EG 651, the Lands Tribunal's decision of site value to represent 25 per cent of entirety value resulted from evidence of both the landlord's and the tenant's valuers adopting the standing house approach as there was no evidence of sales of comparable sites. This case concerned a two bedroom, 1920s, terrace house in Swansea, South Wales, where the unexpired term at the date of valuation under section 9(1) was approximately 44 years.

The 'new for old' approach

In *Farr,* this approach is proposed where the house has an indeterminate future economic life. It is the derivation of site value by what the property as a whole would be worth if a new building was substituted for the existing building, and then taking a proportion of that value, or alternatively subtracting the present day cost of putting up such building.

This approach is seldom used and is widely criticised. The main criticism being that there are too many assumptions to be made in the valuation that consequently would provide wide variations in value.

For example, in *Gajewski v Anderton and Kershaw* (1971) 217 EG 885, the Lands Tribunal determined site value to represent 27.5 per cent of entirety value, adopting the 'new for old' approach. This case concerned a two storey semi-detached house in Chiswick, London W4. The unexpired term was about one year, and as the house was an old one, in the circumstances there was no obvious method to apportion the entirety value between the land and buildings.

Decapitalise the site value

Having established the site value, it is to be decapitalised adopting an appropriate percentage to reach the 'section 15 rent'. To recap, the percentage is the rate of return a freeholder will expect on a site let for 50 years at a modern ground rent, with provision for review after 25 years, and the future prospect of the site and buildings, reverting to the landlord at the end of the term.

Historically, the tribunals have determined the percentage in the range from six per cent to eight per cent, with few exceptions. In the more recent case at *Tsiapkinis*, 4.5 per cent was agreed by the valuers.

The 'adverse differential'

It is important for the valuer to understand the relationship between 'recapitalisation and decapitalisation' in section 15 rent analyses and freehold price computations under section 9(1). As we discuss later, to calculate the freehold price under section 9(1), the section 15 rent is either capitalised in perpetuity or for the 50 years extended term, deferred for the unexpired term of the existing lease.

A valuation 'principle' evolved from early decisions of the tribunals that the percentage adopted to decapitalise the site value to reach the section 15 rent, should not necessarily be the same as that adopted to recapitalise the section 15 rent in the freehold price computation; the lower the decapitalisation and the higher the recapitalisation percentages, being favourable to the tenant.

This is known as the 'adverse differential'; but pursuant to appeal of the Lands Tribunal's decision in *Official Custodian for Charities v Goldridge* (1973) 26 P&CR 191, an enfranchisement claim for the freehold interest under section 9(1) of a four storey terraced house in Hampstead, London NW3, the Court of Appeal held that:

- there may be some cases where the evidence justifies an adverse differential or special incentive, but not in this case;
- the Lands Tribunal should adopt the same percentage for recapitalisation as for decapitalisation; and
- the special incentive was a speculative and uncertain element and should be discarded with the adverse differential.

The special incentive evolved pursuant to the amendment to section 9(1) by section 82 of the *Housing Act* 1969, which introduced the words 'with the tenant and members of his family who reside in the house not buying or seeking to buy'. This led to the argument that a purchaser/investor could buy in existing leasehold interests and thus release the marriage value, in what became known as 'the marriage by sale incentive'.

These points need to be considered in conjunction with the deferment rate appeals in *Sportelli* (see chapter 2). On the face of it, it is the deferment rate that establishes the appropriate decapitalisation rate to be applied to the site value and thus calculates the section 15 rent.

In *Tsiapkinis*, 4.5 per cent was adopted as that was the deferment rate for houses determined in *Arbib*, which in turn was the authority followed at the date of valuation. In the light of *Sportelli*, bearing in mind the house is in within PCL, 4.75 per cent would be adopted.

We now look at examples to calculate the section 15 rent adopting the cleared site and standing house approaches, respectively. Each highlights the approaches only, and they are not based on any particular cases.

Example 3

The cleared site approach:

A two storey late Victorian terrace house in Loughborough has a rateable value in the 1973 list of £220. The site area is 125 sq m; and comparable site values are £400 per sq m.

Site value

125 sq m @ £400 per sq m	£400	
	125	£50,000
Section 15 rent @ 5.5% (see later)		0.055
Section 15 rent		£2,750 p.a.

Example 4

The standing house approach:

A two storey Victorian mews house in central London (PCL) has a rateable value in the 1973 list of £475. The freehold with vacant possession value, modernised in good condition, is £1,250,000.

Entirety value	£1,250,000	
Site value @ 50%, say	0.5	£625,000
Section 15 rent @ 4.75% (see later)		0.0475
Section 15 rent		£29,687.50 p.a.

In Example 3, the site value is decapitalised at 5.5 per cent following *Freehold Properties Limited*; and in Example 4, 4.75 per cent is adopted following *Sportelli*. There is further discussion on the deferment rate, and thus the corresponding decapitalisation rate, later when we discuss valuations under the section 9(1) basis.

Freehold – purchase price

There are three bases upon which the freehold purchase price can be determined, and these are known as:

- section 9(1);
- section 9(1A); and
- section 9(1C).

The latter basis is that which applies to houses which qualified post the *Leasehold Reform, Housing and Urban Development Act* 1993 amendments, and later amendments by the 2002 Act. It allows the tenant to enfranchise during the extended term paying a premium under section 9(1C).

The date of valuation to determine the price is the date of service of notice of the tenant's claim (s.9(1) and (1A) and s.37(1)(d)).

We shall look at each basis in turn, starting with section 9(1).

Valuations under section 9(1)

As outlined at the beginning of this chapter, section 9(1) is the original and most favourable basis of valuation from a tenant's perspective to acquire the freehold interest, with the price principally comprising:

(1) the capitalised value of the existing lease ground rent;
(2) the capitalised value of the modern ground rent; and
(3) the value of the freeholder's reversion at the expiry of the extended lease.

All of the bases of valuation are set out in chapter 5. Once a tenant has established his right to enfranchise, the next important question is 'how much will be paid'? Section 9(1) is the most favourable to the tenant as marriage value is not payable; and as that is the case, establishing that this basis is applicable in assessing the freehold price is the first hurdle to be cleared.

Houses: extended leases and enfranchisement valuation issues

As the right to acquire the freehold interest is borne of section 1 of the Act, the house and premises must fall within certain rateable value limits, and the tenancy is to be a long tenancy at a low rent (i.e. the annual ground rent is to be less than two-thirds of either the rateable or letting values, where applicable). Each of these is discussed, including the current rent tests, in chapter 5 and earlier in this chapter.

The solicitor and valuer are therefore required to establish, on the appropriate date, either the rateable value (in the balance of cases), or letting value, where applicable.

At the outset, and prior to 'starting with a claim', the solicitor should write to the relevant local authority requesting the rateable value in the list. When the legislation was first introduced, domestic rates were paid by households and were based on rateable value. Local authorities maintained lists which, upon request, were available for inspection including details of the valuations and entries therein. Rates for residential property have been replaced, first by the community charge and now the council tax. As a result of those legislative changes, coupled with modern records now predominantly being held on computer archives, those lists and records that were readily available at the onset of the 1967 Act may or may not be so easily accessible, depending on the local authority's archive procedures.

These days, in central London, section 9(1) cases are comparatively rare because of the applicable value limits. Accordingly, it is unlikely that receipt of an enquiry into the historic rateable value history for any one particular house will be at the forefront of the district valuer's office and finance department's minds. Having said that, the solicitor and valuer have to do the best they can, and bearing in mind the effect on price, it is essential to get this right.

In many cases, establishing the rateable value history will be straightforward; typically where similar houses in a terrace have previously been enfranchised, the information may be readily available. The legal and valuation issues arise in those comparatively rare cases where either the letting value is to be established, or a notional reduction in rateable value is sought to meet the limits, which were discussed under extended leases. Outside London, such leases may be more prevalent.

Section 9(1) reads as follows:

9. Purchase price and costs of enfranchisement, and tenant's right to withdraw.

(1) Subject to subsection (2) below, the price payable for a house and premises on a conveyance under section 8 above shall be the amount which at the relevant time the house and premises, if sold in the open market by a willing seller, (with the tenant and members of his family who reside in the house not buying or seeking to buy) might be expected to realise on the following assumptions–
 (a) on the assumption that the vendor was selling for an estate in fee simple, subject to the tenancy but on the assumption that this Part of this Act conferred no right to acquire the freehold, and if the tenancy has not been extended under this Part of this Act, on the assumption that (subject to the landlord's rights under section 17 below) it was to be so extended;
 (b) on the assumption that (subject to paragraph (a) above) the vendor was selling subject, in respect of rentcharges to which section 11(2) below applies, to the same annual charge as the conveyance to the tenant is to be subject to, but the purchaser would otherwise be effectively exonerated until the termination of the tenancy from any liability or charge in respect of tenant's incumbrances; and
 (c) on the assumption that (subject to paragraphs (a) and (b) above) the vendor was selling with and subject to the rights and burdens with and subject to which the conveyance to the tenant is to be made, and in particular with and subject to such permanent or extended rights and burdens as are to be created in order to give effect to section 10 below.

The reference in this subsection to members of the tenant's family must be construed in accordance with section 7(7) of this Act.

Section 7 is 'rights of members of family succeeding to tenancy on death'.

The inclusion of the words 'with the tenant and members of his family who reside in the house not buying or seeking to buy' (section 82, *Housing Act* 1969) in the basis of valuation means that marriage value is excluded. Accordingly, the valuation becomes the investment value of the landlord's interest only.

Houses: extended leases and enfranchisement valuation issues

Pursuant to the House of Lords decision in *Sportelli,* the words also mean that hope value is excluded in the enfranchisement price. As discussed in chapter 4, hope value is only payable in a collective enfranchisement claim where there are non-participating leaseholders.

We now look at section 9, subsections (2), (3), (4), (4A) and (5), as the provisions are common to all of the bases of valuation for the enfranchisement price; the subsections are as follows:

(2) The price payable for the house and premises shall be subject to such deduction (if any) in respect of any defect in the title to be conveyed to the tenant as on a sale in the open market might be expected to be allowed between a willing seller and a willing buyer.

(3) On ascertaining the amount payable, or likely to be payable, as the price for a house and premises in accordance with this section (but not more than one month after the amount payable has been determined by agreement or otherwise), the tenant may give written notice to the landlord that he is unable or unwilling to acquire the house and premises at the price he must pay; and thereupon–
  (a) the notice under section 8 above of his desire to have the freehold shall cease to have effect, and he shall be liable to make such compensation as may be just to the landlord in respect of the interference (if any) by the notice with the exercise by the landlord of his power to dispose of or deal with the house and premises or any neighbouring property; and
  (b) any further notice given under that section with respect to the house or any part of it (with or without other property) shall be void if given within the following 12 months.

(4) Where a person gives notice of his desire to have the freehold of a house and premises under this Part of this Act, then unless the notice lapses under any provision of this Act excluding his liability, there shall be borne by him (so far as they are incurred in pursuance of the notice) the reasonable costs of or incidental to any of the following matters–
  (a) any investigation by the landlord of that person's right to acquire the freehold;
  (b) any conveyance or assurance of the house and premises or any part thereof or of any outstanding estate or interest therein;

(c) deducing, evidencing and verifying the title to the house and premises or any estate or interest therein;
(d) making out and furnishing such abstracts and copies as the person given the notice may require;
(e) any valuation of the house and premises;

but so that this subsection shall not apply to any costs if on a sale made voluntarily a stipulation that they were to be borne by the purchaser would be void.

(4A) Subsection (4) above does not require a person to bear the costs of another person in connection with an application to a leasehold valuation tribunal.

(5) The landlord's lien (as vendor) on the house and premises for the price payable shall extend–
(a) to any sums payable by way of rent or recoverable as rent in respect of the house and premises up to the date of the conveyance; and
(b) to any sums for which the tenant is liable under subsection (4) above; and
(c) to any other sums due and payable by him to the landlord under or in respect of the tenancy or any agreement collateral thereto.

In outline, each provides the following: subsection 2 provides that the price payable is to reflect any defect in title; subsection 3 provides where a tenant withdraws his claim after the price for the house and premises is determined, including a time bar of 12 months before a further notice can be given; subsection 4 covers the reasonable costs to be borne by the tenant, which include 'any valuation of the house and premises' (s.4(e)); and subsection 4A, (introduced by the *CLRA* 2002 amendments) provides that each party is to bear their own costs in an application to the LVT.

The valuation assumptions

We now look at the valuation assumptions in more detail, in order to explain the constituent parts to the price computation.

- An estate in fee simple: fee simple means freehold with vacant possession, accordingly it is the freeholder's reversionary interest to vacant possession which is to be valued; conferring no right to acquire the freehold means that 'the sale is between a hypothetical willing vendor and a hypothetical

willing purchaser and takes place in the market undisturbed by the existence of compulsory powers' *Earl Cadogan v Sportelli* [2008] UK HL; and it is to be assumed that the 50 years extended lease has been taken.
- Rentcharges: the sale is subject to any rentcharge the freehold is subject to.
- Rights and burdens: similarly with rentcharges, the rights and burdens to which the freehold is subject are conveyed to the tenant.

The purchase price of the freeholder's interest under section 9(1) which only applies to lower value houses is made up as follows:

- the freeholder's interest subject to the tenant's unexpired term of the lease (term);
- the right to a further 50 years (ground) lease at a modern ground rent; and
- the present value of the house at the end of the 50 years extended lease.

Following on from the above, the approach to the enfranchisement price is:

- stage 1 – capitalisation of the rent payable under the existing tenancy;
- stage 2 – calculate the section 15 rent (or modern ground rent);
- stage 3 – capitalise the section 15 rent from the term date of the existing tenancy either in perpetuity or to the expiry date of the 50 years extended lease, having regard to the rent review; and
- stage 4 – value of the reversion at the end of the 50 years extended lease, if applicable.

Each of the above are expanded on as follows.

Stage 1 – capitalisation of the rent payable under the existing tenancy

The ground rent payable under the existing tenancy is to be capitalised from the date of valuation to the date of the term of the existing lease. The rate of interest (rate of return) will ultimately depend on market evidence, albeit evidence of transactions is both comparatively rare and difficult to analyse. We considered the factors in the choice of capitalisation rate in chapter 2. In *Tsiapkinis*, the valuers agreed five per cent; and in

Freehold Properties Limited, the valuers agreed 6.5 per cent and seven per cent in the conjoined appeals.

Settlement evidence was regarded as being a good guide to the rate to be adopted until the Lands Tribunal's decision in *Arbib*, which was discussed in chapter 2.

Stage 2 – calculate the section 15 rent (or modern ground rent)

The calculation of the section 15 rent has been considered in detail earlier in this chapter.

Stage 3 – capitalisation of the section 15 rent

It is an established principle to capitalise the section 15 rent either in perpetuity (generally), or to the expiration of the 50 years extension coupled with a separate valuation for the landlord's reversion.

Where a separate sum is not included at Stage 4 (the *Haresign* addition, see later), the section 15 rent is capitalised adopting the years' purchase of a reversion to a perpetuity. If, on the other hand, the *Haresign* addition is included, the section 15 rent is to be capitalised over the term of the extended lease.

Following *Goldridge*, the section 15 rent is to be recapitalised as it is decapitalised. Note that the interests to be valued under stages 1 and 2 are manifestly different; accordingly whereas there may be circumstances where the capitalisation rates adopted for each are the same, it is not necessarily to be so.

As discussed earlier in the chapter, unless there is valuation evidence to the contrary, the capitalisation rate for the section 15 rent will be the same as the deferment rate. The generic deferment rate in *Sportelli* and subsequent cases before the tribunals were discussed at length in chapter 2. We now review those cases under section 9(1) where departure from the generic rate of 4.75 per cent has been sought. Have it in mind that the basis of valuation of the house case in *Sportelli* (13 South Terrace, London SW7) was under section 9(1A), and it is located within PCL.

In *Mansal Securities & other appeals*, (the 'Midlands 22'), the LVT had determined a deferment rate of 5.5 per cent for these various cases under section 9(1); the houses being located in the West Midlands area, thus outside PCL.

At the Lands Tribunal, two issues were highlighted to be decided to determine whether a departure from the 4.75 per cent generic rate in *Sportelli* is justified:

- Are the factors that led to 4.75 per cent in *Sportelli* under section 9(1A) sufficiently different to those under section 9 (1)?
- Is there any evidence to justify a deferment rate for houses in the West Midlands, which is different from that applying to houses in the PCL area?

The tribunal concluded that a 0.25 per cent increase in the risk premium is appropriate to compensate for the increased volatility and illiquidity for a reversion to a ground rent only (section 9 (1)), as opposed to a house standing on the site (section 9(1A)) (para. 27).

As to the second point, the tribunal concluded that the evidence before it was insufficient to displace the *Sportelli* rate of 4.75 per cent. This was discussed in chapter 2.

The tribunal determined a deferment rate of five per cent, an increase of 0.25 per cent, to reflect the increased risk premium an investor would seek for a section 9(1) case as opposed to section 9(1A).

In *Freehold Properties Ltd*, the tribunal upheld the decisions of the LVT for various houses in the West Midlands where the deferment rate was determined at 5.5 per cent under section 9 (1). The increase of 0.75 per cent from the *Sportelli* rate of 4.75 per cent to reflect the lower growth rate in the West Midlands as opposed to PCL, and the differences between section 9(1) and section 9(1A).

Stage 4 – value of the reversion at the end of the 50 years extended lease (the *Haresign* addition)

An established practice in stage 3 of section 9(1) valuations was to capitalise the section 15 rent in perpetuity at a yield to reflect the value of the reversion. In *Haresign v St John the Baptist's College, Oxford* (1980) 255 EG 711, the Lands Tribunal determined an additional sum (known as the *Haresign* addition) for the landlord's reversion, in the freehold price computation of a substantial house in Oxford.

In *Haresign*, the original term date was three years, hence the reversion was 53 years distant. The circumstances of the case will determine as to whether the three stage approach is to be adopted. Evidence that the house will be standing and be of value at the end of the extended lease is required.

Where the unexpired term of the existing tenancy is short, the value of the reversionary interest can be materially different when the *Haresign* addition is included. When this is taken in conjunction with a significant reduction in the deferment rate commonly used by valuers (i.e. post *Sportelli*), it could be a circumstance which justifies a departure from the two stage approach. See *Freehold Properties Limited*, paragraph 16, where in their decision, the Lands Tribunal held that there is no objection in principle to the three stage valuation, but on the evidence before it, upheld the LVT's two stage approach on various claims for existing lease unexpired terms in the region of 25 years to 40 years.

Further considerations

The Delaforce effect

In *Delaforce v Evans* (1970) 215 EG 315, the Lands Tribunal made a deduction from the landlord's settlement evidence of freehold price (equating to approximately 12.5 per cent) to reflect the tenant's perceived overbid. The *Delaforce* effect, as it is known, is the increase in price, 'the overbid', that the tenant will pay if he is anxious to settle the enfranchisement and to limit the proceedings, including having to attend any tribunal. In addition to the anxiety felt by the tenant, it is also argued that he might be reticent to attend a tribunal with the associated stress and costs, as opposed to a landlord who might otherwise be expected to be well versed and 'battle hardened' to the tribunal's process and better able to bear the costs involved.

Of course, this can work the other way around; it can be argued that the landlord will have his own costs to cover in any event, albeit in some cases he may choose to go to the tribunal to establish a particular valuation principle. Ultimately, each case is to be handled on its merits, but it is said in areas of high value property, where both landlords and tenants are professionally advised, the effect is minimal.

Houses: extended leases and enfranchisement valuation issues

Long terms unexpired

The Act does not provide for a different enfranchisement price for leases with long terms unexpired.

Where the unexpired term under the original tenancy was 60 years or more, historically valuers have attributed a nominal value to the prospect of the section 15 rent at the future date, and reversion thereafter. With the lowering of the deferment rate, each case is to be taken on its merits.

We now look at examples of the purchase price under section 9(1).

Example 5

The long term unexpired.

A mid-terrace, Victorian, two storey house in Loughborough, Leicestershire, with a rateable value in the 1973 list of £335. The lease has 115 years unexpired as at the date of service of notice of claim, 25 March 2010, at a fixed ground rent of £75 per annum.

Term

Ground rent	£75 p.a.
Years' purchase in perpetuity @ 9%	11.1111
Freehold price	£833.33
Say (excluding costs)	£835

Note as the unexpired term is 115 years, the reversion to the 50 years extended lease is attributed 'nominal' value.

In the next two examples, we assess the modern ground rent and enfranchisement price on a short term unexpired lease. This is of particular significance where the tenant has to choose between the merits or otherwise of taking the 50 years extended lease or acquiring the freehold.

In addition, as a tenant who has taken a 50 years extended lease now has the right to buy the freehold, it is important to understand: (a) the different bases of valuation if the notice is given during the term of the original tenancy or after the original term date; and (b) the resultant difference in price, assuming market conditions remain stable over the interim.

Example 6

The facts of this case follow on from Example 1.

You are contacted by a solicitor seeking leasehold reform valuation advice on behalf of a client. You are provided with a copy of the lease and carry out your inspection.

The property is a two storey mews house in central London (within PCL), which is now subject to an extended lease under section 14 of the 1967 Act. You establish that the original lease was dated 10 June 1957, for a term of 52.75 years from 24 June 1957 (expiry date 25 March 2010), at a fixed ground rent of £50 per annum. After further enquiries and consultation with the solicitor, you conclude that the house falls to be valued under section 9(1), and firstly you are required to calculate the anticipated order of section 15 rent. The date of valuation you assume for your advice now is 29 September 2009.

The original term date is 25 March 2010, six months hence. As the term of the original lease is within its last 12 months, the freeholder may serve notice on the tenant for the section 15 rent to apply from 25 March 2010.

It is vital to understand that if an enfranchisement claim is to be made for the freehold interest, the claim must be made during the currency of the existing lease.

Calculation of the section 15 rent.

From analysis of comparable sales in the vicinity, you value the freehold with vacant possession, modernised and in good condition, at £1,500,000.

Standing house approach

Entirety value		£1,500,000	
Site value @ 55%		0.55	£825,000
Section 15 rent @ 5%			0.05
			£41,250

So, the anticipated section 15 rent from 25 March 2010 is in the region of £41,250 per annum, with review in March 2035.

The site value is assessed at 55 per cent of entirety value, following *Tsiapkinis*; and it is decapitalised at five per cent, being an increase of 0.25 per cent to the generic rate in *Sportelli* to reflect the different valuation assumptions between section 9(1) and section 9(1A), following *Mansal* and *Freehold Properties Limited*.

Houses: extended leases and enfranchisement valuation issues

> *Example 7*
>
> Following on from Example 6, we now calculate the enfranchisement price, which incorporates the freeholder's reversion to the value of the house and premises in 50.5 years time.
>
> The three stage approach is used (the *Haresign* addition), as the unexpired term of the existing lease is short (six months), the house is situated in a Conservation Area and is expected to be standing in 50.5 years time.
>
> Enfranchisement price
>
> Term
>
> | | | | |
> |---|---|---|---|
> | Ground rent | £50 p.a. | | |
> | YP 6 months @ 5% | 0.4762 | | £24 |
> | Reversion to section 15 rent (from above) | £41,250 p.a. | | |
> | YP 50 years @ 5% | 18.2559 | | |
> | Deferred 6 months @ 5% | 0.9759 | | £734,907 |
> | Reversion to entirety value at the end of the 50 years extended lease | £1,500,000 | | |
> | deferred for 50.5 years @ 5% | 0.0851 | | £127,650 |
> | | | | £862,581 |
> | Enfranchisement price (excluding costs) | | Say | £862,600 |
>
> Note the substantial *Haresign* addition, and compare the enfranchisement price with the freehold vacant possession value of £1,500,000.

Section 9(1A)

The second basis of valuation for the determination of price for the freehold interest in the house and premises is section 9(1A), introduced by the *Housing Act* 1974 and applies, in effect, to higher value houses than those under section 9(1). The freehold price includes a sum for marriage value, as the valuation assumptions do not exclude the tenant and members of his family from the market to purchase (s.1A (a)); the price is principally comprised:

(1) the capitalised value of the existing lease ground rent;
(2) the value of the freeholder's reversion to vacant possession deferred over the unexpired term; and
(3) the freeholder's share of marriage value.

The *Housing Act* 1974 introduced various amendments to the provisions of the 1967 Act, which in outline are as follows.

- The increase in rateable value limits to £500 and £1,000 in the 1973 list were broadly equivalent to their corresponding £200 and £400 in the 1963 list; one intention being to ensure that where new leases had been granted after 1973, which would have otherwise qualified under the original limits, these qualify in any event in the new list.
- The extension of rights to those tenants of houses and premises in higher rateable value bands between £501 to £750, and £1,001 to £1,500 in Greater London.
- Section 118(4) introduced the new basis of valuation, section 9(1A), for those houses and premises in the newly introduced higher rateable value bands, with its associated assumptions; which in turn introduce the concept of marriage value.
- As previously discussed, section 118, subsection (3) introduced s.1(4A) to the 1967 Act to allow the rateable value to be notionally reduced to reflect tenant's improvements; subsection (4) of the 1974 *Act* introduces the corresponding section (1B) for those houses and premises in the higher rateable value band.

Section 9(1A) reads as follows:

(1A) Notwithstanding the foregoing subsection, the price payable for a house and premises–
   (i) the rateable value of which was above £1,000 in Greater London and £500 elsewhere on 31 March 1990, or,
   (ii) which had no rateable value on that date and R exceeded £16,333 under the formula in section 1(1)(a) above (and section 1(7) above shall apply to that amount as it applies to the amount referred to in subsection (1)(a)(ii) of that section)
shall be the amount which at the relevant time the house and premises, if sold in the open market by a willing seller, might be expected to realise on the following assumptions–
   (a) on the assumption that the vendor was selling for an estate in fee simple, subject to the tenancy, but on the assumption that this Part of this Act conferred no right to acquire the freehold or an extended lease, and where the tenancy has been extended under this Part of this Act, that the tenancy will terminate on the original term date;

(b) on the assumption that at the end of the tenancy the tenant has the right to remain in possession of the house and premises;
   (i) if the tenancy is such a tenancy as is mentioned in subsection (2) or subsection (3) of section 186 of the *Local Government and Housing Act* 1989, or is a tenancy which is a long tenancy at a low rent for the purposes of Part I of the *Landlord and Tenant Act* 1954 in respect of which the landlord is not able to serve a notice under section 4 of that Act specifying a date of termination earlier than 15 January 1999, under the provisions of Schedule 10 to the *Local Government and Housing Act* 1989; and
   (ii) in any other case, under the provisions of Part I of the *Landlord and Tenant Act* 1954;
(c) on the assumption that the tenant has no liability to carry out any repairs, maintenance or redecorations under the terms of the tenancy or Part I of the *Landlord and Tenant Act* 1954;
(d) on the assumption that the price be diminished by the extent to which the value of the house and premises has been increased by any improvement carried out by the tenant or his predecessors in title at their own expense;
(e) on the assumption that (subject to paragraph (a) above) the vendor was selling subject, in respect of rentcharges to which section 11(2) below applies, to the same annual charge as the conveyance to the tenant is to be subject to, but the purchaser would otherwise be effectively exonerated until the termination of the tenancy from any liability or charge in respect of tenant's incumbrances; and
(f) on the assumption that (subject to paragraphs (a) and (b) above) the vendor was selling with and subject to the rights and burdens with and subject to which the conveyance to the tenant is to be made, and in particular with and subject to such permanent or extended rights and burdens as are to be created in order to give effect to section 10 below.

Under section 9(1A), the enfranchisement price is made up of the following:

- the freeholder's interest:

the term – the capitalised value of the annual ground rent payable under the lease from the date of notice of claim to expiry, including any provisions for review; plus

the reversion – the value of the freeholder's reversion calculated by applying the appropriate deferment rate to the freehold vacant possession value, thus the present value of the interest; on the assumptions, inter alia, whereas there is no right to acquire the freehold or an extended lease, the tenant has rights (if any) either under Part I of the *Landlord and Tenant Act* 1954 or Schedule 10 to the *Local Government and Housing Act* 1989 to remain in occupation, is not obliged for the house and premises to be in repair and any value attributable to improvements, is disregarded.

- the landlord's 50 per cent share of marriage value (if the current lease does not exceed 80 years);
  the method of calculating the marriage value, and thus the landlord's 50 per cent share, is well established from decisions of the Lands Tribunal. The principles were discussed in chapter 2 for new lease claims in the flats legislation. In short, the aggregate of the values of the landlord's interest and tenant's interest is deducted from the freehold vacant possession value of the house, the resultant sum being the marriage value.

Further considerations:

Similarly with section 9(1), any effect of easements, restrictive covenants and the value (if any) of any other rights under the existing tenancy, extinguished on the acquisition of the freehold, are to be taken into consideration.

The freeholder's interest:

The principles follow those discussed in chapter 2 for a new lease.

The term: the capitalisation rate to be applied to the annual rent will depend on market evidence and the valuer's opinion. Any rent review is to be included, which in turn is to disregard tenant's improvements (*Earl Cadogan v Sharp* (1998) unreported, Lands Tribunal), notwithstanding the fact that generally rent review provisions in residential leases do not include a disregard clause for tenant's improvements.

The reversion: the value of the right to vacant possession of the house at some future date, calculated by applying a deferment rate over the term of the lease to the freehold vacant possession value.

Deferment rates have been discussed and analysed in detail. Be aware that the determination of the price payable for the freehold interest in the house and premises in the enfranchisement claim in the conjoined cases of *Sportelli,* 13 South Terrace, London SW7, was under this basis, section 9(1A).

Norfolk and Lloyd-Jones

(1) *Norfolk v Trinity College, Cambridge,* (1976) 238 EG 421

Norfolk was the first case to be heard at the Lands Tribunal for the determination of price under section 9(1A). The tribunal in their decision outlined the two principal different assumptions between assessing the price under sections 9(1) and 9(1A) as follows:

- the tenant and his family are not to be excluded from the market; and
- the tenant has rights under the 1954 Act as opposed to a reversion to a modern ground rent. This assumption has subsequently been amended to reflect rights under the 1989 Act where applicable.

To recap, section 82 of the *Housing Act* 1969, amended section (1) to the 1967 Act to include the words ('with the tenant and members of his family who reside in the house not buying or seeking to buy'), the purpose of which was to exclude the tenant's overbid in the determination of price. The omission of those corresponding words in section 9(1A) has the effect that the tenant's overbid is not to be excluded and thus the concept of marriage value was introduced.

The Lands Tribunal's determination of price in *Norfolk* comprised sums for:

- the lessor's interest exclusive of 'marriage value'; and
- the lessor's share of marriage value; the share being 50 per cent.

(2) *Lloyd-Jones v Church Commissioners for England*, (1981) 261 EG 471

Lloyd-Jones was the second case to be referred to the Lands Tribunal where the price to be determined is under section 9(1A). The tribunal confirmed the lessor's valuation which followed the approach in Norfolk.

However, the valuation of the lessor's interest includes an adjustment to reflect the tenant's right under Part I of the *Landlord and Tenant Act* 1954, to hold over as a statutory tenant paying a fair rent. This was subsequently amended under Schedule 10 to the *Local Government and Housing Act* 1989, where the cut off point is 15 January 1999, after which the entitlement is to an assessed tenancy. In the calculation of the reversion in the lessor's interest is a deduction of ten per cent to the freehold vacant possession value to reflect the risk that the tenant might hold over under the 1954 Act. This established the '*Lloyd-Jones*' approach to valuations under section 9(1A).

Whereas now that right would be to hold over as an assured tenant, the valuer has to consider on the facts of each case, whether a deduction is appropriate, and if so, what amount. The approach is highlighted in Example 8, chapter 2.

Hope value

Similarly with section 9(1), hope value is to be excluded in calculating the freeholder's interest, albeit for a different reason. Under section 9(1), the tenant's overbid is to be excluded; accordingly there is no marriage value from which hope value can be derived. Whereas under section 9(1A), the tenant's overbid is not to be excluded, the House of Lords in *Sportelli* determined that where marriage value is payable, hope value is not payable, otherwise there would be double counting.

Marriage value

Before we look at examples which include marriage value, be aware of the amending sections 9(1D) and (1E) introduced in the 2002 Act, which follow those under the flats legislation with respect to tenant's share of marriage value (1D); and where at the date of valuation the unexpired term of the existing lease exceeds 80 years, marriage value is 'nil' (1E).

The sections are as follows:

(1D) Where, in determining the price payable for a house and premises in accordance with this section, there falls to be taken into account any marriage value arising by virtue of the coalescence of the freehold and leasehold interests, the share of the marriage value to which the tenant is to be regarded as being entitled shall be one-half of it.

(1E) But where at the relevant time the unexpired term of the tenant's tenancy exceeds eighty years, the marriage value shall be taken to be nil.

Whereas the Lands Tribunal decisions in *Arrowdell* and *Nailrile* to assess the existing lease values for the purposes of the marriage value computation were under Schedules 6 and 13 to the 1993 Act respectively, it is understood that the principles and directions are to apply to enfranchisement claims under sections 9(1A) and (1C) also.

As a general point, it is accepted that 'relativities' may vary between flats and houses in some markets. Relativity was discussed in chapter 2.

Mosley v Hickman (1986) 278 EG 728; and [1986] 1 EGLR 161

Section 9(1A)(a) when originally drafted, provided 'that the vendor was selling for an estate in fee simple, subject to the tenancy'. Subject to which tenancy?

In *Mosley* it was common ground that the valuation fell to be carried out under section 9(1A); the tenant had taken an extended lease under section 14, and thereafter served a notice to acquire the freehold. The question in law was whether the 'tenancy' to be assumed under section 9(1A)(a) was to be the original tenancy or the 50 years extended term? If the tenancy to be assumed was the extended term, the valuation would then fall to be carried out under section 9(1), thereby being more financially advantageous to the tenant.

To recap, the assumption under section 9(1)(a) is that for the purposes of the valuation it is to be assumed that the original tenancy had been extended under section 14. Section 9(1A)(a), as originally drafted, was unspecific as to the 'tenancy' to be assumed; i.e. was it the original tenancy or subject to the extended lease (tenancy), as was the case in *Mosley*. The Court of Appeal upheld the decision of the Lands Tribunal that the enfranchisement price was to be calculated subject to the extended lease, thus the more favourable to the tenant section 9(1) basis of price computation, was to apply.

Leasehold enfranchisement explained

The impact of this decision has been greatly restricted under section 23 of the *Housing and Planning Act* 1986, and subsequently Schedule 14 to the 2002 Act which amended the 1967 Act so as to include the words '…or an extended lease and, where the tenancy has been extended under this Part of the Act, that the tenancy will terminate on the original term date'.

These cases are rare and it is believed that the only circumstances now that might give rise to this loophole being taken advantage of is where the notice of claim for the freehold interest was given before 26 July 2002, the commencement date in Commencement Order No. 1 of the amendments made by the *Commonhold and Leasehold Reform Act* 2002.

We now look at examples of valuations under section 9(1A).

Example 8

Long term unexpired

A 1930s detached house in Brightlingsea, held on a lease dated 19 July 1971 for a term of 99 years from 25 March 1971 (thereby expiring 25 March 2070), at a fixed ground rent of £100 per annum. The house has a rateable value in the 1973 list of £638. The agreed freehold with vacant possession and existing lease values are £250,000 and £202,500 respectively.

The date of valuation is 25 March 2010.

The price computation is as follows:

Value of the freeholder's interest

Term

March 2010 to March 2070

Ground rent at £100 p.a.	£100 p.a.	
Years' purchase for 60 years at 7%	14.0392	£1,404

plus

Reversion

To entirety value, £250,000	£250,000	
deferred for 60 years @ 4.75%	0.0618	£15,450

Value of the freeholder's interest   £16,854

Plus the freeholder's share of marriage value

Difference between:

Value of the interests in the hands
 of the tenant after enfranchisement

freehold vacant possession value   £250,000

Houses: extended leases and enfranchisement valuation issues

less			
The aggregate of values prior to enfranchisement			
the freeholder's interest (from above)	£16,854		
plus			
the tenant's interest	£202,500	£219,354	
Marriage value		£30,646	
50% thereof		0.5	
		£15,323	£15,323
plus the value of the freeholder's interest (from above)			£16,854
Enfranchisement price (excluding costs)			£32,177
		Say	£32,200

The capitalisation rate is derived from market evidence; the generic deferment rate of 4.75 per cent follows *Sportelli*. There should be no deduction to reflect the risk for the tenant holding over in 60 years time as an assured tenant, as the length of the unexpired term is such that the market would treat the risk as nominal.

Example 9

Short term unexpired

A late Victorian terrace house in Chiswick, West London is held on a lease dated 9 May 1956 for a term of 65 years from 25 March 1956 (thereby expiring 25 March 2021), at a fixed ground rent of £50 per annum. The rateable value in the 1973 list is £1,275. The freehold with vacant possession and existing lease values are £500,000 and £135,000 respectively.

The date of valuation is 25 March 2010

The price computation is as follows:

<u>Value of the freeholder's interest</u>

Term

March 2010 to March 2021

Ground rent at £50 p.a.	£50 p.a.	
Years' purchase for 11 years at 6%	7.8869	£394

plus

405

Reversion			
To entirety value, £500,000	£500,000		
Less 5% for the risk of the tenant claiming possession under Schedule 10 of the Local Government and Housing Act 1989, as an assured tenant (5% of £500,000 = £25,000)	£25,000		
	£475,000		
deferred for 11 years @ 4.75%	0.6002	£285,095	
The freeholder's interest		£285,489	

Plus the freeholder's share of marriage value

Difference between

Value of the interests in the hands of the tenant after enfranchisement

freehold vacant possession value		£500,000	
less			
The aggregate of values prior to enfranchisement			
the freeholder's interest (from above)	£285,489		
plus			
the tenant's interest	£135,000	£420,489	
Marriage value		£79,511	
50% thereof		0.5	
		£39,756	£39,756
plus the value of the freeholder's interest (from above)			£285,489
Enfranchisement price (excluding costs)			£325,245
		Say	£325,250

Following on from Example 7, a deduction of five per cent to the freehold vacant possession value is made in calculating the reversion as part of the freeholder's interest, this highlights the approach in *Lloyd-Jones*; the deduction is to reflect the risk of the tenant claiming possession on expiry of the lease.

As discussed in chapter 2, the right to remain in occupation as an assured tenant is less advantageous to the lessee than as a statutory tenant (under the Rent Acts), as the basis of valuation for the rental value under the former excludes the 'scarcity factor' of the latter. That is, the fair rent payable may be less than the market rent payable for an assured tenancy.

Section 9(1B)

Notional reduction in rateable value follows section 1(4A) which applies to houses and premises in the lower value bands, and is as follows:

(1B) For the purpose of determining whether the rateable value of the house and premises is above £1,000 in Greater London, or £500 elsewhere, the rateable value shall be adjusted to take into account any tenant's improvements in accordance with Schedule 8 to the *Housing Act* 1974.

The operation and mechanics of Schedule 8 were discussed earlier in this chapter. The valuer should be aware that there is an inconsistency between the date specified at section 9(1A)(i), being 31 March 1990, and the date under paragraph 3(2) to Schedule 8, which is 1 April 1973.

It is believed that this inconsistency was not the intention of Parliament. Where the valuation officer's certificate requires the date to which the notional reduction in rateable value to be effective is 1 April 1973, the problem does not arise. On the other hand, where the purpose of Schedule 8 is further to section 9(1A)(a), the date required to be applicable is 31 March 1990.

Section 9(1C)

The third basis of valuation for the determination of the freehold price of the house and premises is section 9(1C). In effect, this applies to all those houses that did not qualify for enfranchisement until the amendments introduced in the *Leasehold Reform, Housing and Urban Development Act* 1993 (and subsequently those further amendments under the 2002 Act). That is to say, if the house did not qualify under the 1967 Act coupled with all of the amending legislation prior to the 1993 Act, it is to be valued under section 9(1C).

Section 9(1C) broadly follows section 9(1A) with provision for the payment of compensation under section 9A; accordingly the price is now principally comprised:

(1) the capitalised value of the existing lease ground rent;
(2) the value of the freeholder's reversion to vacant possession deferred over the unexpired term;
(3) the freeholder's share of marriage value; and
(4) any compensation payable under section 9A.

As previously discussed, the section 9(1C) basis also applies where the freehold is claimed pursuant to an extended lease under section 14 having been taken, and the original term date has passed. This latter provision is expanded on later.

The valuer should be aware that the 1993 Act amending qualifications to enfranchisement do not apply to the right to an extended lease. Accordingly, those high value properties that came within the legislation from 1993 onwards do not have the option to take an extended 50 years lease. The right to an extended lease, therefore, only applies to house leases which qualify under the original provisions in the 1967 Act, such as the low rent and upper value limits.

Section 9(1C) and its assumptions are as follows:

(1C) Notwithstanding subsection (1) above, the price payable for a house and premises where the right to acquire the freehold arises by virtue of any one or more of the provisions of sections 1A, 1AA and 1B above, or where the tenancy of the house and premises has been extended under section 14 below and the notice under section 8(1) above was given (whether by the tenant or a sub-tenant) after the original term date of the tenancy, shall be determined in accordance with subsection (1A) above; but in any such case—

(a) (1D)
(b) section 9A below has effect for determining whether any additional amount is payable by way of compensation under that section;

and in a case where the provision (or one of the provisions) by virtue of which the right to acquire the freehold arises is section 1A(1) above, subsection (1A) above shall apply with the omission of the assumption set out in paragraph (b) of that subsection.

The basis of valuation is the same as section 9(1A) with modifications, and where applicable, the freeholder is entitled to compensation under section 9A.

Where the right to acquire the freehold interest is under section 1A(1), the right to remain in occupation under subsection (b) does not apply.

Deferment rate

As discussed in chapter 4, at the time of writing this, there are cases listed for appeal at the Upper Tribunal (Lands Chamber) of LVT decisions under Schedule 6 to the1993 Act, where the appropriate deferment rate is in question post *Sportelli* for unexpired terms less than 20 years (approximately 17 years), at the dates of valuation.

The LVT determined a deferment rate of 5.75 per cent in the enfranchisement claim of 110 Hamilton Terrace, London NW8. The basis of valuation is under section 9(1C); and the property is within PCL. The unexpired term of the lease was 3.38 years, and the date of valuation was November 2007. The tribunal's increase of one per cent to 5.75 per cent reflected a starting point of the generic rate in *Sportelli* of 4.75 per cent, as although the property was sub-divided into flats at the date of valuation, the hypothetical purchaser, on the facts of the case, it determined would buy the property in order to reconvert into a house. The tribunal concluded that at the date of valuation, the hypothetical purchaser would perceive that the market had passed its peak and possibly be in decline; and accepted the tenant's valuer's argument that:

> '...an informed buyer was likely to base his deferment rate on an anticipated real growth of one per cent rather than the two per cent used by Sportelli'; paragraph 267; and accordingly, 'the applicable deferment rate is 5.75 per cent being 4.75 per cent plus a further one per cent to reflect market perception prevailing at the valuation date' (para. 271).

Section 9A – compensation

Where the valuation falls to be carried out under section 9(1C), section 9A also applies, which is as follows:

9A. Compensation payable in cases where right to enfranchisement arises by virtue of section 1A or 1B.

(1) If, in a case where the right to acquire the freehold of a house and premises arises by virtue of any one or more of the provisions of sections 1A, or 1AA and 1B above or where the tenancy of the house and premises has been extended under section 14 below and the notice under section 8(1) above was given (whether by the tenant or a sub-tenant) after the original term date of the tenancy, the landlord will suffer any loss or damage to which this section applies, there shall be payable to him such amount as is reasonable to compensate him for that loss or damage.

(2) This section applies to—
 (a) any diminution in value of any interest of the landlord in other property resulting from the acquisition of his interest in the house and premises; and
 (b) any other loss or damage which results therefrom to the extent that it is referable to his ownership of any interest in other property.

(3) Without prejudice to the generality of paragraph (b) of subsection (2) above, the kinds of loss falling within that paragraph include loss of development value in relation to the house and premises to the extent that it is referable as mentioned in that paragraph.

(4) In subsection (3) above "development value", in relation to the house and premises, means any increase in the value of the landlord's interest in the house and premises which is attributable to the possibility of demolishing, reconstructing, or carrying out substantial works of construction on, the whole or a substantial part of the house and premises.

(5) In relation to any case falling within subsection (1) above—
 (a) any reference (however expressed)—
  (i) in section 8 or 9(3) or (5) above, or
  (ii) in any of the following provisions of this Act,
  to the price payable under section 9 above shall be construed as including a reference to any amount payable to the landlord under this section; and
 (b) for the purpose of determining any such separate price as is mentioned in paragraph 7(1)(b) of Schedule 1 to this Act, this section shall accordingly apply (with

any necessary modifications) to each of the superior interests in question.

In central London, where Georgian and Victorian town houses were traditionally built backing onto their mews cottages to the rear, it has been established in some circumstances that the aggregate of the freehold vacant possession values of the town house and its mews cottage to the rear, is less than the value as one lot. In those circumstances, and where the two houses are enfranchised separately, landlords have argued that compensation should be payable to reflect the fact that, upon reversion, they have lost the opportunity to sell the two as one. This is called 'severance'.

The Lands Tribunal upheld the LVT's assessment of compensation for severance of £6,300 after deferment in *Carl v Grosvenor Estate Belgravia,* [2000] 3 EGLR 79 and [2000] 38 EG 195. This case concerned the enfranchisement of an end of terrace, six storey house, at 46 Chester Square, London SW1. The house and premises included a garage forming part of 46 Ebury Mews to the rear. The premises at 46 Ebury Mews was held by the claimants under a separate, but coterminous, lease to the subject premises.

We now look at examples of valuations under section 9(1C).

Example 10

Medium term unexpired, fixed ground rent reviews and tenant's improvements to be disregarded.

A 1980s terrace house in Oxford held on a lease dated 1 February 1988 for a term of 75 years from 25 December 1987, at an initial ground rent of £500 per annum, doubling every 25 years. The house has a rateable value in the 1973 list of £995. The freehold with vacant possession value is £975,000 of which £57,500 is the value attributed to improvements carried out by the tenant.

The date of valuation is 25 March 2010.

The price computation is as follows:

Value of the freeholder's interest

Term

March 2010 to December 2012

Ground rent at £500 p.a.	£500 p.a.	
Years' purchase for 2.75 years at 7%	2.4254	£1,213

December 2012 – December 2037		
Ground rent at £1,000 p.a.	£1,000 p.a.	
Years' purchase for 25 years at 7%	11.6536	
Deferred 2.75 years @ 7%	0.8302	
		£9,675
December 2037 – December 2062		
Ground rent at £2,000 p.a.	£2,000 p.a.	
Years' purchase for 25 years at 7%	11.6536	
Deferred 27.75 years @ 7%	0.1530	
		£3,566

plus

Reversion

To entirety value, £975,000	£975,000	
less		
value attributable to tenant's improvements	£57,500	
	£917,500	
deferred for 52.75 years @ 4.75%	0.0865	£79,364
Value of the freeholder's interest		£93,818

Plus the freeholder's share of marriage value

That is the difference between:

value of the interests in the hands of the tenant after enfranchisement

freehold vacant possession value		£917,500	
less			
the aggregate of values prior to enfranchisement			
the freeholder's interest (from above)	£93,818		
plus			
the tenant's interest £917,500 @ 76.20%	£699,135	£792,953	
Marriage value		£124,547	
50% thereof		0.5	£62,274

Houses: extended leases and enfranchisement valuation issues

plus the value of the freeholder's interest (from above)	£93,818
Enfranchisement price (excluding costs)	£156,092
Say	£156,100

In this example, the tenant's interest in the marriage value computation represents 76.20 per cent of the freehold vacant possession value (unimproved) of £917,500. This is assessed by applying a graph of relativity, following *Arrowdell and Nailrile*.

Example 11

Section 14 extended lease, where notice of claim served after original term date.

This follows on from Examples 6 and 7 under section 9(1), where the unexpired term of the original tenancy as at the date of valuation was six months.

It is now nine months later, 24 June 2010, three months past the term date of the original tenancy; the valuation for the enfranchisement price now falls under section 9(1C). However, it is to be assumed that the tenant has the right to remain in possession in accordance with Schedule 10 to the *Local Government and Housing Act* 1989. The section 14 rent (as it is known), under the *Housing Act* 1988, is assessed at £425 per week, £22,100 per annum. Accordingly, the rental value is less than the £25,000 per annum limit (in the *Housing Act* 1988), and the tenant has the statutory right to remain in possession.

[The rent payable (section 14 of the 1967 Act) for a 50 years extended lease should not be confused with section 14 of the 1988 Act, which provides for the determination of rental value under an assured tenancy].

From Example 6, the modern ground rent is assessed at £41,250 per annum; it is assumed that market conditions have remained stable over the interim, accordingly the freehold with vacant possession value is £1,500,000.

The valuation for the enfranchisement price is, in effect, the unimproved freehold with vacant possession value, discounted to reflect the tenant's right (if any), to remain in possession as an assured tenant.

It will be recalled that in *Lloyd-Jones*, the freeholder's valuer gave evidence to the effect that tenants in houses on the Grosvenor and Cadogan Estates rarely exercised their rights under Part I of the *Landlord and Tenant Act* 1954 (that was the right to a statutory tenancy under the Rent Acts which applied prior to 15 January 1999); similarly, it is the author's experience that tenants in high value houses rarely exercise their statutory rights under Schedule 10 to an assured tenancy also.

If, under the particular circumstances, the valuer believes a deduction for the risk of the tenant remaining in occupation is inappropriate or as the case may be, the tenant does not occupy the house as his sole or principal residence

Leasehold enfranchisement explained

> (and therefore has no entitlement to an assured tenancy), the enfranchisement price is £1,500,000 excluding costs.
>
> This, when compared with the price at Example 7 (where notice was served six months prior to the term date of the original tenancy), of £862,600 excluding costs, shows the difference in enfranchisement price that can arise adopting the two different bases, albeit where the dates of valuation could be but one day apart.

> *Example 12*
>
> Short term unexpired, rent review, tenant's improvements and compensation for other loss (severance) under section 9A.
>
> A late Victorian terrace house and garage in central London held on a lease dated 12 March 1990 for a term of 40 years from 25 December 1989, at an initial ground rent of £1,000 per annum, with reviews at each 15th anniversary to 0.5 per cent of freehold vacant possession value. The current ground rent is £9,000 per annum, with effect from December 2004. The garage is within a separate mews cottage to the rear.
>
> The house and premises have a rateable value in the 1973 list of £1,868. The freehold vacant possession value is £3,450,000 in its current improved condition, of which £350,000 is attributable to tenant's improvements; the tenant's interest is valued at £1,252,500, unimproved.
>
> The mews cottage, which is not part of the claim, is held on a separate lease which is coterminous with the subject lease; and is held between the same parties. It is agreed that the freehold vacant possession value of the house and mews cottage sold as one lot is £250,000 more than the two sold separately.
>
> The date of valuation is 25 March 2010.
>
> The price computation is as follows:
>
> <u>Value of the freeholder's interest</u>
>
> Term
>
> March 2010 to December 2019
>
> | | | |
> |---|---|---|
> | Ground rent at £9,000 p.a. | £9,000 | |
> | Years' purchase for 9.75 years at 5.5% | 7.3942 | £66,548 |
>
> December 2019 – December 2029
>
> | | | |
> |---|---|---|
> | Ground rent on review to 0.5% of freehold vacant possession value of £3,100,000 | £15,500 | |
> | Years' purchase for 10 years at 5% | 7.7217 | |
> | deferred 9.75 years @ 5% | 0.6215 | £74,385 |

414

Houses: extended leases and enfranchisement valuation issues

plus			
Reversion			
To entirety value, £3,100,000	£3,100,000		
deferred for 19.75 years @ 4.75%	0.3999	£1,239,690	
Value of the freeholder's interest		£1,380,623	
Plus the freeholder's share of marriage value			
That is the difference between:			
value of the interests in the hands of the tenant after enfranchisement			
freehold vacant possession value		£3,100,000	
less			
the aggregate of values prior to enfranchisement			
the freeholder's interest (from above)	£1,380,623		
plus			
the tenant's interest, £1,252,500	£1,252,500	£2,633,123	
Marriage value		£466,877	
50% thereof		0.5	£233,439
plus the value of the freeholder's interest (from above)			£1,380,623
Enfranchisement price (excluding costs)			£1,614,062
Add for 'other loss' (severance)			
Difference in value between the house and mews cottage for sale together and separately	£250,000		
deferred for 19.75 years @ 4.75%	0.3999		£99,975
Enfranchisement price (excluding costs)			£1,714,037
		Say	£1,714,000

In this example, the current ground rent is capitalised using 5.5 per cent tables, and the rent on review is capitalised at 0.5 per cent less to reflect the dynamic nature of the review. The rent on review is based on the unimproved freehold vacant possession value following *Sharp*. The deferment rate of 4.75 per cent follows *Sportelli*.

Leasehold enfranchisement explained

Summary

The *Leasehold Reform Act* 1967 has been subject to a myriad of amendments since enactment. The extended provisions now give rights to tenants of high value houses to enfranchise, which is a considerable departure from the legislation as originally drafted. A brief synopsis of all the amending legislation, since 1967, including that for flats, is as follows (see also, the introductory chapter):

- *Housing Act* 1969: excluded the tenant's overbid from valuations under section 9(1).
- *Housing Act* 1974: extended the 1967 *Act* rateable value limits from £200 and £400 in Greater London, to £500 and £1,000 respectively. Introduced new basis of valuation, section 9(1A), in rateable value bands £501 to £750 and £1,001 to £1,500 in Greater London.
- *Leasehold Reform Act* 1979: prevented the enfranchisement price being increased by the creation of a superior interest.
- *Housing Act* 1980: reduced residency test from five years to three years, introduced the MILI formula, and LVTs set up (and introduced the right to buy).
- *Housing Act* 1985: extended rights to former secure tenants who had exercised the right-to-buy (see the previous point).
- *Housing and Planning Act* 1986: extended rights to lessees under shared ownership (100 per cent), and *Hickman* loophole closed.
- *References to Rating (Housing) Regulations* 1990 (SI 90/434): amended the rateable value and low rent tests further to the abolition of rateable values.
- *Leasehold Reform, Housing and Urban Development Act* 1993: abolished the rateable value test, amended the low rent and long tenancy tests (providing sections 1A and 1B rights to enfranchise), introduced new basis of valuation section 9(1C); and introduced new leases for flats (Schedule 13), and collective enfranchisement for blocks of flats (Schedule 6).
- *Housing Act* 1996: abolished the low rent test for houses held on leases granted for terms in excess of 35 years (providing section 1AA right to enfranchise), (with saving provisions for shared ownership leases granted by registered social landlords).
- *Commonhold and Leasehold Reform Act* 2002: removed the residence test; increased permissible limit on commercial content to blocks of flats for collective enfranchisement to 25 per cent; reduced number of participants required for collective enfranchisement; extended enfranchisement to

lessees under section 14, extended leases; marriage value (where applicable) on all bases to be 'nil' where unexpired term greater than 80 years and landlord's(s') share to be 50 per cent.
- *Housing and Regeneration Act* 2008: which amended the 1967 Act and finally repealed the low rent test (but it is retained as a qualifying condition for extended house leases), and made amendments to the grant of shared ownership leases which are exempt from enfranchisement.

From a valuer's point of view, there remain issues outstanding as to the appropriate deferment rate to apply under sections 9(1), (1A) and (1C). The recent cases referred to the Upper Tribunal (Lands Chamber) in *Mansal* and *Freehold Properties Limited* show the effect of the decisions countrywide in *Sportelli*.

The first question a tenant, having established his rights in leasehold reform, will ask is 'how much will it cost?' With three bases of valuation for the determination of price for the freehold interest, even confirming which is applicable at the outset can be far from straightforward.

As is shown in the examples, the difference in price from one basis to another can vary immensely. Arguably, none more so than where an extended lease has been taken under section 14 to the Act, and submitting a claim for the freehold interest is contemplated; the difference in price where the claim is given either before or after the original term date, can be substantial.

Glossary

Adverse differential: the result of the application of different percentages to decapitalise the site value to reach the section 15 rent, and to recapitalise the section 15 rent in the freehold price computation; the lower the decapitalisation and the higher the recapitalisation percentages, being favourable to the tenant.

Appropriate day: the 23 March 1965 unless the house had no rateable value at that date, in which case the appropriate day is the date on which a rateable value is first shown (s.1(4) of the 1967 Act).

Appropriate sum: the amount to be paid into court pursuant to a vesting order where the landlord is missing as defined in section 27(5) of the 1967 Act and sections 27(5) and 51(5) of the 1993 Act.

Appurtenant property: any garage, outhouse, garden, yard and appurtenances belonging to, or usually enjoyed with, the flat (s.1(7) 1993 Act).

Benefit of the Act or Act rights: the fiscal and non-fiscal value attributable to the tenant's rights in leasehold reform.

Capitalisation rate: the Years' Purchase (return) applied to the rental stream under the existing lease.

Caretaker's or porter's flat: accommodation provided for which the valuation approach and issues will depend on the lease provisions.

Cleared site approach: site value determined by reference to sales of comparable sites for development and redevelopment.

Glossary

Common parts: the structure and exterior of a building (or part of a building) and any common facilities within it (s.101(1) 1993 Act).

Compensation: additional sum payable for any loss or damage; typically loss of development value, and loss of value in two stage collective enfranchisement.

Competent landlord: the landlord for the purposes of Chapter II of the 1993 Act who fulfils the conditions in section 40(1) of that Act, i.e. he has sufficient interest in that flat to be able to grant the new lease and where he is a tenant, the lowest intermediate lease.

Component part: the ILI in relation to the flat as a component part of the whole of that interest.

Counter-notice: a notice given by the reversioner under section 21 of the 1993 Act in response to the initial notice or a notice given by the competent landlord under section 45 of the 1993 Act in response to the tenant's notice.

Decapitalisation: the second stage of calculating the modern ground rent (section 15 rent).

Deferment rate: 'is an annual discount of a future receipt, the vacant possession value of the house or flat at term', *Sportelli*, paragraph 51.

$$DR = RFR - RGR + RP$$

***Delaforce* (1970) effect:** the increase in price, 'the overbid', that the tenant will pay being anxious to settle the enfranchisement and thus limiting the proceedings. It is accepted that it can work the other way around.

Existing lease: the lease in relation to which the claim is made under Chapter II of the 1993 Act (s. 62(1) of the 1993 Act).

Extended lease: a lease for a term of a further 50 years at a modern ground rent provided for under section 14 of the 1967 Act, and which is to be assumed under the section 9(1) basis of valuation.

Freeholder's interest: the freehold (or leasehold) interest subject to the existing leases and any intermediate leasehold interest (where applicable).

Generic rate: in *Sportelli*: 2.25 per cent minus two per cent plus 4.5 per cent equals 4.75 per cent (houses); five per cent (plus 0.25%) (flats).

Greater London: the area comprising the London boroughs, the City of London and the Inner and Middle Temple (s. 2, *London Government Act* 1963).

***Haresign* (1980) addition:** the third stage in the price computation under section 9(1) for the landlord's reversion.

Hope value: the additional value attributable to the prospect of early release of marriage value, as a result of the freeholder selling a new lease or share of freehold (or buying in the leasehold interest), further to arms length negotiations to one or more of the lessees.

ILI: an interest between the existing lease and the competent landlord or freeholder.

Improvements: works carried out by the tenant or any predecessor in title to the flat that add value, which are to be disregarded (Schedules 6 and 13, paras. 3 and 4 of the 1993 Act).

Initial notice: a notice given under section 13(2) of the 1993 Act, claiming the right to collectively enfranchise.

Initial year: the period of one year beginning with the date of the commencement of the tenancy (s.4A(2)(a) of the 1967 Act).

Intermediate leasehold interest: the provisions of Schedule 6 follow those of Schedule 13 of the 1993 Act, including bases of valuation; MILI provisions; share of marriage value, and compensation.

Landlord: the freeholder and any intermediate landlord.

Landlord's interest: the freehold (or leasehold), interest subject to the existing lease and any intermediate leasehold interest (where applicable).

Leaseback: section 36 and Schedule 9 of the 1993 Act, either mandatory or optional; if taken, is on the basis of a 999 years lease at a peppercorn rent (para. 8).

Glossary

Leasehold relativity: the value of a dwelling held on an existing lease at any given unexpired term divided by the value of the same dwelling in possession to the freeholder, expressed as a percentage. (*RICS Research October 2009, Leasehold Reform, Graphs of Relativity*).

Letting value: equals the premium paid for a lease decapitalised over the term of the tenancy, plus the annual ground rent.

Long lease: a lease within the meaning of section 7 of the 1993 Act, which is usually for a fixed term of more than 21 years.

Long tenancy: a tenancy within the meaning of section 3 of the 1967 Act, which is usually for a fixed term of more than 21 years.

Low rent: a rent falling within the financial limits in section 4(1) of the 1967 Act.

Marriage value: the value released by the coalescence of the freehold and leasehold interests.

MILI: an interest with an expectation of possession of not more than one month; and a profit rent of not more than £5, including post any rent review (1967 and 1993 Acts).

Modern ground rent (section 15 rent): that to apply at the term date of the original tenancy under section 14, and a constituent part to the freehold price computation under section 9(1) of the 1967 Act, assessed by decapitalising the site value.

Negative interests: is an interest with a negative value.

New for old approach: site value determined by reference to the value of a new building replacing the existing; and thereafter either taking a proportion thereof, or deducting the costs to build.

No-Act world: the valuation assumption that the rights conferred in leasehold reform are to be disregarded with respect to the interests to be valued.

Nominee purchaser: a person or persons appointed by the tenants to acquire the freehold of premises on their behalf under the 1993 Act (s. 38 of the 1993 Act).

***Norfolk* (1976) and *Lloyd-Jones* (1981) approaches:** the two Lands Tribunal decisions confirming the valuation approach under section 9(1A), where the determination of price incorporates the marriage value.

Notice in reply: a notice under the 1967 Act served in reply to the notice of tenant's claim.

Notice of tenant's claim: notice of the tenant's desire to acquire the freehold of a house under the 1967 Act.

Notional reduction in rateable value: the reduction in rateable value to reflect tenant's improvements; either to bring a house within the higher rateable value limit, thereby qualifying for enfranchisement, or to move the house from one set of valuation assumptions to another, typically from section 9(1A) to section 9(1), thus lowering the enfranchisement price.

Onerous ground rent: an annual rent that has the effect of lessening the capital value of the lease, when compared with the same flat subject to a lease with nominal rent provisions.

Other landlord(s): all landlords who are not 'the reversioner' under the 1967 Act, and under the 1993 Act, landlords other than the competent landlord with a lease intermediate between the interest of the competent landlord and the tenant's lease.

Participating tenant: a tenant who falls within section 14 of the 1993 Act.

Post box: an intermediate lease where the profit rent is nil.

Profit rent: the difference between the rent receivable from the underlessee and the rent payable to the landlord.

Public sector landlord: any of the persons listed in section 171(2) of the *Housing Act* 1985 (s.38(1) of the 1993 Act).

Purpose-built block of flats: a building which, as constructed, contained two or more flats (s.10(6) of the 1993 Act).

Qualifying tenant: a tenant who falls within section 5 or section 39(3) of the 1993 Act.

Real growth rate: the growth in house and flats' prices (values) above the rate of inflation.

Glossary

Relativity: see 'leasehold relativity'.

Relevant date: under the 1993 Act, the date when either the initial notice or the tenant's notice is given (ss. 1(8) and 39(8)).

Relevant date: under the 1967 Act, the date of the commencement of the tenancy, or if the property did not have a rateable value, or had a rateable value of nil on that date, the date on which it first had a rateable value other than nil (s.4A(2)(b)).

Relevant landlord: any person who owns a freehold or leasehold interest which it is proposed to acquire under the 1993 Act (s.9).

Relevant premises: premises in relation to which the right to enfranchise under the 1993 Act is exercised (ss.1(2) and 2(1)).

Relevant services: services provided by means of pipes, cables or other fixed installations (s.3(2) of the 1993 Act).

Relevant time: the time when the tenant gives notice, in accordance with the 1967 Act, of his desire to acquire the freehold.

Rent: rent reserved as such and any part of the rent which is payable in respect of services, repairs, maintenance or insurance is to be disregarded (s.4(1)(b) of the 1967 Act).

Reversion: the value equivalent in lieu of the right to receive vacant possession of the flat (or house, as the case may be), at some future date.

Reversioner: under the 1993 Act, the relevant landlord who conducts proceedings arising out of the initial notice on behalf of the other relevant landlords.

Reversioner: under the 1967 Act, the landlord with the lowest interest of any landlord, who has an expectation of possession of at least 30 years (Sch. 1, para. 2(a)).

Risk-free rate: 'the return demanded by investors for holding an asset with no risk, often proxied by the return on a government security held to redemption' (*Sportelli,* paragraph 16).

Risk premium: 'the additional return required by investors to compensate for the risk of not receiving a guaranteed return' (*Sportelli,* paragraph 16).

Self-contained building: a building which is structurally detached (s.3(2) of the 1993 Act).

Settlements: valuation analyses of prices and premiums of completed leasehold reform claims.

Single rate approach: that to be adopted to value an ILI where the intermediate lease value (profit rent) is negative (single rate).

Site value: see 'cleared site', 'standing house' and 'new for old' approaches.

Specified premises: the premises specified in the initial notice under section 13(3)(a)(i) of the 1993 Act, or if it is later agreed or determined that less extensive premises should be acquired, those premises (s.13(12) of the 1993 Act).

Standing house approach: site value determined by reference to a proportion of the value of the house developed to its best advantage.

Steering group: a tenants' group which can comprise a number of participating tenants; the solicitor; the valuer, and any non-participating tenants' representative, which could include a 'White Knight'.

Tenant's notice: a notice of claim to exercise the right to acquire a new lease of a flat served by the tenant pursuant to section 42 of the 1993 Act.

The right to collective enfranchisement: the right specified in section 1(1) of the 1993 Act.

The terms of acquisition: the terms on which the tenant of a flat is to acquire a new lease (s.48(7) of the 1993 Act) or the terms of the proposed acquisition by the nominee purchaser under Chapter I of the 1993 Act (s.24(8)).

Third party to the lease: any person who is a party to the lease apart from the tenant under the lease and his immediate landlord (s.62(1) of the 1993 Act).

Total profit rent or capitalisation approach: that to be adopted to value an ILI where the intermediate lease value (profit rent) is either positive or nil (dual rates).

Value of landlord's interest: aggregate of the 'term' and 'reversion'.

White Knight: a third party who contributes to funding the non-participator's element of the enfranchisement price under Schedule 6 of the 1993 Act.

Index

a

adjudication
  flat leases: enfranchisement and new claims 27–28
agricultural property
  right to acquire freehold, exception 315–316
applications to court or LVT
  flats: collective enfranchisement 234
    landlord intends to redevelop 240–243
    reversioner fails to serve counter-notice 234–237
    reversioner serves non-admitting counter-notice 237–240
    terms in dispute/failure to enter into binding contract 243–247
  flats: tenant's right to acquire new lease 60–61
    landlord intends to redevelop 66–69
    landlord serves non-admitting counter-notice 64–66
    landlord's failure to serve counter-notice 61–63
    terms in dispute/failure to enter into new lease 69–73
  houses
    tenant's right to acquire extended lease 364–365
    tenant's right to acquire freehold 353–354
Arbib
  deferment rate 88–89, 94
  settlement evidence 94–99

b

business tenancies
  right to acquire freehold, exception 314

c

capitalisation rate
  Schedule 6 255–256
  Schedule 13 84–85
caretaker's flat
  collective enfranchisement, valuation 272–273
charitable housing
  right to acquire freehold, exception 316
collective enfranchisement 196–197
  applications to court or LVT 234
    landlord intends to redevelop 240–243
    reversioner fails to serve counter-notice 234–237
    reversioner serves non-admitting counter-notice 237–240
    terms in dispute/failure to enter into binding contract 243–247
  freehold interests 198–198
  further interests 200–201
  identifying the landlord 208
    finding landlords 210–212
    missing landlords 212–213
    situation one 208
    situation two 208–209
    situation three 209–210
  leasebacks 201–202
  leasehold interests 199–200
  preparation of conveyance 233
  qualifying leases 207
  qualifying premises 202–203
    exclusions 204–206
    self-contained building or part of building 203
  qualifying tenants 206–207
  starting claim 213–214
    initial notice *see* initial notice
  tenants unable to participate 207
  valuation issues *see* valuation

Index

compensation
  flats
    loss arising out of grant of new lease 182–193
    loss resulting from enfranchisement 294
    right to enfranchisement by virtue of section 9(1A) or (1B) 410–415
consecutive tenancies 318
contents of tenant's notice 41–46
  proposed premium 45–46
  proposed terms 43–45
costs
  flat lease claims 11
  houses
    acquisition of extended lease 361–362
    acquisition of freehold 352

d

deferment rate
  appropriate, application to reflect postponement to end of term 86–87
  recent decisions 18–20
  Schedule 6 256–257
  Schedule 13
    Arbib 88–89, 94–99
    definitions 87
    lower rate resulting in higher premium 87–88
    Pockney 88–89, 92–93
    Sportelli 88–91, 99–102
  Sportelli
    analysis 99–102
    Court of Appeal 14–15, 18
    synopsis of decisions 88–91
Delaforce effect 394
development value
  flats: collective enfranchisement 295–303
  Schedule 6, Parts IV–VI 296–303

e

evidence
  valuation, new lease claims 193–195

f

flats
  collective enfranchisement *see* collective enfranchisement
  individual right of tenant to acquire new lease *see* right to acquire new lease
  new lease claims, valuation issues *see* valuation
flat leases
  enfranchisement and new claims 9–11
    adjudication 27–28
    costs 11
    intermediate leases 20, 26–27
    procedures 11
    recent decisions and the meaning of 'house' 21–25
    redevelopment as ground for resisting claim 25–26
    right to acquire new lease 11
    valuation *see* valuation
freehold interests
  flats: collective enfranchisement 198–198

g

garages
  collective enfranchisement, valuation 272
grounds, etc.
  collective enfranchisement, valuation 273

h

hope value *see* valuation
house leases
  extended, right of tenant to acquire *see* right to acquire extended lease
  Leasehold Reform Act 1967 3
    amendments 3–7
  valuation *see* valuation
houses
  definition of house 21
    designed or adapted for living in 22–23, 305–306
    reasonably so called 23–25, 306–307

427

Index

extended leases
  enfranchisement and valuation issues *see* valuation
  right of tenant to acquire *see* right to acquire extended lease
  right of tenant to acquire freehold *see* right to acquire freehold
Housing Act 1988
  flat occupied by assured tenant 181–182

i

initial notice
  copies and giving of 219–220
  effective, restrictions on serving 214
  effect of 220–221
  how to serve 218–219
  nominee purchaser 221–223
  participating tenants 223–224
  receipt of *see* receipt of initial notice
  registration 220
  requirements 214–218
  withdrawal 224–225
intermediate landlords
  intermediate leasehold interests (ILIs) *see* intermediate leasehold interests (ILIs)
intermediate leasehold interests (ILIs)
  amounts payable to owners of 135–136
  checklist 144–164
  compensation for loss on acquisition of interest 279
  interest to be valued 139–142
  intermediate lease reversion 164–170
  owners entitlement to part of marriage value 138–139, 279–280
  price payable 276
  single rate approach 143–144
  total profit rent and capitalisation approaches 142–143
  value 136–138, 277–279
  diminution 136
investment value 12

l

leasebacks
  flats: collective enfranchisement 201–202
  valuation 273–274
leasehold interests
  flats: collective enfranchisement 199–200
Leasehold Reform Act 1967 3
  amendments 3–7
Lloyd-Jones
  determination of price under section 9(1A) 401–402
long tenancy
  qualification for right to acquire tenancy 316–320
low rent *see* valuation

m

marriage value *see* valuation
missing landlords
  flats
    collective enfranchisement 212–213
    right to acquire new lease 38–40
  houses: right to acquire freehold 340–343
mixed-use premises
  right to collective enfranchisement, exclusion 204
multiple concurrent tenancies 319–320
multiple tenancies
  right to acquire freehold, exception 314

n

Norfolk
  determination of price under section 9(1A) 401–402

Index

notice of tenant's claim
  assignment 340
  receipt of 343–346, 359
    landlord's intention to apply for possession 349–350
    landlord's notice in reply 346–349
    redevelopment rights 359
  registration 338
  service of
    bars to serving 337–338
    effect of 338–340
    how to serve 336–337
    who to serve 335–336

o

onerous ground rents 125–132
operational railways
  right to collective enfranchisement, exclusion 206

p

PCL (Prime Central London) 102–103, 104–107
periodical continuation tenancies 319
Pockney
  deferment rate 88–89, 92–93
porter's flat
  collective enfranchisement, valuation 292–293
procedures 7–8
  flat lease claims 11

r

receipt of initial notice 225
  checklist 231
  relevant landlords 225–226
    acting independently 232–233
    reversioner 226–227
      conduct of proceedings 232
      counter-notice 227–231
receipt of notice of tenant's claim 343–346
  landlord's intention to apply for possession 349–350
  landlord's notice in reply 346–349

receipt of tenant's notice 50–51
  checklist for landlords 57
  competent landlord 51–55
    conduct of proceedings 57–58
    landlords counter-notice 55–57
  other landlords 51
    acting independently 58–59
redevelopment rights 359
registration
  initial notice 220
  notice of tenant's claim 338
  tenant's notice 48
relativity
  benefit of Act or Act rights 122–125
  checklist for tenant's valuer 133
  definition 121–122
  onerous ground rents 125–132
renewable tenancies 318–319
rent *see* section 15 rent
Rent Act 1977
  flat occupied by statutory tenant 176–181
resident landlords
  right to collective enfranchisement, exclusion 205–206
right to acquire extended lease 355
  applications to court or LVT 364–365
  meaning of terms used 355–356
  qualification 356–357
  receipt of notice of tenant's claim 359
    redevelopment rights 359
  starting claim 357–358
  terms of acquisition 359–361
    costs 361–362
    execution of new lease 362
    terms of new lease 362–363
    rent 363
right to acquire freehold 305
  applications to court or LVT 353–354

429

Index

basis of valuation *see* valuation
definition of house 305
  designed or adapted for living in 305–306
  divided buildings 308
  extent of freehold to be acquired 309–312
  non-detached buildings 309
  reasonably called a 'house' 306–307
qualification 312–313
  exceptions 313–316
  long tenancy 316–320
  types of tenancy 317–320
starting claim 328–335
  missing landlords 340–343
  serving notice of tenant's claim *see* notice of tenant's claim
terms of acquisition 350–351
  costs 352
  purchase price 351–352
withdrawal 352–353
right to acquire new lease 30
  applications to court or LVT 60–61
  landlord intends to redevelop 66–69
  landlord serves non-admitting counter-notice 64–66
  landlord's failure to serve counter-notice 61–63
  terms in dispute/failure to enter into new lease 69–73
  identifying the landlord 36–38
  missing landlords 38–40
  special categories of landlords 38
  preparing and executing new lease 59–60
  qualification 31
  checklist for tenants 35
  qualifying flat 32
  qualifying lease 32–35
  qualifying tenant 31–32
  starting claim and tenant's notice *see* tenant's notice
right to buy tenancies 320

S

Schedule 6 250–251
  capitalisation rate 255–256
  compensation for loss on acquisition of interest 298–299
  deferment rate 256–257
  freeholder's share of marriage value 257–258
  interpretation and operation of 251
  marriage value 298
  price paid for freehold of specified premises 251–252
  price payable for other interests 296–297
  valuation of freehold and intermediate leasehold interests 300–301
  valuation of freehold and leasehold interests 302–303
  value of freeholder's interest 252–255
  value of other interests 297
Schedule 13 76–81
  amounts payable to owners of intermediate leasehold interest 77
  capitalisation rate 84–85
  compensation
    loss arising out of grant of new lease 182–183
    loss resulting from enfranchisement 294
  deferment rate
    appropriate, application to reflect postponement to end of term 86–87
    Arbib 88–89, 94–99
    definitions 87
    lower rate resulting in higher premium 87–88
    Pockney 88–89, 92–93
    Sportelli 88–91, 99–102
  diminution in value of landlord's interest 78–79, 82
  general 77

Index

intermediate leasehold
   interests (ILIs) *see*
   intermediate leasehold
   interests (ILIs)
landlord's share of marriage
   value 111–112
premium payable in respect of
   grant of new lease 77
reversion 85–86
share of freehold/999 years'
   lease vacant possession
   value 86
statutory provisions 82–83
term 83–84
timing of notice of claim
   81–82
section 15 rent 379–380
   'cleared site' approach 381–382
   methods of valuing site 380
   'new for old' approach 383
   'standing house' approach
     382–383
service of tenant's notice 40
   how to serve notice 47
   restriction 40–41
   who to serve with notice 46–47
shared ownership leases 320
   right to acquire freehold,
     exception 315
split freehold
   right to collective
     enfranchisement,
     exclusion 205
Sportelli 16
   Court of Appeal 14
   deferment rate 14–15, 18
   deferment rate
     analysis 99–102
     Court of Appeal 14–15, 18
     synopsis of decisions 88–91
   House of Lords 15
   summary of decisions 16
sub-tenancies
   right to acquire freehold,
     exception 316

t

telecommunications mast
   collective enfranchisement,
     valuation 293

tenant's notice
   assignment 49
   contents 41–46
     proposed premium 45–46
     proposed terms 43–45
   effect of 48–49
   receipt of *see* receipt of tenant's
     notice
   registration 48
   service of 40
     how to serve notice 47
     restriction 40–41
     who to serve with notice
       46–47
   suspension 50
   withdrawal 50

v

valuation 8–9
   adjudication 27–28
   basis, right to acquire freehold
     320–321, 367–368, 386
   basis of qualification
     322–323
   checklist 321–322
   low rent 323–328
   section 9(1) 386–397
   section 9(1A) 397–407
   section 9(1B) 408
   section 9(1C) 407–409
   section 9A – compensation
     409–416
   collective enfranchisement
     248–249, 303–304
     caretaker's flat 272–273
     checklist for freeholder's
       valuer 291–293
     checklist for tenant's valuer
       274–280
     compensation 293–294
     development value 295–303
     garages, outhouse, garden,
       yard 272
     grounds, etc. 273
     hope value 263–272,
       280–291
     leasebacks 273–274
     marriage value 257–262
     principles 249
     Schedule 6 *see* Schedule 6
     tenant's enquiry 250

Index

deferment rate *see* deferment rate
extended leases   366, 367, 368
  acquiring freehold where extended lease claimed   368–369
  'adverse differential'   384–386
  decapitalised site value   383–384
  letting value   369–371
  rateable value   371–379
  section 1, 'tenants entitled to enfranchisement or extension'   369
  section 4, 'meaning of low rent'   369
  section 15 rent *see* section 15 rent
hope value   13
  all leasehold claims   12
  calculation of freeholder's interest   402
  collective enfranchisement   263–272
  recent decisions   16–18
  relevance in valuing house and flat lease claims   12–13
  Sportelli decisions *see Sportelli*
investment value   12
marriage value   12, 111
  all leasehold claims   12
  collective enfranchisement   257–262

  determination of price payable for house/premises   402–407
  landlord's share   111–121
new lease claims   74, 195
  compensation   182–193
  evidence   193–195
  further issues   170–176
  intermediate landlords – intermediate leasehold interests (ILIs) *see* intermediate leasehold interests (ILIs)
  landlord's view   133–135
  leases below 20 years   103–107
  marriage value   111–121
  occupancy by assured tenant (*Housing Act* 1988)   181–182
  occupancy by statutory tenant (*Rent Act* 1977)   176–181
  outside PCL (Prime Central London)   102–103
  relativity *see* relativity
  Schedule 13 *see* Schedule 13
  section 9(1) v section 9(1A)   107–110
  Sportelli, Arbib, Pockney, Arrowdell, Nailrile et al   75
  starting claim   76
  tenant's enquiry   75–76
proceedings in the tribunal   13–14